T0385490

DUMBARTON OAKS
MEDIEVAL LIBRARY

Jan M. Ziolkowski, General Editor

SAINTS OF NINTH- AND

TENTH-CENTURY GREECE

DOML 54

Saints of Ninth- and Tenth-Century Greece

Edited and Translated by

ANTHONY KALDELLIS

and

IOANNIS POLEMIS

DUMBARTON OAKS
MEDIEVAL LIBRARY

HARVARD UNIVERSITY PRESS
CAMBRIDGE, MASSACHUSETTS
LONDON, ENGLAND
2019

Library of Congress Cataloging-in-Publication Data
Names: Kaldellis, Anthony, editor, translator. | Polemēs, I., editor,
translator.
Title: Saints of ninth- and tenth-century Greece / edited and translated by
Anthony Kaldellis and Ioannis Polemis.
Other titles: Dumbarton Oaks medieval library ; 54.
Description: Cambridge, Massachusetts : Harvard University Press, 2019. |
    Series: Dumbarton Oaks medieval library ; 54 | This is a facing-page
volume: Greek on the versos; English translation on the rectos. |
    Includes bibliographical references and index.
Identifiers: LCCN 2018040033 | ISBN 9780674237360 (alk. paper)
Subjects: LCSH: Christian saints—Greece—Biography—Early works to
1800. | Saints—Greece—Biography—Early works to 1800. | Christian
hagiography—History and criticism. | Christian literature, Byzantine—
History and criticism.
Classification: LCC BX393 .S27 2019 | DDC 274.95/030922 [B]—dc23 LC
record available at https://lccn.loc.gov/2018040033

Contents

CONTENTS

Introduction

The saints' lives translated in this volume are not among the best known, but they have at least two features that compel broader attention: first, they concern a poorly documented but hotly debated period in the history of medieval Greece, the ninth and early tenth centuries; and, second, as a collected corpus they exhibit a great deal of literary variety, presenting students of hagiography with a compact dossier of texts that feature a range of literary modes and tropes. The texts are individually fairly short and have not been previously translated into English.[1]

On the historical side, "Dark Age" Greece is always a topic of interest and even fascination,[2] but the materials for its study (textual and archaeological) are scanty. Major topics have long included the barbarian invasions (Slavic, Avar, and Bulgar); changes in settlement (and resettlement) patterns; the postclassical history of cities, towns, and villages; Arab and pirate raids in the ninth and tenth centuries; ecclesiastical history; and monasticism. The texts included here touch on every one of these themes. They do not provide a sufficient basis for a comprehensive history of the period, but their evidence, which is still generally unknown, fills in crucial parts of the overall picture. Arguably, some of our texts are more historically oriented than others, especially

the *Life of Peter, Bishop of Argos,* which is important for understanding episcopal authority and Church welfare in medieval Greece, and the *Life of Theodore of Kythera,* the most important source for the Byzantine history of that island.[3] The account in the *Martyrdom of Nicholas the Younger* stands between invention and history, possibly combining narrative layers from different periods.

The volume will also be a crucial source for the cult of saints in Greece itself and the topographies of holiness (including holy mountains and the practice of piety in cities). For example, even if it is quasi-fictional, the story of the governor of Thessalonike, who seeks a cure for his leprosy and (vainly) turns to the other saints of Greece before tracking down the body of Nicholas the Younger, shows how new cults sought to establish themselves on the backs of others.

On the literary side, the corpus presents a great variety of approaches, making it a useful instrument for studying and teaching different literary aspects and conventions of hagiography. Along with the traditional *vita* format, there is a hagiographic funeral oration (for Athanasios of Methone) and an encomium (for Nicholas the Younger). Some texts are more historical and others more rhetorical in approach, especially the *Life and Miracles of Theokletos, Bishop of Lakedaimon,* which follows a fairly generic rhetorical template, though its author exhibits a love of metaphor and makes good use of vivid imagery and proverbs. There are also miracle stories of both living and dead saints, and novelistic elements. One text (on Athanasios of Methone) offers multiple comparisons to figures from ancient Greek history and mythology, whereas another, the *Life of Peter, Bishop of Argos,* uses as a template the *Life of Proklos* by his student Marinos,

a rare instance of the recasting of "Neoplatonic hagiography" by a Christian writer. There are also texts associated with the saints' feast days. This collection, therefore, is ideal for studying the varieties of hagiographic rhetoric and aspects of its narrative inventions.

In addition, the *Lives* presented in this volume are composed in a variety of styles, representing the main stylistic tendencies of Byzantine hagiographic prose. The *Life of Peter, Bishop of Argos* is written in an elevated style. Its author, Theodore of Nicaea, a prominent member of the literary circle around the emperor Constantine VII Porphyrogennetos (r. 945–959), was clearly addressing a demanding audience able to appreciate the impeccable syntax of his text and its Attic diction. Written in the first half of the tenth century, this text follows the classicizing tendencies of the ninth century, as represented by the great hagiographic works of the patriarch Methodios and Ignatios the Deacon. The works on Athanasios of Methone, Theokletos of Lakedaimon, and Theodore of Kythera were by contrast written by provincial scholars according to the rules of elevated Byzantine style: good Greek, but clearly inferior to that of the *Life of Peter, Bishop of Argos*. The *Martyrdom of Nicholas the Younger* and the encomium for the same saint written by the priest Achaïkos belong to another category, being representative of low-level, provincial hagiography. Their authors tried to imitate the elevated style of the more ambitious hagiographic works written in their time but were unable to keep their texts under control: their syntax is loose, and grammatical and other mistakes are frequent. Finally, the *Commemoration of Arsenios, Archbishop of Kerkyra* is from a *synaxarion* (a collection of brief readings about individual

saints, arranged by their feast dates in the calendar). This short text was probably read on the saint's feast day. Therefore, this selection of texts nicely illustrates the differences among the main branches of Byzantine hagiography.

As a principle of selection, "Greece" is a valid Byzantine rubric. The region retained its ancient geographical name in Byzantine times and lent it to the military province (or "theme") of Hellas, which was at times combined with the theme of the Peloponnese. Byzantines from Greece were known as *Helladikoi*, "Helladics," rather than *Hellenes*, which in Byzantine times meant "pagans." All the saints in this volume were active in those themes, except for Arsenios of Kerkyra (which was either its own minitheme or belonged to that of Kephallenia). We have decided, however, to exclude the *Lives* of two more famous saints of tenth-century Greece, Loukas of Steiris and Nikon Metanoeite, because these have already been translated and are much longer (each one filling a separate volume);[4] also the *Life of Athanasia of Aigina,* because it is included in the *Holy Women of Byzantium* volume published by Dumbarton Oaks;[5] and the two *Lives of Meletios the Younger* that are also much longer, later than our period, and are about to be published separately in translation as well.[6]

We have retained the chapter numbering of texts in the edition by Ioannis Polemis and Evelina Mineva but subdivided them into paragraphs; texts not included in Polemis-Mineva have new chapter numbering.[7] In the Notes to the Translations we cite passages from both classical and scriptural sources for the quotations and allusions that appear in our texts. Unless otherwise noted, all classical Greek references are to the Loeb Classical Library edition. Our bibli-

cal citations are to the Rahlfs edition of the Septuagint and the Nestle-Aland edition of the New Testament;[8] all translations of scriptural passages are our own. We do not wish to imply that our authors always had those passages in mind or on their desk when writing these texts (though in many cases they clearly did). The sayings, phrases, and ideas in question would often have been known more generally, from their general circulation in Byzantine oral and literary culture (for example, in the liturgy, or anthologies), so we are content to cite here what was likely only their ultimate sources. The mechanics of their diffusion, circulation, and allusion thereafter are too complex to render in our notes.

In the spelling of Byzantine Greek names and place-names, we have generally followed the *Oxford Dictionary of Byzantium*.

SAINT NICHOLAS THE YOUNGER

According to the anonymous *Martyrdom,* Nicholas, a virtuous military man and associate of the emperor Leo VI (r. 886–912), was sent by him to Thessaly to protect the area from the "Avars," who, taking advantage of the emperor's expedition to Asia Minor, had invaded Greece. The saint and his companions arrived at Larissa, Thessaly's main city, but decided to abandon it, retreating to the nearby mountain of Ternavon, where he lived as an ascetic. A short time afterward an angel ordered him to attack the Avars. The companions of the saint were taken prisoner by the Avars, who killed the ascetics after torturing them, but Nicholas managed to escape to Mount Vounaina. There he lived as a hermit for some time, but in the end he, too, was captured

by the Avars and killed. Philip, the bishop of Larissa,[9] found the bodies of Nicholas's companions, who were buried on Ternavon, while sometime later a governor of Thessalonike named Euphemianos, prompted by a dream, discovered the body of Nicholas on Vounaina, where he built a church after being miraculously cured of his leprosy.

It is difficult to determine the historical basis of these events. Several persons mentioned in the text, especially Nicholas and his companions, the governor Euphemianos, and his companion named Horation,[10] are not mentioned in any other source. Also unrecorded is the expedition of the emperor Leo VI to Asia Minor.[11] Scholars disagree about the identity of the Avars referred to in the text. The Byzantines sometimes used that name for the Bulgars; however, the latter had already converted to Christianity by the time of Leo VI. Some scholars have claimed that they were Arabs changed to Avars by a scribal error, Hungarians, or Slavs settled in Macedonia.[12]

The whole story, moreover, is an agglomeration of two distinct narratives: the story of the group martyred on Mount Ternavon and that of the solitary martyr Nicholas on Mount Vounaina. The miraculous discovery of two groups of relics gave rise to each story, and the two were combined at a later stage, possibly by the author of the anonymous *Martyrdom*.[13] Attention has also been drawn to a canon dedicated to Saint Ardomios, written by an Arsenios called *Xenos* ("the foreigner") in the second half of the ninth century.[14] Ardomios and his four companions (Gregory, John, Michael, and Paul) suffered martyrdom at an unspecified time because they refused to bow to idols. This group was certainly related to the group of Saint Nicholas the Younger: all

these names (except for Paul) are recorded in the anonymous *Martyrdom*. Yet if Ardomios was among the companions of Saint Nicholas the Younger, the author of the canon for Saint Ardomios does not mention Saint Nicholas at all. Also, the anonymous *Martyrdom* lists eight more male names and two female ones, and the martyrs referred to in the canon for Ardomios are neither monks nor soldiers, as is the case in the anonymous *Martyrdom*.

Moreover, there exists another witness to the second story, that of Saint Nicholas the lonely soldier. Manuscript 81 of the Transfiguration Monastery of Meteora also preserves an office for the saint containing a *synaxarion* for him. According to this short text, Saint Nicholas was a military man who, at the time of a persecution by a tyrant and some unspecified heretics, was tortured and then exiled. The saint sought refuge on Vounaina, but his torturers followed him and killed him there. His relics were not discovered by a governor named Euphemianos, but by an unnamed barbarian from the east (ἐκ τῶν ἀνατολικῶν μερῶν) who was ill and was cured after discovering the saint's relics on Mount Vounaina.[15] No mention of any companions is made in this short text. The heretics mentioned in the *synaxarion* could be identified with iconoclasts, the only heretics who persecuted the orthodox in this period. Unfortunately, the date of the *synaxarion's* composition is unknown, but it must have been written long before the fifteenth century, when the manuscript was copied. What is more important for our purposes is that there existed a tradition in which Saint Nicholas the Younger had no companions.

Thus, different versions of this story were circulating and different historical circumstances were invented to frame

the saint's life. It is possible that the story's origins go back to the eighth century when emperor Leo III (r. 717–741) had to deal with both the Arabs in the east and the Bulgars in the Balkans, before they converted to Christianity. A hagiographer who wished to conceal the saint's connection to a heretical emperor perhaps decided to place the events in the tenth century under the reign of another Leo. It is difficult to prove such a hypothesis, and it is also difficult to date the *Martyrdom*. It seems to have been written before the occupation of Larissa by the Bulgars in 986, as the relics of Saint Achilleios were still to be found there at this time.[16] The combination of the two stories into one continuous narrative also required that the ascetics of Ternavon become military men, like Nicholas.

The *Encomium* was written by an obscure priest called Achaïkos and is preserved in a twelfth-century manuscript, though it was composed after the anonymous *Martyrdom* on which it is clearly based. It is interesting that Achaïkos takes liberties with his model, reworking embarrassing details, as, for example, the reason for Nicholas's abandonment of Larissa to the mercy of the Avars.

Saint Athanasios of Methone

The *Funeral Oration for Athanasios, Bishop of Methone,* by Peter of Argos is based on a lost *Life* of the saint whose author is unknown.[17] According to the text, Athanasios was born in Catania, Sicily. His family was forced to seek refuge in Patras in the Peloponnese after the invasion of Sicily by the Arabs in 827/8.[18] Considering that the saint was young at the time, his birth has been placed around 818/19.[19] At Patras,

he joined a monastery, but later abandoned it to live as a hermit. However, he was forced to return to the monastery to become its abbot. Against his will he was then ordained bishop of Methone,[20] where he led an exemplary life and died in old age. His death must be placed after 879, because the saint took part in the council of 879, which rehabilitated Photios.[21] His cult was limited and he was soon forgotten, like most of the Peloponnesian saints of our collection, excepting Theodore of Kythera.[22]

One of the sources used by Peter of Argos in writing the *Funeral Oration* was the *Graecarum affectionum curatio (Remedy for the Hellenic Afflictions)* of Theodoret of Cyrrhus.[23]

Saint Peter of Argos

The *Life of Peter, Bishop of Argos*, author of the *Funeral Oration for Athanasios, Bishop of Methone*, was written by his disciple Theodore of Nicaea, a well-known figure of the tenth century,[24] and has been convincingly interpreted as a case of the reemergence of bishops as the subjects of hagiographic literature.[25] The name of the author is preserved only in the manuscript Atheniensis graecus 278, but the attribution may be considered safe: twice in his extant letters, Theodore refers to his saintly spiritual father.[26] Moreover, at the end of the *Life* the author thanks Peter for saving him from the wrath of the emperor. Theodore often refers in his letters to his bad relations with Constantine VII Porphyrogennetos.[27]

According to Theodore, Peter was the scion of a Constantinopolitan aristocratic family renowned for its piety. The eldest son, Paul, became a disciple of a famous ascetic, also named Peter. His example was followed by Dionysios,

the second son. Later on, the entire family joined Paul's monastic community, and he became the spiritual father of his own parents and younger sister. His younger brothers Peter and Plato also became monks. The patriarch Nicholas I (901–907, 912–925) appointed Paul as bishop of Corinth,[28] which at the time was the capital of the administrative district of the Peloponnese. He pressured Peter to become a bishop too, but the saint was adamant in refusing and followed his brother Paul to Corinth, where he lived in a monastery outside the city, writing panegyrical accounts of various saints. After the death of the bishop of Argos, the inhabitants of that area asked Paul to persuade his brother to become their new bishop. After considerable reluctance, Peter yielded to his brother's entreaties and was ordained a bishop of that important city shortly after 912.[29] During his episcopate, he devoted himself to charity. He managed to save many lives during a famine by offering wheat to its victims.[30] Even some barbarians were persuaded by his example to accept Christianity.[31] He also liberated people captured by the Arabs who were plundering the coastal areas of the Peloponnese.

Peter had prophetic powers as well and predicted the invasion of some unidentified barbarians, which took place after his death: more precisely, he said that the Peloponnese would perish at the time of the death either of a certain Theophylaktos or "a man guarded by God" (depending on whether it is a proper name or a descriptive adjective).[32] Scholars have identified this event with an invasion by Symeon's Bulgarians (possibly in 924–927), alternatively with an invasion of Slavic tribes,[33] or with a revolt by unspecified Slavic tribes inhabiting the Peloponnese, put down by the general Krinites Arotras (possibly in 922–924/5).[34]

A later source, the *Life of Theodosios the Younger* written by Nicholas Malaxos (sixteenth century), refers to a journey of Peter of Argos to Constantinople.[35] In all probability, he took part in the Council of 920 that condemned the fourth marriage of the emperor Leo VI. The saint must have died in 921 or 922. According to his *Life,* he was then seventy years old.

Saint Theokletos of Lakedaimon

A certain Theokletos, bishop of Lakedaimon, is mentioned in the Acts of the Council of 869–870, which condemned Photios, and this was almost certainly the same person as the Saint Theokletos of the *Life*.[36] The *Life,* however, does not provide any details concerning the saint's biography. Its author fills in the gaps with generic conventions: initially the saint was a hermit and later he was pressured to become bishop of Lakedaimon. After castigating the powerful magnates of his time for their offenses, he was banned from his bishopric through their machinations but was recalled shortly thereafter. He performed some miracles during his lifetime, which contributed to his fame. His name is also preserved in an inscription on the church of Saint Demetrios in Mesonesia, near the village of Kastorion.[37] He was likely dead by the time of the Council of 879, which rehabilitated Photios, since the bishop of Lakedaimon at that time was called Antony.[38] But given the *Life*'s claim that the saint was expelled from his bishopric, it is possible that Theokletos, an Ignatian supporter, was turned out of his see after 877 but reinstated thereafter. In that case, the saint may have been alive in 879.

As the bishopric of Lakedaimon was elevated to a me-

tropolis in 1082, the *Life* was likely composed before that year.[39] The author of the *Life* was urged to write the text by a bishop of Lakedaimon who wanted to honor his eminent predecessor. As hinted at in the text, the name of that bishop may have been Theodore, possibly the bishop whose name appears on two lead seals of the tenth or eleventh century.[40] But his name may have alternatively been Theodosios, and a certain Theodosios is indeed attested as a bishop of Lakedaimon.[41]

The most historically important part of this text is the passage where the saint castigates those powerful city-magnates (οἱ ἐν ταῖς πόλεσι προέχοντες) who forcefully lay hands on (καταδυναστεύειν) the properties of their poorer brethren. These great proprietors live in cities, a point stressed in other texts of the tenth century as well.[42] The language used by the author reminds us of the laws (called "novels") of the emperors of the tenth century, and most of all the celebrated novel of the emperor Romanos I Lakapenos, promulgated in September 934, against the so-called *dynatoi* (literally, "powerful ones"), who used their authority to exert pressure and buy the lands of their neighbors, and the novel of Constantine VII of 947 against the "powerful."[43]

Saint Theodore of Kythera

According to his *Life,* Theodore of Kythera was born in Korone (in southeastern Messenia). After he was orphaned, a relative, who was a priest at Nauplion, took him under his protection. When he grew up, he married and was ordained a deacon by bishop Theodore of Argos, who admired his vir-

tue. However, soon afterward Theodore left his family to become a monk. He visited the tomb of Saint Peter in Rome and went to Monemvasia, where he lived in the shrine of the Theotokos Diakonia, almost as a beggar. After spending a year there, he asked the *tourmarches* Meliton, the leader of a naval squadron, who was charged by the emperor Romanos I Lakapenos (r. 920–944) with attacking the Arabs of Crete, to take him to the island of Kythera. The sailors left Theodore and his companion, the monk Antony, on the island. Afterward the crew engaged in combat with an Arab ship that was sailing near the island. The Byzantines defeated the Arabs, some of whom sought refuge on the island. The Byzantine fleet returned to Monemvasia, satisfied with their victory. Their only concern was the fate of the two monks who were left on the island and were unaware that some Arabs had taken refuge there and could harm them. But God protected his servants. Theodore spent some time in a chapel of Saints Sergios and Bakchos, while Antony soon left the island, unable to endure its hardships, and returned to Monemvasia. Theodore died on the island eleven months after his arrival. His body was found intact by some sailors who visited the island: he had written the exact date of his death (May 12) on a small tablet found near his head. Curiously enough, the sailors did not bury Theodore's body, but left it where it lay. Sometime afterward, the body was rediscovered by some residents of Monemvasia who went hunting on the island and buried the body properly. This was at the time of an *allagion,* that is, an exchange of prisoners with the Arabs that took place on the initiative of the emperor Romanos I.

The fact that in the *Life* Nauplion lies under the jurisdic-

tion of the bishop of Argos places the ordination of the saint in the period after the council of 879/80, when the two cities still had different bishops.[44] Theodore of Argos is not mentioned among the successors of Saint Peter of Argos, who became bishop between 912 and 920, so he must have been one of his predecessors.[45] Theodore of Kythera must, then, have been born in the last third of the ninth century, because he must have been at least twenty-five years old at the time of his ordination as deacon, if orthodox canon law was observed.[46] The saint possibly died in 922, if the *allagion* took place after the defeat of Leo Tripolites in 924, when many Arabs were taken prisoner by the Byzantines.[47]

The *Life* is based on a lost earlier text, which was written in simple language. The author of our version, a certain Leo, took care to rewrite it, adding to it a long epilogue comparing Theodore to past saints. Some remnants of the style of the previous text are still discernible in the version we have before us. At the time of the redaction, Kythera was no longer a deserted island, as it had allegedly been in the time of Theodore: the cult of the saint was now well established, and the inhabitants of the island were proud of their protector. Leo's redaction of the text must be placed after the liberation of Crete by Nikephoros Phokas in 961, when Kythera was repopulated.[48] But we still do not know when the original *Life* was composed. There is a hint in the text (chapter 5.1): speaking about the arrival of the *tourmarches* Meliton at Monemvasia, the author informs us that this official was sent against the "Hagarenes (Arabs) who were then living on Crete." If the adverb τότε (then, at that time) belongs to the original *Life* of the saint, this means that the original text was also written after the liberation of Crete in 961, and so

at least seventeen years after the death of the saint during the reign of Romanos I (that is, before that emperor's deposition in 944).

Certain elements in the text do not inspire confidence in its historicity. Leo, the redactor, informs us that someone wrote the saint's biography after discussions he had with the saint himself and those who knew him. At the beginning of the text (chapter 1.3), the author informs us that the saint revealed a few things about himself to "us" (ἡμῖν). This is vague and could refer to the author or all the people of Kythera. Later on the author says that he does not know the exact relationship between the saint and his protector, the priest from Nauplion, since he was not there at the time, adding that he wrote down only what the saint revealed to someone in Monemvasia after his trip to Rome. Here again there is no indication that the author knew Theodore personally. At the end he speaks of Theodore's companion, the monk Antony, who preserved information about the saint's sojourn on Kythera. This is the only specific case of a named source of information about Theodore. What astonishes the reader, moreover, is the story of the double discovery of the saint's body. The author tries to reconcile two different versions of the same event: the discovery of a body by the sailors, who did not bury it, and its discovery by the hunters, who buried it properly. This shows that the circumstances of the body's discovery remained unclear.

The *Life* exhibits novelistic traits, which remind us of similar cases of saints whose existence is at least doubtful. The tablet near the head of the saint, where the date of his death was written, was something of a hagiographic *topos*. It can be found in the *Life of Saint Mary the Egyptian* by

Sophronios of Jerusalem: near the saint's body Zosimas found an inscription in the sand written in the saint's own hand, giving the month during which she died and her name.[49] The discovery of a saint's body by hunters is also noteworthy because we encounter this story in the *Life of Saint Theoktiste of Lesbos,* a saint who lived as a hermit on the island of Paros, which was deserted at the time (just like Kythera): the saint's body was found by a hunter, who recognized her, near a church (just like the body of Saint Theodore).[50] The hunter did not initially bury her body, and when he came back to do so it had disappeared.

Any reconstruction of events would be arbitrary. It is possible that everything began with the discovery of a body on Kythera, a largely deserted island. This led to the creation of a life-story: some faint reminiscences of an ascetic called Theodore, who had lived for a time in Monemvasia, were combined with the story of the relic's discovery to create a new saint. The initial text of his *Life* was written many years after the events, when the island was inhabited again. This text was likely composed no earlier than the start of the eleventh century, since the cult of the saint was well-established at that date, a considerable time after the liberation of Crete in 961. The date of its reworking by Leo cannot be established with any certainty.

The *Life* does mention specific persons and concrete events. They need not have been invented, but were used to provide the biography of the new saint with the necessary historical framework. These include bishop Theodore of Argos, the *tourmarches* Meliton, the story of the *allagion* at the time of Romanos I, and the story of the monk Antony who supposedly knew the saint. The *Life* is, moreover, an important source for the precarious situation of the coastal

areas of the Peloponnese in the early tenth century and provides us with valuable information concerning the strate-
gic importance of Monemvasia and the history of Kythera.
However, a text written at least fifty years after the event
cannot be used as a safe basis for the reconstruction of the
life of the mysterious man who was found dead on the island
of Kythera in the reign of Romanos I.

SAINT ARSENIOS OF KERKYRA

This is a short *synaxarion* entry incorporated into the *akolou-
thia* (liturgical rite) in honor of the saint (his feast day was
January 19).[51] Born in the late ninth century in Palestine, Arsenios migrated to Constantinople, where he was probably
appointed *oikonomos* by the patriarch Tryphon (928–931). After being elected metropolitan of Kerkyra in 933, he moved
to the island, where he was taken prisoner by the invading
"Scythians." In just a few condensed pages, this brief biography provides important information about the Byzantine
court's continued reception and promotion to high offices
of Greek-speaking Christian immigrants from Palestine, the
local defenses of islands that were distant from the capital,
the tension between imperial and Church officials in the
provinces and the need for bishops to travel to the capital,
and the contests that continued to take place over the relics
of saints after their deaths.

The Greek texts in this volume were prepared by Polemis,
who also produced the initial translation that was revised by
Kaldellis. The introduction and notes are the result of their
collaboration. The translators are grateful to Alice-Mary

Talbot and Fr. Maximos Constas for their careful review of the texts and translations and their valuable suggestions and corrections that greatly improved the book. They also wish to thank three Tyler Fellows at Dumbarton Oaks, John Zaleski, Jake Ransohoff, and John Mulhall for their meticulous editorial work, and William Little, for his preparation of the index. Finally, we acknowledge with gratitude the contributions of Nicole Eddy, Managing Editor of the Dumbarton Oaks Medieval Library, and her two summer interns, Ned Sanger and Hannelore Segers, who assisted with final review of the volume for the press.

NOTES

1 Three of the texts have been translated into modern Greek; see the Bibliography at the end of the volume for details.

2 See, most recently, Florin Curta, *The Edinburgh History of the Greeks, c. 500 to 1050: The Early Middle Ages* (Edinburgh, 2011); Anagnostakis and Kaldellis, "The Textual Sources for the Peloponnese, A.D. 582–959."

3 Caraher, "Constructing Memories."

4 Carolyn L. Connor and W. Robert Connor, *The Life and Miracles of Saint Luke of Steiris: Text, Translation and Commentary* (Brookline, Mass., 1994); Denis F. Sullivan, *The Life of Saint Nikon* (Brookline, Mass., 1987).

5 Lee F. Sherry, "Life of St. Athanasia of Aigina," in *Holy Women of Byzantium: Ten Saints' Lives in English Translation,* ed. Alice-Mary Talbot (Washington, D.C., 1996), 137–58.

6 By Pamela Armstrong (forthcoming from Brill, accompanied by the Greek text).

7 Ioannis Polemis and Evelina Mineva, *Βυζαντινά υμνογραφικά και αγιολογικά κείμενα* (Athens, 2016). See also the Note on the Texts.

8 Alfred Rahlfs, ed., *Septuaginta,* revised by Robert Hanhart, 2 vols. (Stuttgart, 2006); Barbara Aland, Kurt Aland, et al., eds., *Novum Testamentum Graece: Nestle-Aland,* 28th ed., 4th corrected revised printing (Stuttgart, 2015).

9 Possibly an addressee of a letter by Patriarch Nicholas I Mystikos; Sophianos, Ἅγιος Νικόλαος, 32.

10 However, ὁρατίων or ὡρατίων is an attested word for an address by an official (emperor, consul, etc.). It is possible that our author misunderstood an official address or decree for a person.

11 Kazhdan, "Hagiographical Notes (5–8)," 180.

12 Various proposals: Anna Avramea, Ἡ Βυζαντινὴ Θεσσαλία μέχρι τοῦ 1204: Συμβολὴ εἰς τὴν ἱστορικὴν γεωγραφίαν (Athens, 1974), 89–96; Philippos Philippou, "Ποιοί ἤταν οι Ἀβάρεις' που επέδραμαν στην Θεσσαλία κατά τον 9° αιώνα;", Ἱστορικογεωγραφικά 5 (1995): 123–32; Koulouras, "Σχετικά με τον Βίο του αγίου Νικολάου του Νέου," 113–22.

13 François Halkin, review of Ἅγιος Νικόλαος ὁ ἐν Βουναίνῃ, by Demetrios Z. Sophianos, Analecta Bollandiana 91 (1973): 218–19; Enrica Follieri, "S. Ardomio martire in Tessaglia," Analecta Bollandiana 93 (1975): 313–48, at 327–29, 345–48.

14 Follieri, "S. Ardomio," 343. The canon was simultaneously published by Demetrios Z. Sophianos, "Ἀνέκδοτος κανὼν τοῦ μάρτυρος Ἁρμοδίου, συνταχθεὶς ὑπὸ τοῦ Ἀρσενίου τῆς Κρυπτοφέρρης (ΙΑ΄αἰ.)," Ἐπετηρὶς Ἑταιρείας Βυζαντινῶν Σπουδῶν 39/40 (1972–73): 96–109, at 104–9, and Constantinus [Konstantinos] Nikas, Analecta Hymnica Graeca e codicibus eruta Italiae inferioris Ioseph Schiro consilio et ductu edita, vol. 9, Canones Maii (Rome, 1973), 91–104.

15 This short text has been published by Sophianos, Ἅγιος Νικόλαος, 178–79.

16 Sophianos, Ἅγιος Νικόλαος, 33; also Johannes Koder and Friedrich Hild, Hellas und Thessalia (Vienna, 1976), 138. It seems that the cult of Saint Nicholas developed a rivalry to those of Saint Demetrios in Thessalonike and Saint Achilleios in Larissa, who were unable to heal the governor Euphemianos.

17 Eleni Papaeliopoulou-Photopoulou, "Παρατηρήσεις καὶ προσθῆκες στὸ Dossier ἑνὸς λησμονημένου ἁγίου τῆς Βυζαντινῆς Μεθώνης," in Πρακτικὰ τοῦ Α΄ Συνεδρίου Μεσσηνιακῶν Σπουδῶν (Καλαμάτα 2–4 Δεκ. 1977) (Athens, 1978), 236–58, at 245, identifies him with the author of a liturgical canon written in the saint's honor, preserved in Vaticanus graecus 2571.

18 According to *PmbZ* 1, no. 683, his parents fled from the revolt of Euphemios, which led to the occupation of the island by the Arabs.

19 Germaine da Costa-Louillet, "Saints de Grèce aux VIIIe, IXe et Xe siècles," *Byzantion* 31 (1961): 309–69, at 314.

20 For Methone (Modon) in medieval times, see Enrica Follieri, "Santi di Metone: Atanasio vescovo, Leone taumaturgo," *Byzantion* 41 (1971): 378–451, at 378–99.

21 Joannes Dominicus [Giovanni Domenico] Mansi, *Conciliorum nova et amplissima collectio,* vol. 17 (Venice, 1772), col. 376.

22 Anna Lambropoulou et al., "Μνήμη καὶ λήθη τῆς λατρείας τῶν ἁγίων τῆς Πελοποννήσου (9ος–15ος αἰώνας)," in *Οι ήρωες της ορθόδοξης εκκλησίας: Οι νέοι άγιοι, 8ος–16ος αιώνας,* ed. Eleonora Kountoura-Galake (Athens, 2004), 265–94, at 289–91.

23 Laniado, "Ἅγιος Πέτρος," 134–35.

24 Jean Darrouzès, ed., *Épistoliers byzantins du Xe siècle* (Paris, 1960), 51–57; *PmbZ* 2, no. 27705; also Panayotis A. Yannopoulos, "Ὁ Ναυπλιεύς Θεόδωρος Νικαίας," in Yannopoulos and Savvides, *Μεσαιωνικὴ Πελοπόννησος,* 233–92; Athanasios Markopoulos, "Überlegungen zu Leben und Werk des Alexandros von Nikaia," *Jahrbuch der österreichischen Byzantinistik* 44 (1994): 313–26, at 317.

25 Stephanos Efthymiadis, "Hagiography from the 'Dark Age' to the Age of Symeon Metaphrastes (Eighth–Tenth Centuries)," in *The Ashgate Companion to Byzantine Hagiography,* vol. 1, *Periods and Places,* ed. Stephanos Efthymiadis (Burlington, Vt., 2011), 95–142, at 123.

26 Theodore of Nicaea, *Letters,* 1.55, 14.2, in *Épistoliers,* ed. Darrouzès, 263, 282.

27 For example, Theodore of Nicaea, *Letters,* 40.10–11, in *Épistoliers,* ed. Darrouzès, 308. The strange expression in the *Life,* νόσοις ταριχευθέν (withered by illness), referring to the saint's body, may be compared with similar expressions in *Letters,* 36.4 (p. 302) (ταριχεία φροντίδων, "pickling of cares"), and 37.9 (p. 303) (τῇ ἀηδίᾳ τοῦ στομάχου καὶ τῷ ἀΰπνῳ ταριχευόμενοι, "withered away by nausea in the stomach and sleeplessness").

28 A lead seal of a metropolitan Paul of Corinth: Nikos A. Vees, "Zur Sigillographie der byzantinischen Themen Peloponnes und Hellas," *Vizantiiskii Vremennik* 21 (2014): 90–110, 192–235, at 98–99; Athanasios D. Komi-

nis, Γρηγόριος Πάρδος μητροπολίτης Κορίνθου καὶ τὸ ἔργον αὐτοῦ (Athens and Rome, 1960), 45; Tasos A. Gritsopoulos, Ἐκκλησιαστικὴ ἱστορία καὶ Χριστιανικὰ μνημεῖα Κορινθίας, vol. 1, Ἱστορία (Athens, 1973), 148–49.

29 On Argos, see Anastasia Vassiliou, "Argos from the Ninth to Fifteenth Centuries," in *Heaven and Earth: Cities and Countryside in Byzantine Greece,* eds. Jenny Albani and Eugenia Chalkia (Athens, 2013), 216–23, at 217. For the date of Peter's ordination, see Panayotis Yannopoulos, "Ο επισκοπικός κατάλογος του βυζαντινού Ἄργους," in Yannopoulos and Savvides, *Μεσαιωνική Πελοπόννησος,* 15–24, at 23.

30 According to Vasiliev, "The 'Life' of St. Peter of Argos," 177, the famine was caused by raids by the Bulgarians of Symeon.

31 Vasiliev, "The 'Life' of St. Peter of Argos," 176, identifies them with pagan Slavic tribes of the region.

32 See chapter 18 of the *Life of Peter, Bishop of Argos.* Identified with the *protospatharios* and *tourmarches* of the Peloponnese Theophylaktos, based on a lead seal, by Vasiliev, "The 'Life' of St. Peter of Argos," 185. Another Theophylaktos is mentioned in the "Life of Saint Loukas the Younger" in Connor and Connor, *The Life and Miracles of Saint Luke,* 163.

33 Bulgarians: Nikos A. Vees, "Αἱ ἐπιδρομαὶ τῶν Βουλγάρων ὑπὸ τὸν τζάρον Συμεὼν καὶ τὰ σχετικὰ σχόλια τοῦ Ἀρέθα Καισαρείας," Ἑλληνικά 1 (1928): 337–70, at 349; also Scholz, *Graecia Sacra,* 91–92; Vasiliev, "The 'Life' of St. Peter of Argos," 184. Slavs: Orgels, "En marge," 274–75. Yannopoulos, "Ἱστορικές πληροφορίες," 174–79, questions the claim that the Peloponnese was occupied for three years.

34 Antoine Bon, *Le Péloponnèse byzantin jusqu'en 1204* (Paris, 1951), 48; Dionysios Zakythenos, Οἱ Σλάβοι ἐν Ἑλλάδι: Συμβολαὶ εἰς τὴν ἱστορίαν τοῦ μεσαιωνικοῦ Ἑλληνισμοῦ (Athens, 1945), 52–56; Kyriakopoulos, "Προβλήματα περὶ τὸν Βίον καὶ τὸ ἔργον τοῦ ἁγίου Πέτρου ἐπισκόπου Ἄργους," 262–70. This is mentioned by Constantine VII, *De administrando imperio,* 50.25–70, in *Constantine Porphyrogenitus: De administrando imperio,* ed. Gyula Moravcsik, trans. Romilly Jenkins (Washington, D.C., 1967), 232–34; also the *Life of Saint Loukas the Younger,* 41, in Ἅγιος Νικόλαος, ed. Sophianos, 182; and possibly the *Chronicle of Galaxidi,* a late source that preserves valuable information on much earlier events: Χρονικὸν ἀνέκδοτον Γαλαξειδίου, ἢ Ἱστορία Ἀμφίσσης, Ναυπάκτου, Γαλαξειδίου, Λοιδωρικίου καὶ τῶν περι-

χώρων, ed. Konstantinos N. Sathas (Athens, 1914), 200–202; see Romilly Jenkins, "The Date of the Slav Revolt in Peloponnese under Romanos I," in *Studies on Byzantine History of the 9th and 10th Centuries* (London, 1970), no. 20 (pp. 204–6); Vasiliev, "The 'Life' of St. Peter of Argos," 179. Orgels, "En marge," believes that this passage has nothing to do with the events in the *Life* of Saint Peter.

35 Konstantinos D. Mertzios, "Περὶ τοῦ Ἀθηναίου ὁσίου καὶ ἰαματικοῦ Θεοδοσίου τοῦ Νέου," in *Ἀσματικαὶ Ἀκολουθίαι εἰς τὸν ὅσιον πατέρα ἡμῶν Θεοδόσιον τὸν Νέον λάμψαντα ἐν Ἀργολίδι τὸν Θ΄ αἰῶνα*, ed. Metropolitan Bishop Chrysostomos (Athens, 1969), 30; see Panayotis A. Yannopoulos, "Hosios Théodose le Jeune: Personnage historique ou légendaire?," in *Μεσαιωνικὴ Πελοπόννησος*, 343–81, at 354–55.

36 Vees, "Vie de saint Théoclète," 6–7; also Scholz, *Graecia Sacra*, 50.

37 Vees, "Vie de saint Théoclète," 9; also *PmbZ* 2, no. 28035.

38 Vees, "Vie de saint Théoclète," 7; also Romilly Jenkins and Cyril Mango, "A Synodicon of Antioch and Lacedaemonia," *Dumbarton Oaks Papers* 15 (1961): 221–43, at 237–38.

39 Oikonomides and Nesbitt are probably right to place the text in the early eleventh century: Nicolas Oikonomides and John Nesbitt, *Catalogue of Byzantine Seals at Dumbarton Oaks and in the Fogg Museum of Art* (Washington, D.C., 1994), 2:84–85, no. 2.29.2.

40 Vees, "Vie de saint Théoclète," 12–13.

41 Jenkins and Mango, "A Synodicon of Antioch," 240.

42 Jacques Lefort, "Ἡ ἀγροτικὴ οἰκονομία (7ος–12ος αἰώνας)," in *Οἰκονομικὴ Ἱστορία τοῦ Βυζαντίου ἀπὸ τὸν 7ο μέχρι τὸν 15ο αἰώνα*, ed. Angeliki Laiou (Athens, 2006), 377–494, at 391. See also Chrestou and Nikolaou, "Στοιχεῖα γιὰ τὴν κοινωνία."

43 Paul Lemerle, *The Agrarian History of Byzantium from the Origins to the Twelfth Century: The Sources and Problems,* trans. Gearóid Mac Nincaill (Galway, 1979), 85–108.

44 Oikonomides, "Ὁ Βίος τοῦ Ἁγίου Θεοδώρου," 268–69.

45 Ibid., 269.

46 Ibid., 270.

47 Ibid., 278.

48 Ibid., 279.

49 PG 87:3724C; for English translation, see Maria Kouli, "Life of St. Mary of Egypt," in Talbot, *Holy Women of Byzantium,* 75–93.

50 *Life of Saint Theoktiste,* 16, ed. Theophilos Ioannou, in Μνημεῖα ἁγιολογικά (Venice, 1884), 16 (32–34); for English translation, see Angela C. Hero, "Life of St. Theoktiste of Lesbos," in Talbot, *Holy Women of Byzantium,* 109–14.

51 See *PmbZ* 2, no. 20603.

MARTYRDOM OF
NICHOLAS THE YOUNGER

Μαρτύριον τοῦ ἁγίου ἐνδόξου καὶ μεγάλου μάρτυρος Νικολάου τοῦ Νέου

Δέσποτα, εὐλόγησον.

I

Καὶ τίνι ἂν ἑτέρῳ τὴν ἐκ λόγου εὐφημίαν προσάξωμεν, εἰ μὴ τῷ τοῦ Θεοῦ μάρτυρι, καὶ οὕτω καλῶς στεφανώσωμεν; Αὐτὸς γὰρ καὶ ὄντως ὁ θεῖος Νικόλαος ἐξ ἔργων οἰκείων ἑαυτὸν ἦν εὐφημῶν καὶ τὸν ἐκείνου βίον οἷόν τι κάλλιστον ἄγαλμα ἐν ἡμῖν ἀνιστορῶν, αὐτὸς ἑαυτὸν προτιθέμενος δείκνυται, μήτε τῶν ἡμετέρων ἐγκωμίων δεόμενος μήτε διὰ τεχνικῶν ἀσμάτων εὐφημεῖσθαι βουλόμενος. Οἱ γὰρ τοῦ Θεοῦ ἄνθρωποι, τῆς φθειρομένης ὕλης ἀνώτεροι διακείμενοι καὶ βίον ἄυλον μετὰ σώματος ἔχοντες, ἄγγελοι ἐπὶ γῆς ἀναφαίνονται, τὴν ἐκείνων πολιτείαν ἀσπαζόμενοι καὶ σαρκὸς ἔξω καὶ κόσμου γινόμενοι. Διά τοι τοῦτο ἀτονεῖ μὲν πρὸς τὸν ἐκείνου ἔπαινον ἅπας σοφιστικὸς λόγος, δυστοκεῖ δὲ πρὸς εὕρεσιν αὐτοῦ ἅπας ἀνθρώπινος νοῦς, ναρκᾷ δ' αὖ πρὸς τὴν γραφὴν ἅπασα χεὶρ τεχνική. Οἷς γὰρ ἐξ ἔργων ἡ εὐφημία προσγίνεται,

Martyrdom of the glorious saint and great martyr Nicholas the Younger

Bless this reading, master.

I

Who else merits a speech of praise more than the martyr of God? In this way, we may crown him beautifully. Indeed, the divine Nicholas himself truly brought praise upon himself through his own deeds: by casting his own life as if it were a most beautiful statue placed in our midst, and by putting himself forward so prominently, he thereby indicates that he has no need of our praises and does not wish to be eulogized by artful hymns. For men of God are superior to mere perishable matter and live in the body as if they were bodiless. They resemble angels on earth, embracing the angels' way of life and setting themselves effectively outside the flesh and this world. As a result, every speech written according to the rules of rhetoric falters before the task of praising this saint; the human mind labors in vain to invent a proper speech for him; and even the trained hand grows numb, unable to write about him in a fitting manner. It is superfluous and unprofitable to praise through our speech

τούτοις ἡ διὰ λόγων περιττὴ καὶ ἀνόνητος, ὅτι αἱ τῶν τρόπων ἐπιδόσεις ἔπαινος γίνονται τοῖς ἐργάταις αὐτῶν. Ὁ γοῦν ὁμώνυμος ἐμοὶ ἀθλητὴς καὶ <διὰ> τῆς ἀθλήσεως οἰκειωθεὶς τῷ Θεῷ, ταῖς ἀρεταῖς λάμπων οἷά τις ἀνέσπερος ἥλιος, πάντων ὑπέρτερος διεδείκνυτο, ὑποκλίνας δὲ πρὸς τὴν ἄθλησιν καὶ ταύτης τὸν δρόμον διηνυκώς, διπλοῦν ἐκ τοῦ Θεοῦ τὸν στέφανον εἴληφε. Ἀμέλει καὶ τὸν τούτου βίον διηγεῖσθαι προθυμούμενος ἐγώ, αὐτοῦ τε τὴν ἄθλησιν πᾶσι προθεῖναι βουλόμενος, ὀκνῶ τὸ ἐγχείρημα, ἰλιγγιῶ τὴν ἐξήγησιν, ναρκῶ πρὸς τὴν γραφήν, ὅτι ὑποπτήσσων ὁ ἐμὸς λόγος πρὸς τὴν τῶν νοουμένων ἐξήγησιν, σιγᾶν μᾶλλον ἢ λέγειν προθυμεῖται. Πέφυκε γὰρ τὸ ἀσθενὲς ἀκονιτὶ ὄντως ἡττᾶσθαι καὶ τῶν πρωτείων ἐκείνῳ παραχωρεῖν. Ὧι γὰρ ἥττηταί τις, τούτῳ καὶ δεδούλωται.

2   Λοιπὸν τὰ πλείονα καὶ λεπτότερα τοῖς εἰδόσι παραχωρήσας τοῦ μάρτυρος, αὐτὰ μόνα τὰ μέρη διηγήσομαι, ὅπως ὠφέλειαν μὲν τοῖς ἀκροωμένοις ποιήσωμαι, παράκλησιν δὲ τοῖς ἀνταγωνιζομένοις ἐνθήσωμαι καὶ μίμησιν βελτίστην τοῖς ῥαθυμοτέροις ἐργάσωμαι. Οὐκοῦν καὶ ταῦτα ποιῆσαι προθυμηθείς, οὔτε Ἑλικωνίας ἐπικαλοῦμαι Μούσας καὶ Χάριτας, οὐδὲ τὴν Ὀρφικὴν καὶ θελκτήριον ἠχὴν ἐπιμυθεύομαι, ἀλλὰ τὸν ἀόρατον καὶ ἄσχετον Λόγον, τὴν θείαν οὐσίαν καὶ δύναμιν, ἣ καὶ μογιλάλων γλῶσσαν ἐτράνωσε καὶ τῆς ὄνου τὸ στόμα διήνοιξε καὶ τοὺς ἀγραμμάτους ἁλιεῖς πᾶσαν τὴν οἰκουμένην σαγηνεῦσαι εἰργάσατο. Τούτοις τοίνυν θαρρῶν, τὸν ἀγῶνα ὑπέρχομαι καὶ τὰ τοῦ μάρτυρος πάντα τῷ μαρτυρί<ῳ> τίθημι γνώριμα.

those whose glory stems from their actions, since achievement alone is the praise of him who accomplishes it. The martyr, who is my namesake and drew closer to God through his martyrdom, shining through his virtues like a never-setting sun, was revealed as superior to all men. Submitting, then, to this contest and racing the course to completion, he received a double crown from God. And yet, although I am eager to narrate his life and desire to present his martyrdom to all people, I hesitate to do so. I grow dizzy at the prospect and my hand becomes numb when I try to write, because my speech, hesitant to relate all that I have in my mind, prefers to remain silent rather than to speak. It is natural for that which is feeble to be overpowered without a struggle by that which is stronger and to yield the prize to it. *For whatever overcomes a man, to that he is enslaved.*

Therefore, I shall concede the task of narrating the larger 2 part of the martyr's story and its subtler details to those who knew the martyr, while I will confine myself to narrating only those among the saint's deeds that will benefit my audience, console those who are struggling, and incite those who are sluggish to imitate him in a most perfect manner. Wishing to fulfill this task, I will invoke neither the *Muses* nor the Graces *of Helikon,* nor will I add a fabulous if enchanting Orphic song. Rather, I invoke the invisible and infinite Word, the divine essence and power, which loosened *the tongue of stammerers, opened the donkey's mouth,* and gave unlettered fishermen the power to catch the whole world in their nets. Having confidence in all of them, I embark upon my own contest and begin my narrative of all the martyr's deeds through this account of his passion.

2

Εἰσὶ δὲ ὦδέ πως. Ὁ θεῖος οὗτος ἀνὴρ πατέρα μὲν ἔσχεν ὡς ἀληθῶς οὐδένα, ἅτε τοῦ οὐρανίου Πατρὸς υἱὸς γνησιώτατος ἀναδειχθεὶς καὶ αὐτὸν ἔχων πατέρα τὸν πλάσαντα, πατρίδα δὲ καὶ τὸ γένος τὴν κατὰ τὴν ἑώαν μᾶλλον γῆν, τὴν νοητὴν ἀνατολήν, εἰς ἣν ἡ τῶν προπατόρων τελεῖται πανήγυρις καὶ ἣν ἔχουσιν οἴκησιν πατριάρχαι καὶ προφῆται καὶ ἡ τῶν ἀποστόλων καὶ μαρτύρων θεία ὁμήγυρις. Τοὺς γὰρ σωματικοὺς γεννήτορας καὶ τὴν κάτω καὶ πατουμένην πατρίδα ὑπεριδών, τῇ μόνῃ τῆς θεότητος Τριάδι ἐνήρμοσται, υἱὸς αὐτῆς μεθέξει ἀναδειχθείς, καὶ τῷ ἀγνοτάτῳ αὐτῆς γάλακτι ἐκτραφεὶς τὴν πνευματικήν τε ἡλικίαν ἐκ βρέφους ἀναλαβών, ἐκμαγεῖον τῶν αὐτῆς χαρίτων γεγένηται.

2   Ἀμέλει εἰς ἄκρον ἀρετῆς ἐληλακὼς γνώριμος καὶ τῷ τότε βασιλεῖ καθίσταται. Λέων τοίνυν ὁ Ἀλεξάνδρου αὐτάδελφος, ὁ εὐσεβὴς ἦν βασιλεύς, ὃς διά τε τὸ περιὸν τοῦ ἁγίου καὶ διὰ τὴν ὑπερφερῆ τούτου ἀνδρείαν, τήν τε τοῦ σώματος ὥραν, τοῦ φρονήματός τε τὴν στερρότητα, καὶ τὸ εὐσταθὲς καὶ βεβηκὸς τῶν ἠθῶν αὐτοῦ, διὰ τιμῆς ἦγέ τε τὸν ἄνδρα καὶ πάσης ἠξίου προνοίας αὐτόν, καὶ τοῖς στρατιωτικοῖς καταλόγοις ὥς τι χαράκωμα ὀχυρὸν ἐντάξας τὸν ἅγιον, δεξιὰς αὐτῷ φιλικῶς προσεφέρετο. Οὐ γὰρ τὸ κεκομψευμένον τοῦ λόγου ἠγάπα καὶ πιθανόν, οὐδὲ γελοιαστὴς καὶ ἀγοραῖός τις ἦν, ἀλλὰ γαληνὸς μὲν τὸ εἶδος, ἐμβριθὴς δὲ τῇ γνώμῃ καὶ στερέμνιος τοῖς ἔργοις ἐφαίνετο.

6

2

The story goes as follows. In truth, this divine man had no father at all, as he was revealed to have been a most genuine son of our heavenly Father: the One who created him was also his father. In fact, his true country of origin was that land in the east, I mean the intelligible east, where the celebratory gathering of our forefathers takes place, the abode of the patriarchs, prophets, and the divine assembly of apostles and martyrs. Disregarding his bodily parents and the earthly homeland on which he trod, and united solely with the triune God, he became its son through participation. He was nourished by its most pure milk and was spiritually mature even as a little child, molded by the graces of the Holy Trinity.

Reaching the highest peak of virtue, he became acquainted with the emperor of that time, Leo, the brother of Alexander. That pious emperor, being impressed by the great virtues of the saint, his supernatural courage, the beauty of his body, his firm beliefs, and *his strong moral convictions,* honored him and was solicitous for his welfare. He enlisted the saint in the armed forces as a mighty bulwark, and behaved toward him in a friendly manner. For Nicholas did not care for speech that was refined and persuasive, *nor did he like jokes or behave in a vulgar manner.* Instead, *his appearance was serene,* he was serious of purpose, and his

Καὶ τοιοῦτον ὄντα ὁρῶν ὁ βασιλεύς, ταξίαρχον αὐτὸν λεγεῶνος πεποίηκε στρατιωτικῆς καὶ παραδοὺς αὐτῷ ταύτην, εἰς τὴν προκαθεζομένην τῆς Θετταλίας πόλιν (Λάρισσα δὲ αὕτη κατονομάζεται), παρὰ τοῦ κρατοῦντος ἐξαποστέλλεται, ἵνα διατρίβων ἐκεῖ τοὺς ἐναντίους τῆς πόλεως ἀποτρέπηται. Τοὺς οὖν στρατιώτας ὁ τοῦ Θεοῦ ἄνθρωπος πλεῖον εἰς τὸν τοῦ Θεοῦ φόβον ἐνῆγεν ἢ τῇ ἐμπειρίᾳ ἐπαιδοτρίβει τῆς βασιλείας, καὶ ἦν κατ' ἄμφω δεξιὸς ὁ θαυμάσιος, τοῖς τε στρατιωτικοῖς καὶ τοῖς πνευματικοῖς ἔργοις.

3

Τότε τοίνυν, τότε ζάλη καὶ σκοτόμαινα τὴν οἰκουμένην ἐλάμβανε καὶ ἐξ αἰθρίας καταιγὶς τὴν Ῥωμαίων ἐκάλυπτε γῆν καὶ βαρβαρικὸν ἔθνος, οἱ αἱμοβόροι Ἀββάρεις, οἱ χείρους θηρίων, οἱ τὴν κοινὴν ἀγνοοῦντες φύσιν, οἱ ἄγριοι κύνες, καθ' ἡμῶν ἐπιστρατεύσαντες, διάρπαγμα τὰ ἡμέτερα πεποιήκασι. Καὶ ἦν ἰδεῖν κοσμικὴν ἀνάλωσιν καὶ σκότωσιν ἄφυκτον, πάντων χειρουμένων καὶ σφαττομένων ὑπὸ τῶν αἱμοβόρων τούτων θηρῶν. Συνελαμβάνοντο γὰρ ἄνδρες ὁμοῦ καὶ γυναῖκες, νέοι καὶ πρεσβύτεροι, μοnασταὶ καὶ μιγάδες, ἱερεῖς καὶ ὁ λαός, πάντες ἄρδην φόνου ἐγένοντο παρανάλωμα. Καὶ ἦν βοὴ σὺν οἰμωγῇ καὶ θροῦς ἄσημος, θρῆνος καὶ κοπετὸς καὶ οὐαὶ διαέριον. Αἱ μητέρες

conduct was always steadfast. Seeing all these qualities, the emperor appointed him commander of a military legion. Entrusting it to him, he sent him to Larissa, the capital of Thessaly, with orders to remain there and defend the city from enemy attack. The man of God trained his soldiers to fear God more than he exercised them to obey the crown. Thus this admirable man was successful in both military and spiritual affairs.

3

At that time a tempest broke out and darkness fell upon the entire world. A storm burst out of the clear skies, covering the land of the Romans: a barbaric nation, the blood-thirsty Avars, who were worse than wild animals and igno-rant of human nature, those wild dogs, marched out against us, plundering our territory. The result was widespread de-struction and inescapable death: everyone was taken pris-oner or killed by those bloodthirsty beasts. They took both men and women prisoner indiscriminately, both young and old, hermits and cenobitic monks, priests and laymen. All were utterly destroyed. One could hear cries and lamenta-tions everywhere. Unintelligible groans, dirges, beating of the breast, and wails of despair filled the air. Mothers

ἐθρήνουν τὰ τέκνα, οἱ πατέρες τοὺς υἱούς, τὴν ἄωρον ἡλικίαν οἱ καθ᾽ αἷμα προσήκοντες.

2   Ὁ γὰρ προρρηθεὶς Λέων ἐκεῖνος ὁ πάνυ σὺν τῷ αὐτοῦ αὐταδέλφῳ τοῖς τῆς ἑῴας διατρίβων μέρεσι καὶ τὸν ἐκεῖσε κατὰ τῆς ἀρχῆς ἐγερθέντα πόλεμον καταστέλλοντες. Καὶ γὰρ συνεῖχεν αὐτὰ σφοδρὸς ὢν ὁ πολέμιος καὶ βιαίως ἄπασαν τὴν ἑῴαν λεηλατῶν. Ὡς γοῦν ἐκεῖ τὴν πᾶσαν σχολὴν ἦγεν ὁ βασιλεύς, τὴν ἑσπέραν οἱ Ἄββαροι ἐληΐζοντο. Εὐάλωτον γὰρ φύσει τὸ μόνον καὶ ὑπὸ τοῦ λάθρα ἰόντος ῥᾳδίως κατατροπούμενον, ἂν δὲ καὶ ἰσχυρὸν σὺν τῷ λαθραίῳ ᾖ, μείζονα τὴν καταδρομὴν τοῦ κατατρεχομένου ἐργαζόμενον. Ὅθεν οἱ τῆς κατάρας κληρονόμοι καὶ τοῦ σκότους υἱοί, τὴν μόνωσιν ἡμῶν καὶ τὴν τῆς χώρας ἀφυλαξίαν κατανοήσαντες, τῶν προσοίκων κατέδραμον, <Μυσῶν> λείαν αὐτὴν πᾶσαν πονηρίᾳ κατεργασάμενοι καὶ δεινότατα καγχάζοντες καθ᾽ ἡμῶν καὶ γέλωτα πλατὺν χέοντες, ὅτι δεσπόται ἐρείπιων ἐγίνοντο.

4

Τότε τοίνυν ὁ θεῖος Νικόλαος σὺν τῇ ὑπ᾽ αὐτῷ φάλαγγι τῶν στρατιωτῶν δεῖν ἔκρινε μήτε τῇ πόλει Λαρίσσῃ συγκλεισθῆναι μήτε αὐτῆς τοῖς πολίταις ἐπαχθὴς γενέσθαι καὶ ἀηδής. "Οὐ δέον γάρ," φησίν, "ἄλλων ὄντας ἡμᾶς χειραγωγούς ποτε, παρ᾽ ἑτέρων νῦν τὸ ζωαρκικὸν ἡμᾶς

grieved for their children, fathers for their sons, and relatives for their kinsmen who perished before their time.

The emperor Leo, whom we mentioned above, and his brother were in the eastern part of the empire at the time, trying to defend it from the war that was launched there against our state, since the enemy had attacked those places fiercely, plundering the whole east violently. Since the emperor led the entire regiment there, the Avars took the opportunity to plunder the west. For that which is isolated may be easily captured and defeated by a stealthy attack, and if the attacker is powerful in addition to stealthy, then the disaster brought upon the victim is even greater. Thus, those heirs to the curse, the sons of darkness, perceiving our isolation and that the land was unguarded, attacked the inhabitants of that whole area, wickedly plundering it. They even mocked us and laughed horribly, saying that they were now masters of nothing but ruins.

2

4

At that time the divine Nicholas decided not to blockade himself in the city of Larissa with the phalanx of soldiers under his command, so as not to become burdensome and odious to its citizens. He said, "It is not proper for us, who led others in the past, now to obtain from others the means of

ἐρανίζεσθαι." Τοῦτο μετὰ τῶν σὺν αὐτῷ ἁγίων κρίνας ὁ ὄντως τοῦ Χριστοῦ ἀθλητὴς Νικόλαος, ὅρος τι κατελήφθη, ὃ Τέρναβον ἐγχωρίως ὀνομαζόμενον, ἀσκηταῖς ἀνδράσιν ἦν ἐνδιαίτημα, ἠρέμα πως ὑπανακεχωρημένον, ὃ δρυμοῖς καὶ δάσεσιν ἐναβρύνεται, καὶ πνοιαῖς εὐκράτοις ἀέρων καταπνεόμενον, ὑγείαν ἐκείνοις χαρίζεται. Τὸ δὲ τοῦ ὕδατος πότιμον καὶ ἀγλαὸν τοῖς πίνουσι γίνεται καὶ θέλγον τοὺς πίνοντας ὡς οἶνος, λευκότητι δὲ μερῶν καὶ στιλβότητι διαφανῆ τὴν ἐπιφάνειαν κέκτηται.

2   Τοιοῦτο τοίνυν ὑπάρχον τὸ Τέρναβον καὶ τοιαύταις καλλυνόμενον χάρισιν, οἰκήτορας εἶχε τοὺς ἀσκητὰς καὶ ἦσαν <μόνοι> μόνῳ Θεῷ νοερῶς συγγινόμενοι καὶ τούτῳ κατοπτριζόμενοι, νηστείαις τε σχολάζοντες καὶ στάσεσι παννύχοις, θειοτέρας ἀξιούμενοι ὄψεως. Ἄγγελος γὰρ ἐξ οὐρανοῦ καταβὰς τὸ διὰ μαρτυρίου τέλος αὐτοῖς προεμήνυσε καὶ "δεῦρο, ἀθληταὶ Χριστοῦ," φησί, "πρὸς τὸ μαρτυρῆσαι ἑαυτοὺς εὐτρεπίσατε. Δι' αὐτοῦ γὰρ μέλλετε τὴν βασιλείαν τῶν οὐρανῶν κληρονομεῖν, στεφάνῳ δὲ ἀκηράτῳ τὰς ὑμῶν ταινιωθῆναι κεφαλὰς καὶ μισθὸν λαβεῖν τὸν οὐράνιον. Τοῦ γὰρ εἰς τέλος ἄθλον ὑπομείναντος τὸ σώζεσθαι εἶναι γινώσκετε." Ταῦτα ὁ χρηματίζων τοῖς μάρτυσιν ἐξειπὼν εἰς οὐρανοὺς ἀνελήλυθεν, αὐτοὶ δὲ ὑπὸ τῆς θείας ἐκείνης νευρωθέντες ὁράσεως, προθυμότεροι πρὸς τὴν ἄθλησιν ἀπεγένοντο.

our subsistence." Making that decision, Nicholas, the true athlete of Christ, together with his fellow saints, went to a mountain, which was called Ternavon by the locals and was inhabited by ascetics. It is a somewhat remote and quiet place, priding itself on its forests and woods. With temperate breezes blowing upon it, it grants good health to those hermits. The water there is potable and splendid, delighting those who drink it as if it were wine; being white and shining, this water has a transparent surface.

Such was Ternavon. Adorned as it is with those gifts, its inhabitants were ascetic men. They communed with God alone through their minds, and *transformed themselves into God's mirrors.* They devoted their time to fasting and allnight stations, making themselves worthy of a more divine vision: for an angel came down from heaven, announcing to them that they would end their life as martyrs. He said, "Come now, athletes of Christ, prepare yourselves for martyrdom, through which you will inherit the kingdom of heaven. Your heads will be crowned with imperishable crowns, and you will receive a heavenly reward. Know that *whoever endures* this contest *to the end will receive salvation* as a reward." After saying this to the martyrs, he returned to heaven, while the hermits, fortified by that divine vision, became more eager to suffer martyrdom.

5

Τοίνυν καὶ ὁ θαυμαστὸς οὗτος καὶ θεῖος Νικόλαος, ὁ
ταῖς τῶν ἀρετῶν διαυγάζων μαρμαρυγαῖς ἅπασαν τὴν
ὑφήλιον, σύμβουλος ἄριστος γίνεται τοῖς συνάθλοις αὐτοῦ
καὶ "Ἐξέλθωμεν, φίλοι, πρὸς τοὺς ἐναντίους," λέγει,
"στῶμεν πρὸ προσώπου αὐτῶν, ἐπιδειξώμεθα τὴν πολε-
μικὴν ἐμπειρίαν ἡμῶν, κατασφάξωμεν δι' αὐτῶν τὸν ἀφανῆ
Ἐχθρὸν καὶ πολέμιον, γενώμεθα φίλοι Χριστοῦ τοῦ ἀλη-
θινοῦ Θεοῦ ἡμῶν, ἔργῳ δοκιμασθῶμεν, μετὰ τῆς ἀληθοῦς
ὁμολογίας ἐναποθάνωμεν. Νῦν καιρὸς ἀθλήσεως. Μὴ φει-
σώμεθα ἑαυτῶν, μηδὲ φιλοσωματήσωμεν, ἵνα μὴ τῆς μερί-
δος ἐκπέσωμεν τοῦ Χριστοῦ." Τούτοις ὁ ἅγιος ὀτρύνας
καὶ ζῆλον ἔνθεον ταῖς ἐκείνων ἐνθεὶς ἀγαθαῖς ψυχαῖς, σὺν
αὐτοῖς αὐτομόλως ἐξῄει πρὸς πόλεμον. Καὶ συμπλακέντες
τοῖς ἐναντίοις, πολλοὺς ἐξ αὐτῶν ἀνῇρουν, ἅτε δὴ πεῖραν
στρατιωτικὴν ἔχοντες καὶ τῇ θείᾳ δυνάμει πλέον νευρού-
μενοι. Ἐπεὶ δὲ ἴσχυε μὲν τὸ κράτος τοῦ Θεοῦ, κατέπιπτε
δὲ ἡ πληθὺς τῶν ἀσεβῶν, αὐτοί, ἐπεὶ κατατροπουμένους
ἑαυτοὺς ἑώρων καὶ ἐκλείποντας τῇ ἐπηρείᾳ τῆς τῶν στρατιωτῶν γενναιότητος, ὁμαδὸν †πᾶν† κύκλῳ πάντας ἑαυτοὺς ποιήσαντες ἐμφερεῖς, μέσον τοὺς ἁγίους συνέλαβον.

2 Καὶ χειρωσάμενοι αὐτούς, ποικίλαις τιμωρίαις καθυπέ-
βαλον, τὸν μὲν ὄνυξι ξέσαντες, τὸν δὲ τόξοις κατατοξεύ-
σαντες, ἄλλον τῷ καταπέλτῃ ὑποπιέσαντες, ἕτερον τῷ
τροχῷ ἐπέδουν, καὶ τοῦ μὲν τὴν κεφαλὴν τυμπανίζοντες
καὶ ἄλλου τὰ μετάφρενα σούβλαις διατιτρῶντες καὶ τοῦτον

5

Then the admirable and divine Nicholas, who illuminated the whole earth with the gleam of his virtues, perfectly counseled his companions, saying to them, "Friends, let us march out against our enemies, confront them, and display our military experience. By killing them, we will also kill our invisible Enemy and assailant. Let us become friends of Christ, our true God. Let us put ourselves to a real test, and die confessing the true faith. Now is the time of our trial. Let us not spare ourselves or cherish our flesh, so that we are not separated from the followers of Christ." With such exhortations the saint roused divine enthusiasm in their good souls, and together with them he went out to war of his own free will. They engaged the enemy and killed many of them, since they possessed military experience and, what was more important, they were strengthened by God's power. But at the time of the victory of the power of God, when the multitude of the infidels were being cut down, the latter, realizing that they were being routed and annihilated by the soldiers' bravery, formed themselves all into a circle and trapped the saints in the middle.

After capturing the saints, they subjected them to various 2 tortures: they ripped the flesh of one with iron claws, shot another with bows, and crushed another under a catapult. One was tied upon the wheel, while another was beheaded. The back of yet another was pierced by spits. Yet another

μὲν κοντῷ καταπείραντες, ἐκεῖνον δὲ ξύλου ἀπαιωρήσαντες, ὅπως μεταμάθωσι τὴν εὐσέβειαν. Ἀλλὰ μὴν οἱ μάρτυρες ὡς ἐν ἀλλοτρίοις σώμασιν ἐῴκουν ταῦτα ὑπομένοντες. Ποικίλαις τοιγαροῦν ὑποβληθέντες ἰδέαις βασάνων, ἀμετακίνητον εἶχον τὴν εἰς Χριστὸν πίστιν αὐτῶν καὶ ἐλπίδα, καὶ οἱ τύραννοι, ἐπεὶ τοὺς γενναίους ἑώρων μιᾷ ψυχῇ καὶ καρτερίᾳ φέροντας τὴν ἔκτοπον βάσανον ἔτι ζῶντας, θανάτῳ παρέδωκαν, καὶ τοὺς μὲν μάρτυρας, ἑαυτοὺς δὲ μαρτύρων ἀναιρέτας ἀπέδειξαν. Οὕτω πρὸς ὃν ἐπόθησαν οἱ γενναῖοι διὰ μαρτυρίου διέβησαν Θεόν, οὕτω στεφανῖται οἱ ἀθληταὶ γεγόνασι καὶ τὰ βραβεῖα τῆς νίκης ἠνέγκαντο, τὴν τῶν δαιμόνων ἰσχὺν νικήσαντες καὶ τὸν ἄρχοντα τοῦ σκότους καταπατήσαντες.

6

Ἀλλὰ γὰρ ὁ μάρτυς Νικόλαος, ῥώμῃ σώματος καὶ φρενὸς ἰσχύι εὐτολμίᾳ τε καὶ θράσει χρησάμενος, ἐκ μέσου τῶν κατεχόντων διέδρα. Ταχύτερος γὰρ ἑαυτοῦ γεγονὼς καὶ πτηνοῦ δίκην ἐξαρθείς, φυγὰς ᾤχετο, καὶ τὸ ὄρος καταλαβὼν τῆς Βουναίνης, ἐκεῖσε διῆγε, τὴν προτέραν δίαιταν ἔχων καὶ καθ' ἡσυχίαν ἐμφιλοχωρῶν ἐν αὐτῷ. Ἀλσώδης γὰρ ὁ τῆς κατοικίας αὐτοῦ τόπος ὤν, σπήλαιόν τε κεκτημένος καὶ δρυὶ σκεπόμενος ὑψικόμῳ, ἀρεστὴν παρεῖχε τῷ ἀθλητῇ τὴν δίαιταν. Ἀμέλει γοῦν τὴν ὁλκάδα

was impaled on a pole, while some were hanged from a tree, all to make them deny their true faith. But the martyrs endured all this steadfastly, giving the impression that they were really inhabiting other bodies. Although subjected to diverse kinds of torture, their faith in Christ and their hope in him remained unshakable. The tyrants, seeing that the martyrs who were still alive endured that excruciating torment with their hearts united and with a shared courage, put them to death. In this way they transformed them into martyrs, while becoming themselves the killers of martyrs. Thus, it was through martyrdom that those brave men came to God, whom they had passionately aspired to reach. In this way, the athletes were crowned and received the prize for their victory, after defeating the power of the demons and trampling the ruler of darkness under their feet.

6

The martyr Nicholas, however, through his physical vigor and power of mind, used his courage and prowess to escape from the midst of his captors. He virtually outran himself and, soaring like a bird, escaped quickly and reached the mountain of Vounaina. There he now stayed, having the same way of life as before, dwelling there in spiritual tranquility. The place he inhabited was wooded and had a cave in the shade of *a tall oak,* which formed a pleasant habitat for the athlete. Steering the ship of his soul toward heaven, he

τῆς ἰδίας ψυχῆς εἰς οὐρανοὺς πηδαλιουχῶν, κούφως δι-
έπλει τοῦ βίου τὴν θάλασσαν. Ἐγεγόνει γὰρ <ἀρεταῖς>
ὅλος κατάκομος, τὰ τῶν παθῶν ὑποτάξας σκιρτήματα, καὶ
τὰς τῶν ἐναντίων πνευμάτων βίας καταστορέσας, ὥς τις
ὑπῆρχε μειδιῶσα θάλασσα, μήτε δαιμονικαῖς ἐμβολαῖς κυ-
μαινόμενος, μήτε σωματικαῖς ὁρμαῖς τινασσόμενος, γαλη-
νιῶν ὡς εἰκὸς καὶ μόνη τῇ ἀσκή<σει> προ<στε>τηκώς.

7

Εἶχε μὲν οὕτω ταῦτα καὶ πλήρης χαρίτων θεϊκῶν ἦν ὁ
ἅγιος. Ἀλλ᾽ οὐκ ἤνεγκεν ὁ φθόνος ἠρεμεῖν, οὐδὲ ὁ τοῦ ψεύ-
δους πατὴρ πράως ἤνεγκε τὴν ἀλήθειαν, οὔτε δὲ ἡμέρως
ἦν τόνδε τὸν κρύφιον αὐτοῦ σφαγέα φέρειν. Ἀμέλει, ἵνα
πάντως ἑλκύσῃ τὸν χρηστὸν εἰς ζῆλον αὐτοῦ, ἐν τῷ †φέ-
ρον αὐτοῦ† τὸν μάρτυρα, μᾶλλον αὐτὸς ἐτιτρώσκετο,
ἀκμαιότερον ὁρῶν τὸν εἰς Χριστὸν πόθον αὐτοῦ αὐξά-
νοντα. Τῷ τοι καὶ συνεποδίσθη μᾶλλον ἢ συνεπόδισε καὶ
πτῶμα ἐξαίσιον πέπτωκε καὶ γέλως ὁρᾶται προκείμενος.
Τέως γοῦν λαθραίως τοὺς Ἀβάρρους καθάπερ ποτὲ τὴν
Εὔαν ὑπεισελθών, ἀναψηλαφῆσαι ἐψιθύρισε καὶ εὑρισκο-
μένους τοὺς Χριστιανοὺς μυρίαις ἰδέαις παραδίδοσθαι βασάνων καὶ τέλος τῇ τελευταίᾳ κρίσει τοῦ θανάτου ὑπάγειν
αὐτούς. Ὑπεῖξαν οἱ μιαροὶ τῇ βουλῇ καὶ ἀνηρευνῶντο
κῶμαι, χῶραι, ὀρῶν ἄκρα, ἄλση, ἐσχατιαί, σπήλαια, πάσης

sailed across the sea of life without making waves. For he became rich in virtues, keeping the impulses of his passions under control. Calming the contrary winds, which blew violently, he resembled a smiling sea: he was neither buffeted by demonic passions, nor shaken by bodily urges. Therefore, he was tranquil, being absolutely absorbed by his ascetic practice alone.

7

That was the situation as the saint was filled with the divine graces. But neither could malicious envy stay quiet, nor could *the father of lies* meekly endure the truth, nor could he remain tranquil in the face of his own hidden killer. Trying to convert the pious Nicholas into his own zealous follower, he attacked the martyr, but instead he was wounded himself when he saw Nicholas's love for Christ become greater and greater. Thus, instead of hindering the saint, he himself was hindered: he collapsed in *a spectacular downfall,* and became a laughing stock. Therefore, he approached the Avars in an insidious way, just as he had insinuated himself into Eve's mind secretly in the past, whispering to them that they should try once more to search out and find Christians, subject them to all sorts of tortures, and finally impose on them the ultimate penalty of death. Those vile men followed his advice and started searching through all villages, rural districts, mountain peaks, forests, borderlands, and caves; in short,

Ἑλλάδος κρύφιος τόπος, ἅπας οἰκούμενός τε καὶ ἀοίκη-τος. Συνελαμβάνοντο γοῦν οἱ Χριστιανοὶ καὶ ἀνηροῦντο ὑπὸ τῶν αἱμοβόρων τούτων θηρῶν ποικίλαις <βασάνων εἰδέαις> πρῶτον παραδιδόμενοι, εἶτα καὶ τὸ ζῆν ὀδυνηρῶς ἀφαιρούμενοι.

8

Μετὰ πάντων τοίνυν καὶ ὁ θεῖος ἐχειροῦτο Νικόλαος, καὶ τοῖς τυράννοις ἀντικαταστάς, "Οὐκ ἐξόμνυμαι τὸν Χριστιανισμόν," ἔλεγεν, "οὐχ ὑμῶν γενήσομαι κοινωνός, οὐ τῇ ὑμετέρᾳ θρησκείᾳ προστίθεμαι ὑμῖν, ἀλλὰ Χριστι-ανὸς μενῶ καὶ τῷ ζῶντι λατρεύσω Θεῷ καὶ τοῦτο σέβας ἔσται μοι ἕως ἐσχάτης ἀναπνοῆς." Τούτου μετὰ παρρησίας τῷ ἁγίῳ λεχθέντος, οἱ μιαροὶ Ἀββάρεις ὅλοι γεγόνασι τοῦ θυμοῦ, καὶ πρῶτον μὲν θωπείαις καὶ κολακείαις τὸ εὔτο-νον αὐτοῦ μαλάξαι πειραθέντες, ὡς εἶδον οὐδεμιᾷ προσ-βολῇ τὸν ἅγιον σαλευόμενον, θάνατον αὐτοῦ καταψηφί-ζονται, καὶ μετὰ τῆς ἰδίας λόγχης ὁ ἅγιος λογχευθεὶς μετέστη πρὸς ὃν ἐπόθει Χριστόν, κἂν ἐν τούτῳ τὸν ἴδιον Δεσπότην μιμούμενος, καὶ ὥσπερ ἐκεῖνος ἐπὶ σταυροῦ τὴν ἰδίαν πλευρὰν λογχευθεὶς τὴν σωτηρίαν ἡμῖν ἐπραγματεύ-σατο, οὕτω καὶ ὁ θεράπων αὐτοῦ διὰ τῆς εἰς *τὴν πλευρὰν αὐτοῦ* τρώσεως πρὸς ὃν ἐπόθει διαβάς, θαυμάτων θη-σαυρὸς ἡμῖν ἀναδέδεικται τὸ τίμιον αὐτοῦ καὶ μαρτυρικὸν

they searched through all the hidden places of Greece, both inhabited and uninhabited. Christians were arrested and killed by those bloodthirsty beasts: they took their lives in painful ways, after subjecting them to a variety of tortures.

8

Among them was also captured the divine Nicholas. Confronting the tyrants, he said, "I will not renounce Christianity, I will not go over to your side or adhere to your religion. I shall remain Christian and *I will go on worshipping the living God*. This will be my faith until my last breath." After the saint said that with such outspokenness, the abominable Avars were filled with anger, but they tried first to soften his resistance by flattering him and fawning upon him. However, when they saw that this approach had no effect on the saint, they sentenced him to death. They pierced him with his own spear, and the saint went directly to Christ, whom he had desired. Even in that respect he imitated his own Lord, for at the time of his crucifixion he was pierced in his side, and brought about our salvation. In the same way, after his servant Nicholas was wounded *in his side* he passed over to the one he desired. His precious, martyred body that suffered so much became for us a treasury of miracles. It lay

καὶ πολύαθλον σῶμα. Ἔκειτο γοῦν ἐκεῖσε θείᾳ ῥοπῇ φυ-
λαττόμενον καὶ μηδεμιᾷ προσβολῇ διαρρυέν. Ἡ γὰρ προ-
διαληφθεῖσα ὑψίκομος δρῦς, ἐμπλατυνθεῖσα ὥσπερ ἀπὸ
Θεοῦ καὶ μείζων ἑαυτῆς γεγονυῖα, ἔνδον λαβοῦσα τὸ τίμιον σκῆνος τοῦ μάρτυρος, διεφύλαττε τοῦτο ἀσινῆ καὶ
ἀλώβητον καὶ πάσης βλάβης ἀλλότριον. Καὶ ταῦτα μὲν
οὕτως, νυνὶ δὲ τῆς ἀκολουθίας ἐξώμεθα.

9

Ὁ χριστιανικώτατος βασιλεὺς Λέων τὰ τοῦ πολέμου
ἐν τῇ ἑῴᾳ στήσας τρόπαια καὶ μετὰ νίκης καταλαβὼν τὰ
βασίλεια, τὰ τῶν Ῥωμαίων ἤθη εὖ διέθετο. Οἱ γὰρ Ἀββάρεις τῇ τοῦ βασιλέως ὑποστροφῇ φυγῆς δὴ ἁψάμενοι, τὴν
ἑαυτῶν χώραν ταχὺ κατελάμβανον, καὶ μετὰ πάντων ἡ
Θετταλία πάλιν ἀπολαμβάνει κόσμον τὸν ἑαυτῆς καὶ ἡ
πρὸς μικρὸν χηρεύσασα καὶ στυγνὴ φανεῖσα καὶ ἀκαλλὴς
ἐστεμμένη νύμφη ἐφαίνετο, καὶ ὁ Θετταλίας πρόεδρος
ἐκεῖνος ὁ πάνυ, ὁ τοῦ μεγάλου ἀποστόλου Φιλίππου ἐφά-
μιλλός τε καὶ συνώνυμος, τῷ ἰδίῳ θρόνῳ ἐνιδρυθείς, τῆς
προτέρας αὐτοῦ διαγωγῆς εἴχετο. Ἀμέλει καὶ θειοτέρας
ἀξιοῦται ὄψεως ἐκ Θεοῦ κελευούσης, "ὅτι τάχος," φησί,
"τὰ τῶν μαρτύρων λείψανα τῶν ἐν Τερνάβῳ ὄρει ἀθλη-
σάντων ἁγίων ἀνακομίσασθαι σπεῦσον." Ἃ δὴ καὶ προσ-
εκόμισε τῇ σορῷ, παραδοὺς ἄξια εἰς δόξαν καὶ τιμὴν τῆς

there, protected by God's grace: no force brought against it could weaken it. The *tall oak* we mentioned above—growing even larger than before, as if at God's command—miraculously took the martyr's precious body within itself, and kept it intact, undamaged, and free from harm. That is how it happened. But let us turn now to the sequel.

9

After setting up his war trophies in the east, the most Christian emperor Leo came back to his palace in triumph and governed the territory of the Romans in a good way. For as soon as the emperor came back, the Avars fled and returned to their country in haste. Thus Thessaly, like all other places, was restored again to its former good order: she, who had become a widow for a short time and seemed miserable and ugly, appeared now to be a crowned bride. The great bishop of Thessaly, the namesake and peer of the great apostle Philip, was restored to his metropolitan seat and carried on in his role as before. At that time, he was deemed worthy of a divine vision from God, which told him, "Make haste to bring back the relics of the holy martyrs who suffered on Mount Ternavon, and do so as quickly as possible." The bishop indeed brought the relics back and placed them in a coffin, as was fitting to glorify and honor our holy and

ἁγίας ἡμῶν ἀμωμήτου πίστεως, καὶ γέγονεν ἡ ἀνακομιδὴ τῶν λειψάνων τῶν μαρτυρικῶν τοῖς πολίταις Λαρίσσης νοσημάτων ἰατρεῖον, δαιμόνων φυγὴ καὶ πάσης βλάβης ἀποσοβή.

10

Καὶ ταῦτα μὲν οὕτως. Ἐγὼ δὲ τῆς διηγήσεως τὸ χαρι-έστατον λέξων ἔρχομαι. Ἀλλὰ προσεκτέον τὸν νοῦν ὑμῶν, παρακαλῶ. Ἔχει γὰρ μετὰ τῆς χάριτος καὶ τοῦ θαύματος ἡδονήν, ἣ θέλγειν οἶδε τὰς φιλοθέους ψυχὰς καὶ πρὸς τὸν ἴσον δρόμον διανιστᾶν, ὅτι πεφύκαμέν πως οἱ ἄνθρωποι ἑτερορρεπεῖν καὶ ἢ πρὸς τὸ χεῖρον νεύειν ἢ πρὸς τὸ βέλτι-ον καὶ αὐτίκα καταλαμβάνειν ἐν προβάσει τὴν ἀκρώρειαν τῶν φαύλων ἢ τῶν χρηστῶν. Τὸν οὖν τοῦ Θεοῦ ἄνθρωπον εἰδότες ἡμεῖς ὅπως καλλίστην μὲν πραγματείαν ἐπραγμα-τεύσατο, καλῶς δὲ τὸν *πολύτιμον μαργαρίτην* Χριστὸν ἐκέρδησε καὶ νῦν μετὰ ἀγγέλων συναγάλλεται, μιμησώμε-θα τούτου τὰς ἀρετάς, κτησώμεθα πολλοῖς ἱδρῶσι τὰ ἀπο-κείμενα ἡμῖν ἀγαθά, ἵνα σὺν αὐτῷ αἰωνίως χορεύσωμεν. Ἀλλ' αὖ ὁ λόγος προσθεῖναι μέλλων τὰ λείποντα, παρακα-λεῖ τοῦ προσκεῖσθαι τῷ διηγήματι.

unblemished faith. The transfer of the relics of those martyrs created a veritable hospital for the inhabitants of Larissa, driving the demons away and protecting the people from all harm.

10

That is how things happened. Now I come to recount the most delightful part of my story. Please, I beg you, turn your minds toward it attentively. Besides being graceful and amazing, the story produces the kind of pleasure that satisfies god-loving souls, inciting them to choose the same course as the saint. You see, we human beings are so created that we lean now to one side and now to the other, inclining sometimes toward the worse course and sometimes toward its opposite: we either rush toward an extreme of base behavior, or toward the height of virtue. But now that we know how this man of God made the best possible deal and thereby gained *the pearl of great value,* namely Christ himself, and now shares in the joy of the angels, let us imitate his virtues and let us acquire, even with much toil, the blessings that are reserved for us, so that we may dance with him throughout all of eternity. My speech is now going to add what has been left out, and it begs you to listen to my narrative carefully.

II

Ὁ μάρτυς τοίνυν Νικόλαος τὸ καρτερικὸν αὐτοῦ καὶ πολύαθλον σῶμα εἰς τὸν τῆς Βουναίνης τόπον καταλιπών, ἔνθα καὶ τὸ μακάριον τέλος ἐδέξατο, ἐκρύπτετο ἡ ἐκ Θεοῦ δοθεῖσα χάρις αὐτῷ. Ἀλλ᾽ εἰ καὶ λανθάνον ἦν <τοῖς ἀνθρώ-ποις> τὸ σῶμα τοῦ μάρτυρος, ἀλλ᾽ οὐκ ἦν λανθάνον τῷ θεωρητῇ τῶν καλῶν. Χρόνος διῆλθε συχνὸς καὶ ὁ τῆς Θεσσαλονίκης δοὺξ <Εὐφημιανός>, εἰς προστασίαν φημί, παρὰ τοῦ βασιλέως ταύτην λαβών, μετά τινος ὑπατικοῦ Ὁρατίωνος ἐν ταύτῃ διέτριβεν, ἄλλοις μὲν ἄλλοις κολα-κεύμασι κολακευόμενος, πλείοσι δὲ δορυφορίαις θρυπτό-μενος. Ἀλλ᾽ ἡ θεία δίκη ἅμα μὲν τὸν μάρτυρα στεφανεῖν εὐδοκοῦσα, ἅμα δὲ καὶ δοξάζεσθαι θέλουσα, λέπρα τὸν δοῦκα κατέλαβε καὶ ὡρᾶτο ὁ πρώην λαμπρὸς στυγνὸς καὶ περιαλγής, ὁ ἀλαζὼν ταπεινός, ὁ θρασὺς δειλός, ὁ ἀνδρεῖος ἀσθενής, ὁ ὑπὸ πολλῶν δορυφορούμενος ὑπὸ πολλῶν ἐλε-ούμενος καὶ θρηνούμενος καὶ ἦν πτῶμα κείμενος τοῖς βλέ-πουσι καὶ θρήνων ἐπάξια. Πέφυκε γὰρ συμφερόντως ἡ οἰκονομία καὶ πρόνοια Θεοῦ τὰ ἡμέτερα διὰ πληγῶν καὶ μαστίγων ἀπάγειν μὲν τῶν πονηρῶν, ἐνάγειν δὲ πρὸς ἀρετῶν ἐργασίαν, ἵνα μὴ ἄκρατον τῆς ὀργῆς τοῦ Θεοῦ τὸν τρυγίαν ἐκπίωμεν. Τοιγαροῦν ὁ δοὺξ πληγεὶς θέαμα ἦν τοῖς ὁρῶσι καὶ θρήνων ἐπάξια. Τέως γοῦν τὰς τῶν ἰατρῶν τέχνας ἐσφαλμένας εἰδὼς περὶ τὰ ἀνθρώπινα σώματα, ζημί-αν τε πολλὴν ἢ ὠφέλειαν ἐμποιούσας καὶ οὐχ ὑγίαν περιποιουμένας τῷ κάμνοντι ἐνορῶν, πρὸς ἄλλην ἄγκυ-ραν ἐλπίδος δεῖν ἔγνω καταφυγεῖν προσφοιτῶν, καὶ τῇ

II

The martyr Nicholas left behind at Vounaina his long-suffering body, which had endured so much, there where he had met his blessed end. However, the grace given to him by God remained hidden. Although the martyr's body was unknown to men, it was not hidden to God, who contemplates all good things. Years passed. The governor of Thessalonike, Euphemianos, whom the emperor had entrusted with the protection of that city, was there together with a certain Horation, who held consular rank. Many people rushed to flatter him in various ways, and he was overcome by their obsequiousness. But divine justice, which wanted to crown the martyr and bring glory to him as well, afflicted the governor with leprosy. This man who was formerly so illustrious was now seen to be full of grief and distress. The arrogant man was humiliated, the bold man was now terrified, the manly one was now weak. The man with many bodyguards was now pitied and lamented by most people. He lay there like a corpse and was deemed worthy of lamentations by those who saw him. For divine dispensation and providence, managing our affairs in a way that is profitable to us, keep us away from bad things through blows and flogging, while at the same time inciting us to practice virtue, so that we do not drink the cup of God's wrath unmixed. Thus the governor, stricken by God, was a lamentable spectacle for all who saw him. Realizing that the science of physicians was flawed, that it brought more harm than benefit to human bodies, and that it was not in a position to restore the patient's health, the governor decided to seek refuge in another source of hope, going there frequently: he surrendered

τῶν ἁγίων ἐπισκέψει ἑαυτὸν ἐκδεδωκώς, ὅλος τῆς θείας ἐλπίδος εἴχετο, ἣν ἐξελιπάρει χρημάτων διανομαῖς, πενήτων πλουτισμοῖς, προστασίαις χηρῶν, χορηγίαις ὀρφανῶν, νοσούντων ἐπισκοπαῖς, φόρων ἐκκοπαῖς καὶ τοῖς λοιποῖς, οἷς ὁ Θεὸς ἐπικλᾶται πρὸς ἔλεον.

12

Ἐπεὶ δὲ πολλοῖς μὲν ἁγίοις προσελθών, πλείσταις δὲ καλῶν ἐργασίαις τὸν ἐλεήμονα Θεὸν θεραπεύων, εὕρισκε λύσιν οὐδαμοῦ τοῦ κακοῦ, καὶ πρὸς τὸν περιβόητον ἐν θαύμασι, τῶν ἰατρειῶν τὴν θάλασσαν καὶ τὸ ταμεῖον, τὸ ἄσχετον ῥεῦμα, τὸν θεῖον ὄντως καταφεύγει Δημήτριον καὶ τῷ †περὶ τοῦτον† καὶ οὐρανίῳ τεμένει φέρων ἑαυτὸν δίδωσιν ἐκεῖσε. Τοιγαροῦν διατελέσας χρόνον συχνὸν ἀπώνατο πλεῖον [ἢ] οὐδὲν καὶ ἀπογνοὺς τῆς τοιαύτης ἐλπίδος ἐπὶ τὸν σημειοφόρον καταφεύγει Ἀχίλλειον. Τὴν Θεσσαλονίκην γὰρ λιπὼν τὴν Θετταλίαν κατέλαβε, καὶ τῇ θειοτάτῃ σορῷ τοῦ τρισολβίου πατρὸς προσπεσών, θερμῶς αὐτοῦ ἐπεδέετο, δάκρυα κατάγων ποταμηδὸν καὶ πολλὴν ἀδολεσχίαν ἐκχέων ὡς τὸ εἰκός. Ἠμέλει δὲ ὡσεὶ καὶ ἡ ἐν τῷ πατρὶ Ἀχιλλείῳ θεία χάρις, οὐχ ὡς μὴ θέλουσα εὐεργετεῖν (μὴ γένοιτο· <εἰς> πάντας γὰρ φιλανθρώπως τὸ θεῖον προσφέρεται), ἀλλ᾽ ὡς τῷ Θεῷ δοκοῦν τῷ ἀθληφόρῳ Νικολάῳ τὴν τοῦ δουκὸς ἀπονεμηθῆναι ἴασιν. Καὶ δὴ

himself to the protection of the saints, placing all his hopes in God. He begged for God's mercy by donating money, enriching the poor, protecting widows, making grants to orphans, caring for those who were ill, reducing taxes, and everything else that prompts God to have mercy on us.

12

But although he visited many saints and performed many deeds of charity in service to our merciful God, he could not find release from his illness anywhere. He then sought refuge with the famous wonderworker, the truly divine Demetrios, that ocean and treasury of healing miracles, that stream which cannot be contained. He came to his heavenly shrine and surrendered himself there to the saint. However, even though he stayed there for a long time, he gained nothing. His hopes had been defeated, so he sought refuge with the wonderworker Achilleios. Leaving Thessalonike, he arrived in Thessaly and, falling down before the most divine tomb of that thrice-blessed father, he begged him passionately to cure him, shedding a river of tears and prattling on, as was only to be expected. But the divine grace of father Achilleios did not seem to be effective, not because it did not want to cure him—far from it, for God is always compassionate to everyone—but because God wanted the governor's cure to be attributed to Nicholas the martyr. As the

ἀδολεσχοῦντι ὁ ἐν Τριάδι Θεός, ὁ πάντας δι' ἄμετρον ἔλεος οἰκτείρων, ὁ τοῖς οἰκείοις σπλάγχνοις ἐπικαμπτόμενος
τοῖς εἰς αὐτὸν πεποιθόσιν, ὕπαρ, οὐκ ὄναρ φανεὶς τῷ δου-
κί, "ὅτι τάχος τὸ ὄρος τῆς Βουναίνης καταλαβὼν καὶ περι-
εργότερον ἀνερευνήσας, εὑρήσεις γάρ," φησί, "μέσον ὕλης
δασυτάτης ὑψίκομον δρῦν, ἔξωθεν δὲ αὐτῆς πηγὴν διειδῆ,
μέσον δὲ δρυὸς τὸ πολύαθλον σῶμα τοῦ ἐμοῦ μάρτυρος
Νικολάου. Καθάρας οὖν τὴν τῆς ὕλης δασύτητα, ναὸν τῷ
μάρτυρι οἰκοδόμησον καὶ τρὶς τοῦ πηγαίου ὕδατος εἰς
ὄνομα Πατρός, Υἱοῦ καὶ ἁγίου Πνεύματος λουσάμενος,
ἔσῃ ὑγιής."

13

Ὁ δοὺξ τοίνυν τὸ ὄρος καταλαβὼν τῆς Βουναίνης καὶ
περιεργοτέρως ἀνερευνήσας, εὗρε τὴν ὕλην, εἶδε δὲ τὴν
διειδῆ πηγήν, ἐθεάσατο τὴν ὑψίκομον δρῦν καὶ μεστὸς
φαιδρότητος καὶ χαρᾶς ἐπεδείκνυτο. Μέσον γὰρ τῆς
δρυὸς τὸ πολύαθλον σῶμα τοῦ μάρτυρος ἔκειτο, μυρίζον
εὐωδίαν πνευματικήν. Ἔκειτο δὲ σύνολον, ἀνελλιπές, τέ-
λειον, ἵνα τάχα καὶ ἡ φύσις τῶν δένδρων καθαγιασθῇ,
ὅστις ὑπῆρχε πεῦκος ἢ δρῦς ἢ κυπάρισσος. Ἐπεὶ δὲ ὁ δοὺξ
εἶδε τὸ ἐλπιζόμενον, πόσης ἄν, εἴποι τις, ἐνεπλήσθη χαρᾶς;
Περιχυθεὶς ἠσπάζετο, περιεπτύσσετο, ἔρραινε δάκρυον

governor was talking on and on, the God who exists in Trinity, the One who takes pity on us all because of his immense mercy, and who yields in his heart to those who have faith in him, appeared to the governor, not in a dream but in a waking state, and said, "Go in haste to the mountain of Vounaina and search through it carefully. You will discover a tall oak in the midst of a dense forest and a spring with clear water nearby. Inside that tree you will discover the long-suffering body of my martyr Nicholas. Clear away the thick underbrush there and build a church for the martyr. Afterward, wash yourself three times with the spring water in the name of the Father, the Son, and the Holy Spirit, and you will be cured."

13

The governor went to the mountain of Vounaina, explored the place diligently, and found the forest. He saw the clear spring, observed the tall oak, and was filled with joy and happiness. Inside the oak lay the long-suffering body of the martyr, emitting a spiritual fragrance. The body lay there intact, complete. It was in perfect condition, so that even the trees around it were sanctified—whether they were pine, oak, or cypress. When the governor found what he was hoping for, he was filled with joy, with more joy than one could say. He embraced the body, kissing it, taking it in his arms, and drenching it with tears of joy, saying, "Glory be to

ὑφ' ἡδονῆς, "Δόξα," ἔλεγε, "Θεῷ τῷ πατάσσοντι καὶ ἰω-
μένῳ, τῷ νεκροῦντι καὶ ζωογονοῦντι καὶ ῥυομένῳ ἡμᾶς ἐκ
τῶν ἀνυποίστων θλίψεων. Εὕρηταί μου ὁ ῥύστης, ὁ κα-
θαρισμὸς τῆς δυστήνου μου σαρκὸς πεφανέρωται." Ταῦτα
λέγων ἔργου εἴχετο κτίσεως καὶ ἀνεγείρει οἶκον τῷ μάρτυρι, οὐκ ἄξιον μὲν τῆς ἐκείνου μεγαλειότητος, πλὴν τοῦ
πολλοῦ πόθου καὶ τῆς σπουδῆς αὐτοῦ τὸ κάλλιστον σύμβολον, ὃς καὶ μέχρι σήμερον τεθέαται, καὶ τὸ ἅγιον σῶμα
ἐκείνου ἔνδον ὁ δοὺξ ἐμβαλὼν τὸν αὐτοῦ πόθον ἀφοσιοῖ.

14

Ἐπεὶ δὲ καιρός τε παρῄει συχνὸς καὶ οὐδαμοῦ τῆς
ἱμερτῆς ἰάσεως ὁ δοὺξ παραπέλαυε, ὅλος ἐναγώνιος ἦν.
Ὄναρ τοίνυν ὁ ἅγιος τῷ δουκὶ ἐπιστάς, "Αὔριον," γάρ φησιν, "ἐγερθείς, ἄπιθι πρὸς τὴν πηγὴν καὶ εἰς ὄνομα Πατρός, Υἱοῦ καὶ ἁγίου Πνεύματος λουσάμενος, ἀπολαύσῃ
καθαρᾶς τῆς ἰάσεως." Ταῦτα εἰπὼν ἀφανὴς γεγόνει. Τὸν
ὕπνον τοίνυν ὁ δοὺξ τῶν ὀμμάτων ἐκτιναξάμενος, ὑφη-
γεῖτο τὸ ὅραμα, <...> ἐκπλήξει μὲν ὅπως ὁ Θεὸς διὰ τῶν
θεραπόντων αὐτοῦ θαυματουργεῖ ἐν ἡμῖν, σπουδῇ δὲ ὅτι
τὸν φίλον αὐτῶν ἔμελλον ὁρᾶν ὑγιαίνοντα εἰς τὴν αὔριον,
ὃ κατὰ Χριστὸν γενέσθαι ἱμείροντο. Μετὰ λαμπάδων τοίνυν ἡμμένων τὴν νύκτα πᾶσαν ἐκείνην ἄγρυπνοι διατελέ-
σαντες, ἔωθεν, ὡς ἡμέρα ἧκεν <...> ὕλης τὴν πηγὴν καὶ

God, *who both smites and cures* us, who kills and brings to life, who saves us from our unbearable griefs. I have found my savior. The cleansing of my wretched flesh has been revealed here." Saying these words, he began a construction project and raised up a house for the martyr, which, while not worthy of his magnificence, was yet adequate proof of this man's great love and zeal. The church may be seen even in our days. The governor placed the holy body of the saint inside it, thereby fulfilling his desire.

14

But when much time had passed and the governor did not receive the cure that he desired so much, he grew anxious. Then the saint appeared to him in a dream and said, "Tomorrow when you wake up, go to the spring. Wash yourself in the name of the Father, the Son, and the Holy Spirit, and you will be completely cured." After saying these words, the saint vanished. The governor shook the sleep from his eyes and recounted his dream . . . They were amazed to realize how God works his miracles in us through his servants, but they were also eager to witness on the next morning the imminent healing of their friend, which they so much desired, through the grace of Christ. They passed the whole night in sleepless vigil, holding lit candles. The next morning at dawn . . . they reached the spring in the forest. The

οἱ ἀρχιερεῖς μέσον ἑστῶτα τὸν δοῦκα γυμνοῦσι τῶν ἱματί-
ων καὶ τρὶς τοῦ πηγαίου ὕδατος "Εἰς ὄνομα Πατρός, Υἱοῦ
καὶ ἁγίου Πνεύματος," ἐπειπόντες καὶ αὐτῷ ἐπιχύσαντες
(ὢ θαύματος ἀνυπερβλήτου, ὢ τεραστίου φρικτοῦ, ὢ προθυμίας Θεοῦ), ὑγιῆ τοῦτον εἰργάσαντο. Αἰφνίδιον γὰρ
ὡσεὶ λεπίδες ἀπὸ τοῦ σώματος αὐτοῦ ἀποβληθεῖσαι, καθαρὸν ὅλον τὸ σῶμα καὶ λαμπρὸν ἀνεφάνη, *μὴ σπίλον ἔχον,
μὴ ῥυτίδα, μὴ τὸ τυχὸν τραῦμα, ἀλλὰ μαρμαῖρον ἦν πλέον
ἢ τὸ πρότερον.* Τὰ εἰωθότα τοίνυν ὁ δοὺξ σὺν ἅμα παντὶ
τῷ λαῷ τῷ Θεῷ εὐχαριστήσας καὶ τὴν προσήκουσαν τιμὴν
τῷ ἁγίῳ μάρτυρι ἐνεγκών, χαίρων οἴκαδε ἐπανέστρεψε.

15

Ταῦτά σου, ὦ μάρτυς, τὰ διὰ Θεὸν ἀριστεύματα. Οὕτω
παρέστης εὐχαριστῶν τῷ Θεῷ φαιδρῷ τῷ προσώπῳ καὶ
ἱλαρῷ. Οὕτως ὀπτάνῃ τῷ οὐρανίῳ βασιλεῖ, Χριστῷ τῷ
Θεῷ, καὶ ἐλατὴρ τῶν ἐπερχομένων ἡμῖν νόσων καὶ ἰατὴρ
ἀναδέδειξαι. Καὶ τὰ μὲν θεῖα τῶν συνάθλων καὶ συμμαρ-
τύρων σου ὀνόματα ἡ ἐν οὐρανοῖς τῶν ζώντων φέρει βίβλος ἀνάγραπτα, ἡμῖν δὲ τοῖς ἐπὶ γῆς ταῦτα εἶναι πεφανέρωται. Ὑπῆρχον γὰρ Ἀρδόμιος, Γρηγόριος, Ἰωάννης,
Δημήτριος, Μιχαήλ, Ἀκίνδυνος, Θεόδωρος, Παγκράτιος,
Χριστοφόρος, Παντολέων, [καὶ] Ναβούδιος, <καὶ> Αἰμιλι-
ανός, καὶ γυναῖκες δύο, Εἰρήνη καὶ Πελαγία. Οὗτοι, οἱ τῷ

governor stood among the bishops who removed his clothes and sprinkled water from the spring on him three times, saying, "In the name of the Father and of the Son and of the Holy Spirit." And then—what an unrivaled and tremendous miracle! How eager was God in this!—they cured him immediately! It was as if the scales of leprosy suddenly fell from his body, which became clear and radiant, *without spot or wrinkle* on it, nor any other lesion. In fact, it was more beautiful than before. The governor and all the people recited the customary prayers of thanksgiving to God, honored the holy martyr in a fitting way, and returned home filled with joy.

15

These, O martyr, were your deeds of valor accomplished through God. In this way you stood before God, thanking him with a happy bright face. That is how you make your appearance before Christ our God, our heavenly king. You have proved yourself as one who drives away the illnesses that afflict us, and as our healer. The holy names of your companions, your fellow martyrs, are *recorded in the book of those who live* in heaven, but have been revealed to us who live on earth as well: they were Ardomios, Gregory, John, Demetrios, Michael, Akindynos, Theodore, Pankratios, Christopher, Pantoleon, Navoudios, and Aimilianos, and two women, Eirene and Pelagia. These martyrs, after being

μόνῳ Θεῷ, τῷ ἐν Πατρὶ καὶ Υἱῷ καὶ ἁγίῳ Πνεύματι, οἰκει-
ωθέντες συνήφθησαν καὶ τῆς βασιλείας τῶν οὐρανῶν
κληρονόμοι ἀνεδείχθησαν, οἷς καὶ ἡμεῖς ταῖς πρεσβείαις
αὐτῶν συναφθείημεν ἐν Χριστῷ Ἰησοῦ, τῷ Κυρίῳ ἡμῶν,
ᾧ πρέπει πᾶσα δόξα, κράτος, τιμὴ καὶ προσκύνησις σὺν τῷ
ἀνάρχῳ αὐτοῦ Πατρὶ καὶ τῷ παναγίῳ καὶ ἀγαθῷ καὶ ζωοποιῷ αὐτοῦ Πνεύματι, νῦν καὶ ἀεὶ καὶ εἰς τοὺς αἰῶνας τῶν
αἰώνων, ἀμήν, ἀμήν.

reconciled with the only God, the Father, the Son, and the Holy Spirit, were united with him and revealed as the heirs of the kingdom of heaven. Let us, too, be united with them through their intercessions in the name of Jesus Christ, our Lord. To him, to his eternal Father, and to the all-holy, good, and life-giving Spirit belong all glory, power, honor, and veneration, now and forever and unto the ages of ages, amen, amen.

ENCOMIUM OF NICHOLAS THE YOUNGER BY THE PRESBYTER ACHAÏKOS

Μαρτύριον τοῦ ἁγίου καὶ ἐνδόξου μεγαλομάρτυρος Νικολάου τοῦ νέου, συγγραφὲν καὶ μεταφρασθὲν παρὰ Ἀχαϊκοῦ πρεσβυτέρου

Εὐλόγησον.

I

Εὐφραίνει μὲν καὶ μαρτύρων μνήμη δῆμον φιλέορτον καὶ στεφανοῖ *λαὸν περιούσιον,* ἀγάλλονται δὲ καὶ αὐτοὶ αἰωνίοις σκηναῖς εὐφραινόμενοι, ἔνθα ὁ τῶν ἑορταζόντων ὑπάρχει *ἦχος* καὶ χαρὰ ἀνεκλάλητος, ἐκπλήττει δὲ καὶ τὰς οὐρανίας δυνάμεις, βροτοὺς ὁρώσας πρὸς οὐρανοὺς ἀνιόντας καὶ Θεῷ σὺν αὐταῖς παρεστῶτας, νοερᾷ ψυχῇ τῇ πηλῷ καὶ τῇ ὕλῃ μιχθείσῃ τέχνῃ καὶ δυνάμει τοῦ Κτίσαντος. Ἔδει γὰρ ἡμᾶς καὶ *μαρτύρων* τιμαῖς ἐπιτέρπεσθαι καὶ *ἀθλητῶν* αἵμασιν ἐπαγάλλεσθαι καὶ πρὸς ἡμᾶς οἰκειοῦσθαι τὰ κατορθώματα καὶ προσέχειν ὁμοῦ ταῖς ἐκείνων τιμαῖς τε καὶ πανηγύρεσιν, οὗτοι δὲ μήτε τῶν ἡμετέρων ἐγκωμίων δεόμενοι μήτε τῶν εὐφημιῶν ἡμῶν καλλυνόμενοι, αὐτοὶ ἑαυτοὺς ταῖς ἀρεταῖς κοσμοῦντες καὶ διαλάμποντες,

Martyrdom of the holy and glorious great martyr Nicholas the Younger, written and revised by the presbyter Achaïkos

Bless this reading.

I

The commemoration of martyrs delights the people who are fond of feast days, and it crowns the *chosen people*. At the same time, it pleases the martyrs themselves, who rejoice in their eternal tabernacles, where *the sound of the feasting company* reverberates amid an ineffable delight. It surprises the heavenly powers too, who see mortals ascending to heaven and standing together with them before God as noetic souls united with the clay of material life through the art and power of the Creator. It was right for us *to both take pleasure in the honors of the martyrs and be satisfied with the blood of their martyrdom*. In this way we both appropriate their glorious deeds and also pay close attention to their honors and their feasts. Yet the martyrs themselves have no need of our praises, nor do they become more beautiful when we honor them, since they adorn themselves with their own virtues and shine through them. In this way, they repel the dark

διώκουσι σκοτεινὰ τοῦ αἰῶνος τούτου πλήθη ἀέρια καὶ ζῶντες καὶ μετὰ θάνατον. Ζῶσιν γὰρ ἀληθῶς, θεοὶ καὶ αὐτοὶ γεγονότες ὡς Θεῷ συνεῖναι καὶ πλησιάζοντες, σαρκὸς ἔξω καὶ κόσμου γενόμενοι, τὰ βλεπόμενα τοῖς μὴ οὖσιν ἀντηλλαξάμενοι, ὁλοκαυτώματα ὄντες λογικὰ τῷ Θεῷ καὶ θύματα τέλεια καὶ προσφοραὶ δεκταὶ καὶ ὁλόκληροι, οἱ καὶ κοτύλῃ αἵματος ὡς εἰπεῖν βασιλείαν Θεοῦ κληρωσάμενοι, καὶ ἰῶνται πάθη ψυχῶν καὶ σωμάτων ἐπικαλούμενοι καὶ θαυματουργοῦσιν ἐν κόσμῳ, τὸ πεπαρρησιασμένον αὐτῶν πρὸς Θεὸν ἡμῖν ἐνδεικνύμενοι.

2 Ἀλλὰ καὶ ὃν ἡμεῖς ἑορτάζομεν σήμερον, ἔστω τοιγαροῦν πᾶσιν ἡμῖν ὡς ἄλλο τι τῶν τιμίων ἐπίσημον. Λεπροὺς καὶ αὐτὸς καθαίρει καὶ φυγαδεύει νόσους καὶ μετὰ θάνατον ὡς ἐν ὀνείροις ἡμῖν φανερούμενος, ἵνα κἀνταῦθα δείξῃ τίς καὶ πόθεν ὤν, ἴσως ἂν καὶ Θεὸς δι' αὐτοῦ δοξασθῇ. Τίνα δὲ τοῦτον; Νικόλαον λέγω τὸν νέον καὶ μάρτυρα, Νικόλαον δὲ οὐ τὸν ἐν Μύροις, τὰς ἱερὰς θυσίας καὶ ἀναιμάκτους καθ' ἑκάστην τῷ Θεῷ παρασχών, ἀλλ' ἕτερον μέν, τὴν ἐπωνυμίαν ἐπέχων ἐκείνου, ὃς ἑαυτὸν θυσίαν τῷ ἑαυτοῦ Δεσπότῃ καθαρὰν προθέμενος εἶχεν, οὐ τοῖς ἔξωθεν ῥαντισμοῖς ὡς εἰπεῖν τὸν Ἰσραὴλ ἁγιάσας, ἀλλὰ τοῖς οἰκείοις αἵμασιν ἑαυτὸν Θεῷ οἰκειώσας καὶ ποιήσας τὴν τελευτὴν τελευταῖον μυστήριον, τὸν νέον ὡς λέγειν αὐτὸν Ἀβραάμ, οὐ τὸν υἱὸν ἐν ὄρει θυσιάζειν δοκιμαζόμενος ἢ μᾶλλον ἑαυτὸν ἐν τῷ ὄρει τῷ Θεῷ διδοὺς θῦμα καθαρὸν καὶ ὁλόκληρον, τὸ ἑαυτοῦ αἷμα προθεὶς ὑπὲρ τοῦ ἰδίου Δεσπότου χυθὲν καὶ φίλος αὐτοῦ γενόμενος γνήσιος, τὴν

multitudes of the air that characterize this age, and they do this both during their life and after their death. For they are truly alive, having become gods themselves, since they are in the company of God, drawing near to him after having abandoned the flesh and our world; they exchanged *what is seen for what is invisible.* They transformed themselves into *rational sacrificial offerings* to God: they became *perfect victims for the sacrifice, offerings that were acceptable* and wholly perfect. They have inherited the kingdom of God in exchange for a mere cup of their blood, so to speak. They cure the sufferings of our bodies and souls whenever they are called upon to help us, and they work miracles in this world, proving to us that they are on intimate terms with God.

Let us, then, consider the man whose feast we are celebrating today as *yet another one of our precious and notable possessions.* He too cures lepers and chases away illnesses, appearing in our dreams after his death in order to show us who he really is and where he comes from, and at the same time so that God may be honored as well through him. About whom am I speaking? I am referring to Nicholas the Younger, the martyr, not Nicholas of Myra, who offers the holy, bloodless sacrifice to God every day. This is a different man who only happens to have the same name, who offered himself as a pure sacrifice to his own Lord. He did not in so doing *sanctify Israel with the sprinkling,* but rather he brought himself close to God through the offering of his own *blood. He made his death count as the last mystery.* He was, so to speak, *a new Abraham:* he did not sacrifice his son on the mountain as a test by God, but rather offered himself to God on the mountain as a whole and pure sacrifice, shedding his own blood for the sake of his Lord and becoming his genuine

2

ἑαυτοῦ ψυχὴν ὑπὲρ ἐκείνου τιθέμενος, ὃς οὐ μόνον μετὰ
τῶν ἰδίων οἰκογενῶν κατὰ βασιλέων στρατεύεται, ἵνα καὶ
Λὼτ πανοικεὶ ἐκ χειρὸς ἐκείνων ἐξέληται, ἀλλὰ καὶ πρὸς
ἅπαν οὗτος βαρβαρικὸν δεικνύει τὰ τρόπαια.

3   Οἰκειοῦται τοιγαροῦν αὐτὸς τῷ Θεῷ καὶ πρὸ τῆς ἀθλήσεως. Τὸ σῶμα γὰρ καθαγνίσας, πρὸς τὴν ἀπαθῆ ζωὴν τὴν
ψυχὴν μεταθέμενος, πάσας γὰρ τὰς ἀρετὰς εἰς ἓν συναγα-
γὼν εἶχε, μελίττης ἴσος γενόμενος. Πάντα γὰρ πρὸς ἑαυτὸν συνάγων τὰ κάλλιστά τε καὶ τιμιώτερα καὶ περιέχων
τὰ χρησιμώτατα καὶ ὡς ἐν σίμβλῳ τινὶ τῇ ἐκείνου ψυχῇ
περιθεὶς διεφύλαττε, προφητικῶς τὰ ἔμπροσθεν βλέπων
ὡς καὶ διὰ Χριστὸν μαρτυρεῖν ἔμελλεν. Ναρκᾷ μοι δὲ νοῦς
καὶ γλῶσσα τῶν ἀνεφίκτων ἐφάπτεσθαι καὶ χεῖρα τεῖναι
πρὸς τὰ ἐκείνου ἐγκώμια, εἰ καὶ πάλιν ἐπαινεῖν ἐγχειρήσο-
μαι, μὴ τῇ ὕβρει ἀντηλλάξω τὸν ἔπαινον. Πέποιθα δὲ ταῖς
ἐκείνου εὐχαῖς, αἷς αὐτὸς ἐξιλέει καθεκάστην τὸν Κτί-
σαντα καὶ ὅσα ἐκ τῶν ἐκείνου ἔδει λέγειν, εἰ καὶ μᾶλλον ἐκ
τῶν πολλῶν ὀλίγα, ἐν μικρῷ τῷ λόγῳ τολμήσας ἐφάπτο-
μαι, τὰς ὑμῶν ἀκοὰς αὐτὰ προτιθέμενος.

2

Λέοντος γὰρ ποτὲ τοῦ εὐσεβοῦς βασιλέως καὶ φιλοχρί-
στου τὰ τῶν Ῥωμαίων σκῆπτρα κατέχοντος, τὰ ἀνατολικὰ
μέρη πολλὰ ἔθνη βαρβαρικὰ ἐπόρθει καὶ ἐλυμαίνετο καὶ
κατὰ τῶν Ῥωμαίων σφοδρῶς ἀντεῖχον καὶ παρετάττοντο

friend, as *he lay down his own life on* the latter's *behalf.* Not only did he go out with his household to battle against the kings in order to save Lot together with his whole family from their hands, but he also erected trophies of war against all the barbarians.

He was on intimate terms with God even before his martyrdom, for he purified his body and oriented his soul toward the life that is devoid of any passion. In this way, he had collected all virtues in one place. Just like a bee, he gathered all the best inside himself, all things that are precious and useful, and placed them in his soul as if it were a beehive, keeping them safe. He saw the future like a prophet, knowing in advance that he was going to become a martyr for the sake of Christ. My mind and my tongue are numb, unable to cope with such unattainable things. I do not dare to stretch out my hand to write his praise because if I try again to write his encomium, I am afraid that I may insult the saint instead of praising him. But I am confident in his prayers, through which he appeases the Creator every day. Whatever I will say about him, just a few stories picked out from the many, I will dare to compose in this brief account, which I submit to your hearing.

3

2

During the reign of the pious and Christ-loving emperor Leo, who held the scepters of the Romans, the eastern provinces were taken and plundered by many barbaric nations, who offered strong resistance to the Romans, being drawn

καὶ τὴν ἑῴαν πᾶσαν καταιγὶς ἄλλη τις εἶχεν ὡς εἰπεῖν καὶ σκοτόμαινα, ὑπερνικοῦντες στρατηγοὺς καὶ σατράπας καὶ ὅσον τοῦ βασιλέως στρατόπεδον. Τί δὲ καὶ τὸ ἐν μέσῳ; Κινεῖται δὴ καὶ ὁ βασιλεὺς κατὰ αὐτῶν σὺν Ἀλεξάνδρῳ, τῷ ἰδίῳ ἀδελφῷ καὶ συναίμονι, πέμπονται δὲ παρευθὺς ἐξ αὐτῶν καὶ γράμματα βασιλικὰ πρὸς δυσμάς, "Ὅσοι ἂν ἦτε," λέγων, "τεταγμένοι καὶ πεπειραμένοι τῇ στρατιᾷ, σπεύσατε ἐξ αὐτῆς πρὸς ἡμᾶς, μηδὲν ἀμελήσαντες, τὰ βαρβαρικὰ ἔθνη ἐν τῇ ἀνατολῇ σὺν ἡμῖν παρατάξασθαι." Ἔργον δὲ τῷ λόγῳ εὐθὺς ἠκολούθει καὶ πᾶσα ἡ στρατιὰ ἐκεῖ σὺν τῷ βασιλεῖ ἦν.

2   Τοῦτο δὲ καὶ τὸ τῶν Ἀββάρων ἔθνος μαθόν, κινεῖται πρὸς τὰ ἑσπέρια, ἀκούσαντες ὅσα Ῥωμαίων συμβέβηκε βασιλεῖ, καὶ ληΐζονται παρ' αὐτῶν καὶ τόποι καὶ χῶραι καὶ πόλεις καὶ κῶμαι, μικροῦ δεῖν καὶ ἅπαν τῶν ἑσπερίων μεθόριον, καὶ γίνεται τῆς τῶν Αἰγυπτίων ἐνάτης πληγῆς αὐτοῖς παραπλήσιον, ἢ μᾶλλον καὶ ἀκρίδος καὶ βρούχου καὶ τῶν ἄλλων ἐπιμανέστερον καὶ ἦν ἰδεῖν αἱμάτων ἐπιρροὰς τότε καὶ θρήνους καὶ κωκυτοὺς καὶ ἄλλα ὅσα τὰ λυπηρά. Τοῦτο γὰρ ἦν ἐκείνοις τὸ ἴδιον καὶ οὐδὲν ἄλλο ἢ τὸ κατασφάττειν ἀνθρώπους καὶ χαίρειν ἐν αἵμασι, τῆς ἰδίας ὄντως ἐπιλαθόμενοι φύσεως. Ἠτεκνοῦντο μητέρες, ἀνῃροῦντο πρεσβῦται, ἐσφάττοντο βρέφη καὶ νέοι τὰς κεφαλὰς ἀπετέμνοντο καὶ ἡλικία πᾶσα μακρὰν τῶν ζώντων ἐγένετο, οὓς δὲ πάλιν ῥωγμαὶ γῆς καὶ νῆσοι καὶ θάλαττα διεσώσατο, ὡς κιβωτὸν ἄλλην ταῦτα κατεῖχον, ὡς δι' ἐκείνων σωζόμενοι. Κατακλυσμὸς ἄλλος τὸ βαρβαρικὸν ἐκεῖνο ξίφος τοῖς δυτικοῖς ἦν καὶ θάνατος ἀτιμώτατος.

up in battle order. The entire east was ravaged by a tempest, so to speak, and covered in darkness. The barbarians prevailed over generals, governors, and the whole imperial army. But what happened next? The emperor, along with his brother Alexander, moved against them, and they immediately sent imperial letters to the west saying, "All of you who are enlisted in the army, with military experience, come to us immediately without delay, in order to confront with us the barbarians in the east." No sooner was it said than it was done: the whole army joined the emperor there.

As soon as the Avar nation learned of this—seeing as they 2 were informed about the movements of the emperor of the Romans—they attacked the western part of the empire. They plundered all places, the countryside, the towns, and the villages. Almost all the borderlands of our western regions were ravaged. It was something similar to the ninth plague of Egypt, more furious even than *the locust and the grasshopper* and all the rest. One could see blood flowing, wailing, lamentations, and all manner of woes. For the Avars specialized in killing human beings and took delight in bloodletting, truly forgetting that they too had a human nature. Mothers were deprived of their children, old men were killed, babies were massacred, young men were beheaded, and men of all ages departed from the company of the living. Some others took refuge in crevasses in the earth, islands, and the sea, remaining hidden in these hideouts as if they were a new Noah's ark. These places offered them salvation. The sword of the barbarians was like a second Flood, bringing dishonorable death to the inhabitants of the western regions.

3

Καὶ μηνύεται ταῦτα τῷ βασιλεῖ ὡς παρὰ τοῦ Ἀββαρι-
κοῦ ἔθνους πορθεῖται καὶ ληΐζεται τὰ ἑσπέρια, προσκα-
λεῖται δὲ παραυτὰ Νικόλαον ἐξ ὀνόματος, ὃν οὐ μόνον οἱ
πολλοὶ ἐπὶ στόματος εἶχον, ἀλλὰ δὴ καὶ αὐτὸς ὁ βασιλεὺς
καὶ πᾶσα ἡ σύγκλητος, ὡς πολλὰ κατὰ τῶν ἐθνῶν αὐτὸν
ἀριστεύσαντα, καὶ χειρίζεται τοῦτον στρατηγὸν τοῖς ἄλλοις οἷς εἶχε πρὸς τὴν ἑσπέραν ἐκπέμπειν, ὡς πεπειραμέ-
νον ὄντα τῇ στρατιᾷ καὶ δεξιὸν πρὸς τὸ παρατάττεσθαι
καὶ πρὸς τοὺς ὑπεναντίους μαχητὴν εὐτολμώτατον. Οὕτως
δὲ τῶν πραγμάτων ἐχόντων, Νικόλαος σὺν τοῖς ὑπ᾽ ἐκεῖνον
στρατεύμασιν τὴν τῶν Θετταλικῶν κατέλαβε χώραν, ἣν
καὶ Λάρισον οἱ τοπικοὶ μετωνόμασαν ὕστερον, διὰ τὸ ἱλα-
ρόν, ὡς οἶμαι, τοῦ ἐκεῖσε παραρρέοντος ποταμοῦ ἢ καὶ διὰ
τοῦ τόπου τὸ ἴσον καὶ πεδινόν. Ἐντὸς ὁ μέγας ταύτης τῆς
πόλεως γίνεται καὶ δυναμοῖ ταύτην ἐν ὀχυρώμασιν, ὡσαύ-
τως καὶ τὰ περικύκλῳ πολίχνια, δεξιὰν τὴν ἄνω ἐπικαλού-
μενος. Ἐπεὶ δὲ καὶ τοὺς Ἀββάρους ἔγνω ὑλακτοῦντας καὶ
τῇ πόλει που πλησιάσαντας, τοὺς προκρίτους οὓς εἶχεν ἐξ
ἀνατολῶν μετ᾽ αὐτοῦ, Μιχαὴλ λέγω καὶ Παντολέοντα καὶ
ἑτέρους δέκα τὸν ἀριθμὸν οὗτος προσκαλεσάμενος, κοι-
νολογεῖται ὅσον καὶ μετ᾽ αὐτῶν ποιεῖν ἔμελλεν, "Οὐκ ἔδει
γὰρ ἡμᾶς," λέγων, "οἳ πρὸς οὐδὲ μίαν πόλιν σταλέντες,
ἀλλ᾽ ἐπὶ πολλὰς ἤδη παρὰ βασιλέως καὶ χώρας καὶ τόπους,
ἐν ταύτῃ τῇ πόλει περικλεισθῆναι καὶ τοῖς Ἀββάροις
ἑαυτοὺς παραδοῦναι." Ὀψίας δὲ τῆς ἡμέρας ἐκείνης προσ-
καρτερήσαντες, ἔξεισι τοιγαροῦν ὁ παιδοτρίβης ἐκεῖνος

48

3

It was reported to the emperor that the western provinces were being ravaged and plundered by the nation of the Avars. Immediately the emperor summoned Nicholas, calling him by his name, a man whom not only the common people but also the emperor and all the senators had ready on their lips, since he had gained distinction for valor in fighting against the barbarian nations. He appointed him general of all the other armies that he was to send to the west, since he had military experience and was skillful at deploying armies, and was in addition very brave in battle against the enemy. Such was the situation. Nicholas together with his army arrived in the land of Thessaly, which in later times was renamed Larisos by the natives, because the river flowing nearby was so merry, or because the area was so level and flat. The saint entered the city and reinforced its fortifications as well as those of the nearby small towns, invoking the protection of heaven. But when he realized that the Avars had neared the city, howling with rage, he summoned the officers who accompanied him from the east, I mean Michael, Pantoleon, and another ten officers, and informed them about their further course of action. "Since the emperor sent us to protect many regions and places," he said, "and not one particular town alone, it is not right for us to shut ourselves up in this one city, effectively surrendering ourselves to the Avars." After waiting for the afternoon of that day, that brave trainer went out of the city

ἀνὴρ καὶ γενναῖος μετὰ τῶν δώδεκα, ὡς οἰκείους μαθητὰς αὐτοὺς ἐκλεξάμενος, οὓς ὁ μέγας οὗτος ἅπαν ἦθος αὐτοὺς ἐξεπαίδευσε, καὶ πέραν τῆς ἐκεῖσε γεφύρας σὺν ἐκείνοις γενόμενος καὶ βαδίσας ἕως πρωί, ἐπὶ τὸ ὄρος τὸ Τερνάβου λεγόμενον καταντᾷ καὶ πηγὴν ὕδατος ἐπ᾽ αὐτὸ εὑρηκὼς καὶ ὡς ἀλσώδη τοῦτο κατανοήσας, αὐτὸ καθεκάστην τοῦτον εἶχεν εὐχόμενον.

2   Τὸν οἰκεῖον Δεσπότην ὁ μάρτυς μιμούμενος, ἵλεων αὐτὸν καθεκάστην <γενέσθαι> αἰτούμενος, ἵνα αὐτὸς τῷ τοῦ μαρτυρίου στεφάνῳ αὐτὸν καθοπλίσειεν. Καὶ ὦ σου, Χριστέ, τῶν θαυμασίων. Ἄγγελος γὰρ Θεοῦ ἐπ᾽ αὐτοὺς καταπτάς, ὃς μὴ παριδεῖν οἶδε τοῖς φοβουμένοις αὐτὸν τὰ αἰτήματα, καὶ μηνύει πρὸς αὐτοὺς τὴν μέλλουσαν ἄθλησιν. "Εὐθυμεῖτε," γὰρ ὁ φανεὶς ἐπειπὼν αὐτοῖς καὶ τὸ "διὰ Χριστὸν μαρτυρήσετε" φήσας, εὐθὺς ἐξ αὐτῶν ἀφανὴς γίνεται. Χαρᾶς τε πολλῆς ἐπ᾽ αὐτὸ πάντες γενόμενοι καὶ δὴ θάρσους ἐπὶ τούτῳ πλησθέντες καὶ τῷ τοῦ σταυροῦ σημείῳ περιφραχθέντες, κάτεισιν οἱ γενναῖοι τοῦ ὄρους κατὰ τῶν κυνῶν ἐκείνων βρυχόμενοι καὶ πόλεμον ἐπ᾽ αὐτοῖς ὥσπέρ τοι πεῖραν στρατιωτικὴν ἔχοντες ἐπιπλέξαντες, πολλοὺς τῶν Ἀββάρων κατέλαβον. Εἶτα κύκλον αἱ δυσώδεις ἐκεῖναι μυῖαι ποιήσαντες περιέσχον τοὺς μάρτυρας καὶ τὰ τῶν Χριστιανῶν αὐτοῖς ἐξομόσασθαι πολλὰ βιασάμενοι, οὐδὲν ἄλλο εἶχον αὐτοὶ ἐπὶ στόματος εἰ μὴ τὸ "Χριστιανοί" μόνον "ἐσμὲν καὶ τὸ θανεῖν ὑπὲρ Χριστοῦ προτιμούμεθα ἢ τοῖς ὑμῶν χρανθῆναι μιάσμασι, ζῆσαι ἢ μᾶλλον ἀποθανεῖν τὰς ψυχάς, ὧν ἡμῖν οὐδὲν τιμιώτερον."

followed by those twelve men, whom he had chosen as his own disciples, and had trained in all virtues. He proceeded with them beyond the bridge and marched until dawn, arriving finally at a mountain called Ternavon. He discovered a spring there and, seeing that the place was heavily wooded, he prayed there every day.

He imitated his Lord, asking him daily to show his mercy, 2 so as to arm him with the crown of martyrdom. And, O Christ, what a miracle! An angel of God, who does not overlook the requests of those who fear him, flew down and announced to them their future martyrdom. "Be of good cheer," said the angel who appeared to them, adding, "You will be martyred for the sake of Christ," and then he immediately vanished from their sight. They were all filled with much joy and emboldened by his words. Fortified by the sign of the cross, those brave men descended from the mountain, roaring like lions against those dogs. They waged war against them and, being experienced fighters, killed many Avars. But afterward those foul-smelling flies surrounded them and overcame the martyrs. They pressed them hard to deny Christ, but the martyrs would say nothing except, "We are Christians and prefer to die for Christ rather than to be defiled with your pollutions; we prefer for our souls to live rather than die, as the soul is our most

Παραδίδονται γάρ, φησιν, καὶ δίκαιοι εἰς χεῖρας ἁμαρτωλῶν, ἕως ἄν ἡ τοῦ Θεοῦ χρηστότης κρύπτηται.

3   Οἱ δὲ αἱμοβόροι ἐκεῖνοι καὶ ἀπηνεῖς πρὸς αὐτοὺς μυρίους βασάνους ἀναδειξάμενοι, τέλος τῷ ξίφει κρουσθέντες τὸν τῆς μαρτυρίας ἀπέλαβον στέφανον. Ἔκειντο γὰρ ἐκεῖσε ῥιφέντα τὰ μαρτυρικὰ ἐκεῖνα καὶ τίμια σώματα. Ποῦ γὰρ ἄν τις εἶχεν ἐκ τούτων ἕνα ἢ δύο τῷ Θεῷ ὑπὲρ ἐκείνου πρεσβεύοντα; Ἀλλὰ καὶ γυναῖκες ἦσαν ἐκεῖ δύο καὶ αὐταὶ ἐν τῷ ὄρει κρυπτόμεναι, αἳ καὶ κατῆλθον τοῦ ὄρους θρηνοῦσαι καὶ τρυχόμεναι ἐπὶ τὰ σώματα, Εἰρήνη καὶ Πελαγία καλούμεναι. Συλληφθεῖσαι δὲ καὶ αὗται ὑπὸ τῶν ἀθέων ἐκείνων Ἀββάρων καὶ μὴ πεισθεῖσαι ταῖς αὐτῶν ἐπιθέσεσιν, ἀλλὰ καὶ ταῖς βασάνοις ἐγκαρτερήσασαι, ξίφει τὰς κεφαλὰς ἀποτέμνονται. Αὗται γὰρ πόθεν ἢ τίνες ἡμῖν λέγειν οὐκ ἔστιν, οἶδα δὲ ὅτι Πατέρα μὲν ἔσχον οὐράνιον, πατρίδα δὲ τὰ ἄνω Ἱεροσόλυμα ἢ καὶ τὴν ἄνω καὶ νέαν Σιών, ἣν κατοικοῦσι οἱ πραεῖς καὶ δικαίων τὰ πνεύματα. Μιὰ στρατιὰ καὶ φάλαγξ καὶ σύνταγμα καὶ μιὰ ψυχὴ ἐπὶ τοσούτοις ἐνέκειντο σώμασι.

4

Ὁ δὲ θαυμαστὸς ἐκεῖνος Νικόλαος ῥώμῃ καὶ δυνάμει σώματος περιὼν καὶ τῇ συνοχῇ τοῦ πολέμου μὴ προσσχὼν τοῖς ἑτέροις καὶ τὸ τί ἂν εἴη τὸ ἐπ᾽ αὐτοῖς συμβησόμενον,

precious possession." Sometimes *even the just fall into the hands of sinners,* at least for as long as God's righteousness remains hidden.

After subjecting them to various tortures, in the end 3 those bloodthirsty and relentless persecutors killed them with their swords, and the martyrs received the crown of martyrdom. Their long-suffering, precious bodies lay there, where they had been tossed. If only we had one or two such men to intercede with God on his behalf! There were two women who had also hidden on the mountain, and they now came down, lamenting the bodies, being overcome by grief. They were named Pelagia and Eirene. The godless Avars seized them too. The women did not change their minds as a result of the Avars' assaults, and remained steadfast during the torture; they were then beheaded with swords. We cannot say where they were from or who they were. The only thing I know is that they had a heavenly Father and their native country was the heavenly Jerusalem, the new Zion on high, which is inhabited by the meek and by *the spirits of the righteous.* All those bodies had one soul, resembling a single army, a single phalanx, a single regiment.

4

That admirable Nicholas, however, who excelled in the strength and power of his body, was not near his companions during the battle and did not know what would happen

ἐκ μέσου αὐτῶν διαδρὰς ἐπὶ ὄρος ὀξυδρομεῖ πάλιν ἕτερον, ὃ καὶ τὸ τῆς Βουναίνης οἱ τοπικοὶ λέγειν εἰώθασιν, τὸ φιλήσυχον, ὡς οἶμαι, οὗτος ἐπιποθῶν καὶ θελγόμενος, δρῦν δέ τινα εὐμεγέθη ἐκεῖ ἐντυχὼν καὶ στὰς ἐπὶ τῷ ταύτης κουφώματι, τὰς εὐχὰς ὡς ἔθος τῷ Θεῷ ἐπετέλει. Οὐκ ἔτι γὰρ ὁ στερρὸς ἐκεῖνος καὶ γενναῖος ἀδάμας φεύγων ἦν τὸ μαρτύριον, ὑπὲρ οὗ καὶ μᾶλλον καθ᾿ ἑκάστην ἐπιτυχεῖν ηὔχετο, ἀλλὰ καὶ *νομίμως* οὗτος λαμβάνειν ἐδόκει τὸν στέφανον. Μήτε γὰρ ἔδει κρίνας αὐτομολεῖν ἐπὶ τὸ μαρτύριον, ὡς καὶ τῆς ἰδίας ζωῆς γενόμενος αἴτιος, οὔτε δὲ πάλιν φεύγειν ἐκ τούτου καὶ ποθεῖν τὸ φιλόζωον, ἀλλ᾿ ἢ τοῦτον ὡς εἰκὸς προσκαλεῖσθαι πρὸς τὸ μαρτύριον ἢ κἂν τὸν δήμιον ἀναδραμεῖν πρὸς αὐτὸν καὶ τὸν ποθούμενον ἀναδῆσαι στέφανον, τὸ εὐγενὲς μηδόλως προδοῦναι τὸ ῥάθυμον.

5

Εἶχε γὰρ ἐκεῖ τὸ τοῦ δρυὸς τὸν μάρτυρα ὡς ἔφημεν σπήλαιον, ἦν δὲ καὶ πηγή τις αὐτῷ μικρά τε καὶ πότιμος καὶ χόρτων βοτάναι τροφὴ καὶ κόρος τις ἄλλος αὐτῷ προσευχὴ καὶ ἐγκράτεια. Ἄγγελος γὰρ Θεοῦ ὡς καὶ πρὶν αὐτῷ ἐπιφαίνεται καὶ τὸν τῆς μαρτυρίας στέφανον μηνύει τούτῳ τρανώτερον καὶ τὸ μέλλον αὐτῷ καὶ τὰ συμβησόμενα ἐπειπὼν ἄπεισιν ὁ φανεὶς καὶ τῇ προσευχῇ πάλιν ὁ

to them. He escaped from within the midst of the Avars and quickly took refuge on another mountain, which is called Vounaina by the local people, and he did so because in my view he desired and enjoyed spiritual tranquility. He there found a huge oak and occupied its hollow, offering his prayers to God, as usual. That steadfast and brave man, firm as adamant, did not wish to avoid martyrdom, as after all every day he prayed to become a martyr. But he wished to obtain *the crown* of martyrdom *in a legitimate manner according to the rules.* He judged that it would be wrong for him to receive it of his own accord, as it were, by causing his own death. On the other hand, he had no intention of escaping martyrdom and was not that fond of his life. So he was content either to respond to a legitimate call to become a martyr, or else for the executioner to come to him and bestow upon him that much-desired crown, so that his nobility might not be betrayed by indolence.

5

As we said, the martyr lived in the cavernous recesses of the oak. There was a small spring there, providing him with potable water. His food was wild plants, and he satiated his appetite with prayers and abstinence. An angel of God appeared to him as before and announced to him even more clearly that he would receive the crown of martyrdom. After predicting his future and what would happen to him, the angel vanished, and the martyr devoted himself to his prayers

μάρτυς τῇ προτέρᾳ πλέον ἐξέδοτο. Φθάνει δὲ τὸ βαρβαρικὸν ἐκεῖσε καὶ λυσσῶδες στρατόπεδον καὶ τὸ ἀκρώριον
πλησιάσαντες γυμνὰ τὰ ξίφη καθέλκουσι ὥσπερ ἂν φιλο-
μάκελλοι κῦνες ἰχνεύοντες τὸν μακάριον, καὶ μικρὸν τῷ
ὄρει προσαναβάντες καὶ ὧδε κἀκεῖσε διαδραμόντες, κατα-
λαμβάνουσι προσευχόμενον ἔτι τὸν μάρτυρα καὶ τοῦτον
κυκλώσαντες πρὸς αὐτὸν ἐκινοῦντο κατ᾿ αὐτοῦ τοῖς ξίφε-
σιν ἕλκοντες, τὸν Χριστὸν ἐξομόσασθαι τοῦτον καταναγ-
κάζοντες καὶ ὃς "Μή μοι τοῦτο γενέσθω," λέγων, "εἰ κἂν
μοι δρὰξ αἵματος ἐπιλειφθῇ. Ἑτοίμως γὰρ ἔχω καὶ τοῦτο
τοῖς θέλουσι παρασχεῖν ἢ τὸν ἐμὸν Δεσπότην Χριστὸν
ἐξαρνήσασθαι." Θυμοῦ δὲ πολλοῦ τὸ βαρβαρικὸν ἐκεῖνο
ἔθνος ἐπιπλησθὲν καὶ πολλὰς ἐπ᾿ αὐτὸν βασάνους ἐπιδει-
ξάμενοι, τέλος εἷς ἐξ αὐτῶν, τῶν ἄλλων ὡς οἶμαι δεινό-
τατος, τὸ δόρυ τοῦ δικαίου ἐπὶ χεῖρας ἀναλαβὼν κατὰ
τῆς πλευρᾶς ἐλαύνει τοῦ μάρτυρος (βάσανον γὰρ ἀρετῆς
ὡς εἰπεῖν οἱ βάρβαροι τὴν πληγὴν ὑπελάμβανον), καὶ τὸ
"εἰς χεῖρας σου, Θεὲ Πάτερ παντοκράτορ, τὸ πνεῦμά μου
παρατίθημι," αὐτὸς ἐπειπὼν καὶ πεσὼν ἐπὶ γῆς, ἐξέπνει ὁ
δίκαιος.

6

Ὁ δὲ τῶν βαρβάρων ἐκείνων ἐθνάρχης ἀκούσας ὅτι
ὁ βασιλεὺς ἐπανῄει πάλιν πρὸς τὸ Βυζάντιον ἐπὶ τὰ
βασίλεια, ἀλλὰ καὶ ὅσα τῶν ἐθνῶν κατὰ τῆς ἀνατολῆς κι-

with much more ardor than before. But the rabid, barbaric army came there, approached the peak of the mountain, and drew their swords. Like dogs drawn to butchery, they tracked down the blessed Nicholas. They ascended the mountain a short distance, searched through the whole area, and in the end they found the martyr still praying. They surrounded him and moved toward him with drawn swords, trying to force him to deny Christ. But the saint said, "May such a thing not happen to me as long as a drop of blood remains in my veins. I am ready to offer even that small, final quantity of blood to those who ask it, rather than deny my Lord Christ." That barbaric nation was filled with great anger, and they subjected him to many tortures. In the end, one of them, in my view the worst of them all, took the spear of that righteous man in his own hand and pierced the martyr's side. (For the barbarians *considered that wound a proof of the saint's virtue,* so to speak.) The righteous man said, "*Into your hands, O Father,* almighty God, *I commit my spirit.*" Then the righteous man fell to the ground and expired.

6

The leader of those barbarians then heard that the emperor was returning to his palace in Byzantion, after having defeated together with his brother all the foreign nations

νηθέντα σὺν τῷ ἰδίῳ ἐτροπώσατο ἀδελφῷ, δείσας μήπως καὶ κατ' αὐτοῦ κινηθῇ σὺν τοῖς ὑπ' ἐκεῖνον στρατεύμασιν, ἐπαναστρέφει ἐπὶ τὰ ἴδια. Καὶ παρευθὺς τῷ προέδρῳ τῶν Λαρισσαίων οἱ προαθλήσαντες νυκτὸς ἐπιστάντες, τὰ ἐκείνων σώματα κοσμίως ταφῆναι προστάττουσιν, ἐπὶ τῷ τοῦ Τερνάβου ὄρει τοῦτον παραγενόμενον φήσαντες. Ὁ δὲ τοῦ ὕπνου ἅμα ἐξαναστάς (Φίλιππος γὰρ ἦν τότε ὁ ἁγιώτατος), καὶ τὸν κλῆρον ἅπαντα προσαγαγών, μῦρά τε καὶ σινδόνας ἀναλαβών, ἐπὶ τὸ ὄρος χωρεῖ. Θαυματουργεῖ δὲ κἀνταῦθα Θεός, τοὺς ἰδίους ἱκέτας πᾶσιν ἀναδεικνύων. Στῦλοι γὰρ πυρὸς ὡς καὶ αὐτοὶ δώδεκα ἐπὶ τὰ μαρτυρικὰ ἐκεῖνα ἵσταντο ἄνωθεν σώματα. Ὁμοίως καὶ τῶν δύο γυναικῶν σῶα καὶ χαροποιὰ εὑρόντες κηδεύουσι λείψανα ψαλμοῖς καὶ ὕμνοις ὥσπερ ἦν αὐτοῖς ἄξιον ἐντὸς τῆς πόλεως περιστέλλουσιν, πολλῶν θαυμάτων ἰάσεις μέχρι καὶ νῦν ἡμῖν αὐτοὶ παρεχόμενοι.

7

Δοὺξ δέ ποτε τοῖς Θεσσαλονικέων πολίταις παρὰ τοῦ βασιλέως εἰσπέμπεται, εὐπρεπὴς δὲ ὢν ὁ ἀνὴρ καὶ περικαλλὴς καὶ δεξιὸς ἐπὶ πᾶσιν, ἀλλὰ καὶ ὅσα οἶδεν εὐδοκιμεῖν ἐπὶ τὴν ἀρχὴν οὐδὲν αὐτὸς ὑπελείπετο ἢ καὶ μάλα σοφῶς τὴν ἐγχειρισθεῖσαν αὐτῷ παρὰ τοῦ βασιλέως

that had waged war in the east. So he went back to his own country, fearing lest the emperor march his army against him too. Soon afterward those who were martyred a short time before appeared to the bishop of Larissa at night and ordered him to bury their bodies properly, telling him to go to the mountain of Ternavon. Upon awaking, the most holy man Philip (that was the name of the bishop at the time) gathered all the clergy and, taking perfumed oils and shrouds with him, went to the mountain. God, wishing to make manifest to all people the glory of his servants, performed a miracle there too: for twelve pillars of fire, equal in number to them, appeared above the bodies of those martyrs. Finding the latter as well as the bodies of the two women intact and filled with grace, they performed the funeral service for them, singing psalms and hymns. Then, in a fitting manner, they brought the bodies into the city, where they still work many miraculous cures to this day.

7

At one point a governor was sent by the emperor to the citizens of Thessalonike. He was a distinguished and handsome man and clever in all respects. He was second to none in possessing all those qualities that bring glory to a man in a position of power. He performed the job entrusted to him

ὑπηρεσίαν καλῶς διϊθύνων, μὴ μόνον δὲ τοῦτο, ἀλλὰ καὶ παρὰ τῶν πολιτῶν ἀγαπώμενος καὶ τιμώμενος. Ἐξαίφνης δὲ πίπτει τούτῳ ἀθρόως λέπρα τῷ σώματι καὶ παρευθὺς αἱ τῶν ἰατρῶν αὐτὸν ὑπελάμβανον χεῖραι καὶ οὐδὲν ἄλλο ἢ τὸ λεπρὸν ἐπ᾽ αὐτὸν ἐνεδυναμοῦτο καὶ ἰσχυρίζετο, κέρδος δὲ μόνον ὅσον αὐτὸς ὑπ᾽ ἐκείνοις ἐζημιοῦτο. Καὶ πολλὰ πρὸς αὐτοὺς ἀναλώσας, τέλος δὲ καταγνοὺς αὐτῶν ὡς μηδὲν παρ᾽ αὐτῶν ὠφελούμενος, ἐπὶ τὸν μέγαν καταφεύγει Δημήτριον, ἐκλιπαρῶν ἐπὶ τούτῳ καθεκάστην τὸν ἅγιον, τοῖς ποσὶ τῆς εἰκόνος τοῦ μάρτυρος ἐλεεινῶς κυλινδούμενος, "Σπλαγχνίσθητι ἐπ᾽ ἐμέ," λέγων, "ἅγιε τοῦ Θεοῦ, καὶ τὸ λεπρὸν τῆς σαρκὸς ἀποκάθαρον." Πολλάς τε λιτὰς καὶ δεήσεις ὁ δοὺξ ἐν τῷ ναῷ τοῦ μάρτυρος ποιησάμενος, οὐδαμῶς ἐπέτυχε τοῦ σκοποῦ. Φαίνεται τοιγαροῦν αὐτῷ ἐν ὁράματι ὁ μέγας Δημήτριος, "Εὐφημιανέ," λέγων (τοῦτο γὰρ ἦν αὐτῷ τὸ ὄνομα), "οὐ δύναταί σου τὸ λεπρὸν ἐντὸς αὐτῆς ἰαθῆναι τῆς πόλεως. Θετταλία γάρ σοι παρέξει τὸν θαυματουργοῦντα τὴν ἴασιν."

2   Ὁ δὲ τοῦ ὕπνου ἐξαναστὰς καὶ πεποιθὼς ἐπὶ τὸ λεχθὲν πρὸς τὸν σημειοφόρον ἐν ταύτῃ καταφεύγει Ἀχίλλειον, νομίζων ὡς πρὸς τοῦτον πεμφθὲν διακρίνων πρὸς ἑαυτὸν τὸ ἐνύπνιον. Εὐχαὶ δὲ καὶ δεήσεις καὶ ἀγρυπνίαι τοῦτον εἶχον συχναὶ καὶ πρὸς τῇ τοῦ ἁγίου λάρνακι βλέπων αὐτῷ καθ᾽ ἑκάστην ἐνοχλῶν οὐκ ἐπαύετο, "Τοῦ Θεοῦ," λέγων, "ἅγιε, τὰς ἰάσεις παράσχου τῷ δούλῳ σου. Ἐπὶ σὲ γὰρ παρὰ δικαίου ἀπέσταλμαι, εἰ δὲ καὶ μή, ἐνταῦθα καὶ αὐτὸς θανοῦμαι ὑπεράνω τοῦ τάφου σου." Ἐφιλονίκει γὰρ καὶ αὐτὸς ὡς Ἰὼβ πληγῆναι τὴν ψυχὴν ὡς εἰπεῖν σὺν τῷ

by the emperor in a prudent and proper manner, and not only this but he was also beloved and honored by the citizens. But suddenly his body was stricken with leprosy and he immediately surrendered himself to the care of doctors. However, his leprosy only became even worse. He spent his money in vain, that was his only reward! After spending much money on them, and realizing finally that the doctors could not help him, he resorted to the great Demetrios. He supplicated the saint every day, rolling pitiably on the floor in front of the martyr's image, saying, "O saint of God, have mercy on me and cleanse my flesh of the leprosy." Yet in spite of his numerous prayers and entreaties in the martyr's church, the governor failed to achieve his goal. But the great Demetrios appeared to him in a dream, and said, "Euphemianos" (for that was his name), "your leprosy cannot be cured in this city. It is Thessaly that will provide the one who will cure you miraculously."

The governor then awoke. Trusting in the saint's instruc- 2 tions, he sought the help of Saint Achilleios, the wonder-worker of Thessaly, thinking that it was him to whom he was being sent; that was how he interpreted his dream. He devoted himself to long prayers, solemn petitions, and vigils. He used to gaze at the saint's coffin every day, and relentlessly implored the saint, saying, "O saint of God, give your servant healing. For a righteous saint sent me to you. Otherwise, I shall die here, on your own tomb." For he was eager, like Job, to offer his soul to be tormented in addition to his

σώματι καὶ οὐδὲν ἄλλο εἶχεν ὁ δοὺξ ἢ ὅσον ὑπὸ τῆς νόσου αὐτῷ τῶν σαρκῶν ὑπελείπετο.

3   Τὸ δὲ ὄρος, ὥσπερ ἔφημεν, τῆς Βουναίνης χρόνοις οὐκ ὀλίγοις τὸ τοῦ μάρτυρος περιέκρυβε σῶμα καὶ τοῦτο φυλάττον ἦν ἀσινῆ καὶ ὁλόκληρον ἢ καὶ μᾶλλον εἰπεῖν ἐν ἐκείνῳ τῷ ὄρει διέσῳζεν. Ἵνα δὲ καὶ πάλιν δοξάσῃ Θεὸς τοὺς ἐκεῖνον δοξάζοντας, φαίνεται τοιγαροῦν ἐκεῖ τῷ δουκὶ ἀθυμοῦντι καὶ λογοπραγοῦντι τάχα τῇ λάρνακι. Ἠδύνατο γὰρ τοῦτον ἰάσασθαι καὶ τὸ λεπρὸν ἐξᾶραι τοῦ σώματος, παραχωρεῖ δὲ ὅμως ἑτέρῳ τὴν ἴασιν, ἵνα θαυματουργῶν κἀνταῦθα ὁ μάρτυς φανῇ καὶ ὅσον ἦν ἐπ' αὐτὸν τὸ κρυπτόμενον πρότερον. Καὶ τῆς πλευρᾶς ἁψάμενος τοῦ λεπροῦ, "Ἀνάστα," λέγων αὐτῷ, "καὶ σπουδῇ πρὸς τῷ τῆς Βουναίνης ὄρει προσδραμὼν καὶ μικρὸν ἐπ' αὐτὸ ἀναβὰς καὶ πηγὴν εὑρηκὼς καὶ τρὶς ἐν ταύτῃ λουσάμενος παρ' αὐτὰ τῆς σαρκός σου φεύξηται τὸ λεπρόν." Καὶ ὁ μὲν τίς ὁ φανεὶς ἤρετο καὶ τὸ ὄνομα ἐξαιτεῖτο, ὁ δὲ Νικόλαον ἔλεγεν εἶναι τοῦτον, ὁ ὑπὸ τῶν Ἀββάρων ἐν ἐκείνῳ τῷ ὄρει τὴν πλευρὰν ὑπὲρ Χριστοῦ λοχευθείς. "Εὑρήσεις γάρ με," ὁ λέγων, "ἐκεῖ ἐν αὐτῷ ἐφ' ὑψηλοῦ τινὸς καὶ μεγάλου δρυὸς κάτωθεν ὑποκείμενον." Ἔξυπνος δὲ γενόμενος Εὐφημιανὸς τὸ παρὰ τοῦ φανέντος ἐπυνθάνετο ὄρος καὶ μαθὼν παρ' εὐθὺς εἴχετο τῆς ὁδοῦ, συνεπομένων αὐτῷ καὶ τῶν Λαρισαίων ἄνδρες πολλοὶ τοῖς λόγοις τοῦ ἀνδρὸς ἐκπληττόμενοι. Καὶ δὴ τὸν τόπον καταλαβόντες ἔνθα ὁ μάρτυς ἐν ὁράματι τῆς νυκτὸς τῷ δουκὶ σημειούμενος ὑπεδείκνυεν, θάμνους τε σὺν πόθῳ πολλῷ καὶ ἄλση ἀνακαθάραντες, τῷ φρέατι περιέτυχον, ἄνω δὲ καὶ κάτω

body, so to speak, and the governor had nothing left beyond the flesh of his body that had not yet been ravaged by the disease.

As we said, the saint's body had been concealed in the mountain of Vounaina for many years. The mountain kept it intact and whole, or rather God protected the body in this mountain. But God wanted to glorify again those who glorified him, so he appeared there to the governor, who was lying dejected near the coffin of Saint Achilleios and prattling on at it. Now, Saint Achilleios could have healed him and cleansed his body of his leprosy, but he granted that miracle to another saint so that the martyr Nicholas could be seen as a worker of miracles in spite of being concealed until then. He touched the leper's side and said, "Get up and go to the mountain of Vounaina immediately. After climbing it for a short while, you will discover a spring. Wash yourself there three times and the leprosy will abandon your flesh immediately." The governor asked who it was that had appeared to him, wanting to know his name. The man said that he was Nicholas, whose side was pierced by the Avars for the sake of Christ on that mountain. He added, "You will discover me lying under a tall and big oak." Euphemianos woke up and asked where the mountain was that had been mentioned by the one who appeared to him. As soon as he learned this, he set out on the road, accompanied by many of the inhabitants of Larissa, who were astonished at his words. After reaching the place which the martyr had pointed out to the governor in his dream during the night, they eagerly cleared the area of bushes and trees and found the well. Looking up and down, they discovered that very

3

σκοπεύσαντες, τὴν ὑπερμήκη ἐκείνην ἐθεάσαντο δρῦν, καὶ δὴ πρὸς αὐτὴν πλησιάσαντες, εὐωδίας πολλῆς τῇ ὀσφρήσει ἐμπίπλαντο, ὁρῶσι δὲ καὶ τὸ λείψανον τοῦ δικαίου, νεκροπρεπῶς περικείμενον σταυρικῷ τῷ σχήματι τὰς χεῖρας ἐνστερνιζόμενον καὶ ὡς ἔθος ἐπιμειδιῶν τῷ προσώπῳ καὶ χαροποιὸν ἀνακείμενον.

8

Πεσὼν δὲ ὁ δοὺξ καὶ σύνδακρυς ἤδη γενόμενος, "Οὐαί μοι," λέγων, "πῶς οὐκ ἐνάρκησεν ἡ χεὶρ τοῦ βαρβάρου ἐκείνου ἡ κατὰ σοῦ τὸ ξίφος ἐξακοντίσασα; Ἵνα τί δὲ οὐκ εἰσῆλθε κατὰ τῆς ἐκείνου ψυχῆς, πῶς δὲ καὶ παρ' αὐτὰ τὴν δίκην ὁ τύραννος οὐκ ἐδέξατο;" Ἀναγνωρισθεὶς δὲ καὶ παρὰ τῶν ἀκολουθησάντων ἐκεῖ Λαρισαίων, πίπτοντες καὶ αὐτοὶ πρὸς τοῖς ποσὶ τοῦ ἁγίου ἀνεβόουν μετὰ κλαυθμοῦ, "Ὁ δεσπότης," λέγοντες, "ὁ ῥύστης, ὁ εὐεργέτης, ὁ προστάτης, ὁ φύλαξ, ὁ ὑπερασπιστής, ὁ λυτρωσάμενος ἡμᾶς σὺν Θεῷ τῆς ἀθέου τῶν Ἀββάρων τότε χειρός, οὗτός ἐστιν," ἔλεγον, "Νικόλαος ὁ ἐξ ἀνατολῶν στρατηγός, ὁ πρὸς ἡμᾶς εἰς βοήθειαν παρὰ τοῦ βασιλέως τότε σταλείς."

tall oak. As soon as they came near it, their nostrils were filled with the fragrance that it emitted. They also saw the body of the saint, which was lying in a stately manner befitting the dead: his hands were folded on his chest in the shape of a cross, as is our custom, and his face was smiling and joyous.

8

The governor fell on his knees and said tearfully, "Woe is me! How did the hand of that barbarian who threw the javelin against you not become numb? Why did the spear not pierce his soul? Why was the tyrant not punished immediately?" The inhabitants of Larissa who had followed him there recognized the saint. Falling at the saint's feet with wailing, they cried out, "This is our lord, our savior, our benefactor, our protector, our guardian, our defender, the one who, together with God, delivered us from the godless hands of the Avars. This is Nicholas, the general who came from the east, who was sent at that time by the emperor to help us."

9

Εὐφημιανὸς δὲ καὶ οἱ λοιποὶ τὰς περικύκλῳ κωμοπόλεις διαδραμόντες ἀρχιερεῖς καὶ μονάζοντας τῇ τοῦ ἁγίου λειψάνου εὑρέσει παρεῖναι κελεύουσιν, λάρνακά τε σινδόνας καὶ μύρα οἰκονομήσαντες, τὸ σῶμα τοῦ μάρτυρος περιτίθενται, ψαλμοῖς καὶ ὕμνοις καὶ ᾠδαῖς πνευματικαῖς αὐτὸ περιστείλαντες. Καὶ τὸν τόπον ἔνθα ὁ δίκαιος ἔκειτο, ὁ δοὺξ καὶ οἱ λοιποὶ πάντες ἐπιμελῶς τοῦτον ἀνακαθάραντες, ναὸς εὐθὺς ἀνεγείρετο· αὐτοχείρως τοὺς λίθους καὶ ἄλλα ὅσα τὰ πρὸς οἰκοδομὴν Εὐφημιανὸς μετὰ πολλοῦ προσεκόμιζε πόθου. Δεήσεις τε καὶ λιτὰς ὅσοι τὰ τῆς ἱερωσύνης κατεῖχον, ἀλλὰ δὴ καὶ ἅπας ὁ τῆς μοναχικῆς τάξεως χορὸς σὺν παντὶ τῷ τοῦ Κυρίου λαῷ τῷ Θεῷ ἀναπέμψαντες, τὰς εὐχὰς τοῦ μάρτυρος ἐπικαλεσάμενοι καὶ τῷ δουκὶ μετ' αὐτῶν συλλαβόντες, ἥκασι ἐπὶ τὴν πηγὴν καὶ τρὶς ἐξ αὐτῆς λούσαντες, τὸν λεπρὸν εὐθὺς ἰᾶται τῆς μάστιγος καὶ τούτῳ πάντας ἐκπλήττει τῷ θαύματι, οὐκ ἑπτάκις ἐν τῷ Ἰορδάνῃ ὡς Νεεμὰν ἐπὶ Ἐλισσαίου λουσάμενος τὸ ἑβδομα<. . .>

9

Euphemianos and the others went around the nearby towns, asking the bishops and the monks to attend the celebration of the discovery of the saint's relic. They obtained a coffin, shrouds, and perfumed oils, and placed them around the martyr's body as they sang *psalms and hymns and spiritual songs.* As soon as the governor and all the others diligently cleared the area where the righteous man lay, they started to build a church. Euphemianos, filled with great love, carried the stones and all the other building materials with his own hands. The priests and the entire company of monks, together with all the people of the Lord, offered their prayers and supplications to God and asked for the martyr's intercession. They took the governor with them and came to the spring. There they washed him three times and the leprous man was cured of that affliction. They were all astonished by that miracle, for he was not washed *seven times in the Jordan River* as Naaman was by Elisha . . .

FUNERAL ORATION FOR ATHANASIOS, BISHOP OF METHONE, BY PETER, BISHOP OF ARGOS

Πέτρου ἐλαχίστου ἐπισκόπου Ἀργείων, ἐπιτάφιος εἰς τὸν μακάριον Ἀθανάσιον ἐπίσκοπον Μοθώνης

Εὐλόγησον.

I

Τοὺς ταῖς ὑψηλαῖς ἀρεταῖς τὸν ἑαυτῶν βίον λαμπρύναντας καὶ πάσης ἑαυτοὺς ὑλώδους καὶ χαμερποῦς κακίας χωρίσαντας καὶ πρὸς τὸ θεῖον καὶ οὐράνιον ἐκεῖνο ὕψος ἀπάραντας, ἄξιον μακαρίζειν καὶ ἐπαινεῖν εἴπερ ἄλλο τι τῶν κάτω νομιζομένων καλῶν, ἅπερ τὴν πρὸς τὰ θάτερα *ῥᾷστην ἔχει μετάκλισιν*, τῇ τῶν χρωμένων ῥοπῇ συμμεταβαλλόμενα κἀκείνους ταῦτα μεταφέροντα †πρόσληψιν†. Οὕτω γὰρ ἂν ἐπίδοσιν λάβοι ἡ ἀρετή, τῶν ταύτην μετιόντων θαυμαζομένων καὶ τῶν λαμπηδόνων τοῦ ταύτης φωτὸς ταῖς τῶν συνειλεγμένων ἀκοαῖς κατασπειρομένων διὰ τῆς εὐφημίας καὶ πρὸς τὴν ταύτης ἐγχείρησιν νηφούσῃ καὶ ἐγρηγορίᾳ διεγειρομένων ψυχῇ, κακία δὲ οἰχήσεται καὶ τέλεον μισηθήσεται, τῇ ἐκείνης ἀντιπαραθέσει καταφρονουμένη, καὶ σκότος τῷ τῆς ἡμέρας ὑποχωρήσει φωτί.

Funeral oration for the blessed Athanasios, bishop of Methone, written by Peter, the most humble bishop of Argos

Bless this reading.

I

It is a worthy endeavor to bless and praise those men who polished their lives by their lofty virtues, separated themselves from all material and earthly vice, and raised themselves up to a divine and heavenly height and to God. We should certainly praise them more than anything else here on earth that has a reputation for being good, for such earthly things *tend to switch* easily *either way,* being swayed and taking on the quality of those who use them, as they are adapted to their mental preconceptions. In this way, the cause of virtue may be advanced, because those who practice it come to be admired and, through their praise, the rays of its light are sown among all those who are gathered to listen. The latter are, then, incited to practice virtue with a sober and vigilant soul. On the other hand, vice will disappear and be utterly hated, despised through its comparison to virtue, and darkness will yield to the light of day. For that

Τούτου γὰρ ἕνεκα καὶ ὁ Χριστὸς αὐτός, ὁ τῆς ἡμετέρας φύσεως ὡς ταύτης Δημιουργὸς καὶ διορθωτὴς ἀκριβέστατος, μακαρίζει τοὺς καθὼς ὑφηγεῖται τὸ εὐαγγέλιον. Διὸ καὶ τοῖς μιμεῖσθαι τοῦτον ἐθέλουσιν κατὰ δύναμιν γεραίρειν ὡς τοῖς ἑαυτῶν ἐκεῖνον δοξάσαντας μέλεσιν καὶ προσφέρειν ὥσπερ τι δῶρον, κἂν ἐκ πενιχρᾶς διανοίας, τὸν ἔπαινον ἐποφείλεται.

2

Ἀλλά γε τούτοις ἐμαυτὸν παρενείρων δέδοικα μὴ θράσους ὑποίσω γραφήν, τὸν τῆς ἀθανασίας ἐπώνυμον εὐφημεῖν Ἀθανάσιον. Ὅμως τοιούτῳ γε ὄντι σιγᾶν οὐκ ἔξεστι τὰ καλὰ καὶ μεμυκότι στόματι τὴν ἐκ τούτων κρύπτειν ὠφέλειαν, ὡς μὴ τῷ τὸ ἓν εἰληφότι φανήσωμαι τάλαντον ὅμοιος, εἰς γῆν τὸ πιστευθὲν διὰ τῆς παραλόγου δειλίας κατακρυψάμενος. Ἄλλος μὲν γάρ τις τῶν ἐν κομψείᾳ ῥητόρων, ὃς τοὺς τῶν ἐγκωμίων [μὴ] φυλάττειν ὅρους βουλόμενος ὡς ἐκ τοιούτων ἐπαίνων τὸν εὐφημούμενον δόξειεν ἂν ἐγκωμιάζειν, λαμπρότητά τε βίου καὶ περιφάνειαν λέγων καὶ συνθήκην εὔρυθμον καὶ λέξιν ἐξηνθισμένην καὶ καθαράν, καὶ ἐπὶ πᾶσιν μετὰ τοῦ σοφοῦ τὸ σύντομον ἐπιτετηδευκώς, ὄγκον ἀξιωμάτων καὶ τὰ τούτοις ἐφάμιλλα διηγήσεται, ἵν᾽ ἐκ τούτων πρὸς τὴν τῶν λεγομένων τοὺς ἀκρωμένους ἐπισπάσηται εὔνοιαν ὥσπερ τι ταῦτα προβαλλόμενος δέλεαρ.

reason, Christ himself, who, as its Creator, is the most precise corrector of our nature, pronounced blessed those who follow the way of the Gospel. With regard to those who wish to imitate him, it is our task to praise, to the best of our ability, those who glorified him with their own limbs, and to offer that praise to them as a gift, even if we do so with an inadequate mind.

2

Nevertheless, by involving myself in these affairs, I fear lest I be accused of presumption because I dare to praise Athanasios, he who bears the name of immortality. Yet in spite of my shortcomings, I am not permitted to remain silent about those good things and, by keeping my mouth shut, thereby to conceal the profit that may be gained from them. I fear that I would then be compared to the servant who had hidden under the earth the one talent of money that his master had entrusted to him, simply out of unreasonable timidity. An articulate orator, who wants to stick to the rules of the genre of panegyric in order to give the impression that he is praising someone with encomia, will discuss his illustrious life and prominence, will employ an artful structure of speech and an elevated and pure vocabulary, and, above all, will combine wisdom with brevity. He will mention the dignity of the man's offices and other similar things, in order to dispose his audience favorably toward his speech, using all those qualities as bait.

2   Ἡμῖν δ᾽ οἷς ὥσπερ τἄλλα τοῦ βίου λαμπρὰ καὶ ταῦτα ἐπιλείπεται καὶ διέπτυσται, μόνη δὲ ἡ ἀλήθεια καὶ τὰ τοὺς λόγους ἐμπεδοῦντα ἔργα στέργεται καὶ σπουδάζεται, πῶς εὐαπολόγητος ἡ τοιαύτη γενήσεται πρόφασις, καίπερ εἰδόσι σαφῶς ὡς οὐδ᾽ αὐτοῖς ἐκείνοις, οἷς ἅπας ὁ βίος περὶ τὸ λέγειν τι καὶ ἀκούειν κατετρίβη καινότερον, τῆς ἀξίας τοῦ εὐφημουμένου ἐφικέσθαι δυνατόν; Ἐμοὶ δὲ καὶ ἄλλως εἴη συγγνώμη τῷ ὑπὲρ δύναμιν ἐπιβάλλοντι, τὴν ἐξ ἀνηκοΐας ὀρρωδοῦντι κατάκρισιν καὶ τὸ τῆς ὑπεροψίας ταπεινὸν ἢ ὂν ἢ νομιζόμενον φεύγοντι. *Διδόναι γὰρ τοῖς αἰτοῦσιν οὐ πλούσιοι μόνον, ἀλλὰ καὶ πένητες προστταττόμεθα, εἴπερ οὐκ ἀξιωμάτων καὶ δώρων μισθοί, ἀλλὰ τῶν προθέσεων ἐκ Θεοῦ ἀποδίδονται. Διά τοι τοῦτο θαρρήσας τῷ λόγον ἐν ἀνοίξει διδόντι τοῦ στόματος,* πρὸς τὴν τοῦ παρορμῶντος ἀξίωσιν εἴξαμεν, περιβλέπτου καὶ θείου ἀνδρός.

3

Πατρὶς τοίνυν τοῦ νῦν εὐφημουμένου πατρὸς πρώτη μὲν καὶ ἀληθὴς ἡ οὐράνιος, εἰς ἣν μετὰ τῶν ἀπ᾽ αἰῶνος ἁγίων ἐξ ἁπαλῶν τῶν ὀνύχων ἀπογραψάμενος, τῆς προθέσεως οὐ διήμαρτε, δευτέρα δὲ κἀκείνης τοσοῦτον

74

We, however, omit and reject such things along with all 2
other magnificent aspects of this life, being fond of and caring only for the truth and for deeds that confirm and vali-
date our words. Besides, how could we have justified such an
approach, since we know very well that not even those who
spend their entire life studying the art of speaking and listening closely to novel things are in a position to say anything worthy of the saint we are about to praise here? Moreover, people may forgive my decision to deal with matters
that surpass my powers, seeing as I fear being convicted of
disobedience and want to avoid the accusation of hiding my
arrogance behind a veil of humility, whether that would be
real or only imagined. For it is not only rich men but we
poor ones as well who are ordered *to give to those who beg*
from us, since God does not reward us on the basis of the
offices we possess or the gifts we give, but only of our inner
disposition. For that reason, being confident in the one who
gives the gift of speech as soon as we open our mouth, I yield to the
demand of a most prominent and divine man, who urged me
to do it.

3

The first and true fatherland of the father we are now
praising was heaven. He enrolled in it while he was still of a
tender age, together with the saints of all the ages, and his
hopes were not in vain. His second fatherland, which was as

ἀποδέουσα, ὅσον ἀληθείας σκιὰ καὶ ἰνδάλματα, Κατάνη μὲν προσεχής, Σικελία <δὲ> πόρρω περίπυστος. Ὦν εἰ βουληθείην νῦν ἐπαινεῖν τὰ ἐξαίρετα, θέσιν καὶ κάλλος καὶ μέγεθος, ἀέρων εὐκρασίαν καὶ ὑδάτων τὸ ποτιμώτατον, δένδρων εὐκάρπων τε καὶ ἀκάρπων πλῆθος, ἀνδρῶν ἐπὶ σοφίᾳ τε καὶ φρονήσει καὶ ἀνδρείᾳ καὶ δικαιοσύνῃ λαμψάντων πληθύν, ὡς καὶ τὴν ἐξάκουστον Ἀγάθην τὴν μάρτυρα, ἐν ταύτῃ καὶ γεννηθεῖσαν καὶ τραφεῖσαν καὶ μαρτυρήσασαν διὰ Χριστὸν καὶ τὸ ἅγιον αὐτῆς κατακεῖσθαι λείψανον εὐδοκήσασαν, ὃ καὶ ῥύακες πυρὸς τῆς ὑπερκειμένης Αἴτνης ἠδέσθησαν κατερχόμενοι, τὸ παραδοξότατον, ὡς πάλαι φόρτον εὐσεβῆ καὶ φιλόθεον, πατέρας γέροντας ἐπ᾽ ὤμων φερομένους εὐγνωμόνων υἱῶν, καὶ πρὸς τοὐπίσω χωρεῖν ἐπετάχθησαν, αὐτήν τε τὴν ἐρευγομένην Αἴτνην τὸ πῦρ καὶ καπνὸν παχὺν ἐκπνέουσαν ὕπερθεν καὶ φρικτὸν ὑπηχοῦσαν καὶ λίαν ἐξαίσιον, καίπερ οὐκ ἀθαύμαστον ἐχόντων τὴν ἔρευναν, ἔξω τῆς ὥρας καὶ τῆς προθέσεως δόξομεν φέρεσθαι.

4

Εἰ γὰρ ὁ εὐφημούμενος ἑτέρας πατρίδος ἀπλέτως ἐρῶν, ταύτης ὡς ὑπερορίας κατεφρόνησε καὶ διὰ τοῦτο τοῦ μακαρίου τέλους, ἔνθα ἡμῶν ἡ πρώτη ἑστία καὶ *πάντων*

inferior to the heavenly one as shadows and images are inferior to true objects, was Catania, which was his native town. Speaking more broadly, his fatherland was the illustrious Sicily. Now, one might want to praise the exceptional advantages of that place, such as its location, beauty, and size; its temperate climate, its sweet waters, the number of its trees, some of which bear fruit and some not; the multitude of its men distinguished for their wisdom, prudence, courage, and justice; or the famous martyr Agatha, who was born and raised in that city, was martyred for the sake of Christ, and was fortunate in having her holy body buried there. And what a strange miracle! The streams of fire that flowed down from the mountain of Etna that lies above that city stood still in awe before that body, just as they had once stood still, and were even ordered to flow back, before those grateful sons who were carrying their elderly fathers on their shoulders, a burden proving their piety and love of God. And I might also mention Etna itself, which belches out fire and exhales thick smoke from above, making a horrible and very loud noise. Although it is not without interest to explore these things, we would give the impression of engaging in untimely subjects and going off track.

4

But because the saint whom we are praising was very much enamored of another fatherland, he despised this one as a place of banishment and for that reason he reached his blessed end, which is our original hearth and *the dwelling of*

εὐφραινομένων ἡ κατοικία, τετύχηκε, πῶς, ἦν ὑπεριδεῖν τῶν πρώτων εἶναι καλῶν ἐδοκίμασε, γεραιρόμενος ἐκ ταύτης ἡσθήσεται; Τοίνυν ὥσπερ τις ἑωσφόρος ἐκ δυσμῶν ταύτης ἀνίσχων, τοὺς φύσαντας εὐσεβεῖς καὶ φιλοθέους ἐκήρυσσεν, ἐκ βρέφους καὶ αὐτὸν παρὰ τῶν φυσάντων ἀνατεθέντων Χριστῷ καὶ πρῶτον ἔργον ποιουμένων εὐαρέστως αὐτῷ παρὰ πᾶσαν τὴν ζωὴν ἀναστρέφεσθαι. Καὶ τί δεῖ τὰ τούτων καθ' ἓν ἀριθμεῖν προτερήματα, ἐξὸν ἐκ τοῦ καρποῦ τὸ δένδρον θαυμάζειν γνωρίσαντας; Ἔδειξαν γὰρ αὐτῶν τὸ τῆς ψυχῆς ἀταπείνωτον καὶ γενναῖον οἱ σφοδρῶς προσρήξαντες αὐτοῖς ὡς καταιγίδες καὶ χάλαζαι καὶ μηδόλως παρασαλεύσαντες πειρασμοί. Ὡς γὰρ χωνεία μὲν δοκιμάζει χρυσόν, ἄνεμοι δὲ καὶ βροχαὶ καὶ χάλαζαι καὶ χείμαρροι θέμεθλα, οὕτως οἱ ἀπροσδόκητοι πειρασμοὶ στερρὰν καὶ καρτερικωτάτην ἢ σεσαθρωμένην ἀπελέγχουσι τὴν ψυχήν. Τὸ γὰρ Ἰσμαηλιτικὸν ἔθνος καὶ τῆς Ἄγαρ ἀπόγονον, ἐξ οὗ διὰ τὰς ἡμετέρας ἁμαρτίας <τῇ> προρρηθείσῃ νήσῳ προσεφθάρη, ποινὰς ὥσπερ τις ἡμῖν τῶν παραβάσεων εἰσπραξόμενον δήμιος, ἐπεὶ μηδὲ πατρικῶς εἴξαμεν καὶ εὐήνιον ἐκλίναμεν αὐχένα καλοῦντι Θεῷ, πολλὰς μὲν πόλεις πορθῆσαν ἐδήωσε καὶ τοὺς τούτων μετὰ τῶν περιχώρων οἰκήτορας, τοὺς μὲν πικροτάτω θανάτῳ διὰ ξίφους καὶ λιμοῦ καὶ θαλάσσης παρέπεμψε, τοὺς δὲ δουλείᾳ χαλεπωτάτῃ καὶ δεσμοῖς κατεδίκασε, ἄλλους τῆς θρεψαμένης ἐλεεινῶς ἐκφεύγειν καὶ διὰ τῆς ξένης ἀλητεύειν ἠνάγκασε.

2   Τότε δὴ καὶ οὗτοι μετὰ τοῦ σφετέρου παιδὸς τὰ οἴκοι χαίρειν φράσαντες (οὐ γὰρ ἔφερον ὁρᾶν τὸ Χριστοῦ

all who rejoice. How then would he enjoy being praised for his place of origin? He considered it one of his first tasks to overlook it. Therefore, like the morning star that rises in the west, he proclaimed his parents' piety and love of God: they gave their infant offspring to Christ as a votive offering, and considered it their most important duty to behave in a way that was acceptable to him for as long as they lived. There is no need to enumerate here their great advantages one by one, since one can admire *the tree by getting to know its fruit.* For the temptations that dashed upon them violently, like tempests and hailstorms, did not make them waver and revealed the steadfastness and courage of their souls. Temptations that come unexpectedly test our soul and reveal whether it is steadfast or weak, *in the same way that a smelting furnace tests the quality of gold,* and wind, rain, hail, and swollen torrents test the foundations of a house. Specifically, the Ishmaelites, the descendants of Hagar, invaded that island because of our sins, punishing us like an executioner for our transgressions: God reached out to us like a father and yet we did not heed him, nor bend a compliant neck. So they ravaged and plundered many cities, and either cruelly put to the sword their inhabitants, together with those who lived in the surrounding areas, or killed them through famine, or threw them into the sea. Some they condemned to miserable servitude and fetters, while others were forced to abandon their homeland in a pitiful manner and wander through foreign lands.

At that time, his parents together with their child said farewell to their homeland—for they could not bear to see 2

ποίμνιον, τὸ ἅγιον ἔθνος, τὸ βασίλειον ἱεράτευμα, καταφρυ-
αττομένους δὲ τούτους καὶ κατεντρυφῶντας τῆς αὐτοῦ
συμφορᾶς καὶ κατὰ τοῦ τῶν ὅλων Θεοῦ διατιθεμένους
διαθήκην ὡς ἐξολοθρεύσουσι τέλεον λαὸν τὸν χριστώνυ-
μον καὶ οὐ μὴ τούτου ἔτι μνησθήσεται), εἰς τὰς ἐν Πελο-
ποννήσῳ Παλαιὰς Πάτρας κατῆραν, ἐν αἷς καὶ ὁ πρῶτος
ἐν ἀποστόλοις κληθεὶς Ἀνδρέας καὶ Πέτρον τὸν ἀδελφὸν
καὶ τῆς μακαρίας ἐκείνης ἄρξαντα φάλαγγος καλέσας
πρὸς τὸν καλέσαντα, μετὰ πολὺν τοῦ Εὐαγγελίου δρόμον
τὸ διὰ σταυροῦ μακαριώτατον τέλος ἐδέξατο, τὸν ἴδιον
Δεσπότην κἂν τούτῳ μιμησάμενος ὡς ἐν ἅπασιν. Ἤκου-
σαν γὰρ καὶ αὐτοὶ τῆς θείας τοῦ πατριάρχου ὀμφῆς,
πατρῴαν γῆν καὶ ἑστίαν καταλιπόντας καὶ συγγένειαν,
ἐνταῦθα ἐλθεῖν. Τί οὖν ἐν τούτοις, δισταγμῷ τινὶ ἢ ἀχαρι-
στίᾳ περιεπάρησαν ἢ τῶν θείων κατεγόγγυσαν κριμάτων,
ὡς παρ' ἀξίαν ὧνπερ παρ' ὅλον τὸν βίον εἰργάσαντο
πάσχουσιν; Οὐδαμῶς, πάντα δὲ τὰ οὐκ ἐφ' ἡμῖν ἐκείνῳ
καὶ μόνῳ παραχωρήσαντες, ᾧ ἂν αὐτῷ ἀρεστόν ἐστιν,
εἵποντο.

5

Ὁ δὲ τούτων τῆς ἀθανασίας φερώνυμος παῖς θείῳ
ζήλῳ τὴν καρδίαν ἀναφλεγόμενος, πρὸς τοὺς γενικοὺς
ἀγῶνας, ὥσπερ τῶν ἐν χερσὶν ἐπιλαθόμενος θλίψεων,

the flock of Christ, *that holy nation and royal priesthood,* being treated insolently by the barbarians, who were taking a mad delight in its sufferings. The barbarians had a compact among themselves against the God of all things to kill all Christian people, eradicating all memory of them. Therefore, the saint's parents took refuge in Old Patras in the Peloponnese. In that city, Andrew, the one who is called first among the disciples—he who had summoned his brother Peter, the leader of that blessed company, to join the one who had summoned him—had met his most blessed end: after long travels for the sake of the Gospel, he was crucified, imitating his Lord in this as in all other respects. In fact, the parents of the saint also obeyed the divine commandment given to the patriarch Abraham, abandoning their kin and ancestral land and hearth and going there. What happened next? Did they hesitate? Did they behave in an ungrateful manner? Did they murmur against the divine judgment, believing that they were treated in a way unworthy of their lifelong struggles? Not at all. They let God alone decide all things that do not depend on us, and followed the road that was pleasing to him.

5

Meanwhile their child, who bore the name of immortality and whose heart was burning with desire for God, stripped down for the contest to acquire the cardinal

ἀπεδύσατο. Τοιοῦτο γὰρ ψυχὴ στερρὰ καὶ ἱλύος κεκαθαρ-
μένη τῆς ἐκ παθῶν, οὐ πρὸς τὸν συνειλεγμένον, ἀλλὰ τὸν
ἔτι λειπόμενον πλοῦτον ὁρῶσα, κἀκεῖνον ἐφ᾽ ἑαυτὴν ποι-
ήσασθαι σπεύδουσα, τῶν μὲν ὄπισθεν κατὰ τὸν μέγαν
Παῦλον ἐπιλανθάνεται, τοῖς ἔμπροσθεν δὲ ἀεὶ ἐπεκτείνεται
καὶ πρὸς τὸν οὐρανὸν ὁσημέραι, τὸν χοῦν ἔτι περικειμένη
καὶ τὴν γῆν περιπολοῦσα, ἀναπτῆναι φιλονεικεῖ. Τῷ μο-
ναχικῷ τοίνυν ἑαυτὸν ὑποβάλλει ζυγῷ, οἷα δὴ τῆς τῶν
κοσμικῶν συγχύσεως ἀπαλλάττοντι καὶ τῆς ἀκαίρου περι-
δινήσεως καὶ πρὸς τὸν ἥσυχον βίον καὶ ἀπράγμονα τοὺς
μετιόντας ὡς ἐν ἀκλύστῳ λιμένι προσάγοντι, πάντα χαίρειν φράσας τὰ τῇδε καὶ γονέας αὐτούς, ὅπως ἀμέσως
προσομιλοίη Θεῷ, καὶ τούτῳ διηνεκῶς ἐνούμενος, τῷ θείῳ
ἔρωτι κάτοχος γένοιτο, σχολάσας καὶ γνοὺς ὅτι αὐτός ἐστιν
ὁ Θεός, οὐδὲ πρότερον τῶν χρονισάντων ἐν τοῖς τοιούτοις
φέρων τὰ δεύτερα, καίπερ κομιδῇ νέος ὑπάρχων τῷ σώματι. Ἔξω γὰρ τῶν ἀστικῶν θορύβων καὶ τῆς κοσμικῆς τύρ-
βης ἀποτρέχων, ἐν ἐρημίαις καὶ τοῖς σχολὴν ἐξ ἐκείνων
ἐμάκρυνεν ἄγουσιν. Τὴν γὰρ ἐπίπονον πολιτείαν οἷόν τινα
ζυγὸν ἐκ νεότητος αἴρειν ἐφίετο καὶ κατὰ μόνας καθέζεσθαι.

2   Ἐπὶ πολὺ τοίνυν αὐτὸν ἐν τῷ τοιούτῳ βίῳ κοινωσάμε-
νον καὶ τὴν πάλην οὐ πρὸς αἷμα καὶ σάρκα βλέπων ἀράμε-
νον ὁ τῶν ἐκεῖσε πρόεδρος, ἀλλὰ πρὸς τὰς ἀρχὰς καὶ πρὸς
τὰς ἐξουσίας, πρὸς τὰ πνευματικὰ τῆς πονηρίας (γενναίως
γὰρ κατὰ τοὺς νόμους τῆς μοναχικῆς ἐπαπεδύσατο καταστάσεως καὶ πρὸς τὸ βραβεῖον τῆς ἄνω κλήσεως ἐνδίκως
διὰ τοῦ ὀξυτάτου δρόμου καταλαμβάνειν ἐπείγετο), συ-
στήματος μοναχῶν καίπερ ἀπαναινόμενον, μήπως ἡ περὶ

virtues, as if forgetting his present sorrows. For a steadfast soul, utterly purified of the filth of the passions, behaves in precisely such a manner: it looks not to the wealth that has been already amassed but to the treasures which remain to be gathered, and it strives eagerly to bring them into its possession. Such a soul *forgets what lies behind,* as the great Paul puts it, always *straining forward to what lies ahead,* every day trying to fly up to heaven, even while it is still wearing its material body and wandering about the earth. Therefore, the saint subjected himself to the monastic yoke, since it liberates man from all the turmoil of this life and from all this pointless wandering, bringing all those who submit to it to a spiritually tranquil life devoid of all cares, as if in a well-protected haven. He bid farewell to all the things of this world, even to his own parents, so as to be able to commune directly with God and, being united with him continuously, he wished to be possessed by divine love. He devoted himself to *stillness, knowing that* he is *God.* In this respect, he was not inferior to men who had spent many years living such a life before him, for all that his body was still rather young. Abandoning the disorder found in cities and all mundane cares, he escaped to deserted places, joining those who were likewise free of such cares. *From the time of his youth* he wished *to take on a* life of labor *as if it were a yoke,* and *to live alone.*

The bishop of that place, seeing him absorbed in that life 2 for a long time, and *fighting not against blood and flesh, but against the principalities* and *against the powers, against the spiritual hosts of wickedness,* appointed him leader of a community of monks, even though the saint refused to take that office, lest caring for these monks distract his mind from lofty

τούτων φροντὶς τὸν αὐτοῦ λογισμὸν ἐκ τῆς ὑψηλῆς κατα-
παύσειε θεωρίας, τὴν προστασίαν ἐνεχείρισεν. Οὐ γὰρ δίκαιον ἦν τὸ τῷ χρόνῳ βεβαιωθὲν καλὸν καὶ παγιωθὲν ἐν
αὐτῷ ἀργὸν μένειν καὶ ἀμετάδοτον, μηδὲ κατασπειρόμε-
νον ἐν τοῖς χρήζουσιν. Ὡς γὰρ ὁ τὸν αἰσθητὸν πλοῦτον
παρακατέχων εἰς ἑαυτὸν καὶ μὴ τοῖς ἐνδεέσι τοῦτον ἐκχέων
ψεκτὸς καὶ πηγὴ τοῖς διψῶσιν ἀντλεῖν εἰργομένη τὰ νάματα καὶ γῆ θησαυρὸν ἐν κόλποις κρύπτουσα, οὕτως καὶ
ὁ συσχὼν εἰς ἑαυτὸν πλοῦτον πνευματικὸν καὶ μὴ τοῖς
ἄλλοις προθείς, εἴπερ οὐ τοσοῦτον δι᾽ ἑαυτὸν ὅσον διὰ
τοὺς ἄλλους ἕκαστος ἐκ Θεοῦ εἴληφε χάρισμα. Καὶ διὰ
τοῦτό φησιν ὁ Χριστός, "Λαμψάτω τὸ φῶς ὑμῶν ἔμπροσθεν
τῶν ἀνθρώπων, ὅπως ἴδωσιν ὑμῶν τὰ καλὰ ἔργα καὶ δοξά-
σωσι τὸν Πατέρα ὑμῶν τὸν ἐν τοῖς οὐρανοῖς."

6

Ἐπεὶ δὲ πλέον τὸν ἐν αὐτῷ πλοῦτον ἔβλεπε αὐξανόμε-
νον καὶ πολλοὺς πλουτίζειν ἱκανώτατον καὶ τὸν ἐν αὐτῷ
φωτισμὸν μεταδιδόναι τοῖς προσπελάζουσι, μετὰ τὸ πάντας αὐτὸν ἀμέμπτως τοὺς τῆς ἐκκλησίας βαθμοὺς διελθεῖν
πρὸς τὸ τῆς ἀρχιερωσύνης μέγιστον ἀγαγεῖν ἀξίωμα

contemplation. For he had stripped himself bravely for combat, according to the rules of monastic life, and was eager to obtain *the prize of the upward call* in the right way, by the fastest and most direct path. But it was not right for his spiritual gift to remain unexploited and to be kept from other people, and not to be sowed among those who needed it, seeing as it had been confirmed through the passage of time and consolidated firmly inside him. A person who keeps material wealth for himself, and does not share it with those in need, is worthy of criticism; the same applies to a spring that is prevented from giving its water to those who are thirsty, and to the earth that hides a treasure in its bosom. Also to be blamed is he who keeps his spiritual wealth for himself and does not place it at the disposal of his fellow men, since, after all, everyone is given a certain gift by God not so much for his own sake as for the sake of his brethren. For this reason Christ said, *"Let your light shine before men, that they might see your good works and give glory to your Father who is in heaven."*

6

After seeing that the saint's internal wealth was steadily growing and that he was in a position to enrich many people and to transmit the light within him to those who approached him, the bishop considered the possibility of elevating him to the highest office of a bishop, after he had passed through all other ranks of the priesthood without

διασκέπτεται, ἵν᾿, ὥσπερ ἐξ ὑψηλοτάτης περιωπῆς πλεί-
στους αὐγάζων, τὴν ἀληθινὴν ὁδὸν ὑποδείκνυσι καὶ πρὸς
ταύτην ἀπροσκόπως βαδίζειν ὡς ἐν ἡμέρᾳ παρασκευά-
σειεν. Οὐ γὰρ θέμις ἐν γωνίᾳ μικρᾷ μέγα φῶς κατακρύ-
πτεσθαι, οὐδὲ ποταμὸν ἀέννα ῥέοντα μικρὸν κατάρδειν
παράδεισον.

2   Διὰ τοῦτο τὴν τῆς Μεθώνης προεδρείαν λαχών (περιφανὴς δὲ αὕτη πόλις τῆς κατὰ Πελοπόννησον Μεσσή-
νης), πολλοῖς αὐτὴν οἷά τις ἐμμελὴς γεωργὸς τοῖς τῆς
εὐσεβείας φυτοῖς κατάκομον ἀπετέλεσεν καὶ καρπὸν
ὡραῖον καὶ ἐδώδιμον φέρειν ταῖς τῆς διδασκαλίας ἀεν-
νάοις ἀρδείαις τῷ πάντων Δεσπότῃ καὶ ἐρασμιώτατον
παρεσκεύασεν. Οὐ γὰρ ὡς μισθωτὸς ῥαστώνῃ καὶ νωχε-
λείᾳ τὸ πιστευθὲν ἔργον ἐξήνυεν, ὡς ποιμὴν δὲ καλὸς τὰ
τοῦ δεσπότου γινώσκων ὡς ἴδια πρόβατα, τὴν ψυχὴν οὐ
παρῃτεῖτο τιθέναι καλοῦντος καιροῦ, ἐν περιστάσεσι προ-
ϊστάμενος, ἐν ἀνάγκαις ὑπερμαχῶν, ἀσθενοῦσιν ἰατρὸς
εὑρισκόμενος ἐμπειρότατος, γυμνητεύουσι σκεπαστής,
πεινῶσι τροφή, θλιβομένοις παραψυχή, ἀθυμοῦσι θυμηδία
καὶ μόνον ὁρώμενος, πατὴρ ὀρφανοῖς, χήραις ὑπερ-
ασπιστὴς καὶ ἁπλῶς τοῖς πᾶσι πάντα γινόμενος, ἵνα κερδάνῃ
τοὺς πλείους. Καὶ τίς τὰς ὑπὲρ αὐτῶν ἀγρυπνίας αὐτοῦ
διηγήσεται, τὰς συνεχεῖς φροντίδας, τοὺς κόπους, μήπως
ἐν ἐξ αὐτῶν γένηται θηριάλωτον ἢ τῇ νοητῇ μὴ σαλπίσαν-
τος ῥομφαίᾳ ἀποσφαγῇ καὶ αὐτὸς παρὰ τοῦ πιστεύσαντος
τὸ αἷμα τοῦ σφαγέντος ἀπαιτηθήσεται; Οὐδέ τις ἦν ἐκείνων τῶν κατασφαττόντων τὰ πίονα καὶ ἀπεμπολούντων τὰ

blame. From that position, as if from a lofty mountain peak, the saint would be able to enlighten many men, showing them the true path and preparing them to walk upon it as if under the light of day, without encountering obstacles. For it was not right to keep such a great light source hidden away *in a* small *corner,* nor for a river that flows continuously to water only a small garden.

So, after being appointed bishop of Methone (this was a prominent town of Messene in the Peloponnese), like an industrious gardener he made his bishopric luxuriant with the plants of piety and made it yield a ripe, edible, and most desirable harvest to the Lord of all things, by constantly watering it through his teachings. He did not perform the task entrusted to him like a hired worker, that is, carelessly and lazily, but instead like *the good shepherd* who considered his master's sheep as his own; nor would he hesitate to *lay down his own life,* if the times called for it. He protected them in difficult circumstances, championed them when they were in need, and showed himself to be an experienced doctor when they were ill. He cloaked those who were naked, gave food to the hungry, consoled those in grief, and encouraged the dejected through his appearance alone. He became a father to orphans, a protector of widows, and generally speaking, *he became everything for everyone in order to win over* as many people as possible. Who will describe his vigils for their sake, his constant cares and labors to ensure that not one of them was caught by wild beasts or killed with the spiritual sword, all because he failed to warn them clearly? And then the one who had entrusted them to him would demand from him the blood of the slain. But he was not one of *those who slaughter the fat sheep* and sell off those that are

2

ἰσχυρὰ καὶ περιβαλλομένων τὰ ἔρια, ὡς ὁ προφήτης φησίν, καὶ λεγόντων, "Εὐλογητὸς Κύριος, πεπλουτήκαμεν," ἀλλὰ τῶν ἐνισχυόντων τὸ ταπεινόν, τῶν ἀνορθούντων τὸ καταπίπτον, τῶν καταδεσμούντων τὸ χωλὸν καὶ τρέχειν παρασκευαζόντων καὶ ἄλλεσθαι. Ἡγεῖτο γὰρ οὐκ ἀνέσεως τὸ ἀξίωμα, ἀγῶνος δὲ μᾶλλον καὶ κόπου πλείονος τῆς προτέρας ζωῆς, ὅσῳ καὶ πλειόνων ἐπιστασίαν ἐπεπίστευτο, καὶ διὰ τοῦτο οὐ λόγῳ μόνον ὑπετίθει τὰ δέοντα, ἔργῳ δὲ μᾶλλον εἷλκε πρὸς τὰ ἐκ λόγων ὑποτιθέμενα.

7

Τὰς μὲν οὖν γενικὰς οὕτω κατώρθωσεν ἀρετὰς καὶ σὺν αὐταῖς τὰς ἑπομένας αὐταῖς, ὡς μηδέποτε ταῖς μαχομέναις αὐταῖς ὑπερβολαῖς καὶ ἐλλείψεσι τῆς βασιλικῆς ἐκκλίνειν ὁδοῦ ἢ τῶν ἐσκαμμένων ἔξω βαίνειν ὁρᾶσθαι πόρρωθεν. Φρονήσει μὲν τὸ λογιστικὸν ἐνεύρωσεν, ὡς πάσας τὰς τούτου κινήσεις πρὸς τὸν Θεὸν καὶ οἷς αὐτὸς ἀνάγειν ἐφίεται, σωφροσύνῃ δὲ παιδαγωγήσας τὸ ἐπιθυμητικόν, ἐκ τῶν κάτω πρὸς τὰ οὐράνια ἀνεπτέρωσε, καὶ πάντα πόθον ἐκεῖσε κενώσας, νεκρός τις ἐν τούτῳ τῷ μέρει πρὸς τὰ γήινα ἦν καὶ τὸν ἐκ τούτων τοῖς ἀπαιδεύτοις ἐγγινόμενον ἔρωτα. Κατωχύρωσε καὶ τῇ ἀνδρείᾳ τὸ θυμικόν, ὡς κατὰ

strong in order to *wear their wool,* as the prophet says. He did not say, "*Blessed be the Lord, for we have become rich.*" To the contrary, he was one to encourage the humble and raise up the fallen. He put bandages on the lame, preparing them to run and leap. For he did not regard his office as an opportunity for relaxation, but for an even greater struggle and more toil than before, insofar as he was now responsible for many more souls. For that reason, he not only taught his people their duties through words, but, much more through his own deeds, drew them toward the tasks that he set before them.

7

He acquired the four cardinal virtues, as well as those that follow upon them, to such a great extent that he was never seen to deviate from the straight and narrow, or to step outside the line, and this held true for either extreme, that is, either by going too far or not going far enough. He fortified the rational part of his soul with prudence, and in this way he managed to direct all of its movements toward God and toward those goals which God wishes us to attain. He educated the desirous part of his soul with moderation, raising it up from the earth toward heaven and emptying it of every desire that may lurk there. He became dead with respect to earthly things and to the passionate desires that they give rise to in the souls of uneducated men. He also fortified the irascible part of his soul with courage, so as to di-

μόνον τοῦτο κινεῖσθαι τοῦ ὄφεως, τοῦ τῷ γένει ἡμῶν θάνατον καὶ φθορὰν ἐπεισάξαντος, καὶ πρὸς τὰς τῶν παθῶν
ὁρμὰς καὶ τοὺς ταῦτα δαίμονας ὑποσπείροντας ἀνδρείως
ἀντικαθίστασθαι. Κατηύνασε καὶ τῇ δικαιοσύνῃ τὸ περιττὸν καὶ νόθον τῶν μερῶν τῆς ψυχῆς, καὶ ἰσονομίαν τούτοις βραβεύσας, πᾶσι τὰ πρόσφορα κατὰ καιρὸν ἐπρυτά-
νευσε, ψυχῇ λέγω καὶ σώματι, φυλάττων ἀρρεπῆ καὶ
ἀπαρέγκλιτα τὰ τῆς δίκης ζυγὰ καὶ πᾶσι τὰς ψήφους ἐκ-
φέρων ὀρθάς, βιαίων συναλλαγμάτων λύων στραγγαλιάς,
πιπτόντων στάσις γινόμενος, ἱσταμένων ἐρυμνότατον
ἔρεισμα, λειπομένοις πᾶσι χορηγία ἡ ἀφθονώτατος, ποῦς
τῶν κατὰ ψυχὴν χωλευόντων καὶ σώματι. Ἀνέῳκτο καὶ
παντὶ ἀνθρώπῳ κατὰ τὸν θεῖον Ἰὼβ ἡ θύρα αὐτοῦ. Ἐθέρ-
μαναν καὶ ὤμους γυμνῶν τὰ ἐξ αὐτοῦ διαδιδόμενα ψυχῇ
τε καὶ σώματι περιβόλαια. Διά τοι τοῦτο καὶ τῆς παρὰ τοῦ
Θεοῦ τετύχηκε <. . .>, ὡς ἄμεμπτος, δίκαιος καὶ ἀληθινὸς
μαρτυρούμενος.

2   Μετὰ συνέσεως ἤλεγχε τοὺς ὑψοῦ τὸν τένοντα αἴρον-
τας καὶ τῷ χρηστῷ ζυγῷ τοῦτον μὴ ὑποβάλλοντας, παρακαλῶν, νουθετῶν, ἐπιτιμῶν, λόγῳ διαγράφων τὸ φοβερὸν
δικαστήριον καὶ τὸν ἐπὶ τοῦ βήματος φρικτῶς δικαστὴν
ἐφεζόμενον, καὶ κατ᾽ ἀξίαν ἑκάστῳ τὴν ποινὴν εἰσπραττό-
μενον καὶ τοὺς ἀγγέλους βλοσυρὸν καὶ πυρῶδες τοῖς
καταδεδικασμένοις ἐμβλέποντας καὶ οὐδένα τούτοις οἰ-
κτείραντας, ὡς οὐ μετανοίας ἀλλ᾽ ἀνταποδόσεως πεφθα-
κότας καιρόν. Τούτοις ἥρει πολλοὺς καὶ εἴσω τῆς ἑαυτοῦ
συνεῖχε σαγήνης καὶ τῷ Δεσπότῃ, ὃς πολλοῦ τὴν τῶν ἀνθρώπων τιμᾶται σωτηρίαν, ὀψώνιον ἔφερε κάλλιστον.

rect it solely against the serpent that brought death and ruin to our race, and to resist bravely the passionate impulses that assault us and the demons that sow them within us. He also used justice to calm the useless and adulterated parts of his soul. He placed all parts of his soul under an equitable regime, giving what was appropriate to each—I mean to his body and to his soul—at the proper time. He kept steady the balance scale of justice, which did not waver under his watch, making the right decisions for everyone. He managed *to untie the knots of those violent quarrels.* He propped up those who were falling and became a mighty bulwark for those who could stand. He gave abundantly to all those in need, and himself became *the feet of those who were lame,* whether in body or soul. His *door was* always *open to all,* like the door of the divine Job. The clothes that he gave away warmed the shoulders of those whose bodies or souls were naked. For that reason he received God's . . . , being declared *blameless, righteous, and true.*

He castigated with prudence those who were arrogant and unwilling to submit to his *easy yoke,* and he did so with entreaties, admonitions, and criticism. He painted with words a vivid picture of that frightful future tribunal and the judge who would preside over it in a fearful manner and would punish everyone as he deserved. He also described the angels who would gaze upon the condemned with grim and fiery eyes, being pitiless toward them, because that would be a time of revenge, not repentance. In this way, he captivated the souls of many people and kept them inside his net, bringing an excellent bounty to the Lord, who places the greatest value on human salvation.

8

Οὕτως τὸ δοθὲν πολυπλασιάσας τάλαντον Ἀθανάσιος, ἐπάνω πολλῶν ὡς πιστὸς γεγένηται πόλεων. Οὕτως εἰς τὴν χαρὰν τοῦ ἑαυτοῦ Κυρίου ἐλήλυθεν, ἑαυτὸν καὶ τὰ δεδωρημένα παιδία δεικνὺς ἄσπιλα καὶ ἀλώβητα. Διὰ ταῦτα καὶ κλέος εὐρὺ δέδεκται παρὰ Θεοῦ καὶ πάντες τῶν ὑπηργμένων τούτῳ καλῶν τὸ πλῆθος ᾄδουσιν ἄνθρωποι, παράκλησιν οὐ τὴν τυχοῦσαν ἐκ μόνης τῆς μνήμης καρπούμενοι. Ὡς γὰρ ἡ τῶν ἀπηγορευμένων ἐνθύμησις καὶ διήγησις τοὺς ἀκροωμένους καὶ λέγοντας ἢ λογιζομένους πολλάκις κατέβλαψεν, οὕτως ἡ τῶν ἀγαθῶν ὠφελείας ἐγένετο πρόξενος. Οὕτω διδάσκων καὶ πράττων, διδακτοὺς ἅπαντας Θεοῦ κατὰ τὸν θεῖον χρησμὸν ἀπετέλεσε καὶ διακριτικοὺς καλοῦ καὶ τοῦ χείρονος, οὐ καθάπερ Ζάμολξις καὶ Ἀνάχαρσις, οὓς ἐπὶ σοφίᾳ, καίτοι βαρβάρους ὄντας, ἐθαύμασαν Ἕλληνες, οὐ Μίνως Κρήταις νόμους ἐνθείς, οὐ Λυκοῦργος τοῖς Σπαρτιάταις καὶ Μνησίων Ἀργείοις, οὐ Νέστωρ Πυλίοις, οὐ τοὺς λόγους μέλιτος γλυκυτέρους ἐκάλεσεν Ὅμηρος, οὐ Σόλων καὶ Κλεισθένης Ἀθηναίοις νομοθετήσαντες, οἵτινες οὐ μόνον ἀγχιτέρμονας Ἕλληνας τοὺς αὐτῶν δέξασθαι νόμους καὶ κατ᾽ αὐτοὺς πολιτεύεσθαι, ἀλλ᾽ οὐδ᾽ ἐκείνους, οἷς τούτους ἐξέθηκαν, μέχρι τέλους ἔπεισαν κατασχεῖν (ἅπαντες γὰρ νῦν τοὺς ἐκείνων ἐρίῳ στέψαντες ἢ μύρῳ καθάπερ τοὺς χελιδόνας ἀλείψαντες, οὐδόλως τούτων ἐπαΐειν ἀνέχονται), ἀλλὰ τοὺς τοῦ Χριστοῦ καὶ τῶν αὐτοῦ παθημάτων νόμους τῇ ἑαυτοῦ

8

In this way Athanasios managed to multiply the sum that he was given by God and, being a faithful servant, he was appointed to preside over numerous cities. Thus he entered *into the joy of* his *Lord,* showing both himself and the children entrusted to him to be unblemished and safe. Because of that, he is greatly glorified by God, and all men sing the praises of his numerous good deeds. Even by simply remembering those deeds men are comforted in no small way. Just as the memory and retelling of forbidden things often harms those who hear them, whether they repeat them or merely think about them, so too does the memory of good things bring us a great benefit. In this way, through his teaching and his deeds, he transformed *all men* into *men taught by God,* as the Holy Scripture puts it, enabling them to distinguish between good and bad. He did not act like Zamolxis or Anacharsis, who, though barbarians, were admired by the Greeks for their wisdom. He did not legislate as Minos did for the Cretans, Lycurgus for the Spartans, Mnesion for the Argives, or Nestor for the people of Pylos, whose words are called *sweeter than honey* by Homer; he did not resemble Solon and Cleisthenes, who gave laws to the Athenians. For they were unable to persuade even their neighboring Greeks to receive and abide by their laws, and even those to whom the laws were directly given were not persuaded to keep them forever. (For all those people crowned their lawgivers with crowns of wool, or anointed them with perfumed oil like swallows, but could not bear to listen to them anymore.) By contrast, our Athanasios brought the laws of Christ and

ποίμνῃ προσενηνοχὼς ὁ ἡμέτερος Ἀθανάσιος, λίαν περι-
χαρῶς ἀσπάσασθαι πέπεικε καὶ μέχρι τέλους ἀλωβήτους
τηρεῖν. Ὄντως μακάριος οὗτος, ὡς φόβον Θεοῦ τὸν τελει-
οποιὸν καὶ οὐκ εἰσαγωγικὸν κτησάμενος. Ἐφίλησε γὰρ
σφόδρα Χριστόν.

2   Τούτου τεκμήριον ἀληθέστατον ἡ εἰς τὸ ποίμνιον αὐτοῦ
ἐπιμέλεια, ἥν, πολλῶν ὄντων τῶν τῆς ἀρετῆς εἰδῶν, ὁ
Δεσπότης προτίθησι, τῷ Πέτρῳ διαλεγόμενος καὶ ταύτην
ἐγχειρῶν ὡς θερμοτέρῳ τῶν ἄλλων ὑπάρχοντι. Ἠθέλησε
κατὰ τὸν προφήτην σφόδρα ἐν ταῖς ἐντολαῖς καὶ διὰ τοῦτο
ἔστη ἐν τῇ τῶν ἐντολῶν γῇ τὸ σπέρμα αὐτοῦ, εἴτε ὁ διδα-
σκαλικὸς λόγος διὰ τῆς ἀρίστης πράξεως ἐν τῇ τῶν ἀκου-
όντων καὶ ὁρώντων κατασπειρόμενος γῇ, εἴτε καὶ αὐτοὶ οἱ
διὰ τούτου οἱονεὶ κυοφορηθέντες καὶ γεννηθέντες καὶ
τραφέντες καὶ τέκνα τοῦ σπείραντος χρηματίσαντες. Ὄντως δόξα καὶ πλοῦτος μέγιστος ἐν τῷ οἴκῳ, τῇ Ἐκκλησίᾳ
λέγω, αὐτοῦ, ὡς τῆς δικαιοσύνης αὐτοῦ μενούσης εἰς τοὺς
αἰῶνας, οὐ κενή τις δόξα καὶ οἷόν τις πομφόλυξ ἐπαιρο-
μένη καὶ τάχιστα ῥηγνυμένη, οὐ πλοῦτος ὁ τοῖς εἰς βασιλείαν οὐρανῶν εἰσελθεῖν βουλομένοις ἀντίπαλος, οὐχ ὁ
τοῖς ἐφιεμένοις αὐτὸν μυρίων πρόξενος συμφορῶν καὶ
πρὸς λόχους καὶ παγίδας ἀπάγων τοὺς τούτῳ δουλεύειν
διὰ τῆς ἀκορέστου ἐπιθυμίας ἐθέλοντας, οὐχ ὁ τῶν ἁμαρ-
τάδων ἕτοιμος ὑπηρέτης ἀφθόνως ὑποβάλλων ὕλην τῷ
τούτων πυρί, ἀλλὰ δόξα μὲν ἡ πρὸς τὴν τῶν ἀγγέλων ὁμο-
τιμίαν ἀνάγουσα, ἡ Θεὸν παρασκευάζουσα, τὸν ἐν ἁγίοις
ἀναπαυόμενον ἅγιον, παρὰ τῶν γεηρῶν καὶ φθειρομένων
ἡμῶν ἁγιάζεσθαι, ἡ ἀρραβὼν τῆς ἐκεῖθεν δόξης τῶν ἁγίων

the stories concerning his passion to his flock, persuading them to accept them with great joy and to preserve them intact until the end. He was a truly *blessed man,* since he had acquired *the fear of God,* which does not merely introduce us to the Christian life but perfects us in it, for he loved Christ very much.

The truest proof of this is his concern for his flock. There   2
are many forms of virtue, but the Lord puts that particular one before all others in his discussion with Peter, who had a more ardent love for him than the others and was therefore entrusted by the Lord with that particular virtue. Our saint too *delighted greatly in the commandments* of the Lord, just as the prophet says, and thus *his seed put down roots in the earth* of his commandments. I mean by this either that his teaching was sowed into the earth of those who listened and looked at him, and did so through his excellent deeds, or that those who were conceived, born, and raised by him became the sons of the one who sowed them. Indeed, *there is glory and* great *wealth in* his *house,* I mean the Church, as the saint's *justice abides eternally.* It is not a vain glory, or like a bubble that swells up and quickly bursts. It is not that kind of wealth that prohibits those who wish to enter the kingdom of heaven from doing so, or that type of wealth that causes countless hardships to those who want to acquire it, drawing those who are enslaved to it into various ambushes and traps through their insatiable desire for it. His wealth is not the willing servant of sinful desires, pouring fuel onto the fire of hell for those who possess it. No, his is a glory that makes men equal in honor with the angels, it makes us, who are earthly and perishable creatures, to hallow God, *who reposes among the saints.* It is a glory that *pledges* the future

ὑπάρχουσα, ἡ χαρᾶς τὸν ἐντὸς ἡμῶν ἄνθρωπον πληροῦσα
καὶ ἀϊδίου ἀγαλλιάσεως, πλοῦτος δὲ ὁ μὴ κενούμενος, ὁ
μὴ λῃσταῖς καὶ κλέπταις διορυττόμενος.

3   Μακάριος ὡς ἀληθῶς ὁ ἱερὸς Ἀθανάσιος. Οὐ γὰρ ἐν
συνεδρίῳ ἀσεβῶν καὶ καθέδρᾳ λεγόντων καὶ πραττόντων
αἰσχρὰ κεκάθικε πορευθείς, ἀλλ᾽ ὡς ἀθανασίας φυτὸν
παρὰ τὰ ζωηρὰ τοῦ Σωτῆρος ἐμπεφύτευτο νάματα, ἅπερ
ἐκ κοιλίας τῶν εἰς αὐτὸν πιστευόντων ῥεύσειν ὑπέσχετο,
οὐδὲ δόλος ἐν τῷ αὐτοῦ εὑρέθη στόματι, λόγος δὲ μόνος
Θεοῦ, ᾧτινι καθάπερ τι καθαρώτατον ἀφώριστο ἐνδιαίτημα. Νοηθείη καὶ Ὄρος Σιὼν ὁ τρισόλβιος. Οὐκ ἐσαλεύθη
γὰρ παρ᾽ ὅλον αἰῶνα, τὴν νέαν κατοικῶν Ἰερουσαλήμ, καὶ
πρὸς Θεὸν αἴρων τοὺς ὀφθαλμούς, τὴν μὴ βραδύνουσαν
ἐκεῖθεν ᾐτεῖτο βοήθειαν. Διὰ τοῦτο χαρὰ καὶ εὐφροσύνη
σήμερον τοῖς συνειλεγμένοις προστέθειται, οὐ πρόσκαιρα
τέρπουσα, ἀλλ᾽ αἰώνια. Τὰς γὰρ ψυχὰς ἐνηδύνουσα, πρὸς
Θεὸν διὰ τῆς εἰς ἐκεῖνον μιμήσεως ἀνυψοῖ, ὅτι κἀκεῖνος
ἔτι τὸν χοῦν περικείμενος, εἰς τόδε τὸ τῆς ἀρετῆς ὕψος ὡς
δένδρον ὑψίκομον ἔφθασε, πρὸς τοὺς τῷ Θεῷ εὐαρεστή-
σαντας βλέπων καὶ τῷ τούτων βίῳ οἷόν τινι φωτὶ ποδη-
γούμενος.

glory of the saints, filling our inner selves with joy and eternal happiness. His wealth, moreover, is not one that can be emptied or *stolen by thieves* and robbers.

Blessed indeed is the holy Athanasios. He neither took 3 counsel with *impious men* nor sat on the *seat* of those who spoke blasphemous words and committed sins. Like a vine of immortality, the saint was planted near the life-giving waters of our Savior, which *flow out of the belly* of those *who believe* in him, as he had promised them. *No guile was found on his lips,* only the word of God. Indeed, his mouth resembled a most pure place consecrated to God. That thrice-blessed father may be compared with *Mount Zion* as well: for *he was not shaken* throughout the whole of *time,* as he *inhabited* the New *Jerusalem. Lifting up his eyes* to God, he sought his help, and it came to him without delay. That is why all those who are gathered here today are filled with joy and happiness. That joy is not temporary, but eternal. Satisfying our souls, it raises them up to God through imitation of the saint, since Athanasios, while he still wore his earthly flesh, managed to reach that peak of virtue like a towering tree, as he himself looked upon the example of those who had satisfied God; their life was like a light that guided him.

9

Τίς γὰρ τὸ τούτου φιλόξενον, τὸ τῆς πίστεως εἰλικρινές τε καὶ ἄληπτον βλέπων, τὸν πατριάρχην οὐκ ἐδόκει καθορᾶν Ἀβραάμ; Τίς τὸ καρτερικὸν καὶ εὐήνιον ἐν πᾶσιν, οἷς ἐπιτάττει Θεός, τὸν Ἰσαὰκ βλέπειν ἐκεῖνον οὐκ ἂν ὑπετόπησε; Τίς ἐν ταῖς περιστάσεσι τὸ στερρὸν καὶ μακρόθυμον καὶ τὸ τοῦ ἤθους ἄπλαστον καὶ ἀκέραιον, τὸν Ἰακὼβ ἤδη παρεῖναι οὐκ ἂν ἐνενόησε; Τίς τὸ σῶφρον τοῦ Ἰωσὴφ καὶ ἀνεξίκακον οὐκ ἐδόκει σπενδόμενον τοῖς μισήσασι καὶ πωλήσασιν ἀδελφοῖς καθορᾶν; Τίς τὸ γενναῖον καὶ ἀταπείνωτον ἐν τοῖς ἀπροσδοκήτοις προσπίπτουσι λυπηροῖς ὑπ᾽ ὄψιν παρεῖναι τὸν γενναῖον οὐκ ἂν εἶπεν Ἰώβ; Ἐμιμήσατο Μωσέως καὶ Ἀαρὼν τὸ πρᾶον καὶ ἀνεπίληπτον καὶ πρὸς θεοπτίαν ἀνηγμένον καὶ ὑψηλότατον, τὸν ζῆλον τοῦ Φινεές, οὐ ζιβύνῃ παρανομήσαντας ἐκκεντῶν, ἀλλὰ λόγῳ τῷ στύφοντι καὶ μαλάσσοντι, καὶ τὸν τῆς ἁμαρτίας δρόμον ἱστῶν καὶ τὴν ἐπὶ τὰ πρόσω φοράν, οὐδὲ τὴν γῆν ὑπορραγῆναι καὶ τοῖς εἰς τὴν μεγάλην ἱερωσύνην τολμηρῶς ἐξυβρίσασι πολυάνδριον ἐργαζόμενος, οὐδὲ πυρὶ παραδοθῆναι ὅπερ παρανόμως ἐβάσταζον (ἀπήτει γὰρ ὁ τότε ταῦτα καιρός), ἀλλὰ τὸν ὅμοια δεδρακότα ἐκείνοις, τῶν ἀναισθήτων ἀπογυμνῶν διὰ τῆς προσευχῆς καὶ μόνων τριχῶν, αἵπερ ἐκ τῶν περιττευμάτων τοῦ σώματος φύουσαι, οὔτε παροῦσαι πρὸς τὴν τῆς οὐσίας συντελοῦσι σύστασιν,

9

Who did not believe, when seeing his hospitality and his sincere and blameless faith, that he was gazing upon the patriarch Abraham? Was there anyone who, upon seeing his endurance and patience in carrying out all of God's commandments, did not believe that he was seeing that Isaac of older times? Who did not believe that he was beholding Jacob upon seeing his steadfastness in difficult circumstances, his long-suffering patience, the *authenticity* of his character, and his sincerity? Who did not make the comparison with the prudence and forbearance of Joseph, when he was reconciling himself with his brothers who hated him and had sold him off? Who would not say that he had a new courageous Job in front of him, seeing his courage and refusal to yield in the face of unexpected suffering? He imitated the mildness, blameless life, and lofty ascent to divine contemplation exhibited by Moses and Aaron; also the zeal of Phinees, not in killing sinners with his spear, but rather through his word, which reprimanded, encouraged, and stopped them from going any further along the path toward more sin. He did not make the earth open up and swallow those who dared to insult the great priesthood, thereby creating a mass grave, nor did he deliver over to the fire all that they were holding illegally. The circumstances prevailing at the time called for precisely such measures. Instead, however, using prayer alone he merely painlessly deprived of his hair a man who behaved in such a way. The latter is something created out of bodily secretions; its presence does not add anything to man's true essence, nor does its absence do

οὔτε παραβλάπτουσιν ἀφαιρούμεναι, μόνον δὲ τὸ τῆς πράξεως ἄγος τῷ τολμητίᾳ δεικνῦσαι πρὸς μετάμελον ἄγουσι
καὶ τὴν τοῦ μύσους φυγὴν καὶ ἀπόκαρσιν.

2   Ἐζήλωσε καὶ Δαυὶδ τὸ ἀνεξίκακον καὶ φιλόθεον καὶ διὰ
τοῦτο κατεπῇδεν οὐ δαιμόνων μόνων, ἀλλὰ καὶ τῶν ἐκ
τούτων ὑποβαλλομένων καὶ κρατυνομένων παθῶν, καὶ
τούτων πολλοὶ μάρτυρες, ὧν τοὺς μὲν ἔτι τῷ βίῳ περιὼν
ἐθεράπευσε, τοὺς δὲ μεταστὰς πρὸς ὃν ἵετο ποθῶν ἀεὶ τὴν
ἀνάλυσιν, ὡς καθαρώτερον καὶ τρανώτερον συνών, ἐπαπο-
λαύοι Χριστοῦ, τῇ τούτου προσερχομένους μετὰ θερμῆς
πίστεως καὶ πόθου σορῷ. Ἠλιοὺ καὶ Ἐλισσαίου τὸν ἀσκη-
τικὸν βίον καὶ αὐχμηρὸν ἐμιμήσατο καὶ ζῆλον ὡς πῦρ ἀπο-
πνέοντα, οὐ πῦρ ἄνωθεν κατάγων καὶ δυσσεβεῖς ἐμπιπρῶν,
οὐδὲ θηρίοις αἱμοβόροις θοίνην ποιούμενος τοὺς ὑβρίζον-
τας (καὶ ταῦτα γὰρ ὁ τότε καιρὸς ἀπῄτει, Θεοῦ τὰς ἰα-
τρείας ἐπάγοντος πρὸς τὰ τραύματα), ἀλλὰ λόγῳ τῷ διδα-
σκαλικῷ ἅλατι ἠρτυμένῳ καὶ βίῳ ἀλήπτῳ πρὸς ἐπιστροφὴν
ἄγων τοὺς ἁμαρτάνοντας. Ἠπίστατο γὰρ κατὰ τὸν Δεσπότην Χριστὸν εἰρηνοποιεῖν τοὺς τοῦ Πνεύματος. Ἐγένετο
κατὰ τὸν μακάριον Δανιὴλ καὶ ἀνὴρ ἐπιθυμιῶν τῶν τοῦ
Πνεύματος, ἀνδρείως κατὰ τῶν παθῶν ἱστάμενος τῆς σαρκὸς καὶ μόνα τὰ θεῖα καὶ οἷς εὕροι Θεὸν καθαρώτερον
ἐφιέμενος. Κατεφρόνησε καὶ αὐτὸς κατὰ τοὺς τρεῖς ἐν Βα-
βυλῶνι νεανίας τὴν κάμινον τῶν σαρκικῶν ἡδονῶν, ὥσπερ
τινὰ τέφραν τὸ ἐκ τούτων καταπατῶν ἀναπτόμενον πῦρ,
διὰ τὸ μὴ συσχεῖν ἐν καρδίᾳ τὰς τούτων εἰκόνας καὶ
προσκυνεῖν εἴδωλα πορνικὰ καὶ ὀλέθρια.

him any harm. The loss of his hair was, for this man, just a marker of his insulting behavior, urging him to repent, to avoid pollution, and to shave it off.

He also imitated David's forbearance and piety. Accordingly, he subdued not only demons through his song, but even the passions that are incited and strengthened by them. There are many witnesses to this. Some of them the saint cured when he was still alive, while others were cured by coming to his grave with an ardent faith and love. This happened after he had departed for the one he loved, as he had always yearned for his death, since he would then enjoy the company of Christ, communing with him in a more perfect and clear way. He imitated also the ascetic and severe life of Elijah and Elisha and their fire-breathing zeal. He did not bring fire down from heaven, burning up the impious, nor did he turn those who insulted him over to flesh-eating beasts for their supper. (For these responses too were demanded by the special circumstances of that time, as God would apply a proper cure to each particular wound.) Instead, the saint led sinners to repentance through his *speech, seasoning it with the salt* of pedagogy, and also through the example of his unblemished life. For like Christ our Lord, he knew how to pacify men of the Spirit. Like the blessed Daniel, he became *a man truly desirous* of the Spirit, and forcefully resisted the passions of our flesh; he wanted to possess only things divine, through which he might find God in a purer way. Like the three young men in Babylon, he despised the furnace of our fleshly pleasures, trampling underfoot the fire lit by them as if it was ashes, and he did this by not keeping in his heart the images created by those pleasures and by not worshipping these idols of prostitution that ruin men.

3   Εἰ δὲ καὶ Ἰωάννου τοῦ πάνυ, οὗ μείζων ἐν γεννητοῖς οὐκ
ἐγήγερται γυναικῶν, τοῦ προδραμόντος ἐν βίῳ καὶ ἐν Ἅιδῃ
Χριστοῦ, ἵνα κηρύξῃ Σωτῆρα καὶ Λυτρωτὴν ἐλθόντα, καὶ
ἐν Ἰορδάνῃ τοῦτον βαπτίσαντος, ὅτε τὴν ἡμετέραν ἁμαρτίαν ἐκεῖσε κατέκλυσεν, ἐν τούτῳ χαρακτῆρας ἐθέλεις
ἰδεῖν καὶ μιμήματα, σκόπει τὸ πρὸς τὰ κάτω ὑπέροπτον, τὸ
ἀπέριττον, τὸ παρρησίας ἀνάπλεων, τὸ ἀκατάπληκτον τοῦ
φρονήματος, τὸ πρὸς δυνάστας ἐλεγκτικόν, ὅτε νόμοι
Θεοῦ ἐν δευτέρῳ τιθέμενοι παρωθοῦντο καὶ παρεκρού-
οντο, τὴν τῆς μετανοίας εἰσήγησιν, τὸν ὑπ᾽ ἐκείνου βαπτι-
σθέντα Χριστὸν ὑποδεικνῦντα πάλιν κρῖναι πάντας ἐρχό-
μενον καὶ ἑκάστῳ κατὰ τὰς πράξεις ἀποδιδοῦντα τὰς
ἀμοιβάς.

10

Εἰ δέ τῳ καὶ τῶν μαθητῶν Χριστοῦ κἀν τούτῳ μεσιτεύ-
ειν ἐφίεται σύμβολον, ἴτω καὶ βλεπέτω τὴν τοῦ βίου παντὸς
καταφρόνησιν, ἵν᾽ εὕρῃ κερδήσας Χριστόν, τὸ σύντονον
ἐν τῷ τοῦ Εὐαγγελίου κηρύγματι, τὸ μεγαλόψυχον ἐν ταῖς
ὀχληραῖς περιστάσεσι, τὸ συνεῖναι διὰ τῆς μνήμης ἀεὶ τῷ
Χριστῷ καὶ παρὰ μηδενὸς ταύτης ἀφέλκεσθαι, ἀλλ᾽ αἴρειν
αὐτὸν διὰ βίου παντὸς τὸν σταυρὸν καὶ ἀκολουθεῖν αὐτῷ,
πάντα ἡγησάμενον σκύβαλα. Ὧν Ἀθανάσιος τὸν βίον ζη-
λώσας, εἰκόνα τὸν ἑαυτοῦ ζῶσαν ὡς ἀπ᾽ ἀρχετύπου τοῦ

You may also wish to see in him the characteristics and ₃
special traits of that great John, he than whom *no one greater
has arisen among those born of women,* who was Christ's forerunner both in this life and in Hades in order to proclaim
him as Savior and Redeemer, and who baptized him in the
Jordan River, where Christ washed away our sins. Observe
Athanasios's contempt for all things mundane, his simplic-
ity, the frankness with which his speech was filled, his im-
perturbable mind, and the way he rebuked those in power
when they violated and despised the laws of God and put
them in second place. Observe his admonitions to repentance and his declaration that Christ, who was baptized by
John, is returning to judge all people and *reward everyone
according to his deeds.*

IO

If anyone wishes to see the characteristics of Christ's disciples in him, let him come and see how the saint held in
contempt our life in this world, because he wanted to find
and gain Christ. See his ardor for preaching the Gospel, his
magnanimity in difficult circumstances, how he used his
memory to be in constant communion with Christ: no one
could detach him from that. See also how he *carried the cross*
throughout his entire life, following in the footsteps of our
Lord and *considering all other things to be as refuse.* Imitating
the life of the apostles, Athanasios made his own life a living

ἐκείνων ἀπηκριβώσατο, ὡς εἴ τις ἐθέλοι ἑκάστου χαρακτῆρας ἰδεῖν, ἐν τούτῳ κατοπτεύσας εἰλικρινεστάτους εὑρήσῃ καὶ σχεδὸν οὐδὲν ἀποδέοντας.

II

Ἀλλ' ἧκεν ὁ τῆς ἐκδημίας καιρός. Οὐ γὰρ ἄλλο τι τὴν ἐκείνου τελευτὴν ὀνομαστέον ἢ ἐξ ὑπερορίας πρὸς τὴν ἐνεγκοῦσαν μετάστασιν. Καὶ δὴ τὰ κατ' αὐτὸν ἐπισκήπτοντι παρῆσαν πολλοί, σφόδρα παθαινόμενοι καὶ ὡς ζημίαν μεγάλην τὸν αὐτοῦ χωρισμὸν ἀπολοφυρόμενοι. Ἀλλ' ἤκουον ἐκείνου κατακειμένου τῷ σκίμποδι, οὐ χρημάτων διαταττόμενον εἴνεκα, οὐ χρυσοῦ καὶ ἀργύρου βαλάντια τοῖς ἐπιτρόποις καταλιμπάνοντα, ὧν τὴν ἀκτησίαν ὡς ἄλλοι τὴν κτῆσιν ἐδίωξεν, οὐ γῆς καὶ δένδρων καὶ ἀμπελώνων καὶ βοσκημάτων, ὧν ξένος ἕως ἦν ἐτύγχανεν ἐπὶ γῆς, ἀλλ' ἐκείνων περὶ ὧν ἀεὶ διελέγετο, συντόμως διὰ τὴν ἐκ τῆς νόσου συνοχὴν ὑπομιμνήσκοντα. Ἄνθρωπος γὰρ ἦν, εἰ καὶ τοῦ τῆς ταπεινώσεως ὑψηλότερος διὰ τὴν προθυμίαν ἐγίνετο σώματος, "Ἔδει με," λέγων, "εἰς ἐμαυτὸν συστραφέντα καὶ μόνον τὰ νῦν, περὶ τῆς ἀποδημίας σκοπεῖν καὶ τὸ φοβερὸν καὶ φρικτὸν ἐκδέχεσθαι πρόσταγμα καὶ τοὺς παραληψομένους μου τὴν ψυχὴν τούς τε τόπους

and exact copy of those models. If anyone wishes to know the character of each of the apostles, he may look upon the saint to find exact copies of them, with almost no defect.

11

But the time has come for his departure. I cannot use any other word when referring to his death, for it was like a return to his homeland after living abroad. Many people were present when he was giving his last instructions concerning his own affairs, and they were overcome with sadness, lamenting his departure as a great loss. But as the saint was lying on his bed, no one heard him give instructions about money; he did not leave bags full of gold and silver to his stewards, and even took as much care not to possess any of those things as other people take to acquire them. He did not say anything about land, trees, vineyards, or cattle, for he had remained a stranger to all these things for as long as he had lived on this earth. He merely reminded them of all those matters about which he always used to speak in the past, though briefly this time because of the grip of his illness. He was a human being after all, although he was raised above the abasement of his body through his sheer eagerness. He said to them, "It would be right for me *to turn inward* and think only about my present condition, namely my imminent death, and to await that frightful, awesome decree and those who will gather up my soul. It would be

οὓς διέρχεσθαι μέλλω καὶ τοὺς λοχῶντας ἀεὶ δυσμενεῖς τὴν πορείαν ἡμῖν ὡς φῶράς τε καὶ λῃστὰς ἐμποδίζοντας. Ἀλλ᾽ ἐπεὶ τοῦ ἐμαυτοῦ τὸ ὑμέτερον συμφέρον ὡς ἀεὶ καὶ νῦν ἐκζητῶ (τοῦτο γὰρ νόμος Θεοῦ), ὅσα ὁ καιρὸς ἐπιτρέπει καὶ τὸ λειπόμενον ἐν ἐμοὶ ζωτικόν, φράσω καὶ νῦν. Ἐγὼ μὲν ὡς ὁρᾶτε πρὸς τοὺς ἐμοὺς πατέρας πορεύομαι καὶ οὐκ ἔτι ἐν τούτῳ με τῷ βίῳ θεάσεσθε. Ἀλλ᾽ εἰ τῶν ἐμῶν μὴ ἐπιλάθεσθε παραινέσεων ἃς ὑμῖν προσῆγον, διαπύρῳ φίλτρῳ πρὸς ὑμᾶς ἀγάπης κινούμενος, ἔσομαι ἀδιάστατος ὑμῖν, μᾶλλον δὲ Χριστὸς αὐτὸς σὺν τῷ Πατρὶ καὶ τῷ Πνεύματι, καὶ οὕτω κατοικητήρια θεῖα γενήσεσθε καὶ ναοὶ ἔμψυχοι τοῦ τὸν οὐρανὸν ἔχοντος θρόνον καὶ τὴν γῆν ὑποπόδιον. ᾽Ἐγώ,᾽ γάρ φησιν ὁ Σωτήρ, ᾽καὶ ὁ Πατὴρ πρὸς αὐτὸν ἐλευσόμεθα,᾽ δῆλον ὅτι τὸν τηροῦντα τὰς ἑαυτοῦ ἐντολάς, ᾽καὶ μονὴν παρ᾽ αὐτῷ ποιήσομεν.᾽

12

"Γενικωτέρα δὲ καὶ πρώτη τῶν ἐντολῶν ἀγαπᾶν τὸν Θεὸν ἐξ ὅλης ψυχῆς καὶ ἰσχύος καὶ διανοίας καὶ τὸν πλησίον ὡς ἑαυτόν. Ταύτῃ γὰρ ἕπονται πᾶσαι, ἑτέρα τῆς ἑτέρας ἐχόμεναι, ἡ ἀγαπᾶν κελεύουσα τοὺς ἐχθρούς, τιθέναι δὲ ὑπὲρ φίλων, καιροῦ καλοῦντος, τὴν ἰδίαν ψυχήν, ἀφιέναι τοῖς ὀφειλέταις τὰ ὀφειλήματα, ὅπως ἡμῖν καὶ τὰ ἡμέτερα

proper for me to think about those places through which I have to pass; to be concerned about those enemies who always lie in ambush, like robbers and thieves, who block us from proceeding further. However, I care now not only about my own self-interest but also about yours, as I always have, because this is the law of God. Therefore, at this time too I shall speak about that as far as circumstances and the spirit that remains inside me permit. As you can see, I am about to go join my fathers, and you will no longer see me alive. But if you do not forget the commandments I gave you, moved by my burning love for you, then in that way I will remain among you, in fact inseparable from you. Actually, it will be Christ himself together with his Father and the Spirit who will be among you. In this way, you will become dwelling places and living sanctuaries of God, *whose throne is heaven and whose footstool is the earth.* For the Savior said, '*My Father* and I *will come to that man,*' meaning the one who keeps his commandments, '*and we will make our home with him.*'

12

" *T he first* and most encompassing *of the commandments* is *to love God with our entire soul, power, and mind, and to love our fellow men as we love ourselves.* All the other commandments follow upon this one, coming one after the other. I am referring to the one ordering us *to love our enemies; to sacrifice our life for our friends,* when circumstances call for that; *to forgive*

παρὰ τοῦ οὐρανίου πατρὸς ἀφεθῇ, τὴν φοβερὰν ἐννοουμέ-
νους ἀπόφασιν τοῦ τὰ πλεῖστα συγχωρηθέντος καὶ τῷ
συνδούλῳ κατάγχοντος διὰ τὰ ἐλάχιστα, ἐπικλίνειν τοῖς
δεομένοις διὰ τῆς συμπαθείας εὐήκοον οὓς, ὅπως οἱ γήι-
νοι καὶ φθαρτοὶ κατὰ τὸ ἡμῖν ἐφικτὸν Θεοῦ, τοῦ εἰς βασιλείαν τοὺς τοιούτους εἰσάγοντος καὶ ἑαυτὸν εἶναι τὸν ἐλέ-
ους δεόμενον λέγοντος, γενώμεθα ὅμοιοι, τοὺς δὲ τὸ
θηριῶδες νοσήσαντας καὶ ἀπάνθρωπον ὡς αὐτὸν παρεω-
ραμένους εἰς πῦρ τὸ αἰώνιον ἀποπέμποντος μετὰ τοῦ ἀρχε-
κάκου Σατὰν καὶ τῶν ἀγγέλων αὐτοῦ.

2   "Ἀναμιμνησκώμεθα οὖν συνεχῶς τὸν ἡμέτερον Δεσπότην κριτὴν ἀδέκαστον ἐπὶ θρόνου φρικτῶς καθεζόμενον καὶ
ποταμὸν πυρὸς ἔμπροσθεν αὐτοῦ πορευόμενον καὶ τετραχη-
λισμένους εἰσαγομένους εἰς τὸ κριτήριον εὐθύνας εἰσπρα-
ξομένους ὧν εὖ ἢ κακῶς εἰργασάμεθα. Ὅσοι εἰς Χριστὸν
ἐβαπτίσθημεν, Χριστὸν ἐνδεδύμεθα. Μὴ οὖν διὰ τῆς πρὸς
τὰ γήινα συμπαθείας τὸ τοιοῦτον ἀποβαλώμεθα ἔνδυμα,
ἵνα μὴ τοῦ νυμφῶνος ἔξω ῥιφῶμεν, τοῦτ᾽ ἔστιν τῆς τῶν
δικαίων ἀγαλλιάσεως. ῾Λόγος σαπρὸς ἐκ τοῦ στόματος ἡμῶν
μὴ ἐκπορευέσθω,᾽ φησὶν ὁ θεῖος ἀπόστολος, ῾ἀλλ᾽ εἴ τις πρὸς
οἰκοδομὴν τοῦ πλησίον καὶ ὠφέλειαν.᾽ Λόγον γὰρ οὐ μόνον περὶ πραγμάτων, ἀλλὰ καὶ λόγων ἀργῶν δώσομεν τῷ
Θεῷ καὶ τῶν πονηρῶν ἐνθυμήσεων. Ἕκαστος τῷ πλησίον
ἀρεσκέτω εἰς τὸ ἀγαθόν. Χρεωστεῖ γὰρ ἕκαστος τὸν πέλας
ἡμῶν ὠφελεῖν. Οὐδεὶς ἡμῖν μάτην προβαλλομένοις τὴν
ἄγνοιαν τῆς δίκης ἐξαιρήσεται. Πάντες γὰρ καθ᾽ ἑκάστην
σχεδὸν τῶν θείων Εὐαγγελίων ἀκούομεν καὶ τῶν ἀποστο-
λικῶν καὶ προφητικῶν παραινέσεων."

our debtors, just as *our heavenly Father may forgive* our own debts too, bearing in mind the horrible condemnation of the servant who did not hesitate to pressure his fellow servant over some trivial debts, when his own great debts had been discharged by their master. We are also admonished to lend a benevolent ear of compassion to those who are in need, so as to become like God as far as is possible for such earthly and perishable creatures as ourselves, seeing as it is God who admits those in need into the kingdom of heaven, saying that he is the one who needs our mercy. By contrast, those who, like rabid beasts, hold their brethren in inhuman contempt are thrown by him *into the eternal fire* together with Satan, the originator of evil, *and his angels.*

"Let us continually remember that our Lord will be our 2
impartial judge, *sitting* terrifyingly *on a throne before a river of* flowing *fire,* and all of us, laid bare, will be hauled before the tribunal in order to be rewarded for our good deeds or punished for our sins. *As many of us as were baptized into the name of Christ have put on Christ.* Let us not toss that garment aside because of our passion for things mundane, lest we be thrown out of the wedding chamber, by which I mean the rejoicing of just men. '*Let no foul word come out of* our *mouth,*' says the holy apostle, '*only words that are edifying* and useful to our neighbor.' For we will have to render an accounting before God not only for our deeds, but also for the words that came out of our mouth in vain and also for our evil thoughts. *Let each of us please his neighbor for his good.* For each of us is required to be of benefit to his fellow man. No one will be able to claim ignorance and thereby avoid punishment, since we all hear the words of the holy Gospel almost every day, as well as the admonitions of the apostles and the prophets."

13

Τί μοι Σωκράτους τὰ τελευταῖα πρὸς ταῦτα φιλοσοφήματα νομιζόμενα, πρὸς ἃ τὰς ὀφρῦς ἐπαίρουσιν Ἕλληνες, ὅτιπερ, ὡς αὐτοί φασιν, κρείττων ὁ φιλόσοφος τῆς τοῦ θανάτου δειλίας γεγένηται; Κενοῦ γὰρ δοξαρίου καὶ σκηνῆς τὰ γινόμενα, προσωπεῖον καὶ μόνον φιλοσοφίας ὑποδυόμενα, ὡς εἰς ἑαυτόν, οὐκ εἰς τοὺς ἄλλους περιιστῶντος τὸ πραττόμενον. Καὶ τοῦτο κράζει ὁ τῷ Ἀσκληπιῷ τυθεὶς ἀλεκτρύων καὶ τὰ τούτου ἀνθρωπαρεσκείας γέμοντα ῥήματα, ἅπερ, τῶν μαθητῶν εἰσηγουμένων τὸν πειρασμὸν ἐκφυγεῖν, ὃν Ἄνυτος αὐτῷ καὶ Μέλητος ἐξήγειραν, ἀπεφθέγγετο. Ἀλλ᾽ οὐχ οὕτως ὁ ἡμέτερος Ἀθανάσιος, πάντα δὲ τότε λιπών, ἑνὸς καὶ μόνου γίνεται, δεῖξαι τῷ πάντων ἐφόρῳ Χριστῷ ὡς οὐδὲν αὐτῷ περισπούδαστον, ὡς ἡ τοῦ ἐμπιστευθέντος ποιμνίου σωτηρία γεγένηται, δι᾽ ἣν καὶ αὐτὸς ἄνθρωπος γίνεται, τὸ παραδοξότατον, καὶ τῶν αὐτὸν φιλούντων σύμβολον τοῦτο καθίστησιν ἐναργέστατον. Διὰ τοῦτο, καίπερ ἐν δυσμαῖς τοῦ βίου γενόμενος καὶ τὴν λύσιν τοῦ φυσικωτάτου δεσμοῦ, ψυχῆς λέγω καὶ σώματος, ὑφιστάμενος, ἅπερ παρὰ πᾶσαν τὴν ἀρχιερωσύνης ζωὴν μυῶν διετέλεσε ὑπεμίμνησκεν. Οὕτως τὴν εἰς τὸν Θεὸν καὶ τὸν πλησίον ἀγάπην τελείαν κατώρθωσεν Ἀθανάσιος. Οὕτως ἡμῖν οὐ δι᾽ ἔργων μόνον, ἀλλὰ καὶ λόγων μέχρις ἐσχάτης ἀναπνοῆς καταλέλοιπεν ὑποδείγματα. Πρὸς ἃ βλέποντες, οἷα οἱ ἀσελήνῳ νυκτὶ ναυτιλλόμενοι πρὸς τοὺς ἀστέρας, πάσας τὰς ἐπανισταμένας ἐν βίῳ

13

Can the final, so-called philosophical words of Socrates, of which the Greeks are so proud, be compared with the words of that man? Although they say that the philosopher did not show cowardice in the face of death, in fact what he did was due to vainglory and histrionics. His words were but a mask: he made a pretense of philosophy, caring only about himself in what he did, not about his fellow men. This is proved by the cock sacrificed to Asklepios, and by the pandering words he addressed to his students who urged him to avoid the temptation placed before him by Anytos and Meletos. Not so our Athanasios. He abandoned everything and turned his attention to just one thing, to prove to Christ who oversees everything that he had no other concern but the salvation of the flock entrusted to him. It was for the sake of that salvation that Christ himself became man, a most extraordinary miracle, and so caring for others is a clear sign that someone loves Christ. For this reason, although the saint was near the end of his life and was imminently expecting the dissolution of that most natural bond that united his soul to his body, he went on reminding them of the lessons into which he had initiated them as long as he had been bishop. That was the extent to which Athanasios attained that perfect love for God and his fellow men, leaving to us exemplars of virtue not only through his deeds but through his words as well, and that until his very last breath. Let us look upon these exemplars as sailors do who look to the stars on a moonless night, and let us sail past all the

τρικυμίας καὶ ζάλας ἐξ ἐπιβουλῆς τοῦ κοινοῦ Δυσμενοῦς
ὑπερπλεύσωμεν καὶ πρὸς τὸν γαληνότατον τῆς Χριστοῦ
βασιλείας λιμένα προσορμισθείημεν, οἷόν τινα κυβερνή-
την τὸν διδάσκαλον ἔχοντες ἐμπειρότατον, πρύμνιον
ἑστηκότα καὶ τῶν οἰάκων ἐπειλημμένον καὶ θάρσος ἡμῖν
ἐντιθέμενον καὶ πρὸς τὰ ἐξ ὧν τὸ σώζεσθαι περιγίνεται
διεγείροντα.

14

Τοιοῦτον τοῖς ἑαυτοῦ παισὶ κλῆρον λιπὼν ὁ ἱερώτατος
Ἀθανάσιος, ἐξάρας τοὺς ὡραίους πόδας καὶ τὰς ἀθῴας
χεῖρας περιστείλας εὖ καὶ σεμνῶς τὸ ὄμμα τε τείνας πρὸς
οὐρανὸν καὶ τελευταῖον, "Εἰς χεῖρας σου, Δέσποτα, παρατίθημι τὴν ψυχήν," ὑπειπὼν τοῖς ἀπάγουσιν ἀγγέλοις, χαρί-
εις τε καὶ μάλα φαιδρὸς ἐναπέψυξεν, πλήρης μὲν ἡμερῶν
τῶν τοῦ Πνεύματος, πλήρης δὲ τῶν ἐξ αὐτοῦ χαρισμάτων
γενόμενος. Ἔλιπε μετάμελον κατὰ τὸν σοφόν. Τὰς γὰρ τῶν
ἀγώνων ἀντιδόσεις ἐκεῖσε βλέπων, οὔμενουν πρὸς μετάμελον ἥξει, ἀλλ' εὐφρανθήσεται, ὡραῖός τις καθάπερ σῖτος
εἰς τὰς θείας ἀποθήκας συγκομισθεὶς καὶ πᾶσαν ἐγγινομέ-
νην τοῖς ἀτελεσφορήτοις βλάβην ἐκπεφευγώς, καὶ διὰ
τοῦτο ζῇ μετὰ δικαίων τὴν ὄντως ζωὴν καὶ ὁ μισθὸς αὐτοῦ
πολὺς παρὰ τῷ ὑψίστῳ Θεῷ. Ἀνθεῖ καὶ ὡς φοῖνιξ καὶ κέδρος
πληθύνεται, πολὺν ἡμῖν τοῖς εἰς αὐτὸν διὰ τοῦ ζήλου

tempests and storms of life that are caused by the malice of our common Enemy. Let us reach the most calm haven of Christ's kingdom, guided by our teacher who, in this respect, resembled an experienced captain, standing by the stern and holding the helm, filling us with courage, and admonishing us to perform the deeds that secure our salvation.

14

Such was the inheritance that the most holy Athanasios left to his children. Then he stretched out his *beautiful feet* and, crossing his innocent hands, solemnly lifted his eyes up to heaven, speaking his final words, "O Lord, *into your hands I commend* my soul." Then, full of joy and happiness, he surrendered his soul to the angels who had come to take him away. He was *full of the days* of the Spirit, filled with the gifts that come from it. Therefore, *he left regret behind him,* as the wise man said. Seeing the rewards for his struggles that await him in heaven, he will not regret his departure from the earth. On the contrary, he will rejoice, resembling the ripe grain that has been harvested for the storehouses of God, and having escaped the harm suffered by those who yielded no fruit. Therefore, he now lives the true life in the company of the righteous, and *the reward that* he *received* from the highest God *is great indeed. He blossoms like a palm tree and he grows ever taller like a cedar,* offering his many fruits

βλέπουσι τὸν καρπὸν παρεχόμενος καὶ σκιὰν σχεδιάζων καυσουμένοις ἐκ πειρασμῶν, ὅθεν καὶ εἰς μνημόσυνον αἰώνιον καὶ ἄσβεστον κλέος γεγένηται.

2 Ἡμῖν δὲ τὸν τάφον μετὰ τοῦ τρισολβίου καταλέλοιπε σώματος, πηγὰς ἰαμάτων τοῖς πίστει προσιοῦσιν ἅπασιν ἀναβλύζοντα. Ὅθεν αὐτὸν ἐν τούτῳ νομίζοντες καθορᾶν, ἀσχέτῳ πόθῳ τοῦτον κατασπαζόμεθα ὡς πατέρα τιμῶντες καὶ στέργοντες, ὡς εὐεργέτην εὐχαριστοῦντες, ὡς ἰατρῷ τὰς τῆς ψυχῆς καὶ τοῦ σώματος νόσους ἐπιδεικνῦντες καὶ πρὸς τὴν τούτων ἐπισπεύδοντες ἴασιν. Ἐνταῦθα καὶ οἱ μακρὰν ἀποδημίαν στελλόμενοι παραγίνονται, καλῶς ἀναστρέψαι δεόμενοι οἴκαδε καὶ γυναῖκες ἀνδράσιν ἢ παισὶν ἴασιν καὶ ἀνάκλησιν ἐξαιτούμεναι. Οἱ καταδυναστευόμενοι ὑπὸ στερρεωτέρας χειρὸς ζητοῦσι τὸν βοηθόν, οἱ συκοφαντούμενοι καὶ ἀδίκως ἑλκόμενοι τὸν ὑπέρμαχον καὶ ἁπλῶς οἱ πάντες τὸν πάντα <τοῖς πᾶσι> γινόμενον, οἳ καὶ χερσὶ τὸ αἰτούμενον διὰ τῆς ἑτοίμου κατέχοντες λήψεως χαίροντες ὑποστρέφουσιν. Βλέπομεν γὰρ τοῦτον ἕτερον Σιλωὰμ παντοίων παθῶν σβεστήριον ἡμῖν ἐκβλύζοντα καὶ πάντων ταῖς μυριπνόοις ἀρδείαις ψυχάς τε καὶ σώματα κατευφραίνοντα. Ὧν καὶ ἡμεῖς εὐξώμεθα μετασχεῖν, τῷ πάντων καλῶν αἰτίῳ καὶ <ἐν> τοῖς ἁγίοις αὐτοῦ δοξαζομένῳ εὐχαριστοῦντες Θεῷ, ὅτι αὐτῷ πρέπει πᾶσα δόξα, τιμὴ καὶ προσκύνησις τῷ Πατρὶ καὶ τῷ Υἱῷ καὶ τῷ Ἁγίῳ Πνεύματι νῦν καὶ ἀεὶ καὶ εἰς τοὺς αἰῶνας τῶν αἰώνων, ἀμήν.

to us who look upon him with fervor. He also provides us with a place of shade for when we are burned by the fire of temptation. Therefore, *his remembrance will be everlasting* and *his glory inextinguishable.*

He has left his grave behind for us, along with his thrice-blessed body, which gushes forth a fount of healings for all who come to it with faith. Believing that we are looking at him when we gaze upon it, we embrace it with irrepressible desire, honoring and loving him as a father, thanking him as our benefactor, showing him the afflictions of our body and our soul, as if he were a doctor, and asking him to cure us quickly. Those who undertake long journeys come here too, asking him to safeguard their return. Women come as well, asking the saint to cure their husbands or children, or to bring them back to them. Those who suffer injustice *at the hands of the powerful* seek his help, those who are calumniated or arrested unjustly seek their champion. Simply put, all people come to *him who becomes everything for everyone,* and all come away satisfied, after readily receiving what they ask for. We look upon him as a new Siloam: the streams gushing out of him extinguish all sorts of passions and satisfy all souls and bodies with their fragrance. Let us too pray to God, the Father, the Son, and the Holy Spirit, who is the cause of all good things and is glorified in the midst of his saints, and let us thank him so that we may partake of those graces as well. To him belong all glory, honor, and veneration, now and forever and unto the ages of ages, amen.

LIFE OF PETER, BISHOP OF ARGOS, BY THEODORE, BISHOP OF NICAEA

Θεοδώρου ἐλαχίστου μητροπολίτου Νικαίας εἰς τὸν ἐν ἁγίοις πατέρα ἡμῶν καὶ θαυματουργὸν Πέτρον ἐπίσκοπον Ἄργους

Δέσποτα, εὐλόγησον.

I

Καὶ πάντας μὲν προσῆκε τοὺς ἀρετῇ τῶν ἄλλων διενεγκόντας τῶν κατ᾽ ἀξίαν ἐπαίνων τυγχάνειν, πολλῷ γε δήπου τοὺς ὅσοι ταύτης εἰς ἄκρον ἀφίκοντο καὶ ὥσπερ ἐν ἱερῷ χωρίῳ συνήθροισαν τῇ ψυχῇ πᾶν ὅ,τι τῶν ἐκείνης καλῶν, οἳ καὶ τοῖς ἄλλοις πρόξενοι τιμῶν ἀθανάτων ἐγένοντο τοῖς μιμεῖσθαι τούτους φιλονικήσασι. Καὶ πῶς οὐ περὶ πρωτείων ἤρισεν ἂν πολλοῖς ἀρχέτυπον ἀρετῆς γεγονώς, εἴ γε φιλότιμος ἦν ὁ νῦν εὐφημούμενος καὶ μὴ τὸ ἦθος ἐκέκτητο μέτριον καὶ τὴν ἐσχάτην ἀεὶ χώραν ἀπένεμεν ἑαυτῷ; Ὃν καὶ πάλαι μοι προθυμουμένῳ κατὰ δύναμιν ἐπαινεῖν, ὡς πρὸ τῶν ἄλλων ἐμοὶ προσῆκον ἀποτιννύναι τὰ τροφεῖα παιδείας τε εἵνεκα καὶ τῆς ἄλλης ἐκ παιδὸς ἀγωγῆς καὶ αὐτῆς ἱερωσύνης εἰς ἄνδρα ἥκοντι, ἀπεῖργον

Life of our father among the saints, the miracle-worker Peter, the bishop of Argos, written by Theodore, the most humble metropolitan bishop of Nicaea

Bless this reading, master.

I

It was proper that all men who excel in virtue among their fellow men should be praised in a fitting way, and this is all the more true for those who reached the highest peak of virtue and gathered all its goodness inside their soul, as if in a holy place. These people, moreover, served as intermediaries for others who were eager to imitate them and acquire these immortal honors. Had the man I am praising now been ambitious and not so humble in character, always ranking himself last, he would certainly have a claim to the first prize, seeing as he served as a paragon of virtue for many people. It was for a long time my intention to write an encomium for him, the best that I could, since it was more appropriate for me than for others to repay him for educating me, for training me in other respects when I was a child, and for ordaining me priest when I reached adulthood.

αἱ συχναὶ περιπέτειαι. Ἄλλως τέ με καὶ δέος ὑπεισῄει τοσοῦτον ἀναρριπτεῖν κίνδυνον καὶ τὸ τῆς ὑποθέσεως μέγεθος κατασμικρύνειν ὅσον ἐπὶ τῷ τῶν ἡμετέρων λόγων
χαμαιπετεῖ. Ἀλλὰ μὴ στέγων τὸ ὄνειδος τῶν εἰς τοῦτό με
παρορμώντων ἀεί, εὐλαβούμενός τε μὴ καὶ ἀχαριστίας
γραφὴν ἀπενέγκωμαι καὶ μήποτε οὐδὲ ὅσιον ᾖ, πολλῶν εἰς
τοῦτο ἐπιχειρησάντων, ἐμὲ σιωπᾶν, ἐμαυτὸν ἐδοκίμασα καθ-
εῖναι πρὸς τὸ τἀκείνου γράφειν, ταῖς ἐκείνου πρεσβείαις τε-
θαρρηκώς, οὐ πάντα καθεξῆς (τίς γὰρ ἂν ἐφίκοιτο λόγος
κατὰ μέρος ταῦτα διεξιέναι;) διά μοι καὶ τὸ τῆς μακρᾶς
σιωπῆς ἀποδειλιῶντι τὸ πλῆθος, ἀλλ᾽ ὅσα χαρακτηρίζειν
οἶδε τὸν ἄληπτον ἐκείνου βίον καὶ ὅσα ἡ μνήμη ἀποσχεδι-
άζει, ὧν καὶ τὰ καίρια σιωπώμενα κινδυνεύει τῷ χρόνῳ
διαρρυῆναι.

2

Οἱ μὲν οὖν πλεῖστοι τῶν ἐπαίνους ἐπιχειρούντων
ἐξυφαίνειν τισὶ πολὺν ἀναλίσκουσι χρόνον μακρὸν ἀπο-
τείνοντες λόγον περί τε πατρίδος καὶ γένους καὶ πατέρων
εὐκλείας καὶ ὄλβου καὶ περιφανείας τῶν ἐπαινουμένων, ἐκ
τούτων δοκοῦντες ἐξαίρειν αὐτούς. Ἐμοὶ δὲ πῶς οὐκ εὔηθες τὸν ἀοίδιμον Πέτρον ἀποσεμνύνειν ἐκ τῶν κάτω καὶ

However, I was prevented from doing so by the vicissitudes of fortune that I frequently encountered. Moreover, I was afraid *to incur such a great risk* and trivialize my magnificent subject, given that my speech is so pedestrian. However, I could not endure the reproach of those who were always urging me to compose this encomium. I was also afraid that I might be accused of ingratitude, and that it might be considered *unholy for me to remain silent* when so many other people have tried to deal with this subject. Therefore, *I decided to make the attempt and compose his life,* placing my confidence in his intercessory prayers. I will not write everything in a linear order, for what speech could succeed in enumerating all his deeds in detail? Besides, I shrink from this task because for a long time now I have kept silent. So I will write down only whatever distinguished his irreproachable life and *whatever my memory prompts me to write offhand.* The greater risk is that, if we remain silent, all of his important deeds may be destroyed by the tides of time.

2

Most of those who try to weave the praises of others spend a lot of time talking about their homeland, family, ancestral glory, and the wealth and renown of those whom they are praising, believing that they are glorifying them in this way. But it would be silly for me to extol that famous Peter through such base and mundane matters, a man who

τῶν τῆς γῆς, τὸν τούτων ἀφέμενον καὶ μόνα τὰ ἄνω καὶ
μόνιμα στέρξαντα, ὡς, εἰ καὶ τούτων ἐχρῆν διαμνημονεύ-
ειν νόμῳ τῆς τέχνης, πολλῆς ἄν μοι λόγων εὐπορίας ἐδέ-
ησε περὶ τῆς Κωνσταντίνου διεξιόντι μεγαλοπόλεως, ἣν
ἔλαχε πατρίδα θεῖος ἀνήρ, τῆς τῶν ἄλλων ἁπασῶν προκα-
θημένης ἅτε δὴ βασιλίδος, ὅσας ἥλιος ἐφορᾷ, καὶ πλούτῳ
καὶ δόξῃ κομώσης καὶ συγκλήτῳ περιφανεῖ καὶ σοφῶν
πληθούσης ἀνδρῶν, ἐν ᾗ λόγων ἅμιλλαι καὶ ἀρετῶν ἰδέαι
παντοίων, ἐν ᾗ μεγέθη καὶ κάλλη ναῶν καὶ ἀναθημάτων
πολυτέλειαι καὶ θεραπεία τοῦ θείου τὸ ταύτης ἐξαίρετον.

3

Πατέρων δὲ ἔφυ μακρῷ τῶν ἄλλων ἐπ᾽ εὐσεβείᾳ γνω-
ρίμων, οὐ τῷ πλούτῳ πρὸς ἡδονὰς ἀποχρωμένων, ἀλλὰ
τοῦτον ὡς ἐν ἀσύλῳ ταμείῳ ταῖς τῶν πενήτων ἐναποτιθε-
μένων χερσίν. Οὐδ᾽ ἔστιν εἰπεῖν ὅσον ἀφειστήκεσαν φιλοχρηματίας. Οὐδὲ γὰρ αὐτοῖς κιχρῶσι τὴν χεῖρα πρὸς ἔλεον
παρήλλαττεν ἡμέρα καὶ νύξ, ἀλλ᾽ ἡ μὲν τῇ τραπέζῃ συνευ-
ωχουμένους εἶχε τοὺς ἐνδεεῖς, αἱ δὲ νύκτες αὐτοῖς τῇ πρὸς
τὰ ἱερὰ προόδῳ πόσην οὐκ ἐνεποίουν τοῖς πενομένοις
παραψυχὴν λανθάνειν ἐθέλουσιν; Ἡ δὲ πρὸς τοὺς παῖδας
συχνὴ νουθεσία καὶ τῶν Ἱερῶν Λογίων ἐξάπλωσις καὶ
πειθὼ τὸ εὔκολον ἐσωφρόνιζε τῆς νεότητος καὶ ὅλον

renounced all of them, choosing instead only heavenly things, which are permanent. Besides, if it were necessary for me to observe the laws of rhetoric and mention those things, I would have needed a host of speeches to describe the great city of Constantine, which was allotted to that holy man as his birthplace. It is superior to all other cities under the sun, because it is a royal city and very rich and famous as well, and the seat of the illustrious senate. It is full of wise men; contests in the art of speech take place there, and all sorts of virtues are found there, in addition to *large and beautiful churches* and precious votive offerings. Its most outstanding aspect is the worship of God.

3

He was born to parents distinguished for their piety, surpassing all other people in this respect. They did not abuse their wealth for the sake of voluptuous pleasure, but deposited it into the hands of the poor as if into a most secure treasury. *It would be hard to exaggerate how much they avoided any thought of greed.* Day and night, their hand was always extended in charity: daytime saw the needy feasting with them at their table, while the nights brought great consolation to the poor, as they proceeded to the churches, even though they did not want other people to see them doing this. Their constant admonitions to their children, the explication of Holy Scripture to them, and the power of their arguments curbed the frivolity of the young, turning their minds fully

ἀνῆγε τὸν νοῦν πρὸς Θεόν, ὡς κατεστάλθαι μὴ μόνον
αὐτοὺς καὶ σωφρόνως βιοῦν, ἀλλὰ καὶ αὐτὸ τὸ οἰκετικόν.
Τοῦτο δὴ πλέον ἀνέπεισε τοὺς υἱεῖς τῷ κρείττονι προσ-
ανέχειν μᾶλλον ἢ τοῖς γονεῦσι.

2   Καὶ δὴ πρῶτος Παῦλος ὁ τὰ πρεσβεῖα λαχὼν τῆς γενέσεως καὶ πρῶτος λύσας τὴν ὠδῖνα τὴν μητρικήν, περικαῶς
ἔχων πρὸς τὰ θεῖα, αὐθόρμητος ἀφῖκτο πρὸς Πέτρον
ἐκεῖνον, τὸν ἐπὶ προφητείᾳ καὶ προγνώσει καὶ θαύμασι
διαβόητον, ὡς ἡ περὶ αὐτοῦ διέξεισι βίβλος. Ὃν καὶ βασιλεὺς τῆς ἀρετῆς ἀγασθείς, πολλαῖς ἱκετηρίαις τοῦ ὄρους
ἀπαναστάντα σὺν τοῖς περὶ αὐτὸν ἀνέπειθεν ὡς αὐτὸν
ἥκειν. Δι᾽ ὃν καὶ φροντιστήριον φιλοτίμως δειμάμενος ἱε-
ρόν, οὗ τὸ βαθύπλουτον καὶ ὁ καθ᾽ ἡμᾶς μαρτυρεῖ χρόνος,
αὐτῷ ἐνεχείριζεν. Ἐφ᾽ ᾧ τὴν κόμην πρῶτος ἀποκειράμενος
Παῦλος ὁ θεῖος καὶ πᾶσι χαίρειν εἰπὼν καὶ πάντων ἀπει-
πάμενος τῶν ὅσα τὸν νοῦν ἐντρέπειν οἶδε πρὸς τὰ τῆς γῆς,
ὥσπερ τι πρωτόλειον προσῆκτο Θεῷ, καὶ μετ᾽ αὐτὸν ὁ
δεύτερος Διονύσιος. Οὓς καὶ πατὴρ καὶ μήτηρ ἐκμιμησά-
μενοι καὶ ἀδελφὴ παρθένος ἔτι νεάζουσα, τὸν μοναστικὸν
ἡροῦντο βίον καὶ τὴν ἐπίπονον ἄσκησιν. Ὧν Παῦλος ἐγεγόνει διδάσκαλος καὶ πατήρ, τὸ παράδοξον. Ἀλλ᾽ ἐκεῖνοι
μὲν τῇ φύσει λειτουργήσαντες μετὰ τῶν μυρίων ἐκείνων
καμάτων, μετὰ τοὺς ἀσκητικοὺς ἱδρῶτας ἐπ᾽ ἐλπίσι χρησταῖς ἀπέτισαν τὸ χρεὼν μακαρίως ἀναπαυσάμενοι.

toward God. Therefore, it was not only their children but their servants too who were constrained and lived prudently. This persuaded their sons to devote themselves much more to God than to their parents.

In this way, Paul, who was the oldest and the first to 2 emerge from his mother's womb, was also the first to ardently desire the religious life and went to that famous Peter of his own volition. According to the book narrating his life, Peter was renowned for his prophecies, his gift of predicting the future, and his miracles. The emperor, admiring his virtue, used many supplications to persuade him to leave the mountain and come down to him with his disciples. For his sake he built a holy monastery, at great expense, and offered it to him. Its great wealth is renowned down to our own time. In that monastery, the divine Paul was tonsured first, renouncing all else and bidding farewell to all those things that distract the mind by turning it to mundane things. He was offered to God as the firstfruits of the harvest. The second son, Dionysios, was tonsured after him. Their father, mother, and sister (who was still a young maiden), imitated them, embracing the monastic life and the laborious regimen of an ascetic. Paul became their teacher and spiritual father, which was indeed a strange turn of events. However, after these countless labors and ascetic toils, the parents paid their debt to nature and died, taking their repose in a blessed manner and cherishing good hopes for the future.

4

Ὑπολέλειπτο δὲ Παῦλος καὶ Διονύσιος τὴν ἄσκησιν ἐπιτείνοντες, ὧν κατὰ ζῆλον καὶ μίμησιν καὶ Πέτρος αὐτὸς ἅμα Πλάτωνι τἀδελφῷ, νέαν ἄγων ἔτι τὴν ἡλικίαν, ἐξ αὐτῆς ἀφετηρίας κατέβη πρὸς πάλην ἀσκητικήν, καὶ τὸν ἀγῶνα ὑποδύς, τοσοῦτον ἐφιλονείκησεν ὑπερβαλέσθαι τῷ φερεπόνῳ τοὺς ἥλικας, ὡς ἀρχετύπῳ τούτῳ χρῆσθαι αὐτούς τε καὶ τοὺς ἄλλους καὶ πᾶν εἴ τι τῶν ἐκείνῳ προσόντων καλῶν μετεγγράφειν καὶ μεθαρμόζειν πρὸς τὸν οἰκεῖον βίον. Οὐδὲ γὰρ ὡς τῆς ἔξωθεν παιδείας περιχειλής, ἐφρόνει τι μέγα καὶ μετέωρον, ἀλλὰ πρὸς μὲν τὰς τοῦ σώματος ἡδονὰς ὑπερηφάνως εἶχε (καὶ γὰρ ἦν ἀγνείας ὅτι μάλιστα καὶ σωφροσύνης φίλος), πρὸς δὲ τἆλλα καὶ μάλα μέτριος, εἰ καί τις ἄλλος, ὡς καὶ τῷ πειθηνίῳ μηδὲ παραιτεῖσθαι καὶ τὰς εὐτελεῖς τῶν λειτουργιῶν, καὶ πρὸς μὲν γέλωτα ἄχρι μειδιάματος τῷ προσώπῳ διαχεόμενος, πρὸς ὀργὴν δὲ δυσκίνητος, περὶ τὰς ἐντεύξεις εὐπρόσιτος. Τὸ δ' ἐν συνουσίαις αὐτοῦ ἀστεῖον καὶ εὔχαρι οὐκ ἔξω τοῦ σεμνοῦ τοὺς συνόντας ἐπήγετο, ὡς, εἴ ποτε δεήσοι διαλεχθῆναι μικρόν, σοφῶν ἀνδρῶν ἀποφθέγματα καὶ συνετῶν πατέρων εἰς μέσον προὐτίθετο, ὡς τῷ ἀστείῳ μᾶλλον παρέπεσθαι τὸ ὠφέλιμον καὶ τοὺς κατηκόους τῶν ἐξ ἐκείνου τοῦ σωφρονοῦντος στόματος ἰόντων λόγων κρίνεσθαι μακαρίους.

2   Ἀλλὰ καὶ σχῆμα καὶ βάδισμα καὶ βλέμμα καὶ μειδίαμα θαυμάζειν ἦν αὐτοῦ καὶ ἀγαπητόν, εἴ τις μιμήσαιτο, ἰδεῖν τε

4

Thus Paul and Dionysios were left alone, intensifying their ascetic labors. Emulating and imitating them, Peter, who was still very young, together with his brother Plato, took up the ascetic struggle from the starting point. Throwing himself into the contest, he was so eager to surpass in endurance of hardship all who were about the same age that they, and all others, held him as their model, copying all his virtues and adapting them to their own lives. *Although his secular knowledge was abundant, he did not think highly of himself and did not boast of it.* He felt contempt for bodily pleasures, being as *good a friend as possible of* chastity and *temperance,* and he was restrained in all other respects, more so than everyone else. He was so obedient that he did not avoid even the most humble chores in the monastery. When it came to laughter, he went only so far as to show an imperceptible smile on his face. On the other hand, he was not quick to anger, and was most approachable for conversation. His wit and charm in social contacts, combined with his modesty, won over all those who became acquainted with him. When he was obliged to chat for a while, he brought forward the brief sayings of the wise men and the prudent fathers of old, so that profit might be combined with wit; as a result, those who heard the words that issued from his wise mouth were deemed most blessed.

His bearing, gait, glance, and smile may also be admired, and 2 many were content merely to imitate him. He was a very

ἦν καὶ λίαν ἐράσμιος. Εἶχε γὰρ τῷ ψυχικῷ κάλλει συναπο-
στίλβουσαν θαυμάσιον ὅσον καὶ τὴν ὥραν τοῦ σώματος,
ὅπερ, εἰ αἴσθοιτο σκιρτῶν καὶ κατεπαιρόμενον, νηστείαις
καὶ παννύχοις ἀγρυπνίαις ἐδάμαζε καὶ προσευχῇ ἐκτενεῖ
καὶ ἀμετεωρίστῳ καὶ στάσει ἐπιτεταμένῃ καὶ μελέτῃ συχνῇ
καὶ ὥσπερ πῶλον ἦγχε δυσήνιον. Καὶ τίς τῶν πόνων καὶ
κόπων, οὓς νύκτωρ τε καὶ μεθ᾽ ἡμέραν ἐξήντλει, διεξέλθοι
τὸ πλῆθος καὶ μέγεθος, ὃ καὶ ἀνδρίας τεκμήριον ἐναρ-
γοῦς; Ἐπὶ τοσοῦτο δὲ φιλαλήθης ἦν, ὡς μηδ᾽ ἐν μέρει παι-
διᾶς τὸ ψεῦδος προσίεσθαι, οὐδ᾽ ἔστι τις ὃς ἠνωτίσατο τῆς
μακαρίας ἐκείνης γλώττης ὅρκον οὐ μικρόν, οὐ μέγαν
προϊεμένης ποτέ. Τῇ μέντοι εὐλογιστίᾳ τὰ μόρια τῆς
ψυχῆς πείσας μὴ στασιάζειν καθ᾽ ἑαυτά, πῶς οὐκ ἂν τῇ
συνέσει διαιτητὴς κρίνοιτο δίκαιος; Καὶ τούτῳ μὲν ἀγαθῷ
φύντι ἐξ ἀγαθῶν ἐκ πρώτης γενέσεως συγγενεῖς ἦσαν αἱ
γενικαὶ ἀρεταί. Ἀλλὰ τοῦ φῦναι καὶ αὐξηθῆναι καλῶς
μᾶλλον αὐτῷ τὸ γενέσθαι καλῷ διεσπούδαστο, ἐπεὶ καὶ
πολλοῖς τῶν φαύλων τὰ τοιαῦτα τῶν ἀγαθῶν πρόσεστιν,
ἀλλ᾽ οὐκ ἐκ τούτων ὁ σπουδαῖος, ἀλλ᾽ ἐξ οἰκείων γνωρίζε-
ται προαιρέσεων. Αὗται γὰρ ἀξιοῦνται παρὰ τῶν καλῶς τὰ
πράγματα κρίνειν εἰδότων πλείονος δόξης προεδρίας τε
καὶ τιμῆς. Ἄλλως τε καὶ τὰ τῆς ἀρετῆς ἔργα μόνου ἐστὶ
τοῦ δράσαντος καὶ ὁ ἐκ τούτων ἔπαινος ἀληθὴς καθεστώς,
ἴδιός ἐστι τοῦ κεκτημένου. Τὸ δὲ μεγαλοφυὲς αὐτοῦ καὶ
γόνιμον μὴ καὶ περιττὸν ᾖ γράφειν, ὃς πολλῶν ἐγκύμων
ἐγένετο σοφῶν μαθημάτων καὶ ταύτην ἀπέτεκε τὴν καλὴν
ὠδῖνα τῶν λόγων, ὡς καὶ αὐτὰ δηλοῖ τὰ τούτῳ ἐκπονη-
θέντα συγγράμματα.

pleasing spectacle for all to see, since his physical beauty, combined with the beauty of his soul, shone in an admirable way. If he perceived that his body was becoming unruly and arrogant, he would tame it through fasting, all-night vigils, long, undistracted prayers, prolonged standing vigils, and continuous study. In this way he brought it under control, as if it were an unruly colt. Who could recount the multitude or magnitude of the labors and pains that he endured day and night? That was a clear sign of his bravery. He was so honest that he never told lies, not even in jest. No one ever heard an oath, big or small, coming out of his blessed mouth. Since through reason he persuaded the different parts of his soul not to wage war against each other, how might he, in all his wisdom, not be considered a just arbitrator? Being a virtuous man, born of virtuous parents, he grew up from infancy together with the cardinal virtues. But he paid less attention to his good birth and proper rearing than he strove to become a good man, since after all many depraved persons possessed the former assets. A truly virtuous man, however, is not marked by these external things but by his inner disposition. It is this which is considered more worthy of glory, prominence, and praise by those who know how to judge everything properly. Besides, virtuous deeds belong only to the one who performs them, and so the praise for them is real and his exclusive possession. *It may be pointless* to write about how magnificent and *prolific* he was: being pregnant with many wise lessons, he gave birth to the good offspring of words, as his writings themselves testify.

5

Τούτων ἁπάντων πυθόμενος ὁ τότε ἀρχιερεύς (Νικόλαος δ' ἦν ὁ Ἰταλός, ἀνὴρ λόγιος καὶ αὐτός, οὐδὲν ἧττον κατ' ἀρετὴν ἐπαινούμενος, δι' ἣν καὶ ὑπερορίαν κατεδικάσθη, εἰ καὶ δόξης ὕστερον ἡττηθείς, τοῖς τὰ βασιλέως φρονήσασιν ἐπὶ τῷ τετάρτῳ γάμῳ συνείπετο καὶ συνῳκονόμει, εὐπροσώπως τὸ μῦσος ἀποσκευαζόμενος), καὶ τὸν ἄνδρα τῆς ἀρετῆς καὶ λογιότητος ἀγασθείς, ἐβούλετο καὶ διὰ σπουδῆς ὅτι πλείστης εἶχεν ἀρχιερωσύνῃ τιμῆσαι καὶ τοῖς πρώτοις τῶν θρόνων ἐγκαθιδρύσαι, πολλῶν ἀπεληλαμένων τότε ἀρχιερέων, τῶν δὲ καὶ ἀπορραγέντων. Ὁ δὲ καὶ τὸ τοῦ πράγματος ἐπικίνδυνον εὐλαβούμενος καὶ τὴν ἡσυχίαν φιλῶν, πρὸς δὲ καὶ τοῖς τότε τελουμένοις ἀπαρεσκόμενος, ἀνένδοτος ἦν. Μεταπέμπεται δὴ Παῦλον τὸν ἀδελφόν, ἄνδρα δι' ἄσκησιν ἀρετῆς προεστῶτα τότε τῆς μονῆς καὶ τῶν ἄλλων κατάρχοντα, καὶ τὰ μὲν παραινέσεσι καὶ λόγοις μειλικτηρίοις, τὰ δὲ καὶ ἱκετηρίοις πείθει καὶ ἀρχιερέα τῇ Κορινθίων καθίστησιν Ἐκκλησίᾳ. Ὡς δὲ καὶ αὖθις κατηναγκάζετο Πέτρος παρὰ τοῦ τῆς βασιλίδος προέδρου, τὴν βίαν ἀποδιδράσκων συγκατήει μὲν ἐν Κορίνθῳ τῷ ἀδελφῷ, χρόνῳ δὲ συχνῷ ἐφ' ἑνὶ τῶν ἔξω τῆς πόλεως φροντιστηρίων καθ' ἑαυτὸν ἠσκεῖτο, τῶν προτέρων ἐχόμενος καὶ τῇ μελέτῃ σχολάζων ἐπὶ μᾶλλον καὶ πολλοὺς τῶν θείων μαρτύρων καὶ ἄλλων ὁσίων ἀνδρῶν ἐξυμνῶν ἐγκωμίοις. Πολλοὶ γὰρ αὐτὸν πρὸς τοῦτο ἐξεβιάζοντο.

5

The chief bishop of that time, Nicholas of Italy, learned all these things. He was a learned man himself and no less praised for his virtue, because of which he was exiled. Later, however, he succumbed to a desire to secure a good reputation and joined those who supported the emperor's view concerning the fourth marriage and made an accommodation with them, trying to disguise that abomination under a decent pretext. Admiring both Peter's virtue and learning, he decided—in fact he was quite eager—to honor him with the rank of bishop and give him one of the preeminent sees, because many bishops were exiled at this time, while others had defected from his side. However, Peter was adamantly opposed to this, fearing the dangers involved and loving the quiet, spiritual life. Moreover, he did not approve of the whole situation at the time. Therefore, Nicholas summoned his brother Paul, who had become abbot of the monastery and had been appointed a leader of the other monks on account of his practice of ascetic virtue, and managed to persuade him to become bishop of the church of the Corinthians, partly through admonitions and soothing speeches, and partly through entreaties. Peter once again had to endure the pressures that were coming from the archbishop of the imperial city, and so in order to escape this stress he went down to Corinth with his brother. For a long time he lived alone as an ascetic in a monastery outside that city. He followed the same path as before: he was even more devoted to his studies, praising many of the divine martyrs and other holy men with his encomia. For many people were urging him to do that.

6

Ἀλλ' οὐκ εἰς τέλος ἀπώνατο τοῦ σκοποῦ. Παραπόδας γὰρ ὁ τῶν Ἀργείων ἀπεβίω πρόεδρος καὶ ἦκον αὐτοί τε Ἀργεῖοι καὶ Ναύπλιοι πανδημεί, ναὶ μὴν καὶ οἱ τῆς περιοι-κίδος Κορινθόθι, μακρὰν ἱκετείαν πρὸς τὸν ἀοίδιμον Παῦλον ποιούμενοι δοθῆναι αὐτοῖς ἀρχιερέα τὸν ἀδελ-φόν. Καὶ τοῦτο μὲν καὶ αὐτὸς προτεθύμητο, ἀλλ' οὐδὲν εἶχεν ἀνύειν, ἐκεῖνον ὁρῶν ἐπὶ πολὺ ἀνανεύοντα, τὸν εἰς τἆλλα καταπειθῆ καὶ εὐήκοον, ὡς καὶ φυγῇ χρήσασθαι χρόνῳ ἐφ' ἱκανῷ, καὶ τοῦτο δηλοῖ καὶ ὁ περὶ τῆς φυγῆς αὐτῷ λόγος γραφείς. Ὡς δὲ ἐπανῆκεν, οὐκ ἠναγκάζετο μὲν παρὰ τοῦ ἀδελφοῦ, παρὰ μέντοι τῶν Ἀργείων ἠνω-χλεῖτο συχνότερον, ἐπομνυμένων μὴ ἂν ἕτερον καταδέξα-σθαι, εἴ τι καὶ συμβῆναι δεήσοι, διεξιόντων ὅσα πρὸς πειθὼ φέρειν οἶδε, καὶ ὡς ἐρημίᾳ ἱερέων πολλὰ τῶν ἀρτιγενῶν βρεφῶν ἀνηρπάσθη ἄωρα στερηθέντα τοῦ θείου λουτροῦ, πολλοὶ δὲ τῶν ἐξοδευόντων τῶν συνήθων οὐκ ἔτυχον ὕμνων ἐπιταφίων. Τούτοις καὶ ἄλλοις κατὰ μικρὸν ὑπεν-δοὺς καὶ καταμαλακισθείς, τὴν προστασίαν αὐτῶν ἀνεδέ-ξατο. Οὕτως ἀφιλότιμος ἦν καὶ πρὸς μόνην ὁρῶν τὴν τῶν ψυχῶν ἐπιμέλειαν.

6

Bᵤt his plan did not work in the end. For after a short time the bishop of Argos died, and the inhabitants of Argos and Nauplion, along with the inhabitants of the countryside of Corinth, all came together and begged that most memorable Paul at length to give them his brother as bishop. Paul himself was eager to do this, but powerless, seeing as his brother, who was so obedient and agreeable in other respects, refused the offer for a long time; he even fled for a while. This can be proved by the speech that he composed regarding his flight. After he returned, his brother stopped pressuring him, but the citizens of Argos kept on pestering him more often than before. They even took an oath that they would not accept any other man as their bishop, no matter what happened. They used all sorts of arguments that might persuade him: they said that in the absence of priests many newborn babies who were carried off by death before their time would be deprived of holy baptism, while many men who passed away would be denied the customary funeral hymns. On account of these and other similar arguments he started to give in, little by little. Finally, he relented and agreed to be their spiritual guide. Thus he had no ambition at all, and his only concern was the care of the souls.

7

Ὡς δὲ ἐπὶ τῶν ἔργων ἐγένετο, εὐθὺς μὲν ἐπεμελήθη τῆς εὐταξίας τῶν ὅσοι τοῦ βήματος καὶ τοῦ λοιποῦ κλήρου καὶ τῆς ἄλλης τοῦ ἱεροῦ εὐκοσμίας καὶ καταστάσεως, εἶτα τῶν πολιτῶν καὶ τῶν ἁπάσης τῆς ὑπ᾽ αὐτὸν ἐφορείας, καὶ εἴ τι μῦσος καὶ εἴ τι μίασμα, πάντα μακρὰν ἀπεώσατο, τὰ μὲν παραινέσεσιν, οἷος ἐκεῖνος, μέλιτος γλυκυτέραις, τὰ δὲ τομαῖς ταῖς μετὰ φειδοῦς ἐκκόπτων τὸ σεσηπὸς καὶ τῇ τῶν λόγων καταιονῶν σπογγιᾷ καὶ τὸ νόσημα καταλλήλοις ἐμπλάστοις ἐπαφώμενος καὶ θεραπεύων ἐπιμελῶς, πολὺ τῶν Ἀσκληπιαδῶν ἐμπειρότερον, ὅσῳ σωμάτων ἐκεῖνοι, οὗτος δὲ ψυχῶν ἰατρός. Εἶπες ἂν αὐτὸν ἀποστολικώτατον ἄνδρα, σοφίᾳ λόγων καὶ παραινέσεσιν ἐκμοχλεύοντα χρόνια πάθη ἐνδομυχοῦντα καὶ σχεδὸν ἀνιάτρευτα. Ἐπεὶ δὲ Θεὸν ἐλέῳ μᾶλλον τῶν ἄλλων ᾔδει θεραπεύεσθαι, τοσοῦτον ἐξέτεινε τὴν χεῖρα πρὸς ἔλεον, ὡς μηδ᾽ αὐτοῦ φείδεσθαι τοῦ πυθμένος. Οὐ γὰρ ἀνέμενε τὸν σῖτον ἤ τι τῶν γεωργίων τιμιουλκεῖσθαι, ἀλλ᾽ αὐτὸ καθ᾽ αὑτὸ τῶν ἐπετείων καρπῶν καὶ τῶν ἄλλων εἰδῶν, ὁποῖον ἂν ᾖ, διεδίδου τοῖς πένησιν, οὐ τοῦ καιροῦ στοχαζόμενος τῆς ἐνδείας, οὐ τὴν βίαν τῶν ἐπηρεαστῶν ὑπειδόμενος, ὡς, εἰ δεήσοι, δανείῳ χρῆσθαι πολλάκις, κἀκείνων κορεννῦναι τὸ ἄπληστον. Καὶ εἶδες ἂν τὴν αὔλειον καὶ προαύλιον στενοχωρουμένην δι᾽ ὅλης ἡμέρας πενήτων, γερόντων, νέων,

7

As soon as he assumed office, he ensured the orderly behavior of the priests and all other clergymen. He also paid
attention to all other matters concerning the good conduct
and orderly state of affairs among the clergy. Then he concerned himself with the conduct of the laity and all who fell
under his jurisdiction. He utterly removed all sorts of foul
pollutions, either through his habitual admonitions, which
were sweeter than honey, or through surgical treatments, by
cutting out all the rotten parts, but doing so in a merciful
manner; he then placed his healing speeches upon the
wound like a sponge and sterilized the ailing part of the
body, wrapping plasters around it and curing it carefully. In
this he was a more experienced healer than the followers of
Asklepios, insofar as they cured the body, while he cured the
soul. You might call him a most apostolic man indeed: with
his wise speeches and admonitions he dislodged all the old
passions that had entrenched themselves inside and were,
by this point, almost incurable. Being aware that we serve
God more through merciful almsgiving than anything else,
he stretched out his hand and gave alms in an extraordinary
way, holding back not even what was left at the bottom of
the bin. He did not wait for the wheat or other crops to be
stored up, but rushed to offer to the poor all crops of the
season or anything else, whatever it might be, neither caring
about the season of need, nor fearing the pressures brought
to bear by the tax collectors. If he needed the money, he did
not hesitate to borrow it in order to satiate their avidity. All
day long you could see the courtyard and forecourt of his
house crowded by the poor, the old, the young, orphans,

ὀρφανῶν, χηρῶν, ἀναπήρων τὸ σῶμα, τὰς ὄψεις λελωβη-
μένων, οἷς ἀφθόνως ἐπήρκει σπουδῇ. Καὶ εἴ γέ τις τῶν
διακονουμένων μικρὸν παρημέλησε πρὸς τὸν ἔλεον, ὁ δὲ
πένης ἐλθὼν εἰς τὴν αὔριον κατεῖπε τῆς βραδυτῆτος, διπλοῦν εἰληφὼς ἀπήει τὸ διωρισμένον, ὡς καταναγκάζε-
σθαι τοὺς ἐξυπηρετουμένους, ὅτε μὴ τύχοιεν ἔχοντες,
μεταιτεῖν ἐξ ἑτέρων καὶ οὕτω τὸ κελευσθὲν ἐκπληροῦν.

2   Εἰδὼς δὲ Θεὸς τὸ τῆς τούτου χειρὸς ἀφειδές, εὐετηρίαν
ἐδίδου καὶ καρπῶν ἀφθονίαν καὶ τοὺς σιτῶνας ἐνεπίμπλη
τοσοῦτον, ὡς δεδυνῆσθαι καὶ τὸ δάνειον ἀποτιννύειν καὶ
τῇ Ἐκκλησίᾳ καὶ τοῖς ἐνδεέσι καὶ ἄλλοις τοῖς ἔξωθεν ἐπαρκεῖν. Πολλοὶ γὰρ οἱ ἐπιξενούμενοι καὶ μάλιστα μοναχοί,
ὡς, εἰ καὶ ὅλον τις ἐνιαυτὸν ἐπιξενωθείη, μηδ᾽ ἀνακρίνε-
σθαι ἢ διερωτᾶσθαι πόθεν ἀφῖκται καὶ ποῖ πορεύοιτο.
Ὀρφανοὺς δὲ καὶ προστασίας ἐστερημένους ἀποτρέφων
ἀεί, ἔστι δ᾽ οὓς καὶ τῆς οἰκείας ἀπαναστάντας ἐφόδοις βαρ-
βαρικαῖς, πᾶσι μὲν αὐτάρκως τὰ χρειώδη παρεῖχε, τοὺς δὲ
νέους οὐκ ἀμοίρους εἴα παιδείας, τοὺς ὅσοι δὲ ἀνεπιτη-
δείως εἶχον πρὸς μαθημάτων ἀνάληψιν, ἀφώριζεν αἷς ἠρέ-
σκοντο τῶν τεχνῶν. Εἰ δεήσοι δὲ μεταβῆναι πρὸς πόλιν
ἑτέραν ἢ ἀγρὸν ἢ προάστειον, ἡλίκον τὸ χρῆμα τῆς εὐποιΐας, αὐτὰ τὰ πρὸς ὑπηρεσίαν σκεύη χρειώδη τοῖς δεομένοις ἐδίδοτο. Στρωμναὶ δὲ καὶ μανδύαι καὶ ἄμφια μέχρι
καὶ αὐτοῦ τοῦ χιτῶνος ἀωρὶ τῶν νυκτῶν ἄνωθεν ἐρρι-
πτεῖτο τοῖς πενομένοις ἀψοφητί, ὡς ἀνάγκην εἶναι τοῖς τὰ
ἐκείνου χειρίζουσιν ὁσημέραι πολλάκις αὐτὰ τὰ ἴδια ἐξω-
νεῖσθαι, εἰ τύχοι, ἢ ἕτερα.

widows, and people crippled of limb or impaired in their sight, whose needs he satisfied in abundance. If one of his servants was negligent when it came to charity, even in a small way, and a poor man came to report his procrastinations the next day, the latter would leave after receiving a double portion. Thus his servants, when they did not have enough, were forced to ask for it from other people, in order to fulfill his commandments.

God, seeing that his hand was generous, granted a good 2 season and an abundant harvest, and filled up his granaries in such a way that he was able to pay off his debts and, at the same time, cover the needs of the Church, the poor, and those who came from outside. For many travelers, and especially monks, were offered hospitality by Peter, and even if somebody stayed with him for a whole year, he neither asked him questions, nor wondered where he came from or where he was going. He always fed the orphans and all who had lost their guardians, as well as people who had left their homes because of the barbarian incursions. He offered sufficient supplies to them all, and did not neglect the education of the young. He steered those who lacked a natural bent for lessons toward whichever craft they liked. If someone was obliged to travel to another town, field, or estate in the suburbs, his generosity knew no bounds. He gave to those who asked even the necessary implements to do their job. Mattresses, cloaks, clothes, even undergarments were thrown to the poor from above at night, without any fuss. Because of this, his servants were obliged to buy back their own clothing, or buy other clothes, and this happened daily many times.

8

Ἀλλὰ πῶς ἄν τις παρέλθοι καὶ τὸ δι᾽ ὑπερβολὴν ἀπι-
στούμενον; Λιμὸς ἐπίεζε τὴν τοῦ Πέλοπος, ἐπὶ τοσοῦτο δὲ
ταύτην ἐπεβόσκετο καὶ κατέτρυχεν, ὡς τὰς οἰκίας καὶ στε-
νωποὺς καὶ ἄμφοδα καὶ πλατείας, ἔτι δὲ καὶ τὰ ὕπαιθρα
ἐμπλησθῆναι νεκρῶν, μὴ τῶν ζώντων ἐξικανούντων ἔτι τῇ
γῇ κατακρύπτειν τὰ σώματα, καὶ πλήρη μὲν τὰ πολυάν-
δρια, πλήρεις δὲ χῶραι τῶν κειμένων, τῶν μὲν ῥίζαις βο-
τανῶν ἐνασχολουμένων, τῶν δὲ καὶ ἔτι ποηφαγούντων τὸ
πνεῦμα ἐναφιέντων. Ἀλλ᾽ ὁ ἡμέτερος Ἰωσὴφ ἀρτοποιοὺς
ἐπιστήσας καὶ ὅσος σῖτος ἐνῆν εἰς ἄλευρον διεργασάμενος
καὶ κεραμείοις ἀγγείοις ἐναποθείς, ὡς ἂν μηδ᾽ ἐν τούτῳ
ἀπασχολοῖντο οἱ τῷ λιμῷ κατειργασμένοι, τὸ δὴ λεγόμενον *ἀληλεσμένον* αὐτοῖς ἐποίει τὸν *βίον* καὶ ἀρτοποιῶν διεδίδου τοῖς συρρέουσι πλήθεσι ἔκ τε τῶν οἰκείων καὶ τῶν
ὁμόρων πόλεων καὶ κωμῶν καὶ ἀγρῶν.

2   Ἐπιλείποντος δὲ τοῦ ἀλεύρου τῇ ἀφειδίᾳ καὶ τῷ τῆς
εὐποιΐας ἀπλήστῳ καὶ ἱλαρῷ, ὡς ἐφ᾽ ἑνὸς πίθου πυθμένι
καὶ μόνον ἡμιμέδιμνον ὑπολελεῖφθαι καὶ τῶν εἰς τοῦτο
τεταγμένων μηδὲ πρὸς τὴν ἔνδον πληθὺν λεγόντων ἄρ-
τους ἔχειν ἡμέρας μιᾶς, ἀγανακτήσας ὁ μέγας, ἠπειγμένως
ἐνεκελεύετο τὰ δεδογμένα πληροῦν. Ὡς δὲ τῇ λύπῃ κατά-
σχετοι πρὸς τὸ σιτανεῖον ἀφίκοντο καὶ τὸν πίθον ἀλεύρου
πλήρη κατεῖδον, ὑπὸ δέους τε καὶ ἐκπλήξεως εἰς ἀφασίαν
ἐνέπιπτον καὶ τῷ ἀρχιερεῖ τὸ παράδοξον διεσάφουν καὶ

8

We cannot overlook one other thing, which is unbelievable in its sheer magnitude. A famine was pressing hard upon the Peloponnese at the time. It was stalking and oppressing that region so grievously that houses, alleys, streets, squares, and even the countryside were full of dead bodies, and there were not enough survivors to bury the corpses in the ground. The cemeteries were filled to capacity, while the open spaces were teeming with people lying on the ground. Some were foraging for plant roots, while others died while eating grass. But our new Joseph appointed bakers: he took all the wheat that had already been milled into flour and placed it in ceramic vessels, so that those who were exhausted by the famine would not even have to do this. Thus he created *life* for them, *using ground wheat* according to the proverb. Then, making bread, he distributed it to the crowds who poured in from the cities under his jurisdiction and from the towns, villages, and fields that lay near to it.

In the end, all the reserves of flour were consumed because of Peter's generosity and his insatiable and cheerful desire to offer charity to the poor. Finally, only half a measure of flour was left at the bottom of one jar. Those entrusted with that job told him that they did not have any more bread for the multitude gathered inside, not even for one day. The great man was dismayed, and instructed them to hurry up and carry out his orders. The servants, overcome with grief, went to the granary, and found that the jar was full of flour. They were amazed, terrified even, and rendered speechless. They explained this miraculous occurrence to

τῆς ὀλιγωρίας ἠτοῦντο συγγνώμην. Ὁ δὲ μικρὸν ἐπιπλή-
ξας αὐτοῖς ὡς ῥαθύμως καὶ μικρολόγως τὰ πρὸς τοὺς πένητας ἔχουσι, σιγᾶν ἐνεκελεύετο καὶ περὶ τούτου ἐχεμυ-
θεῖν. Ἀλλ' οὐκ ἦν ἄρα λαθεῖν τῷ τὸν πίθον ἐφ' ἱκαναῖς
ἡμέραις κενούμενον μὴ κατακενοῦσθαι καὶ τὸ πραττόμενον κηρύττειν καὶ δίχα φωνῆς. Ἐπὶ μὲν τῷ Θεσβίτῃ τοσοῦτον οὐκ ἐπιλελοίπει τὰ τῆς ὑδρίας, ὅσον ἐπαρκεῖν αὐτῷ τε
καὶ τῇ Σιδωνίᾳ χήρᾳ καὶ τοῖς ἐκείνης παισί, τὰ δὲ τοῦ πίθου πολλοῖς ἀπέχρησε καὶ πολίταις καὶ ξένοις τὰ πρὸς
τροφήν, καὶ ζήλῳ μὲν κινουμένου τοῦ προφήτου καὶ θυ-
μουμένου κατὰ τῶν ἀσεβῶν, εἰς στενὸν τὰ τοῦ ἀλεύρου
περιεγράφετο, Πέτρου δὲ συχναῖς ἱκετηρίαις τὸ θεῖον ἐκ-
καλουμένου πρὸς οἶκτον λαῶν εὐσεβῶν λιμῷ καταδαπα-
νωμένων, εἰκότως ἐπεδαψιλεύετο καὶ τὰ τῆς τροφῆς.

9

Ταῦτα θρυλλούμενα σχεδὸν ἀνὰ τὴν ὑπ' οὐρανόν, ὑπη-
γάγετο καὶ βαρβάρους, οἳ κατὰ κλέος τῆς αὐτοῦ ἀρετῆς
ἀφικνούμενοι, ἐξώμνυντο μὲν τὰ πάτρια καὶ τὴν ἐκ προγό-
νων θρησκείαν, τῇ δὲ ἡμετέρᾳ μετετάττοντο καθαιρόμενοι
καὶ μεταπλαττόμενοι τῷ θείῳ λουτρῷ. Καὶ Κρῆτες δὲ πει-
ρατικαῖς ναυσὶ χρώμενοι, ἅτε δὴ ληστρικὸν διαζῶντες
βίον καὶ νήσοις καὶ πόλεσι καὶ κώμαις ταῖς παραλίοις
νυκτὸς ἐνεδρεύοντες καὶ τοὺς παρατυγχάνοντας ληϊζό-
μενοι, οὓς μὲν τῶν γρῦξαι τολμώντων ἔργον ἐποιοῦντο

the bishop and begged him to forgive their neglect of their duty. He reproved them slightly for treating the poor in a lazy and stingy way, and instructed them to remain silent, keeping the event confidential. But since the jar remained full of flour over the course of many days, even though they were emptying it out daily, the voiceless jar itself proclaimed the miracle, which could not be hidden! In the case of Elijah of Thisbe, the bucket was not emptied so as to suffice for his own daily needs and those of the widow of Sidon and her children. But Peter's jar was enough to supply food to many people, both native and foreigners. When the prophet was filled with divine fervor and became angry against the impious, the supplies of flour were reduced to a mere minimum. However, Peter, asking the Lord to have mercy on the pious people who were devastated by the famine, fittingly safeguarded their sustenance through his continuous entreaties.

9

These stories spread almost throughout the whole world and attracted even some barbarians to him. They came because of the fame of his virtue, and they foreswore their own customs and ancestral faith and embraced our own, having been cleansed and transformed through holy baptism. Let me also tell you about the inhabitants of Crete, who had pirate ships and lived like robbers. They staged night attacks on the islands and seaside towns and villages, ambushing and robbing anyone they encountered. They killed those

μαχαίρας, τοὺς δ᾽ ὅσοι κατεπτηχότες εἵποντο σιγῇ, εἷλκον εἰς δουλείαν οἰκτρῶς. Πυνθανόμενοι δὲ τὸν εἰς ἄκρον ἔλεον τοῦ ἀνδρὸς τῇ Ναυπλίᾳ καταίροντες καὶ πίστεις λαμβάνοντες καὶ διδόντες, τοὺς αἰχμαλώτους ἀπεδίδοσαν λύτρων, καὶ τοῦτο ποιοῦντες ἀνὰ πᾶν ἔτος οὐ διελίμπανον.

2 Καὶ δή ποτε περιτυχόντες σώφρονος γυναικὸς ἀγαθῆς τὴν ὄψιν καὶ τὴν ὥραν διαπρεποῦς, ἧκον ἄγοντες μεθ᾽ ἑτέρων, καὶ τοὺς μὲν ἄλλους ἄνδρας τε καὶ παῖδας καὶ γύναια ἐξῆγον τῆς νεὼς εἰς τὸ πωλητήριον, αὐτὴν δὲ μόνην ἔνδον παρακατεῖχον τῷ ἑαυτῶν φυλάρχῳ ἀποίσειν προφασιζόμενοι. Ἡμῶν δὲ ἰσχυρῶς ἐγκειμένων ὅσοι παρῆμεν πρὸς τὸ κἀκείνην λαβεῖν καὶ τὸ πολὺ τῆς ἡμέρας τριβόντων καὶ πᾶν ὅ,τι βούλοιντο διαβεβαιουμένων διδόναι, βαρβαρικώτερον γυμνοῖς ἐπελθόντες τοῖς ξίφεσι καὶ τοὺς ἄλλους διαρπάσαντες, εἰσῆγον ἐν τῇ νηῒ καὶ τὸν ἀπόπλουν ἐποιοῦντο. Διαμαρτόντες δὲ τῶν ἐλπίδων ἡμεῖς καὶ τῆς ὅλης ἀποτυχόντες πράξεως, πρὸς τὸν μέγαν εἰσῄειμεν διεξιόντες τὸ πεπραγμένον. Τί δαὶ ἡ συμπαθὴς ἐκείνη καὶ μακαρία ψυχή; Τοσοῦτον συνεχύθη τῇ λύπῃ, ὡς μηδ᾽ ἀνέχεσθαι φθέγξασθαι. Δάκρυον αὐτῷ κατέρρει τῶν ὀφθαλμῶν ὡς ἀπό τινος κρήνης, κατάβροχος ἦν τὴν παρειὰν καὶ αὐτὸ δὲ τὸ πεπολιωμένον γένειον, καὶ τῷ κοιτωνίσκῳ εἰσδὺς ὡς ἐν ἀδύτῳ ἱερῷ, ἔνθα τὰς παννύχους εἰώθει προσαναφέρειν εὐχὰς τῷ Θεῷ, διεκαρτέρει μέχρις ἑσπέρας. Οὔπω τὰ τῆς εὐχῆς ἔληξε καὶ ἧκον ἄγγελοι θέοντες μετὰ δύσιν ἡλίου, ὡς ἅμα τῷ τὴν ληστρικὴν ναῦν ἀκρωτηρίῳ προσχεῖν, μία τῶν φυλακίδων τριήρης ἀπό τινος τῶν κύκλῳ νησιδίων φανεῖσα, ὥρμησεν ἐπ᾽ αὐτήν, ἡ δὲ

who dared to protest, while they took as slaves those wretches who were terrified and followed them in silence. But being informed about Peter's great mercifulness, and anchoring near Nauplion, they gave and received guarantees and released the prisoners in exchange for ransom. They never failed to do this every year.

On one occasion, they encountered a chaste woman who was beautiful and had a noble bearing. So when they came that time with the other prisoners, and brought them, men, children and women, out of the ship to the slave market, they kept the woman alone inside, on the pretext that they would offer her to their leader. We who were present at the time persisted in wanting to ransom her too. We spent most of the day in these discussions and promised to give them whatever they wished. In the end, they drew their swords in a barbaric manner, rounded up all the other prisoners into the ship, and sailed off. Having lost all hope and failed abjectly, we went to the great man and explained to him what had happened. And how did that merciful, blessed soul react? He was so overcome by sorrow that he was unable to utter a word: tears flowed from his eyes as if from a fountain, so that his cheeks and white beard were drenched. He entered his small chamber, where he used to offer his prayers to God all night, and stayed there until evening as if it were a holy sanctuary. Before his prayers were finished, after sunset some people ran in saying that, as soon as the pirate ship had reached the promontory, a guard-ship, a trireme, made its appearance from one of the nearby small islands that encircled us, heading toward it. The pirate ship tried to escape it,

ταχυναυτοῦσα ἐχρῆτο συντονωτέρᾳ φυγῇ καὶ οἱ τῆς τρι-
ήρους πῦρ αὐτοῖς ἐπαφέντες, τῆς εἰρεσίας ἐπέσχον καὶ
τούτων ἐκράτησαν. Τούτου δὴ ἀγγελθέντος, εὐχαριστηρί-
ους ᾠδὰς δι᾽ ὅλης νυκτὸς ἤδομεν τῷ Θεῷ, καὶ ἅμα ἡμέρᾳ
ἧκεν ἡ τριήρης ἐστεφανωμένη καὶ τὴν πολεμίαν ἀναδησα-
μένη ναῦν καὶ ταύτην ὡς ἐφόλκιον ἕλκουσα, αὐτούς τε
τοὺς πολεμίους ἄγουσα καὶ τὰ αἰχμάλωτα σώματα. Οὕτω
Θεὸς εἶχε τὸ οὖς ἐπικλινὲς ἀεὶ ταῖς ἐκείνου εὐχαῖς καὶ οἱ
πρότερον μηδὲ τιμήματος ἀνεχόμενοι προέσθαι τοὺς
αἰχμαλώτους, αἰχμάλωτοι ἤγοντο τὸ ἔμπαλιν, οἱ Κρῆτες,
ὡς λόγος, πρὸς Κρῆτας κρητίζοντες.

10

Πῶς ἂν κἀκεῖνο παρέλθοιμι τὸ τῆς ἀπελευθέρας κόρης
διὰ μόνην ὥραν τοῦ σώματος ὑπὸ τοῦ τότε στρατηγοῦντος
εἰς δουλείαν ἑλκομένης καὶ τῷ ἱερῷ προσφυγούσης καὶ
πρὸς ἄμυναν τοῦτον τὸν μέγαν ἐκκαλουμένης; Ὃς ῥύεσθαι συνήθως ἔχων τοὺς ὑπὸ στερεωτέρας ἑλκομένους χειρός, τὸ τοῦ πράγματος ἄτοπον ἐλευθέρᾳ γλώσσῃ διήλεγ-
χεν, ἡττώμενος δὲ τῆς κόρης ἐκεῖνος ὡς ἐξ ἀμάρας δυσῶδες
ἀπέβλυσε ῥῆμα τοῦ στόματος. Ὁ δὲ πραείᾳ φωνῇ, "Εἰ τὸν
Θεὸν οὐ δεδίαμεν," εἶπεν, "οὐκ ἀνθρώπους αἰδεσθησό-
μεθα," καὶ εἰπὼν ἀπηλλάττετο. Καὶ ὃς τῷ λόγῳ πληγεὶς
ὥσπερ μάστιγι συνείχετο ῥίγεσι καὶ πυρετοῖς ἐξητάζετο,

sailing as quickly as possible. But the crew of the trireme hurled fire at them, forced them to stop rowing, and prevailed over them. When news of this reached us, we sang hymns of thanksgiving to God throughout the night. In the morning, the trireme arrived, crowned with the garlands of victory and tugging the enemy ship behind, as if it were a small boat. Inside it were both our enemies and their prisoners. In such a way was God always listening to Peter's prayers. Those who had refused to free their prisoners, even in exchange for money, were taken prisoner themselves. Cretans *speak like Cretans to Cretans,* as the proverb says.

10

How could I omit the story of the young freedwoman who was dragged into slavery by the general of that time solely because of her physical beauty? The girl sought refuge in the church, calling on the great man to protect her. It was his custom to save those who were victimized by *the stronger arm,* and he reproached that impropriety quite frankly. But the general, overcome by his desire for that girl, emitted an obscenity from his mouth as if from a sewer. Peter responded in a gentle tone, "If we do not fear God, we will show no respect toward men," and left. The general was struck by the saint's words as if by a whip, was gripped by a chill, and tormented by fever. So he sent men to ask for the

καὶ πέμπων ἠντιβόλει συγγνώμην αἰτῶν καὶ τὴν ἱκέτιν τοῦ
Θεοῦ ἀφεῖσθαι ἐνεκελεύετο καὶ τοῦ ἱεροῦ ἀπανίστασθαι.
Ἧς ἀφειμένης καὶ τῆς συγγνώμης ἐφεπομένης (ἐπεκλᾶτο
γὰρ ταῖς ἱκετείαις καὶ περὶ ταύτας ἦν λιπαρὴς ὁ θεῖος
ἀνήρ), παραυτίκα μὲν ὑπελώφα τὸ λάβρον τοῦ πυρετοῦ,
αὐτὸς δὲ ῥάων ἐγεγόνει καὶ ὅσον οὔπω τῆς ὑγείας τυχών,
τὸν εὐεργέτην ὥσπερ ἐξ ἐκείνου τὴν πνοὴν ἕλκων διὰ στόματος ἦγε καὶ τῆς αὐτοῦ ἐξεκρέματο πρεσβείας, μανθάνων
μηδὲν ἔτι μικρὸν ἡγεῖσθαι τῶν ἁμαρτανομένων, ἀλλ᾽ ἐξευ-
λαβεῖσθαι καὶ προσέχειν ἐν ἅπασι.

11

Καὶ παρθένῳ δέ τινι νόμῳ γάμων ἀνδρὶ συζυγείσῃ καθ᾽
ὥραν, μῖσος ἄλεκτον ἐνέπεσε καὶ πρὸ τῆς ὁμιλίας πρὸς τὸν
ὁμόζυγον ἐξ ἐνεργείας τοῦ Πονηροῦ, τοσοῦτον ὥς, εἴ που
τοῦτον κατίδοι ἢ καὶ μόνον ἔρχεσθαι πύθοιτο, κατὰ γῆς
ῥιπτεῖσθαι καὶ σπαίρειν καὶ τὰ τῶν δαιμονώντων διενερ-
γεῖν, κεῖσθαί τε ἄφωνον ἐφ᾽ ὥραις ἱκαναῖς, καὶ ὅτε ἀναφρο-
νήσοι, μηδὲν τῶν γενομένων ἐπαισθάνεσθαι. Ὁ δὲ ταύτης
πατὴρ συμπαθείᾳ τῇ πρὸς τὴν παῖδα ἀφίκετο πρὸς τουτονὶ τὸν θαυμάσιον, δακρυρροῶν καὶ τίλλων τὸν πώγονα
καὶ τὸ πάθος διεκτραγῳδῶν καὶ πρὸς ἄμυναν ἐκκαλούμε-
νος τοῦ τοσούτου δεινοῦ. Ὁ δὲ τὸν ἄνθρωπον ἀπολοφυ-
ρόμενον ἠλέει μέν, ἀπεπέμπετο δέ, Θεοῦ μόνου λέγων

saint's forgiveness, ordering them to release the suppliant of God and permit her to depart from the sanctuary. The girl was released, and the saint's forgiveness followed closely afterward, for the divine man was moved to pity by supplications and persistent entreaties. The general's high temperature dropped immediately, his condition improved, and soon he was restored to health. Thereafter, he could not stop talking about his benefactor, as if he were drawing his own breath from him. He was dependent on the saint's intercessions to God, and since he had learned that no trespass was too small, he was now extremely careful and attentive not to give offense in any respect.

II

A virgin was married to a man at the right age, but through the action of the Evil One an indescribable hatred for her husband fell upon her before they had sexual intercourse, to such an extent that, if she but saw her husband or heard that he was coming, she would fall to the floor, quivering violently like those possessed by evil spirits, and lie there speechless for many hours. But when she regained her senses, she did not remember anything that had happened. Her father, full of compassion for his daughter, came to the saint, shedding tears and pulling out the hairs of his beard. He described her affliction and asked for help against this great misfortune. The saint, although he felt pity for the weeping man, dismissed him, saying that only God and the

εἶναι καὶ τῶν ἐκεῖθεν χάριν εἰληφότων τὰ τοιαῦτα ἰᾶσθαι. Ὡς δ᾽ ἱκετεύων ἐνέκειτο, μεταπεμψάμενος ἱερέας καὶ ἅμα τούτοις εὐχὴν ἐπ᾽ ἐλαίῳ πεποιηκὼς καὶ τὴν θείαν μυσταγωγίαν τετελεκώς, προὔτρέπετο τὴν κόρην ἐκ τούτου ἀλείψασθαι. Οὗ γενομένου ἐν ὅλαις ἡμέραις ἑπτά, καὶ τὸ πάθος ἀπεδιοπομπεῖτο καὶ συνδιῆγεν ἐκείνη ἔκτοτε τῷ ἀνδρί, πρὸς τοῦτον ἥμερον βλέπουσα καὶ φανεῖσα οἰκουρὸς ἀγαθή.

12

Πολλὰ τοιαῦτα καὶ μείζω παρῆκεν ὁ λόγος τῆς συμμετρίας φροντίζων, ἃ μηδ᾽ ἐκείνῳ διεσπούδαστο, λανθάνειν ἐθέλοντι καὶ τὸ φιλότιμον ἐκκρουομένῳ καὶ πρὸς μόνην τούτῳ χρωμένῳ τὴν ἀρετὴν καὶ τὸ ἀγαθόν. Ἃ καὶ περιστάντα με καὶ πρὸς ἑαυτὰ ἕλκοντα, παρῃτησάμην, τῆς τῶν πολλῶν φειδόμενος ἀκοῆς. Καὶ τί θαυμαστὸν ἀνδρὶ τῶν χειρόνων μακρὰν ἀφεστηκότι καὶ τῶν τοῦ σώματος μικρὸν ποιουμένῳ λόγον καὶ ἁγνείαν ἐκ παιδὸς ἠσκηκότι καὶ παρθενίας ἐραστῇ καὶ ἀληθείας φίλῳ καὶ σωφροσύνην τετιμηκότι καὶ ἀνδρείως κατὰ παθῶν ἀριστεύσαντι καὶ δικαιοσύνην ἐς ἄκρον ἠγαπηκότι καὶ φρονήσει τὴν τῆς ψυχῆς καλῶς διαιτησαμένῳ τριμέρειαν καὶ πᾶσαν ἰδέαν ἀρετῆς μετιόντι, μὴ τὸν νοῦν ἔχειν διαφανῆ καὶ ταῖς τούτου

men who had received God's grace could cure such afflictions. But because this man kept begging the saint, in the end he summoned some priests and performed the office of Holy Unction. After completing the divine service, he urged them to anoint the girl with the blessed oil. This was done for seven days. In the end, her affliction was cured and from then on the young woman lived together with her husband, being gentle toward him and a good housewife.

12

My narrative has omitted many such miracles, even greater ones than those I have described, since I am concerned to maintain due proportion in my account. But even Peter himself did not make a great fuss about them, as he wished to remain unobserved. He renounced ambition, using it only in order to become virtuous and perform his good deeds. Although those miracles surround me and draw my attention, I have refrained from writing them down so as not to impose on my audience. Why should we be surprised that this man long avoided base behavior, paying little attention to his body? He had practiced chastity from childhood, being a lover of virginity and a friend to truth. He honored prudence, bravely prevailed over the passions, loved justice to the highest degree, and was able, through his reasonable judgment, to govern the three parts of his soul in a fitting way, pursuing every kind of virtue. Why should we deem it as strange that he had a *luminous mind* and that he

ἐνεργείαις ἁπλαῖς ἐπιβολαῖς ὥσπερ ἐν ὄψει τῶν μακαρίων
ἐκείνων θεαμάτων γινομένῳ θεατῇ χαρισμάτων καταξι-
οῦσθαι καὶ τὰ μέλλοντα προορᾶν;

2   Καὶ γὰρ δὴ καὶ τὸ πᾶσαν ὑπεραῖρον τραγῳδίαν πάθος
τῆς Πέλοπος καὶ αὐτὰ δὲ τὰ τοῦ τέλους αὐτῷ δι᾽ αἰνιγμά-
των δεδήλωτο. Ὄναρ ἐδόκει τὸν παρθένον καὶ φιλούμε-
νον τῷ Χριστῷ μαθητὴν Ἰωάννην ὁρᾶν καὶ διαπυνθάνε-
σθαι περὶ τῆς ἐν ἀρχῇ τοῦ Λόγου γεννήσεως καὶ ὅτι φησί,
"πολλῶν εἰς τοῦτο ἐξηγησαμένων καὶ μὴ πρὸς τὸ βάθος
τῶν νοημάτων ἐξικνουμένων τῶν σῶν, αὐτὸς ἂν διαλευκα-
νεῖς μᾶλλον ἁπάντων καὶ διασαφήσεις, ὡς τῷ ἀκηράτῳ
στήθει ἀναπεσὼν κἀκεῖθεν τὴν περὶ τούτου γνῶσιν ἑλκύ-
σας ἀψευδῆ τε καὶ ἀπλανῆ."

3   Τὸν δὲ πρὸς τῷ μὴ λῦσαι τὸ διαπορούμενον, ἀπορώτε-
ρον αὐταῖς λέξεσι φάναι ὡς "ἐπὶ τῷ τέλει θεοφυλάκτου
ὀλεῖται ἡ Πελοπόννησος" καὶ ἅμα τῷ λόγῳ οἴχεσθαι. Καὶ
τότε μὲν ἡμῖν ἠγνοεῖτο τὸ ῥηθέν, πρὸς ἕτερον ἀναφέρουσι
τοὔνομα, ἐκείνῳ δὲ διεξιόντι τὸν ὄνειρον, δάκρυα τῶν
ὀμμάτων προὔπιπτεν ἀστακτί, τὸν ὄλεθρον τῆς τοῦ Πέλοπος ἐγνωκότι καὶ τὸ πέρας τῆς ἑαυτοῦ τελευτῆς, καθὸ καὶ
τῷ ἀποβιῶναι τὸ ἄπορον λύεσθαι, τῶν βαρβάρων μετὰ
μικρὸν κατασχόντων τὴν νῆσον ἐφ᾽ ὅλοις ἔτεσι τρισὶ καὶ
τοὺς πλείους διεργασαμένων καὶ πάντα λῃσαμένων τὰ
αὐτῆς καὶ πεδίον ἀποφηνάντων ἀφανισμοῦ, ὡς μηδ᾽ ἔτι τῆς
παλαιᾶς εὐδαιμονίας ἴχνη ἐκεῖσε ὁρᾶν ἢ τῆς τῶν τότε
ἀνθρώπων εὐταξίας καὶ καταστάσεως.

was able, through its operations, to contemplate those blessed spectacles in a simple way, as if he had them right before his eyes? Thus, he was deemed worthy of divine gifts and was able to know the future in advance.

In this way, the disaster that befell the Peloponnese, 2 which was more horrible than any tragedy, was revealed to him in riddles, and so was his own end. He had a dream in which he saw John, the beloved disciple of Christ, who was a virgin. He asked John about the generation of the Word who was in the beginning, saying, "Many people have tried to interpret that passage, but no one was able to grasp the full meaning of your words. Only you yourself, more than anyone else, would be in a position to elucidate and interpret them, since you had leaned upon the pure chest of Christ, and drew from there an infallible and unwavering understanding of the matter."

The evangelist did not answer his question, but uttered 3 some incomprehensible words to the effect that "the Peloponnese will be destroyed by the time of the death of the man protected by God." As soon as he said that, he disappeared. We were not able to understand these words, because we had in mind another man whose name actually means "protected by God." But the saint's eyes were full of tears as he was narrating his dream, since he realized that the Peloponnese would be destroyed and that his own death was approaching. His death elucidated the meaning of that obscure prophecy, since after a short while the barbarians occupied the land for three whole years, killing most of its inhabitants, plundering the entire area, and transforming it into *a plain of destruction*. As a result, no signs of its former prosperity or of the orderly and calm life of its citizens can be seen there any longer.

13

Προσεπετείνετο γοῦν αὐτῷ τὰ τῶν κόπων ὡσεὶ καὶ χθὲς τῶν ἀγώνων ἀρξαμένῳ ἀνθρώπῳ καὶ τῇ συντρόφῳ νόσῳ δεδαπανημένῳ καὶ τῷ γήρᾳ τρυχομένῳ (καὶ γὰρ ἦν ἔτη γεγονὼς ἑβδομήκοντα), καὶ ταῖς ἄλλαις κακοπαθείαις κατεσκληκότι τὸ σῶμα, περὶ ὧν τί δεῖ λέγοντα διατρίβειν ἐπεκδιηγούμενον ἕκαστα; Ἀλλ᾽ ἧκεν ὁ τῆς ἀναλύσεως προσδοκώμενος καιρὸς καὶ συνέρρει τὰ πλήθη τῶν πόλεων καὶ κωμῶν. Αὐτοῦ δὴ παρῆσαν καὶ μοναζόντων ἀγέλαι καὶ τὸ κόσμιον τῶν μοναζουσῶν καὶ παρθένων αἰδὼς σώζουσα τὸ σεμνὸν ἄχρι καὶ ὄψεως καὶ γυναῖκες σώφρονες καὶ νέοι καὶ γέροντες, πάντες καὶ πᾶσαι τῆς ἐκείνου ἡδίστης καὶ ὄψεως καὶ φωνῆς ἐμφορηθησόμενοι καὶ ἀκούσοντες καὶ τὴν εὐλογίαν ὡς ἀσφάλειαν καὶ φρουρὰν τῆς ζωῆς κομισόμενοι. Ὁ δέ, μέχρι τὰ τῆς φωνῆς διετράνωτο καὶ ὁ λόγος διήρθρωτο, νουθεσίαις ὑπεστήριζε καὶ τῶν παρόντων καταφρονεῖν ὑπεμίμνησκε καὶ μόνων ἔχεσθαι τῶν μελλόντων ὡς μενόντων ἀεί, καὶ τοῦτο ἐφ᾽ ἡμέραις τρισίν. Εἶτα διεξήει καὶ τοὺς ἐξιτηρίους. Ὡς δὲ τὰ τῆς φωνῆς ἐνεκόπτετο, χειρὶ καὶ τύπῳ σταυροῦ κατοχυρῶν πάντας, ἀπιέναι διένευε. Καὶ ἡμᾶς δὲ τοὺς περὶ αὐτὸν τῷ Θεῷ ἀναθεὶς καὶ μικρὸν καθ᾽ ἑαυτὸν ὑποψιθυρίσας καὶ τὸν σταυρὸν τῷ προσώπῳ περιγραψάμενος καὶ ἱλαρὸν ἐπιβλέψας γεγανωμένῳ καὶ χαίροντι ἐοικώς, ὥσπερ ὑπομειδιῶν, τὰ ὄμματα μύσας, ἀταράχως διαφῆκε τὸ πνεῦμα.

13

He intensified his ascetic struggles, as if he had just started them the day before, although he was exhausted by illness and wasted away by old age. For he was seventy years old. Moreover, his body was weakened by his other privations. There is no reason to say anything about them and procrastinate by describing everything in detail. But the anticipated time for his departure finally arrived, and multitudes from nearby towns and villages streamed to him. Monastic brotherhoods, decorous nuns, chaste virgins whose solemnity was reflected on their faces, temperate women, young and old men, were all gathered there, to fill themselves with the sight of his beloved face and the sound of his voice, to receive his blessing as a guarantee and protection for their own lives. As long as his voice was clear and his speech articulate, Peter sustained them with his admonitions, reminding them to hold in contempt the things of this world and to pay attention only to the things of the future life, because only these abide forever. This lasted for three days. Afterward he delivered his parting words. Then his voice fell away, so he blessed them all with his hand, fortifying them with the sign of the cross, and sent them on their way with a nod. He dedicated us, his close associates, to God. Then he whispered something to himself, made the sign of the cross on his face, looked upon us cheerfully with a faint smile as if he was very happy and glad, closed his eyes, and serenely released his spirit.

14

Καὶ πάλιν ἠθροίζετο τὰ πλήθη καὶ συστήματα ἱερὰ καὶ χοροὶ μοναστῶν περιστάντες τὸ ἱερὸν ἐκεῖνο σῶμα ὕμνοις ἐγέραιρον καὶ ψαλμοῖς, καὶ τὸν ἱεροφόρον ἄραντες σκίμποδα, ὑποβασταζόντων ἱερέων, διὰ μέσης τῆς πόλεως ὑπὸ λαμπάσιν ἤεσαν ᾄδοντες καὶ περὶ δείλην ὀψίαν ὑποστρέφοντες τὸ θεῖον τῆς Θεοτόκου κατειλήφεσαν τέμενος. Καὶ τῆς ἱερᾶς τελετῆς καὶ μυσταγωγίας τελουμένης, εἰωθὸς τοῦτο ἐπὶ τοῖς ἀρχιερεῦσι γίνεσθαι, ἀθρόον φωτὶ τὸ πρόσωπον περιελάμπετο τοῦ θείου ἀνδρὸς καὶ λεπτὸς αὐτῷ περιερρεῖτο ἱδρὼς καὶ τὸν χρῶτα εἶχεν ἐρυθαινόμενον ὡσεὶ ζῶν καὶ ὑπνῶν. Τότε δὴ καὶ Ναύπλιοι τοῖς Ἀργείοις διενεχθέντες καὶ πρὸς ἑαυτοὺς ἕλκειν τὸ μακάριον ἐκεῖνο φιλονεικοῦντες λείψανον καὶ τῇ Ναυπλίᾳ μετακομίζειν καὶ πρὸς ὅπλα χωρήσαντες, τῇ πολυπληθείᾳ τῶν Ἀργείων καὶ ἄκοντες ἐξέπιπτον τῆς ὁρμῆς καὶ τοῦ σκοποῦ διημάρτανον. Καὶ κατετίθετο τῇ σορῷ, ἣ τῷ λαιῷ μέρει τοῦ θείου νεὼ κατεσκεύαστο, τὸ πολυπαθὲς ἐκεῖνο καὶ νόσοις ταριχευθὲν καὶ εἴ τι μικρὸν ἐξ ἑαυτῆς ἀπροαιρέτως ἢ ὕλη τυχὸν ἐπεσπάσατο δι᾽ αὐτῶν καὶ τῶν ἄλλων τῆς ἀρετῆς ἱδρώτων καθηράμενον. Ὃ καὶ διαδήλους εὐθὺς ἐδείκνυ τὰς ἐνεργείας, μῦρα προχέον ὡς ἐκ πηγῆς καὶ δαίμονας ἀπελαῦνον καὶ νόσους παντοίας ἰώμενον καὶ ὑποφαῖνον τὴν ἐκεῖθεν ἐκδεξομένην ἀϊδιότητα.

14

Again a multitude gathered. Many priests and monastic choirs encircled the holy body, honoring him with hymns and psalms. They lifted up *the bed on which the holy man was lying,* and priests carried it through the town, holding candles and singing. As night approached, they returned to the holy church of the Mother of God. As the holy office and sacrament was being performed in accordance with custom, namely the liturgy for a deceased bishop, suddenly the holy man's face started to shine with light; it was also dripping with a fine sweat. The color of his skin became pink as if he were alive and sleeping. Then a quarrel broke out between the citizens of Argos and those of Nauplion, as the latter wanted to carry the blessed relic into their own town and transfer it to Nauplion. They even drew weapons, but their rush was checked by the multitude of the inhabitants of Argos. So they yielded unwillingly and failed in their purpose. Accordingly, the long-suffering body of the saint, which had been withered by illness, was buried in the tomb that was constructed on the left-hand side of the holy church. This was all that matter had been able to preserve for itself in spite of the saint's will, even though it had been cleansed through the saint's sweaty labors and his other toils toward the attainment of virtue. That part of his material self revealed its hidden energies immediately: there flowed from his body, as if from a fountain, perfumed oil, which cast out demons, cured every kind of illness, and was a proof of the eternal blessedness that would be enjoyed by the saint in heaven.

15

Ὁ τοίνυν οὕτω καὶ ἐκ τοιούτων γεννηθεὶς καὶ τραφείς, παιδευθεὶς δὲ καὶ βιώσας, ὡς ὁ λόγος ἀπέδειξε, καὶ τοῖς πράξει καὶ θεωρίᾳ καθόσον οἷόν τε προσῳκειωμένοις Θεῷ διαμιλληθείς, οὐ καὶ τῶν ἴσων ἀμοιβῶν τεύξεται καὶ μετ᾽ ἐκείνων τετάξεται; Καὶ τίς ἀντερεῖ; Παραβαλλόμενος γὰρ τῷ δικαίῳ καὶ φιλοξένῳ τῷ τε θεοσεβεῖ καὶ παντὸς ἀπεχομένῳ κακοῦ οὐκ ἀποίσεται τὰ δευτερεῖα. Ἀντεξεταζόμενος δὲ τῷ σώφρονι, τῷ τε πρακτικῷ καὶ θεωρητικῷ, πολλῷ δήπου τῶν πρεσβείων ἀνθέξεται. Οὕτω συνέψεται τῷ προῖκα χρηστῷ καὶ μεγαλοψύχῳ καὶ πρὸς ἔλεον ἑτοίμῳ. Καὶ μὴν τῷ πράῳ καὶ συμπαθεῖ, τῷ ἀνεξικάκῳ καὶ ἀοργήτῳ καὶ μὴ προχείρῳ πρὸς ἀλόγους θυμοὺς ὑπερβαλεῖται τοὺς πλείονας. Τῷ παιδευτικῷ καὶ διδακτικῷ τοῖς πρώτοις τῶν διδασκάλων συστήσεται. Ἀγαπητὸν τοῖς ἀληθέσι ποιμέσιν εἰ συνδιαιτήσονται τῷ συμποίμενι. Οὐκ ἀπολειφθήσεται τῶν κατ᾽ ἐπίγνωσιν τῷ ζήλῳ χρησαμένων κατὰ καιρόν, ἐπεὶ καὶ αὐτὸς τὰς ἀδίκως ἐκτεινομένας χεῖρας κατὰ τῶν ἀκληρούντων τῷ ξίφει τῆς παρρησίας ἐξέτεμε. Τῷ δὲ συγκεραννῦναι τὸ πρᾶον τῷ στύφοντι πόσων οὐχ ὑπερέξει; Τῷ δὲ τῶν λόγων εὐφραδεῖ καὶ σαφεῖ ἔστιν ὅτε καὶ διηνθισμένῳ μετὰ μεγέθους πῶς οὐκ ἐξισωθήσεται τοῖς οὓς ἐμιμήσατο; Καὶ οὕτω τοῖς μὲν ἀμιλληθείς, τοὺς δὲ

15

Was it not only to be expected that Peter, who was born to such parents and raised by them, was educated and led his life in the way we described, who emulated as much as possible those who had drawn near to God through both deeds and contemplation, would not also receive the same rewards that are accorded by God to the other saints, among whom he is now registered? Who will deny this? If we compare his justice, hospitality, piety, and abstinence from all evil to that of the other saints, he would certainly not take second place. But if we take into account his wisdom, I mean both its practical and its theoretical aspect, he would certainly take first place. The same applies to his *disinterested generosity,* his magnanimity, and his readiness to show mercy. However, he surpasses many saints when we take into account his mildness, compassion, patient endurance, lack of anger, and avoidance of all irrational sentiments. His ability to educate and instruct others will recommend him to the most important teachers of the faith. The true shepherds will be very happy to live together with their colleague. He will not be left behind by those who conscientiously showed their ardor at the appropriate time, since he too used the sword of his outspokenness to cut off the hands of unjust men when they were extended against the poor. His ability to combine mildness with severity exceeded that of many others. Likewise, how can he not be considered the equal of those writers whom he imitated, given the correctness of his language and his clear style, which was sometimes adorned with loftiness? *He contended against some,* and imitated others. Overall,

μιμησάμενος, τῶν δὲ μὴ ἀπολειφθείς, τοὺς δὲ πλείους ὑπερελάσας, χρῆναι σκοπεῖν ὅσων ἀξιωθήσεται τῶν ἀναρρήσεων καὶ γερῶν.

16

Ἐγὼ μέν, ὦ μακάριε, κατὰ δύναμιν ἐξέτισα τὰ τροφεῖα, κατὰ πολὺ μὲν ἧττον τῶν σῶν καλῶν καὶ τοῦ μεγέθους τῆς ὑποθέσεως, οὐκ ἔλαττον δὲ τῆς προθέσεως. Σὺ δὲ ἀλλ᾽ ἄνωθεν ἐποπτεύοις ἵλεως καὶ τὰς καθ᾽ ἡμῶν ἐπεγειρομένας τοῦ Πονηροῦ καταιγίδας καὶ ἄγρια κύματα καταπραΰναις ταῖς πρὸς τὸ θεῖον ἐντεύξεσιν. Εἰ γὰρ ἔτι περιὼν καὶ κρυπτόμενος τῷ προκαλύμματι, διαφανεῖς ἐκέκτησο τὰς ψυχικὰς ἐνεργείας καὶ τῷ τοῦ νοῦ διαυγεῖ τὰ ὑπὲρ κατάληψιν ἐφαντάζου, τῶν ἐλύτρων περιρραγέντων καὶ καθαρῶς τῷ καθαρῷ συνὼν καὶ θεώμενος ἀσωμάτως σὺν ἀσωμάτοις ἐκεῖνα τὰ πολλοῖς ἀθέατα, πολλῷ γε δὴ μᾶλλον ἐπαμυνῇ τοῖς ὡς ἐπ᾽ ἀσφαλεῖ ἀγκύρᾳ τὰς ἑαυτῶν ἐλπίδας ἐξαψαμένοις σοι. Σὺ καὶ βασιλέων ἡμῖν θυμοὺς σφοδρῶς ἐπιπνέοντας κατευνάσας, ἐστόρεσας τὸ κῦμα τῶν συμφορῶν καὶ φθόνου περιπαρέντας ὀδοῦσιν ἐξέσπασας καὶ τῶν κακοῦν ἐθελόντων ἐπέσχες ὁρμὴν ἀκατάσχετον. Ἀλλ᾽ ἔτι καὶ νῦν μὴ ἐλλίποις τὸ νωθρὸν ἡμῶν διεγείρων ὡς εἴωθας, εὐμενῆ τε καθιστῶν τοῖς οἰκέταις καὶ φοιτηταῖς, ὃν ἐκ καρδίας

he was not left behind by any, and surpassed the majority. Accordingly, one must wonder with how much distinction and how many praises he will be rewarded by God.

16

O blessed father, I have repaid you, to the best of my ability, for the nourishment that you gave me. It is true that this text is not equal to your virtues or the magnitude of its subject, but it does not fall short of its intention. *May you watch* over me kindly *from above,* using your prayers to God to calm the tempests and fierce waves that are roused up against me by the Evil One. Even while you were still alive, when your soul was encased in the body, you possessed the purest spiritual energies: with the clarity of your mind, you contemplated things that surpass human understanding. Now that your outer shell has fallen away, you associate with God, who is pure, in a purer manner; being bodiless, you behold in the company of equally bodiless spirits those visions that remain unseen by the multitude. Accordingly, you may now protect us, who place all our hopes in you, as in a more secure anchor. You saved us from the violent wrath of emperors, calmed the waves of adversity, saved us from the teeth of envy, and restrained the irresistible charge of those who wanted to harm us. But even now may you continue to spur us on, we who are sluggish, even as you used to do in the past. Make the Lord, whom you loved with all your

ἠγάπησας Κύριον, βασιλεῦσι πρεσβεύων διαμονὴν καὶ ἐχθρῶν ἐπικράτειαν, τῷ ὑπηκόῳ τὸ ἀστασίαστον, τῇ Ἐκκλησίᾳ τὸ εἰρηναῖον καὶ ἀδιάσπαστον, τῇ σῇ ποίμνῃ ποιμένος εὐμοιρεῖν ἀγαθοῦ καὶ πρὸς τούτοις καλῶς καὶ ἀξίως τῶν ὑμετέρων προρρήσεων ποιμαίνειν καὶ διϊθύνειν τὸ τοῖς εὐτελέσιν ἡμῖν καταπιστευθέν, οἷς εὐδόκησε κρίμασι Κύριος, ποίμνιον καὶ ἀκυμάντως διαπερᾶν τὸ βαθὺ τοῦτο τοῦ βίου καὶ ἀσέληνον πέλαγος, ὡς ἂν καὶ αὐτοὶ καταντήσαιμεν εἰς ὃν καὶ αὐτὸς λιμένα κατήντησας, καὶ σὺν σοὶ χαριστήρια καὶ σωτήρια θύσωμεν τῇ Ἁγίᾳ Τριάδι, τῷ μόνῳ Θεῷ, ᾧ πρέπει πᾶσα δόξα, τιμὴ καὶ κράτος νῦν καὶ ἀεὶ καὶ εἰς τοὺς αἰῶνας τῶν αἰώνων, ἀμήν.

heart, gracious toward us, your students and disciples. Grant to our emperors perseverance and victory against our enemies, and pray that their subjects do not rebel against them. Preserve the unity and peace of the Church and give a good shepherd to your flock. In a way worthy of your prophecy, help me to shepherd and guide the flock entrusted to my unworthy self by the Lord's decision. Help me cross this deep sea of life, upon which the light of the moon does not shine, without being buffeted by its waves, so that I too may reach the harbor that you have already entered, where together with you I may offer a sacrifice and express my gratitude to the Holy Trinity, the only God. All glory, honor, and power to him now and forever and unto the ages of eternity, amen.

LIFE AND MIRACLES
OF THEOKLETOS,
BISHOP OF LAKEDAIMON

Βίος καὶ πολιτεία καὶ μερικὴ θαυμάτων διήγησις τοῦ ἐν ἁγίοις πατρὸς ἡμῶν Θεοκλήτου ἐπισκόπου Λακεδαιμονίας

Εὐλόγησον, πάτερ.

I

Οὐδὲ τὸν καθ᾽ ἡμᾶς βίον, οὐδὲ τὰς ἐπὶ τέλει τῶν αἰώνων γενεὰς ἀφῆκεν ἀβοηθήτους εἰς ἀρετὴν ὁ πάντων ἀεὶ φιλανθρώπως ἐπ᾽ ἀγαθοῖς προμηθούμενος Κύριος, ἀλλ᾽ ἔδωκε πολλὰ τῆς ἀρετῆς παραδείγματα γειτονοῦντα καὶ τοῖς χρόνοις τῆς ἡμετέρας ἀναδείξεως καὶ εἰς τὸν βίον προόδου, ὡς ἂν πᾶσα περιαιρεθείη πρόφασις τῶν κακίζειν ἐθελόντων καὶ αἰτιᾶσθαι τὰ ἀναίτια, εἴτουν ἡμέρας καὶ ἐνιαυτούς. Ἐπεὶ γὰρ οὐχ οὕτως ἐπάγεται πρὸς ἀρετὴν εὐγενῶν ἀνδρῶν ὑπέρλαμπρος βίος καὶ θαυμαζόμενος, ἀλλὰ δοκοῦμεν οἱ τυφλοὶ τὰς κρίσεις καὶ φρονοῦντες ὑλικὰ καὶ ἠλίθια ὡς ἑτέρα τις ἐπέλαμπε τῷ βίῳ χάρις τὰ παλαίτερα, καὶ ὥσπερ ἀπογνόντες τὴν κατὰ Θεὸν εὐδοκίμησιν, ἀναπίπτομεν καὶ ῥαθυμοῦμεν, οὐδὲ βραχὺ ζώπυρον ἀρετῆς

The life and conduct and a partial account of the miracles of Theokletos, our father among the saints, bishop of Lakedaimonia

Bless this reading, father.

I

The Lord, who is always benevolent toward mankind and ensures that we are adequately prepared to attain good ends, did not abandon us to live our daily lives without help in these, the final generations before the end. He provided us with many examples of the virtuous life, men who lived near the time of our own emergence into the world and our subsequent progress through life, so that any and all pretext may be removed from those who want to assault and cast blame on guiltless things, namely our days and our times. The illustrious and admirable life of noble-minded men of the past does not lead us to virtue, but we are blind in our judgment and desire only material and stupid things, thinking that a different kind of grace shone on life in older times. As if we had no hope of winning God's approval, we lie back and remain inactive, kindling no spark of virtue, not even a

ταῖς ψυχαῖς ὑποκαίοντες, διὰ τοῦτο προσεχῆ δίδωσι καὶ ὡς εἰπεῖν ἀγχίθυρα τῆς εἰλικρινοῦς πολιτείας τὰ ὑποδεί- γματα, ἵνα πᾶσα μὲν σκῆψις καὶ ἅπαν ῥαθυμίας προκάλυμ- μα ἐκποδὼν γένηται, τῶν πιστῶν δὲ ἕκαστος ἢ πρὸς ἔν- θεον διαθερμανθείη ζῆλον, ἢ διαμέλλων πρὸς τὰ καλὰ καὶ ἀναδυόμενος, γυμνὸν φέρῃ τὸν ἔλεγχον τῆς οἰκείας βλα- κείας κατήγορον καὶ τὴν γλῶσσαν πεδοῖτο, πρὸς τηλαυγῆ καὶ φανερὰν ἀλήθειαν ἀναισχυντεῖν μὴ δυνάμενος.

2   Ὅτι δὲ καὶ νῦν πολλοὺς ὁ βίος καρποφορεῖ Θεῷ τοὺς εἰς ἀκρότατον τῶν καλῶν δι' ἀρετῆς ἀναδραμόντας καὶ κατὰ πᾶσαν πρᾶξιν θαυμαστωθέντας καὶ θεωρίαν, αὐτὰ μαρτυρεῖ τὰ πράγματα. Ἀλλὰ τούτων ἄλλους μὲν ἄλλαι προβάλλονται χῶραι καὶ πόλεις οἷόν τινα ἑαυτῶν ἀγάλ- ματα καὶ σεμνολογήματα, ἡ δὲ ἀοίδιμος Λακεδαίμων καὶ περιβόητος, ἣν πᾶσα γραφή τε καὶ ποίησις θαῦμα πεποίη- ται, μεῖζον ἑαυτῆς θαῦμα προβάλλεται καὶ καλλώπισμα τὸν ἱερὸν Θεόκλητον, ἄνδρα περιφανῆ καὶ περιώνυμον τοῖς οἰκείοις κατορθώμασι καὶ οἷον ὁ λόγος προϊὼν ἀπο- δείξει. Τί γὰρ τὰ παλαιὰ τῆς Λακεδαίμονος διηγήματα πρὸς τὴν τούτου ἀντεξεταζόμενα ἀρετήν; Ἢ δῆλα δὴ ἐκεῖνα μὲν οὐδὲν ἄλλο ἢ ξίφη καὶ πόλεμοι καὶ σφαγαὶ καὶ χύσις αἵματος καὶ ἄνδρες πολεμικὸν καὶ φόνιον πνέοντες καὶ τὴν ἐν ὅπλοις ἐπίδειξιν διὰ βίου μελετήσαντες παντός, ἃ καὶ διὰ γῆς καὶ θαλάσσης τεθρύλληται, τὰ δ' ἐμὰ καὶ τοῦ ἐμοῦ ἀριστέως διηγήματα οὐ πόλεμοι καὶ σφαγαί, οὐδὲ ὁπλομανία τις καὶ ἀκόρεστος φόνων ἐπιθυμία, ἀλλὰ πάλαι καὶ ἀριστεῖαι κατὰ δαιμόνων χωρὶς αἵματος

small one, to burn inside our souls. For this reason God provides us with examples of a genuine way of life that may be found close to us, right beside our doors, so to speak, so that any pretext and disguise of our laziness may be removed. In this way, each one of the faithful may acquire either an ardent zeal for things divine or else, by putting off good deeds and avoiding them, he may be exposed to a merciless testing of his own stupidity: his tongue will be paralyzed in the face of such a clear and evident truth and he will be unable to behave shamefully.

Events themselves bear testimony to the fact that even now life can produce, as an offering of fruits to God, numerous examples of men who have attained the peak of goodness through their virtue and who have become admirable through both their actions and contemplation. Different lands and cities produce different men and exhibit them like statues of themselves, as objects of pride, but the famous and much-vaunted Lakedaimon, which is admired by all authors and poets, produced a miracle and adornment that was superior to itself, namely the holy Theokletos, an illustrious man made famous through his accomplishments. My speech will offer proof of this. For how can the old tales about Lakedaimon be compared to the virtue of this man? It is clear that those tales deal only with swords, wars, massacres, and bloodshed; they concern warriors filled with a desire for battle and slaughter, men who devoted their entire lives to feats of arms. All this is common talk all over the earth and across the seas. But my stories and my hero have nothing to do with wars and massacres, nor the mad love of arms, and the insatiable desire for slaughter: they have rather to do with prowess and struggles against demons,

2

κατορθούμεναι, ἀφ' ὧν ὁ ἐμὸς κηρύττεται Θεόκλητος, τὸ τῆς ἀρετῆς ἄνθος, ὁ τῆς ἱερωσύνης κανών, τὸ σεμνολόγημα τῆς Χριστοῦ Ἐκκλησίας.

2

Τὰ τούτου τοίνυν καὶ διηγητέον ἡμῖν καὶ ἀνάγραπτα ταῖς τῶν πιστῶν φιλαρέτοις ποιητέον ἀκοαῖς, εἰ καὶ μὴ πάντα συλλαβεῖν ὁ λόγος δεδύνηται. Τὰ πολλὰ γὰρ ὁ διαρρεύσας μετὰ τὴν ἐκείνου ἐκδημίαν ὑπέκλεψε χρόνος καὶ λήθης ἐναφῆκε βυθοῖς, οἷος ἐκεῖνος οὐ καλὸς τῶν καλλίστων ἐν πολλοῖς ἐπίβουλος καὶ τὰ ἄξια μνήμης καὶ φωτὸς τῇ τῆς σιωπῆς παραπέμπων νυκτὶ καὶ μελαίνων τὰ τῆς ἀρετῆς χρώματα, κἂν μὴ ταχεῖαν ὑπέτεινε τὴν σύμμαχον χεῖρα καὶ θερμὴν τὴν σπουδὴν εἰσηγάγετο ὁ νῦν ἱερὸς τῆς Λακεδαίμονος ποιμὴν καὶ πολλοστὸς μὲν τῷ ἀριθμῷ μετὰ τὸν θεῖον Θεόκλητον, τῷ τρόπῳ δὲ καὶ τῇ ζέσει τοῦ πνεύματος εὐθὺς μετ' ἐκεῖνον καὶ Θεοῦ δῶρον ὡς ἀληθῶς τῇ Λακεδαίμονι καὶ ὢν καὶ καλούμενος, εἰ μὴ οὗτος ἐτάχυνε τὴν βοήθειαν, οὐδ' ἂν λείψανόν τι κἂν βραχύ, οὐδὲ λόγος τις τῶν τοῦ θείου ποιμένος Θεοκλήτου κατορθωμάτων εἰς τὸ μέλλον ὑπελείφθη τῷ βίῳ. Τί δ' ἄν τις αἰτιάσαιτο ἕτερον, δίκαιος ὢν καὶ ἀδέκαστος δικαστής, ἀλλ' ἢ τὴν τῶν προγεγονότων ἐπισκόπων οὐκ καλὴν ἐπὶ τοῖς μεγίστοις, οὐκ οἶδα πῶς εἴπω μετρίως, εἴτε λήθην εἴτε ὀλιγωρίαν, εἴ

won without bloodshed, on account of which my Theokletos is extolled, that flower of virtue, exemplar of the priesthood, the pride of the Church of Christ.

2

Now, then, we must recount his life and make a record of it for the ears of the faithful who love virtue, although my discourse cannot describe everything, since the time that has passed since his demise has swept away the majority of his deeds and cast them into the depths of oblivion. Time is the worst enemy of the best deeds in many instances, sending things that are worthy of remembrance and light into the night of silence, obscuring the bright colors of virtue. If the current holy shepherd of Lakedaimon, who served many episcopal successions after the holy Theokletos in the same position, but who came a close second to him when it came to his manner of life and the ardor of his spirit, being a true "gift of God" to Lakedaimon, and thus called by this name— if, then, he had not swiftly offered a helping hand and zealously promoted the issue, not a single remnant, not even a small one, nor any memory of the achievements of the holy shepherd Theokletos would have remained among us for the future. If you are a righteous and impartial judge, you will blame no one other than the former bishops for their reprehensible forgetfulness and neglect of such important matters. I do not know how to put it more mildly. How

γε ἠνέσχοντο τηλικαύτην ἀνδρὸς ἀρετὴν ἐᾶσαι τῇ τοῦ χρόνου συγκαλυφθῆναι φορᾷ καὶ ὑπὸ τῇ πολλῇ τούτου μαρανθῆναι σκιᾷ;

2 Οὐ μὴν ὁ θεοφιλὴς οὗτος καὶ φιλόκαλος ἀνήρ, ὁ ταῖς θείαις καταπλουτιζόμενος δωρεαῖς, ἠνέσχετο τὸ παθεῖν τοῖς ἄλλοις παραπλήσιον, ἀλλὰ τὴν φιλεργὸν ἐκμιμούμενος μέλισσαν, ἀνένδοτός τέ ἐστι πρὸς πᾶσαν ἐργασίαν ἀρετῆς καὶ ἀήττητος, τοῦτο μὲν οἴκους ἀνεγείρων θείους, οἷος καὶ οὗτος ἐστὶν ὁ τὴν Λακεδαίμονα περικοσμῶν, αὐτὸς ἑαυτὸν θεατρίζων καὶ ἐκπυρσεύων ὥσπερ τινὰς ἀκτῖνας τὰ οἰκεῖα κάλλη καὶ τὸ μέγεθος ἐπιδεικνύμενος, τῆς ἐκείνου φρενὸς καὶ χειρὸς ἔργον, τοῦτο δὲ καὶ τοὺς τῶν ἁγίων βίους ἐπιὼν καὶ συλλέγων ὡς ἐκ πολυανθῶν τινῶν λειμώνων τὰ κάλλιστα καὶ τὴν ψυχὴν ἐξευγενίζων καὶ καθωραΐζων. Ἐπεὶ δὲ εὗρε καὶ τῶν τοῦ θεσπεσίου πατρὸς Θεοκλήτου κατορθωμάτων ἀμυδράν τινα μνήμην ἄγραφον διαφοιτῶσαν, οὐδὲ ἐνταῦθα τοῦ καθήκοντος ἠμέλησεν, ἀλλὰ μετὰ θερμοῦ τοῦ ζήλου διαναστὰς καὶ διχνεύσας τὴν τοῦ ἀνδρὸς πολιτείαν, ὅσα περισχεῖν οἷός τε ἐγένετο, ἀνάγραπτα θεῖναι διηγωνίσατο, μέγα τε ὄφελος τῷ βίῳ περιποιούμενος καὶ ζήλου τι κέντρον ἀγαθοῦ τοῖς ὕστερον γενησομένοις ἐναπολείπων.

could they have allowed such a virtuous life to be concealed by the passage of time and to wither away in the dark shadows that it casts?

But our present bishop, who loves God and all good 2 things, who is abundantly enriched by divine gifts, could not bear to behave likewise, but instead, imitating the industrious bee, is unyielding and invincible when it comes to every performance of virtue. First, he builds holy churches, such as this one which adorns Lakedaimon, displaying and illuminating its own beauty like the rays of the sun, and exhibiting its great size. It is the product of his mind and the deed of his hand. And second, perusing the lives of the saints and gathering up the best parts like a bee flying over meadows full of flowers, he thereby ennobles and adorns his soul. Since he came across a faded, unwritten memory of the deeds of the divine father Theokletos that was circulating, he did not neglect his duty in this case too, but, filled with ardent zeal, rose up, made inquiries concerning that man's life, and took care that whatever he could ascertain was written down. In this way, he rendered a great service to our life, leaving an incentive for virtuous deeds to future generations.

3

Εἰ δὲ ὅσα εἰς γένος ἥκει τοῦ ἀνδρὸς καὶ τίνων γεννητόρων τὸ καλὸν τοῦτο προελήλυθε φυτόν, ὁ λόγος ἀπορεῖ, ἀλλ᾽ ὑπεκλάπη ταῦτα τῷ χρόνῳ καὶ σεσίγηται, μικρὰ παρὰ τοῦτο ἡ ζημία. Εἰ δὲ δεῖ τεκμήρασθαι *ἐκ τοῦ καρποῦ τὸ δένδρον* καὶ *ἐκ τοῦ ῥεύματος τὴν πηγήν*, φαίη ἄν τις οὐκ ἀπὸ τοῦ πρέποντος καὶ <τοὺς> τοῦ ἱεροῦ τούτου πατρὸς πατέρας κομῶσαν ἔχειν τὴν ψυχὴν καὶ θάλλουσαν τοῖς καλοῖς τῶν ἀρετῶν ἄνθεσι κἀντεῦθεν ἀξίους γενέσθαι τὸν εὐγενῆ τοῦτον καὶ ὡραῖον προενεγκεῖν καρπόν. Οὐ μὴν ἀλλὰ βουλομένοις μὲν ἦν ἡμῖν δήλην ἔχειν τὴν ὅλην περὶ τούτων ἱστορίαν, εἰ δὲ καὶ ταῦτα ὁ χρόνος ὑφείλετο, ἕλκων καὶ τὰ κάλλιστα ὥσπερ ποταμὸς τὰ ῥεύματα καὶ τοὺς μὴ ταχύναντας διαφεύγων, ὅμως οὐ περὶ τὰ καίρια ἡμῖν ἡ ζημία. Τί γάρ τοι καὶ προσθήσομεν εἰπόντες τῷ ἀθλητῇ τούτῳ καὶ γενναίῳ εἰς ἀρετὴν γένος καὶ πατρίδα καὶ ὅσα ῥευστὰ καὶ ἐπίκηρα καὶ ἱστοῦ ἀράχνης ἀδρανέστερα, ἃ μόνοις τοῖς φιλοσάρκοις καὶ φιλοζώοις εἰσὶν ἐπέραστα καὶ ποθούμενα; Τούτῳ γὰρ ἐξ αὐτῶν τῶν σπαργάνων κἀκ πρώτης ἡλικίας τὴν κατὰ Θεὸν πτωχείαν ἑλομένῳ, καὶ τὸ τοῖς Ναζιραίοις κολλᾶσθαι καὶ τὰς αὐτῶν μανθάνειν καὶ σπᾶσθαι διαθέσεις καὶ ἀρετάς. Ἐντεῦθεν γὰρ πολλὴν ἐκαρπώσατο τὴν ὠφέλειαν, οὐχ ἧττον ἢ μᾶλλον ἐρημικὸς ἢ κοινωνικὸς γενόμενος. Ὅθεν εἰς προσθήκην καθάρσεως καὶ ὑψηλοτέρας θεωρίας ἑαυτὸν ταῖς ὁλονύκτοις στάσεσιν καὶ μακραῖς καὶ ἐπιτεταμέναις νηστείαις ἐκδούς, *μονάζων*

3

My narrative is unable to say anything about the saint's family or the parents from whom that beautiful plant sprouted: all this has been stolen away by time and swallowed up in silence—but it is also no great loss. Nevertheless, if we were to pass judgment on *the tree based on the fruit that it produced,* or on the spring based on its water, we might fittingly say that the parents of this holy father had adorned their blossoming souls with the beautiful flowers of virtue, and thus became worthy to produce such a noble and beautiful fruit. Our wish was to have laid before us the entire story of their life, but no vital interest has been harmed now that time has eliminated these details too, sweeping all good things along like a river in its current, leaving behind those who are unable to rush after it. Besides, would we really add anything of substance to the praise of that athlete, who was so noble in his virtue, if we were to mention his family, his homeland, and all those perishable and mortal things, which are more ephemeral than a spiderweb? Such things are loved and desired only by men who are fond of their fleshy and even animalistic existence. This man preferred to be poor for the sake of God from as early as the time of his swaddling bands, the very beginning of his life, and to associate with monks, learning and imitating their dispositions and virtues. He gained great profit from these acquaintances, not the least of which was that he preferred the solitude of the desert to the society of men. Therefore, wishing to become purer and to attain a higher level of contemplation, he dedicated himself to all-night vigils and to long and intense

ἐπὶ δώματος ὡς ὄρνις ἐν ἀβάτοις τόποις καὶ μηδεμίαν ἔχουσιν ἀναψυχὴν ἐποιεῖτο τὴν διατριβήν, τὸ πενιχρὸν ἐκεῖνο
ῥάκος ἁλουργίδος ἡγούμενος τιμιώτερον. Τῷ γὰρ τρύχε-
σθαι τῷ κρύει καὶ τῷ παγετῷ ὡς πρὸς θάλψιν τὴν αἰθέριον
χωροβατῶν ἐπευφραίνετο, τὴν ἐρημίαν δὲ πόλιν εἶχεν,
ἀγγέλοις συνδιαιτώμενος καὶ Θεὸν ἔχων ἐν πᾶσι τῶν ἀγώνων συλλήπτορα.

2   Καὶ πονοῦσι μὲν ὡς τὰ πολλὰ οἱ τὴν μεταλλικὴν μετερ-
χόμενοι τέχνην, ὀρύγματά τινα ὀρύσσοντες ὑπόγαια καὶ
βαθύτατα τῇ ἀβύσσῳ πλησιάζοντα, ἵνα τί γένηται ἢ τί
κερδήσουσιν, ἐκ μὲν τῆς ἐπιμονῆς καὶ μεγαλοψυχίας, ὅλην
ἐκείνην φανταζόμενοι τὴν ἐν τῷ βάθει γῆν χρυσῖτιν εἶναι
καὶ ὄλβου μεστὴν καὶ πλούτου οὐ πολλοστοῦ ἐμπορίαν
σπουδάζοντες. Μέσον τοίνυν τῶν τοιούτων πόνων καὶ τοῦ
ἀφορήτου κόπου καὶ τῶν πολλῶν ἐκείνων καμάτων πολλά
εἰσι τὰ ἐμποδίζοντα. Ἀντὶ γὰρ ψηγμάτων χρυσέων, χαλκοῦ
τυχὸν ἢ μολίβδου φλέβα εὑρίσκοντες ἠκηδίασαν, καὶ
ἄργυρον ζητοῦντες, θείου ἐπέτυχον αὔλακας, ὕδωρ τε ἐκ
τοῦ βάθους ἀναδοθὲν τὴν ἐκείνων ὁρμὴν καὶ σπουδὴν
ἤμβλυνε. Ἀλλὰ καὶ τούτων καὶ τοιούτων ἐπισυμβάντων
τοῖς ἀγωνιζομένοις, οὐκ ἄν ποτε παύσωνται τῶν ἔργων
ἐχόμενοι, ἐν ἐλπίσι χρησταῖς πυκαζόμενοι, πλοῦτον ἐπίκη-
ρον καὶ φθειρόμενον ἐντεῦθεν θησαυρίσαι πειρώμενοι ἢ
βασιλεῖ φθαρτῷ γῆς κρατοῦντι καὶ μόνον ἀρέσαι σπεύδον-
τες. Οὔμενουν ταῦτα καὶ Θεοκλήτῳ ἁρμόδια, τῷ κατα-
πτύσαντι πάντα καὶ ἅπαξ ἀπορραγέντι κόσμου καὶ τῶν ἐν
βίῳ καὶ βασιλεῖ αἰωνίῳ οἰκειωθῆναι σπεύδοντι. Ὄρυγμα
γὰρ αὐτῷ πόνοι καὶ μόχθοι καὶ ταλαιπωρίαι καὶ χαμευνίαι

fasting. Resembling a bird *dwelling alone on a roof,* he lived in desolate places, having no comfort at all. He deemed his poor, ragged garment as more precious than the royal purple. He rejoiced in his suffering from the cold weather and the frost, as if he had ascended to the balmy warmth of heaven; he lived in the desert as if in a city, enjoying the company of angels and the protection of God, who helped him in all his struggles.

Miners work hard to open up very deep channels underground, reaching to the very depths of the earth so that they may profit from their persistence and noble toil, imagining that deep inside the earth everything is made of gold and is full of treasures, which they are eager to trade in order to acquire a wealth which is not negligible. However, there are many obstacles in the way of their labors and unbearable toils and hard work: instead of gold dust, they find veins of copper or lead, and so become disappointed. Searching for silver, they find channels of sulfur, or water comes out of the depths, quenching their zeal and ardent desire. But in spite of these and similar obstacles, these struggling men do not interrupt their endeavors, as they are driven on by good hopes and seek to obtain from them a temporary and perishable wealth, or else they wish to obtain the favor of a mortal emperor who is merely a ruler of this earth. But none of these goals was fitting for Theokletos, who held all mortal things in disdain. He had renounced this world and its way of life once and for all, trying to gain intimacy only with the eternal emperor. His toils, labors, and hardships, as well as

καὶ νηστεῖαι καὶ γυμνότης καὶ ἀγρυπνίαι καὶ ἐλπίδες ἦσαν,
οὐ κατῃσχυμμέναι τυχὸν καὶ δυσέλπιστοι ἢ ἀντὶ χρυσοῦ
τοῦ μόνην τὴν ὄρασιν ἐκ τῆς ὄψεως θέλγοντος χαλκὸν
εὑρίσκειν οἰομένῳ ἢ ἀντὶ ἀργύρου μόλιβδον ἢ θεῖον ἄπυ-
ρον ὄζοντα, ἀλλὰ πάντων τῶν τοιούτων ἀποταξάμενος,
τὰς γενικωτάτας ἐτήρησεν ἀρετάς, ἐξ ὧν τὸ πᾶν ὡς ἔοικε
κατορθωκὼς εἶχε. Δόξα μὲν αὐτῷ ἦν ἡ τελεωτάτη καὶ γε-
νικωτάτη τῆς μακαρίας ἀπολαύσεως τῶν σῳζομένων λαμ-
πρότης, ἧς οὐκ ἂν ἐπινοήσασθαι θέμις ὑψηλότερόν τι καὶ
λαμπρότερον, πλοῦτος δὲ αἱ εἰς Θεὸν ἐλπίδες καὶ τὸ πάντα
μισῆσαι τὰ τοῦ βίου λαμπρὰ καὶ περίδοξα καὶ τὴν περιττὴν
ὕλην ἀποτινάξασθαι καὶ πάντων τούτων ἀνταλλάξασθαι
τὸν τίμιον μαργαρίτην Χριστόν, τὸν ἀληθῆ πλοῦτον, τὸν
γλυκὺν θησαυρόν.

4

Οὗ τρωθεὶς τῷ ἔρωτι, ὁ καλὸς οὗτος ἔμπορος, νέος ἔτι
τὴν ἡλικίαν, πολιὰν ἐνέφανε φρόνησιν, οὐ μόνον οὐδὲν
ζηλῶν ἢ ζητῶν χαμερπὲς καὶ συρόμενον, ἀλλὰ καὶ ὡς φαύλης καὶ παιδικῆς φρενὸς δελεάσματα τὰ ὑλικὰ πάντα καὶ
πρόσκαιρα λογισάμενος καὶ τῷ τῆς θείας ἀγάπης πυρὶ
ἀποτεφρώσας, χρυσὸς ἦν δόκιμος, καθαρῶς λατρεύων τῷ
μόνῳ καθαρῷ καὶ τοῖς χαμαιζήλοις ἀπροσπελάστῳ Θεῷ,
ἐκεῖνον δόξαν, ἐκεῖνον πλοῦτον, ἐκεῖνον ζωὴν καὶ πνοὴν

his sleeping on the bare ground, fasting, nakedness, and vigils, resembled those mines, but his hopes were not shameful or unfulfilled, nor did he think that he found mere copper instead of gold, whose gleam, after all, merely entices our eyes with its outward appearance, or that he found lead instead of silver, or noxious mineral sulfur. Having renounced all these things, he took care to acquire the cardinal virtues, through which, it appears, he accomplished everything. His glory was the most perfect and shining beatitude of those who have found salvation, compared to which nothing higher and nobler may be imagined. His wealth consisted of the hopes that he placed in God, his disdain for all the illustrious and glorious things of this life, his rejection of all matter that is useless, and exchanging all these for the *precious pearl,* that is Christ himself, the true wealth, that sweet treasure.

4

Stricken with love for Christ, that still youthful *good merchant* displayed a sagacity proper to an old man: he neither strove for nor sought things that were crawling on the ground, but considered all ephemeral matter as a temptation for those with stupid and childish minds. He burned all that up into ash through the fire of his love for God, and so came to resemble authentic gold. He purely worshipped God who alone is pure, who is unapproachable to all who crawl on the ground. He regarded God as his glory, his

τιθέμενος. Πῶς δὲ καὶ ἦν λαθεῖν τοιοῦτον ὄντα καὶ οὕτω
βιοῦντα, ποῦ δὲ καὶ Θεοῦ τοῦ φιλαγάθου ὑπεριδεῖν τηλικαύτην ἀρετὴν ὑπὸ μοδίῳ κρυπτομένην, ἀλλὰ μὴ ἐν περι-
ωπῇ τινι θεῖναι, ὅπερ καὶ γέγονεν, ὥστε ἀρχέτυπον γενέσθαι παντὸς ἀγαθοῦ, οὐ μόνον τῇ Λακεδαίμονι, ἀλλὰ καὶ
πάσῃ τῇ τοῦ Πέλοπος, ἤδη δὲ καὶ τῆς Ἑλλάδος τῷ πλεί-
ονι; Οὐ γὰρ αὐτὸς ἐδεῖτο δόξης ἀνθρωπίνης καὶ τιμῆς τινος, ἀλλ' οἱ τότε καιροὶ ἔχρῃζον ἀνδρὸς τὴν πολλὴν ἀνα-
κόπτοντος τῶν πολλῶν κακίαν καὶ ποιμαντικῶς ἄρχοντος.

2   Γίνεται δὴ καταφανὴς θείᾳ βουλήσει καὶ εἰς τὴν τῆς
Ἐκκλησίας περιωπὴν ἀνάγεται, ἵνα διαπυρσεύσῃ πολλοῖς
τὸ τῆς σωτηρίας φῶς, οὐ ζητήσας τὴν τιμήν, οὐδὲ διώξας,
οὐδὲ χάριτος ἀνθρωπίνης ἢ εὐνοίας ἀλόγου δῶρον λαβών.
Ποῦ γὰρ ἐκείνου ταῦτα, τοῦ καταπτύσαντος πάντα δι'
εὐλάβειαν καὶ εἰδότος ὅσον μὲν τὸ θεῖον ὕψος, ὅσον δὲ τῆς
ἀνθρωπίνης φύσεως τὸ χαμαίζηλον καὶ οἷον τῆς ἀρχιερωσύνης τὸ ἀξίωμα, ἐπεὶ μηδὲ καθ' ἕνα τινὰ ἐζήτει γενέσθαι
ἐκείνων τῶν μόνας προσόδους περιβλεπόντων, ψυχῶν δὲ
ἀμελούντων καὶ διὰ τοῦτο ἐπὶ τὰς βαθυπλούτους καὶ πο-
λυχρύσους τῶν ἐκκλησιῶν εἰσωθουμένων, ἵν' ἔχοιεν ἐπι-
γαυριᾶν χρήμασι καὶ κτήμασι καὶ πλείονος ἀποπνεῖν τῆς
κοσμικῆς ὕλης; Οὓς ψυχῶν προστασίαν δεξαμένους
κακῶς, χρημάτων ταμίας ἡ φιλοπλουτία μετεχειροτόνησε,
κἂν μὴ ἔχοιεν ἁδρὰ κέρδη καὶ βαρυταλάντους ἀπαριθμεῖν
προσόδους, ἴλιγγος τὸ λοιπὸν καὶ ἀπορία καὶ ἀπόγνωσις
καὶ τῆς οἰκείας ἱερατείας κατάγνωσις καὶ δυστυχίαν
ἑαυτῶν καταλέγουσι καὶ ἀποφράδας τὰς τῆς ἀρχῆς

wealth, his life, his breath. Was it possible for such a man, who led such a life, to escape attention? Was it possible for God, who loves goodness, to overlook such a virtuous man, to let him be hidden under a bushel basket and not place him on a pedestal? And that is exactly what happened: he became an exemplar of every good thing, not only for Lakedaimon but for the whole Peloponnese and the major part of Greece as well. For he had no need of human glory and honors, and the times themselves cried out for a man who would rule as a shepherd and inhibit the numerous bad actions of most people.

Thus, through the will of God, Theokletos became 2 known to all and was elevated to the apex of the Church, in order to blazon the light of salvation abroad to many people as if by beacon fires. He neither asked for such an office, nor pursued it, nor did he obtain it through men's favor or receive it as a gift through misplaced favoritism. For how could he act in this way? He despised all material things because of his piety, being well aware of the loftiness of divinity and the baseness of human nature; he was also aware of the importance of the episcopal dignity. He did not wish to become one of those who seek only a large income, who neglect the souls of their brethren and as a result try to take over very wealthy churches that are full of gold so that they can boast of money and property and inhale the smell of earthly matter. Such men wickedly agree to become pastors of human souls, but greed transforms them into mere treasurers. If they do not make huge profits and large incomes, they grow dizzy and are at a loss as to what to do. They become so disappointed that they curse their own bishopric, tally up their misfortune, and consider the days of their

ἡμέρας, ὥσπερ φορολόγοι τινὲς προβληθέντες ἢ χρημάτων πράκτορες, τῆς δὲ λογικῆς ποίμνης καὶ τῶν προβάτων
τοῦ Χριστοῦ λόγος οὐδείς, οὐ μᾶλλον ἢ τῶν θανόντων.
Ἀλλ᾽ ἤδη τις τῆς μὲν τῶν ἀλόγων ποίμνης ἐπεστράφη καὶ
ὅση τὸ πλῆθος καὶ ὁποία τὴν ὄψιν καὶ ποῦ τὰς νομὰς ποι-
εῖται τημελῶς ἐφρόντισε, πρὸς τὸ κέρδος ἀποσκοπῶν, τῶν
δὲ ἀθλίων ψυχῶν πᾶσαν ἀπείπατο φροντίδα, ὧν καὶ τὰς
εὐθύνας ἀπαιτεῖσθαι μέλλει.

3   Οὐ μὴν ἁπάντων ἡμῖν ὁ λόγος κατατρέχει, οὐδὲ πᾶσιν
ἐγκαλεῖ τὸ τῶν ποιμνίων ὀλίγωρον. Οὐδὲ γὰρ ἂν εἴη δίκαιος κριτής, οὐδὲ φίλος τῆς ἀληθείας, εἰ μὴ φείδεται τῶν
δεξιῶν ποιμένων, πολλῶν ὄντων καὶ περιδεξίως τῆς ποίμνης προϊσταμένων, οἳ καὶ περὶ ἐπιμέλειαν ψυχῶν ποιμαν-
τικήν τινα καὶ φερέπονον ἐπιδεικνύντες τὴν ἐμπειρίαν,
συντηροῦσι ταῖς ἐκκλησίαις καὶ τὴν ἔξωθεν ἀπὸ τῶν χρημάτων ἰσχὺν ἀμείωτον, ἑκατέρωθεν αὐτῶν τὸ εὐδόκιμον
ἐνδεικνύμενοι. Τούτοις οὖν οὐ μόνον οὐ σφοδράν τινα
καταδρομὴν ὁ λόγος ἐπεγείρει, ἀλλὰ καὶ προσαποδέχεται
καὶ τὸ διὰ πάντων ἄγρυπνον καὶ ἀήττητον ἐκθειάζει, εἰ
μὴ πλέον τοῦ δέοντος ἢ πρὸς τὰ ρευστὰ ἐπιμέλεια καὶ
περικλῶσα ἢ καὶ ὑπ᾽ ἀγκῶνα τιθεῖσα τὴν ἀναγκαίαν καὶ
ἀπαραίτητον τῶν ψυχῶν φροντίδα. Ὅσοι δὲ μηδ᾽ ἴκταρ τὸ
τοῦ λόγου πρὸς ταυτηνὶ τὴν φροντίδα βάλλουσιν, ὅλοι δὲ
τῷ πηλῷ καὶ τῇ πλινθείᾳ προστετήκασι (τοιαῦτα γὰρ τὰ
γήϊνα), τούτους καὶ μέγα ἂν συμπαθὴς καὶ ἥμερος κατα-
θρηνήσειε ψυχή, ὅτι δὴ μηδὲ τοῦτο αὐτὸ ἴσασιν, οἷος
αὐτοῖς τῆς ἀμελείας ἐπικρέμαται κίνδυνος.

office as unlucky. They resemble men who have been appointed as tax collectors or money dealers, not caring about
their rational flock, the sheep of Christ, any more than
about those who are dead. Instead, they pay attention to
their actual flock of irrational animals, investigating diligently their numbers, their appearance, and where they pas-
ture, concerned for their profit. On the other hand, they pay
no attention at all to the wretched souls of their spiritual
flock, for which they will be called to render an account in
the future.

My speech, of course, does not target all bishops, and 3
does not blame them all for neglecting their flock. He would
not be a righteous judge and lover of truth who did not ex-
empt good shepherds, the many who expertly preside over
their sheep. Those men exert much effort and display experience in caring for souls. At the same time they keep the
material income of their churches intact, showing their ability in both respects. Not only does my speech not accuse
those men vehemently, but rather it commends them, extol-
ling their vigilance in all respects and their steadfastness,
provided their concern about perishable things is not
greater than it should be, which would confuse them and
prevent them from caring for human souls, which is their
proper and indispensable job. But a compassionate and calm
soul may still shed many tears on behalf of those who *do not
care at all* about these matters, who are totally absorbed in
clay and brickmaking (for such are worldly things), as they do
not even know what a great danger threatens them because
of their neglect.

4   Ὃν ὁ μέγας ὑφορώμενος Θεόκλητος καὶ εἰδὼς φο-
βεῖσθαι οὗ ἐστι φόβος, οὐκ ἐπεπήδησε τῷ θρόνῳ καλούμενος, οὐδ' ἕρμαιον τὴν κλῆσιν ἐποιήσατο, ἀλλ' ἀνεδύετο καὶ
ὑπεχώρει τῆς τιμῆς καὶ παρῃτεῖτο, ἀντιβολῶν τοὺς κα-
λοῦντας ἐπ' ἄλλον τινὰ τραπέσθαι τὸν τοῖς θείοις θελήμα-
σιν ὑπηρετεῖν ἱκανώτατον, αὐτῷ δὲ ἄσυλον τὴν ἡδίστην
ἡσυχίαν χαρίσασθαι. Πολλῶν δὲ λογάδων ἀνδρῶν ἰσχυρῶς
ἐπικειμένων καὶ Θεῷ δοκοῦν εἶναι τοῦτο διατεινομένων
καὶ δεδιέναι παρεγγυωμένων, μὴ καὶ τὸ θεῖον παροξύνειεν
ἐπὶ πλέον ἀντερείδων καὶ ἀπειθῶν, οὐκ ἔτι ἀντειπών,
εἵπετο τοῖς καλοῦσι, καὶ ἐπὶ τὴν ἐκκλησίαν ἐλθὼν καὶ τῷ
θείῳ τελεσθεὶς χρίσματι, τῷ θρόνῳ τῆς Λακεδαίμονος
ἀποδίδοται. Οἶμαι δὲ λαμπράν τινα φανῆναι τὴν ἡμέραν
τῆς ἐκείνου τελειώσεως καὶ πανήγυριν κοινὴν τῶν οὐρανίων καὶ ἐπιγείων. Πάντως γὰρ καὶ αἱ οὐράνιαι δυνάμεις
φιλάνθρωποι οὖσαι τὰ τοιαῦτα συνεορτάζουσι τοῖς ἀνθρώποις καὶ συνευφραίνονται.

5

Ὁ δὲ ἐπὶ τὴν ὑψηλὴν ταύτην ἀναχθεὶς καθέδραν καὶ
τοὺς τῆς Ἐκκλησίας οἴακας ἁγίαις χερσὶ δεξάμενος, οὔμενουν ὑφῆκέ τι τῆς προτέρας προθέσεως ἢ μαλακώτερον
διετέθη, οὐδὲ τὴν συνήθη καὶ ἐπιτεταμένην ἐγκράτειαν
ὁπωσοῦν ὑπετέμετο, ἀλλὰ προσθήκην καὶ ἑτέρων ἀγώνων

But the great Theokletos, knowing this threat and *fearing* 4
things that should cause a justifiable fear, did not jump at the
chance to occupy the episcopal throne when he was called
to it. He did not regard that summons as an unexpected
piece of luck, but shrank back, declined the honor, and renounced the dignity, asking those who summoned him to
turn to another man, who would be far more able to fulfill
God's wishes, leaving him to enjoy the refuge of his beloved
spiritual tranquility. However, many important persons put
great pressure on him, arguing that this was the will of God.
They urged him to be careful lest God become angry with
him, if he went on resisting and disobeying for too long. So
Theokletos did not put up any more resistance and followed
those who summoned him. He came to the church, was
anointed with the divine chrism, and was delivered up to the
throne of Lakedaimon. I think that the day of his consecra-
tion was a shining day and a joint festival of heavenly powers
and human beings, since the former, who love mankind, join
with men in such celebrations and all rejoice together.

5

After ascending that lofty throne and taking the helm of
the Church in his own holy hands, the saint did not moderate his former behavior or ease up, nor did he reduce his customary intensive ascetic regimen at all. Instead, he rightly
considered the office of bishop to be an opportunity for

καὶ πολυειδῶν φροντίδων τὴν ἀρχιερωσύνην, ὡς ἔδει, καὶ
λογισάμενος καὶ ποιησάμενος, ἄτρυτος ὢν καὶ ἀνένδοτος
οἷά τις ἄριστος κυβερνήτης, ἄγρυπνον τείνων τὸ ὄμμα καὶ
ὀξυδερκὲς καὶ ὅλος προστετηκώς, μήπου τὸ σκάφος αὐτῷ
τῶν φίλων τῷ Χριστῷ ψυχῶν ὑφάλῳ τινὶ προσοκείλῃ
πέτρᾳ ἢ σπιλάδι, ὁποῖα πολλὰ περὶ τὴν τοῦ βίου θάλασσαν
σατανικῆς ἐπινοίας εὑρέματα, καὶ ἢ περιτραπείη ἢ καί τινα
τῶν ἐμπλεόντων τὰ ἐμφωλεύοντα τοῖς ὕδασι θηρία ὑφαρ-
πάσειε καὶ ἐπαγάγοι, φεῦ, τὸν τῆς ψυχῆς θάνατον, πρὸς ἃ
τὴν διάνοιαν ἔχων, πάντα περιεσκόπει καὶ πάντων ἐκήδε-
το καὶ θερμὴν ὡς εἰκὸς καὶ πατρικὴν ἐνεδείκνυτο τὴν
στοργὴν καὶ προσήγετο πάντας καὶ προσῳκείου Θεῷ τε
καὶ ἑαυτῷ, ἐκκλείων καὶ ἀποκρουόμενος τὸν κοινὸν
ἀνθρώπων Ἐχθρὸν καὶ πολέμιον, ὡς ἐκεῖνον μὲν τὰς ἐπιβουλὰς συνήθως ἐξαρτύειν καὶ τὰς ἐνέδρας ὑποσπείρειν
μετὰ τῆς οἰκείας κακουργίας καὶ πλοκῆς, τὸν δὲ μέγαν
πάντα καταφωρᾶν καὶ περιτρέπειν ἐκείνῳ εἰς κενὸν τὰ
βουλεύματα.

6

Ἀλλὰ πῶς ἐκείνου πάντα διηγήσομαι, ὃν οὐδεὶς οὐδαμῶς καιρός ποτε διέφυγεν ἄπρακτος, ἢ τινὰς ἐπισκεπτό-
μενον τῶν συμφοραῖς περιπεσόντων καὶ τὰ εἰκότα παρα-
καλοῦντα καὶ ἀνακτώμενον, ἢ διδάσκοντα τὰ σωτήρια ἢ

more struggles and new cares, and he conformed to that principle. He was indefatigable and unyielding, resembling the good captain of a ship. He kept his eyes open, being sharp-sighted, and took all precautions lest his ship of souls, those friends of Christ, run aground on an underwater rock or shoal. I am referring to the numerous satanic traps that infest the sea of life. He also took care that none of his passengers might be seized by the monsters which lurk in that sea and led off, alas, to the death of his soul. Focusing his attention on all these things, he observed everything carefully and took care of everyone. As was only reasonable, he showed a warm and paternal affection toward them. In this way, he attracted all people, acquainting them both with God and with himself. He thwarted and drove away the common Enemy and adversary of mankind, for the Evil One had prepared his plots in advance and laid his traps with his usual villainy and cunning, but that great man detected the plotter and brought his plans to naught.

6

But how could I recount everything about him? There was no time when he was idle: he was either visiting someone who had fallen into misfortune, giving him reasonable consolation and reviving his spirits, or teaching what

διατρέφοντα τοὺς λιμώττοντας, οἷον βούλει λιμόν, εἴτε τὸν εἰς σῶμα εἴτε τὸν εἰς ψυχὴν περιϊστάμενον, ἤ τι τῶν ὁμοίως ἀξιοπρεπῶν διαπραττόμενον; Ὀρφανοῖς μὲν ἴσα καὶ πατὴρ ἐχρημάτιζε, χήραις δὲ τὴν τῶν ἀνδρῶν ἀπεπλήρου κηδεμονίαν, τοῖς τὰ σώματα κακῶς διακειμένοις καὶ νοσερῶς ἔχουσιν ἀντὶ τῶν ὑστεριζομένων μελῶν ἐγίνετο, ὀφθαλμὸς μὲν τυφλῶν, ποὺς δὲ χωλῶν καὶ ὢν καὶ ὀνομαζόμενος καὶ πᾶσι πάντα γινόμενος, ἵνα πάντας κερδήσῃ ἢ μᾶλλον εἰπεῖν τῷ Χριστῷ συντηρήσῃ.

2   Οὐδὲ ἡ νεότης τὴν ἐκείνου ἠγνόησεν ἀρετήν, ἀλλ᾽ ἔσχεν αὐτὸν σωφρονιστὴν παιδευτικώτατον, παραινοῦντα τῇ χρυσῇ γλώσσῃ μὴ τὸ τῆς ἡλικίας ἄνθος ταῖς τῶν ἐπιθυμιῶν ὑβρίζειν αἰσχρότησι, μηδὲ τὴν ἐπιλάμπουσαν ὥραν ἀτιμοτέραν ποιεῖν τῇ τῶν ἀτίμων παθῶν δουλείᾳ, ἀλλ᾽ ἐνταῦθα μᾶλλον τὴν ἀνδρείαν ἐπιδείκνυσθαι καὶ ὁπλίζεσθαι κατὰ τῶν ἐπιθυμιῶν τῶν βεβήλων καὶ τὴν εὐγένειαν τῆς ψυχῆς διατηρεῖν ἀδούλωτον. Τί δὲ τὸ γῆρας; Καὶ τοῦτο τὰ προσήκοντα ἐδιδάσκετο, μηδὲν ἀπᾷδον τῆς ἐπανθούσης ὄψεως πράττειν, ἀλλὰ πολιὰν κτᾶσθαι τὴν πολιάν, φρονήσει καὶ ἀρετῇ κεκοσμημένην καὶ νέοις εἶναι πρεσβυτικὸν τῷ ὄντι καὶ ἀξιοζήλωτον τῶν καλλίστων ἀρχέτυπον, ὡς, εἰ μὴ τὸ κόσμιον τοῦτο καὶ σεμνὸν ἡ πολιὰ ἐν ἑαυτῇ περιφέρει, οὐδὲν ἂν ἔχοι τίμιον. Τίνος ἐκεῖνος οὐκ ἐφρόντιζε, τίνος οὐ περιεκαίετο; Ἄλλος ἠσθένει καὶ αὐτὸς τὰς ὀδύνας ἐδέχετο, οἵαν βούλει ἀσθένειαν, εἴτε τὴν τοῦ σώματος εἴτε τὴν τῆς ψυχῆς, ἣν καὶ μᾶλλον ἐθρήνει,

contributed to salvation, or giving food to those who were hungry, I mean both those whose body was hungry and those whose soul was in need of spiritual sustenance. At any rate, he was always busy with such tasks worthy of his dignity. He was like a father to orphans, while for widows he fulfilled the tasks of a husband as a good steward. For all those whose bodies were in a bad condition and who were ill, he supplied the function of the missing or handicapped organ: he really was, and was called, *the eye of the blind and the foot of the lame.* He *became all things to all people, in order to win over everyone,* or rather to keep them in the company of Christ.

Young men were not unaware of his virtue: they had in   2 him a most pedagogically effective tutor in morality who urged them with his golden tongue neither to sully the flower of their youth through their shameful desires, nor to dishonor their shining beauty through enslavement to dishonorable passions. He admonished them instead to show their manliness in that respect, fighting against their impure desires and keeping the nobility of their souls intact. And what about old age? The elderly were also given proper lessons: he asked them not to behave in a way unbecoming to their white hair, which adorned them like a flower, but to be truly venerable old men, adorning their advanced years with temperance and virtue, to be true models of sage elders for the young and enviable models of the best behavior, since, if old men lack decency and moderation in themselves, they are worth nothing. Was there anyone neglected by the saint? Was there anyone about whom he did not care ardently? If someone was ill, whether in body or soul, the saint suffered from his pains, though he shed most tears for illnesses of the

τὴν ἁμαρτίαν φημί, καὶ ὡς Ἰακὼβ ἐπὶ τῷ Ἰωσὴφ ἢ ὡς
Δαυὶδ ἐπὶ τῷ <Ἰω>νάθαν ἐκόπτετο καὶ ἀπαράκλητον εἶχε
τὸ πένθος. Τὴν γὰρ τῆς σαρκὸς ἀσθένειαν οὐκ ἠγνόει
πολλάκις καὶ ἀφορμὴν σωτηρίας γινομένην, ἐκείνην δὲ
πικρῶς ἀπεκλαίετο, καὶ πλέον εἰ δυσίατος ἦν καὶ δυσανά-
κλητος καὶ μήτε μάλαγμα δεχομένη μήτε ἐπίδεσμον μήτε
φάρμακόν τι ἕτερον.

7

Τί τὰ καθ᾽ ἕκαστον διεξέρχομαι, τὴν θέρμην τῆς πίστεως, τὴν ὑπὲρ τῶν ἀδικουμένων παρρησίαν, τὴν ἐλευθέραν
κατὰ τῶν ἀδικούντων φωνήν, τὴν ἱλαρὰν μετάδοσιν καὶ
ὡς ἐκ πηγῶν ῥέουσαν, τὸ ἥμερον, τὸ πρᾷον, τὸ ἄτυφον, τὸ
μετριάζον ἐν ἅπασι, καὶ οὐ μόνον, ἀλλὰ καὶ τὰς ἐπηρμένας
ὀφρῦς καταστέλλον καὶ τὰς πλεονέκτιδας ἀνακροῦον
χεῖρας, εἰ μὲν δύναιτο, τοῖς ἠπίοις καὶ προσηνέσι φαρμά-
κοις, εἴτουν παραινέσεσι καὶ διδασκαλίαις, εἰ δὲ δεήσοι,
καὶ τραχυτέροις ῥήμασι;

2   Τί γὰρ ἔλεγεν ἡ μελισταγὴς ἐκείνη καὶ χαρίτων μεστὴ
γλῶττα, "Τί τὸ ἐξογκοῦν ὑμᾶς καὶ διοιδαίνειν τοῖς φρονή-
μασι παρασκευάζον; Μή τι τῶν ἄλλων ὧν καταπτύετε
πλέον ὑμῖν ἡ φύσις πεφιλοτίμηται, μᾶλλον δὲ ὁ Κτίστης
τῆς φύσεως; Οὐχ εἷς χαρακτήρ, οὐ μία σφραγὶς πᾶσιν, οὐχ
εἷς Πλάστης, οὐ μία φύσις, οὐ τὸ αὐτὸ σχῆμα; Οὐχ αἱ αὐταὶ

soul, I mean, sin. He mourned like Jacob for his son Joseph. He mourned for them as David mourned for Jonathan, and his grief was inconsolable. He was not unaware that in many cases bodily illness can prove salvific, but he wept bitterly over illnesses of the soul, especially if they were incurable and health could not be easily restored through spiritual emollients, bandages, or other medicines.

7

Why am I enumerating each item separately? His ardent faith; his outspokenness on behalf of those who were treated unjustly; his bold speech before those who had acted unjustly; his cheerful generosity, resembling a flowing spring; his mildness; his gentleness; his lack of pretension; his moderation in all respects. And not only that, he also calmed those whose eyebrows were arched in arrogance and he restrained greedy hands, if possible, with mild and gentle medicine (I am referring to his admonitions and his teaching), or, if necessary, through sterner words.

For what were the words of that graceful tongue that 2 dripped honey, that was so full of graces? "What is puffing you up," he would say, "what is making your spirit arrogant? Did nature, or rather the Creator of nature, endow you with more gifts than those whom you disdain? Do we not all have a common character, a common baptism, a *single Creator,* one nature, and the same form? Do we not have the same

χεῖρες, οὐχὶ καὶ ἡ διάρτισις ὁμοία τοῦ σώματος καὶ ἐκ τῶν ὁμοίων; Τί περιττὸν ὑπὲρ τοὺς ἄλλους ἔχοντες, καταφρυάττεσθε τῶν ταπεινοτέρων καὶ αἴρετε τὰς ὀφρῦς ὑπὲρ τοὺς κροτάφους καὶ οὐδὲ ἀξιοῦτε προσρήσεως, ὥσπερ αὐτοὶ ἄλλην τινὰ ἔχοντες διατριβὴν ὑπερφέρουσαν καὶ μετέωροί τινες ὄντες καὶ ὑψιβάμονες, ὁρῶντες δὲ τοὺς ἄλλους ἡμᾶς ταπεινοὺς καὶ προσγείους καὶ τοῦτο ὄντας ὅπερ ἐσμέν; Ὡς εἴθε καὶ ἄλλην τινὰ οἱ ἀκόρεστοι τὰς φιλοπλούτους ἐπιθυμίας ἐλάχετε διατριβὴν καὶ ἄλλην κατοίκησιν, ἵνα μὴ καὶ τὰ μικρὰ ταῦτα τῆς ζωῆς τῶν ἀθλίων λείψανα διαρπάζοντες, εἰς ἀπαραμύθητον τούτους ἀπορίαν ἠλαύνετε. Ἀλλ' ἴσως αἱ λαμπραὶ ὑμᾶς μετεωρίζουσιν ἐσθῆτες καὶ τὰ τῶν σκωλήκων γεννήματα, ἃ τοὺς καλῶς ὑμῶν καὶ τεθραμμένους περιστέλλουσιν ἀνδριάντας, ἤγουν τὰς τρυφερὰς ταύτας καὶ περιττὰς σάρκας, ἃς ἐπὶ κακῷ τῆς ὑμετέρας πιαίνετε κεφαλῆς, καὶ διὰ τοῦτο φυσᾶτε τὰ μεγάλα καὶ ὑπερφρονεῖτε ῥακενδυτούντων τῶν ἀδελφῶν, καὶ οὐδὲ αἰδεῖσθε, οὐδὲ ἐγκαλύπτεσθε κατεσκληκότα πολλάκις μέλη καὶ ἐρρικνωμένα καὶ εἰς ἔσχατον ταλαιπωρίας ἥκοντα, ἐπιτρίβοντες, φεῦ, καὶ ἐπὶ πλέον ἐκτρύχοντες διὰ μανικὴν ἀτεχνῶς ἀπληστίαν καὶ ἀόριστον, ὑφ' ἧς καὶ ταῖς μικραῖς εἰς τὸ ζῆν ἀφορμαῖς τῶν πενήτων ἐπιβουλεύετε, ἐξ αὐτῶν ἔσθ' ὅτε τῶν φαρύγγων καὶ ταύτας ἁρπάζοντες θηριωδῶς, καὶ οὐδὲ τὸν Λάζαρον καὶ τὸν πλούσιον ἐννοεῖτε, γείτονα παραδείγματα καὶ ἱκανὰ τὴν πάντολμον κατασεῖσαι ψυχὴν καὶ ἀναχαιτίσαι τὴν ἀπόνοιαν." Ἀλλὰ τούτων μὲν τὸ πλεονεκτικὸν τῆς χειρὸς καὶ βαρὺ τοῦ φρονήματος τοιαύταις κατέστελλεν ἐπῳδαῖς.

hands? Has not the body of all human beings been created in the same way and from similar parts? Do you have something more than your fellow men that you behave so insolently toward your humble brethren? You raise your eyebrows at them so high and refuse to greet them, as if you lived in some different place, loftier, suspended in the air, and looking down with contempt on all of us humble folk who live on the earth, we who have no pretensions to be something more. I even wish that you, who have such an insatiable desire for wealth, had another place of residence, a different dwelling, so that you might not snatch up these small remnants of the life that is left to these miserable men, driving them into a poverty that admits no consolation. Perhaps you elevate yourselves with false hopes because of your shining garments, made of a silk that is actually a product of worms. These garments adorn those beautiful, well-fed statues of yours, I mean your delicate and fat bodies, which you make even fatter to the detriment of your own head. This is the reason for your great arrogance, for the contempt that you feel toward your brethren clothed in rags. You do not hesitate, you are not ashamed to crush the often skeletal limbs of those men, which are already shriveled up and reduced to utter misery, and to exhaust them because of your mad greed, which knows no limits. You even plot ways to deprive the poor of their small means of subsistence, sometimes grabbing it from their mouths as if you were wild beasts. You forget the parable of Lazarus and the rich man, which is an example most appropriate for you: it should shake your shameless soul and restrain your madness." Through such spellbinding words he tried to restrain their greedy hands and their arrogance.

8

Ἐπεὶ δὲ οὐδὲ ὁ κλῆρος αὐτῷ ἅπας ἐκτὸς ἐχρημάτιζεν αἰτίας, ἀλλ' ἦσάν τινες καὶ ἐν τῷ καταλόγῳ τούτῳ τεταγμένοι, βαθεῖαν μὲν περικείμενοι τὴν ἔξω εὐλάβειαν, ἔνδον δὲ περικρύπτοντες οὐ καλά, οὐδὲ ἀκόλουθα καὶ συνᾴδοντα τῷ φαινομένῳ σχήματι τὰ ἐπιτηδεύματα, ἀλλ' ἄλλο μὲν ὡς ἔφην προφαίνοντες τὸ προσωπεῖον, ἄλλην δὲ ὑπ' αὐτῷ τὴν ψυχὴν <...>

9

<...>μένος καὶ περικνιζόμενος. Τίσι γάρ που καὶ ἔμελλον τὸν οὐρανοπολίτην ἐκεῖνον ἄνθρωπον, τίνων ἀποστεροῦντες, ποίαν ἀτιμίαν ἐπάγοντες, ᾧ γε τὸ πάσχειν μὲν διὰ Χριστὸν τὰ ἀτιμότατα, τιμῆς ἦν ἁπάσης ἐπέκεινα, ἡ μηλωτὴ δὲ ὁ πᾶς πλοῦτος καὶ τὰ ῥάκια, οἷς τὸ ἀσθενὲς τῆς φύσεως περιεκάλυπτε, καὶ ῥάβδος ἀφελῶς οὕτως καὶ ἀγροικικῶς ἔχουσα, οὐ τρυφώσης χειρὸς κατήγορος, ἀλλὰ γηραιῶν ποδῶν ὑποστήριγμα, ὑφ' ᾗ βαδίζων μακράς τε διήνυεν ὁδοὺς καὶ τὰ τοῦ Δαυὶδ ἠρεμαίᾳ ὑπέψαλλε φωνῇ, συνοδοιπόρους ἑαυτῷ καὶ συνεργοὺς τῆς ᾠδῆς καὶ παῖδας ποιούμενος; Ἦσαν δὲ αὐτῷ ὡς τὰ πολλὰ τῆς ταλαιπωρίας ταύτης ἀφορμὴ οἱ νοσοῦντες, οἱ δεσμὰ περικείμενοι καὶ δεσμωτήρια οἰκοῦντες, οἱ ἀδίκως πάσχοντες, καὶ μᾶλλον

8

But even his clergymen were not blameless in their entirety. Some who were in these ranks maintained a pious veneer, but their bad character was concealed within, and their actions were at variance and not in accord with their outward appearance. As I said, the mask that they showed to the world was different from their soul that was concealed by it . . .

9

. . . being harassed. But with what means could they do any harm to that man whose citizenship was in heaven? Could they deprive him of anything? What insult could they bring against him, whose ignominious suffering for the sake of Christ was for him an honor beyond all honors? His sheepskin cloak and the rags that covered the frailty of his body were the sum of his riches. His simple rustic staff was not the sign of a hand that sought luxury, but merely a crutch for his old legs when he undertook a long journey on foot, softly singing the Psalms of David. He even took children along as his fellow travelers and assistants in these chants. In most cases, he undertook those arduous journeys for the sake of those who were ill, or who were in chains and lived in prison, who were suffering unjustly, and especially those who were

ὅσοι ὑπὸ πολλῇ τῇ πενίᾳ καὶ νόσῳ κατετρύχοντο. Ὧν ὑπο-
τρέχων τὰ φαῦλα οἰκήματα, ἀνηρώτα μὲν περὶ τῆς νόσου,
φιλοσοφεῖν δὲ ἔπειθεν ἐπὶ τοῖς ἀνιαροῖς, πολλήν τινα τὴν
παραψυχὴν καὶ λόγῳ καὶ ἔργῳ τοῖς ἀνδράσι προσεξευ-
ρίσκων.

2   Πῶς δὲ καὶ ἔμελλεν ἀνεκτῶς ὁ φθόνος οἴσεσθαι ταῦτα,
μᾶλλον δὲ ὁ τοῦ φθόνου Πατήρ, ὁ τῶν ζιζανίων σπορεύς,
ὁ τῆς Ἐκκλησίας πολέμιος; Πῶς δ' ἂν καὶ ἀνθοῦσαν ὁρᾶν
ἐκαρτέρησε τὴν Ἐκκλησίαν καὶ μή τι γνήσιον τῆς κακίας
εὑρεῖν τέχνασμα καὶ τὴν πολλὴν γαλήνην καὶ τὴν ἐπ' ἀγαθοῖς εὐδοκίμησιν φιλονεικῆσαι ἐπισχεῖν καὶ λυμήνασθαι;
Ποῦ γὰρ ἐκείνου τὸ μετριάζειν ἐν τοῖς τοιούτοις; Ἀλλὰ
λυττήσας ὁ Πονηρὸς πόλεμον οἷον βαρύτατον ἐπὶ τὸν
καλὸν τῆς ἀρετῆς φυτοκόμον, ἐπὶ τὸ ἱερὸν τῆς Ἐκκλησίας
ἄνθος ἐξήγειρε· καὶ ὁ πόλεμος τίς; Ἴσασι πάντες τοὺς ἐν
ταῖς πόλεσι προέχοντας, ὅσον εἰσὶ βίαιοι τὰς ὁρμὰς καὶ
ὅπως τῇ τοῦ πλείονος ἐπιθυμίᾳ δελεαζόμενοι, καταδυναστεύειν τῶν ταπεινοτέρων ἀγριαίνονται, καὶ ὅσον ὁ πλοῦτος αὐτοῖς πρόεισι, τοσοῦτον καὶ ἡ πλεονεξία συναύξεται,
ὥσπερ φασὶ τοὺς ὑπὸ τῆς διψάδος δηχθέντας, ὅσον ἂν
πλέον πίνοιεν, τοσοῦτον καὶ τῇ δίψῃ ἐκκαίεσθαι. Διά τοι
τοῦτο καὶ ἀγρίους καὶ ἀκορέστους ὀφθαλμοὺς τοῖς τῶν
γειτόνων ἐπιβάλλουσιν, εἴτε κτήμασιν εἴτε οἰκήμασι, κἂν
μὴ προσμίξαιεν τὰ ἀλλότρια τοῖς σφετέροις καὶ προσλά-
βοιεν ὥσπερ αἱ χαράδραι καὶ οἱ ῥύακες τὰ παραρρέοντα,
ἀδικεῖσθαι νομίζουσι καὶ δυσχεραίνουσι καὶ βούλονται
μηδὲν εἶναι τὸ ἀνθέλκον καὶ προσιστάμενον, ἀλλ' εἰ μὲν
εὐοδοῖντο τούτοις αἱ ὁρμαὶ ἐπὶ τοὺς ἀκαθέκτους τούτους

suffering from extreme poverty and illness. He went into their poor huts, asked them about their illness, urged them to endure their sufferings like philosophers, and, in sum, provided these men a great consolation through both his deeds and his words.

Was it then *possible that envy,* or rather the Father of envy, 2 the sower of weeds, the enemy of the Church, *could endure all this* without reacting? How could he bear to see the Church flourishing and not strive to find a device, typical of his villainy, to counter and dishonor that great calmness, and the saint's good reputation? It was impossible for him to be moderate in such a situation. Seized by frenzy, the Evil One started a fierce war against the good gardener of virtue, against the holy flower of the Church. What sort of war? Everyone knows the magistrates of the cities and how their inclination is toward violence. Tempted by their desire to acquire more and more, they become wrathful and oppress the members of the lower classes. The more wealth they accumulate, the greater their greed becomes in tandem. They resemble those who are bitten by a venomous serpent: as they say, the more water they drink, the more they burn with thirst. For that reason they look upon their neighbors' property, whether dwellings or land, with raging eyes full of greed. They actually think that they suffer a great injustice if they do not add the property of others to their own, as if they were mountain streams to be united with rushing torrents. Annoyed in this way, they do not want anything to resist them and stand in their way. If their rush toward these ungovernable and illegitimate desires attains its goal, they

καὶ ἐκθέσμους ἔρωτας, σιγῇ παρ' αὐτοῖς καὶ πολλή τις
ἡδονὴ ληϊζομένοις κατὰ πολλὴν ἄδειαν τὰ ἀλλότρια, εἰ δέ
τι φανείη τὸ ἀντιπίπτον ταῖς αὐτῶν ἀδικίαις καὶ ἀντιτεῖνον
καὶ μὴ ἐπιτρέπον κατὰ ῥοῦν αὐτοῖς φέρεσθαι τὴν τῆς πλε-
ονεξίας ῥύμην, οἱ σπινθῆρες εὐθὺς ἀναφλέγονται τῆς μα-
νίας καὶ σφοδρὰ πρὸς τὸ ἀντιπίπτον ἡ ἔχθρα καὶ αἱ ἐπι-
βουλαὶ καὶ οἱ θυμοὶ ἀφανῶς τε καὶ φανερῶς.

10

Ταῦτα δὴ ταῦτα καὶ τῷ μεγάλῳ Θεοκλήτῳ πολλοὺς
ἐξήγειρεν ὥσπερ λυσσῶντας τινὰς κύνας διαξαίνειν, φεῦ,
καὶ διασπαράττειν ἀπαναισχυντοῦντας, ὅσοι δήπου κακὸν
ἑαυτοῖς καὶ ἐπιζήμιον πλοῦτον ἀθροίζειν κακῶς καὶ ἀθέως
ἐφιλονείκουν καὶ εἰς τοὺς ἀθλίως γειτονοῦντας καὶ ἰδιώτην ἕλκοντας βίον τὸν λίχνον καὶ ἐπίβουλον ἐπέστρεφον
ὀφθαλμὸν καὶ κίνδυνον ἐπῆγον περὶ τῶν ἰδίων, διὰ πάσης
χωροῦντες μηχανῆς καὶ πάντα στρέφοντες ἢ διαστρέφον-
τες, ὥστε ἐπιβῆναι τῶν ἀλλοτρίων καὶ τῆς ἑαυτῶν κἀκεῖνα
θέσθαι ἀπλήστου δεσποτείας, οἱ πλεονέκται ταῦτα καὶ
ὠμοὶ τὰς ψυχὰς καὶ τὰς ὁρμὰς ἀνεπίσχετοι καὶ μήτε τὴν
φύσιν αἰδούμενοι μήτε τὸν μέλλοντα Κριτὴν ἐννοούμενοι.
Τί δὲ ὁ μέγας τὴν ψυχὴν καὶ πολὺς τὴν ἀρετὴν καὶ θερμὸς
τῶν ἀδικουμένων προστάτης, ἆρα κατενάρκησε τῆς

keep quiet, and take great pleasure in plundering the property of others without hindrance. But if an obstacle to their unjust endeavors should appear, something that blocks the rushing torrent of their greed from proceeding along its course, the sparks of their madness then burst into flames immediately, they become bitterly hostile to the one who hinders them, and they angrily plot against him, both openly and secretly.

10

Those very passions roused many people to action against the great Theokletos. They behaved like mad dogs, shamelessly wishing to shred and tear him to pieces. Woe to them, I mean those who strove in an ungodly fashion to hurt themselves by evilly accumulating harmful wealth. They turned their greedy and malevolent eyes upon their wretched neighbors, who were merely living out private lives, and endangered their property. They invented all sorts of nefarious schemes and turned everything upside down, or distorted it, in order to take possession of other people's property and subject it to the tyranny of their insatiable ownership. The souls of those grasping men were cruel, their desires uncontrollable. They neither respected our common nature, nor took thought for the one who shall judge us. But how did that man react, he who was great of soul, abundant in virtue, and zealously protected the victims of injustice? Did he remain passive in the face of their great

πολλῆς τούτων πονηρίας ἢ μικρόν τι καὶ ἀνθρώπινον ὑπε-
λογίσατο; "Τί δεῖ τοσούτοις μάχεσθαι καὶ βαρεῖαν κινεῖν
τὴν ἔχθραν καὶ πρὸς πολλὰς γλώττας καὶ δεξιὰς διαπλη-
κτίζεσθαι, δέον εἰρήνην ἄγειν καὶ πᾶσι συμπεριφέρεσθαι
καὶ τὴν παρὰ πάντων κερδαίνειν εὔνοιαν;" Οὔμενουν,
οὐδὲν τούτων οὔτε ἐλογίσατο, οὔτε μὴν διεπράξατο, ἀλλὰ
τὴν μὲν ἐν τούτοις ἡσυχίαν τοὺς πέτρας ὑπελθόντας καὶ
σπήλαια δεῖν ἄγειν νομίσας, αὐτῷ δὲ τὴν ὑπὲρ τῶν ἀδικουμένων παρρησίαν ὀφειλόμενον εἶναι καὶ ἀπαιτούμενον
(τοῦτο γὰρ πρὸς τοῖς ἄλλοις ἔργον ἱερωσύνης), παρίστατο
τοῖς ἀδικουμένοις, προσίστατο τοῖς ἀδικοῦσι, νουθετῶν,
παρακαλῶν, ἄγχων αὐτοῖς τὴν πλεονεξίαν, κέντρον ὢν
ἄθραυστον κατὰ στόμα ἀπαντῶν καὶ περιτρέπων τὰς εἰς
τὸ πλεονεκτεῖν φοράς.

II

Οἱ δὲ ὃ πάσχουσιν οἱ σφοδρῷ τῷ ῥεύματι φερόμενοι
ποταμοί, εἴ τι διάφραγμα εὑρεθείη ἀνακροῦον αὐτοῖς τὴν
τῶν ῥοθίων φοράν, κατ' αὐτοῦ τὴν πλημμύραν αὐξάνουσι
καὶ ἢ συναρπάσαντες κατὰ τὴν πρόσθεν φέρονται ὁρμὴν
ἢ στερροτέρῳ ἐντυχόντες κατὰ κορυφὴν αὐτῷ τὸν ῥοῦν
ἐκτοξεύουσι καὶ τὸν ἀφρὸν πολὺν παραπτύουσι, τοῦτο
καὶ αὐτοὶ ἀτεχνῶς πάσχοντες ἐξηλέγχοντο. Τῆς γὰρ
ἐπιθυμίας ἐξειργόμενοι καὶ τὴν ἄκρατον λύσσαν τῆς

villainy? Did he make a petty, all-too-human calculation? "Why should we take up arms against such a multitude and arouse their formidable enmity, fighting against so many tongues and so many right hands? Is it not more desirable to make peace, and more profitable to maintain good relations with everyone, to win everyone's goodwill?" No such thought entered his mind—not at all—nor did he act in that way. He was convinced that such quiet behavior was proper to those who inhabit grottos and caves, while his own task and duty was to raise his voice on behalf of those who were treated unjustly; this, among others, was the work of the priesthood. Therefore, he stood by those who were wronged, resisting those who acted unjustly, admonishing them and begging them, suppressing their greed. He was like an unbreakable horse bit in their mouth, restraining their desire to acquire more and more.

II

But they behaved like rivers swept along by a rapid current which come across a dam that breaks the flow of their waves: they raise their flood tide against it and either manage to flow on as before, sweeping the dam away, or, if the dam offers strong enough resistance, they strike at its top, foaming vehemently. And this is what happened to them when they were stopped in their tracks. Prevented from fulfilling their desires, and seeing their rabid lust for money

φιλοχρηματίας ἐγκοπτόμενοι, σφοδρὸν τὸν θυμὸν καὶ
ἀνήμερον τὴν ὀργὴν ἐπὶ τὸν θεῖον ἀνέκαιον Θεόκλητον,
φονᾶν ἄντικρυς ἐνδεικνύμενοι. Ἀμέλει καὶ τὴν Ἰουδαϊκὴν
ἐκείνην ἐκμιμούμενοι συναγωγήν, πολλὴν συγκροτοῦσι
περὶ αὐτοὺς θεομισῆ ἑταιρείαν, ἐκ τῆς αὐτῆς ὅ φασι κερα-
μείας, καὶ Κερκώπων ἀγορὰ γενόμενοι, οὐδὲν ἕτερον ἢ τῷ
ἁγίῳ τὰς ἐπιβουλὰς ἤρτυον. Καὶ συνιόντες ἐπὶ τὰ τῆς πονηρίας συμπόσια, σύνδειπνόν τε καὶ ὁμοδίαιτον τὴν κατὰ
τοῦ θείου ποιμένος ἐποιοῦντο σκαιωρίαν καὶ αἱ ἐν σκοτο-
μήνῃ πλοκαὶ μεθ᾽ ἡμέραν ἐτοξεύοντο, καὶ τοσαῦται τῷ
πλήθει καὶ οὕτω χαλεπαὶ ταῖς ἐπινοίαις, ὥστε καὶ ἐδόκουν
οἱ τὴν κακίαν ἀνίατοι ἄπορον ἐκείνῳ καὶ ἐπαχθῆ τὴν ζωὴν
καταστήσεσθαι, τὸ πᾶν διαμαρτάνοντες τῆς μεγαλόφρο-
νος ἐκείνης καὶ ἀκαταπλήκτου ψυχῆς, ἣν ἐλάνθανον
λαμπροτέραν τοῖς πειρασμοῖς τιθέντες καὶ Θεῷ μᾶλλον
γειτνιάζουσαν.

2   Ὡς δὲ πᾶσαν ἄλλην κακίας ὁδὸν διεξελθόντες, ἄπρακτα
πονοῦντες ἠλέγχοντο, τελευταίαν ταύτην τελεωτέρας μο-
χθηρίας ἀπόδειξιν ἀναρρηγνύουσι καὶ βλασφημίας (ὦ μα-
νίας ἀκρατοῦς εἰς ὅσον προχωρεῖ κακίας ἐπ᾽ ἀτιμίᾳ τοῦ
δικαίου), καὶ μυρίαν ὕβριν ἐκείνου κατέχεον, κἂν ἐν οἰκίᾳ
μένῃ τῆς φίλης ἐχόμενος ἀγωγῆς, κἂν ἐπ᾽ ἀγορὰν προέλ-
θοι ἐπισκεψόμενος τινὰ τῶν ἀσθενῶν ἢ ἐπὶ σύναξιν θείαν
ἀπίοι, οἵδε, αἱ πονηραὶ γλῶσσαι καὶ ἄθεοι καὶ ἐπάρατοι, οἱ
τῷ Πονηρῷ ἀγελάρχῃ χρώμενοι, συρρέοντες παμπληθεῖς
ὡς ἔκ τινος συνθήματος καὶ παικτικήν τινα καὶ γελοιώδη
δορυφορίαν ὑπερχόμενοι, προεπορεύοντο τοῦ ἱεροῦ
ἀνδρὸς καὶ περιεβόμβουν αὐτὸν καὶ τὰς ὁσίας ἐκείνας

checked, they became inflamed with an implacable, wild anger against the divine Theokletos; they were even prepared
to kill him. Imitating that Jewish assembly, they gathered
around themselves a large band hated by God, which consisted of men of the same make, thereby becoming *a knaves-
market,* and they did nothing other than scheme against the
saint. They met at their evil banquets, feasting in the company of their conspiracy against the divine shepherd, so to
speak. During the day they shot against him like arrows the
wicked plots that they had hatched in the darkness of night.
These were so numerous and so malicious in intent that
those men, whose villainy was incurable, believed that they
would thereby make the saint's life unbearable and burdensome. But they utterly failed to understand that magnani-
mous and undaunted soul, and did not realize that it became
even brighter and drew closer to God because of their temptations.

After trying every other path of villainy, and doing so in   2
vain, they offered one last proof of their perfect wickedness
and irreverence—oh, the extent of uncontrollable madness
to which their depravity went in order to tarnish a righteous
man's reputation!—pouring upon him all sorts of calumnies.
Either when the saint was at his home, leading his own beloved way of life, or when he went out to the market in order
to visit someone who was ill, or when he went to the holy
service, those wicked, godless, accursed tongues, who had
the Evil One as their leader, gathered together in a crowd as
if by prior agreement and assumed the role of a mocking
and jeering bodyguard: they walked ahead of this holy man,
buzzing all around him; they flooded those holy ears, which

ἀκοὰς καὶ ὑπὸ πολλῇ ἁγνείᾳ καὶ τραφείσας καὶ παιδευθεί-
σας κατέπλυνον ἀνάγνοις τισὶ καὶ ἀπηχέσι ῥήμασι καὶ ταῖς
ἐξ ἀγορᾶς βωμολοχίαις καὶ οἷα φιλεῖ λαλεῖν τὰ χείλη τὰ
δόλια τὰ ἐν παντὶ καιρῷ βεβηλούμενα. Τί γὰρ ἂν καὶ εἴποι
ποτὲ σεμνὸν καὶ ἐμμελὲς γλῶττα μιαρὰ καὶ βδελυροῖς
ἤθεσι ἐντραφεῖσα καὶ ῥήμασι; Πρότερον ἄν, οἶμαι, μυρί-
πνους ἐκ τάφου σεσηπότος ὀδμὴ διαπνεύσειεν ἢ ἐκ βδε-
λυροῦ λάρυγγος εὐώδης λόγος καὶ ἥδιστος. Οὔμενουν
ἐκεῖνον <οὐδὲν> τούτων διετάραττεν, ἀλλ᾽ ἄλλως μὲν ἐπὶ
τῇ ἀκράτῳ τῶν ἀνδρῶν πωρώσει ἤλγει τὴν ψυχὴν καὶ
ἐσπαράττετο, φιλόθεον οὖσαν καὶ φιλάνθρωπον καὶ οὐ
μόνον τὸ ἴδιον μαθοῦσαν περισκοπεῖν συμφέρον, περικαι-
ομένην δὲ καὶ τῆς τῶν ἀδελφῶν σωτηρίας, τοῦ δὲ γέλωτος
τῶν γελοίων ἐκείνων, μᾶλλον δὲ καταγελάστων νέων καὶ
τῆς ἀναισχύντου μωκίας καὶ χλεύης τοσαῦτα φροντίζων
ἦν, ὅσα καὶ κώνωπος Ἰνδικός φασιν ἐλέφας, εἰ μὴ καὶ
μᾶλλον ἐνωραΐζεσθαι τούτοις καὶ ἐναβρύνεσθαι εἶχε, φιλοσοφίας ἀρκοῦσαν ἀφορμὴν καὶ ταῦτα οἰόμενος.

12

Ἐς τοσοῦτον δὲ ἄρα τοὺς φρενοβλαβεῖς ἐκείνους καὶ
ἀποφράδας ἐξέμηναν οἱ θυμοί, ὥστε οὐδὲ λυσσῶντες
ἐπαύσαντο, ἕως ἐπιστοιβάσαντες ἑαυτῶν τὴν κακίαν καὶ
συστήσαντες τὴν πονηρίαν καὶ κρατύναντες τὴν μιαιφο-
νίαν, ἐξήλασαν τῆς ποίμνης τὸν ἅγιον, τέλος τοῦτο τῶν

were brought up in purity, with all sorts of filthy, coarse words, and with the obscenities of the marketplace; and they generally spoke in the way of treacherous lips that remain unclean at all times. For can a profane tongue, brought up on shameful habits and words, ever utter something holy and harmonious? It is easier, I think, for a fragrant odor to waft forth from a rotting grave than for a filthy throat to utter a fragrant and sweet word. However, nothing of all this disturbed the saint. He only felt pain in his soul and was rent asunder by the unrestrained and blind malice of those men, since he loved God and his fellow men. He learned to seek not only his own profit, but burned with anxiety for the salvation of his brethren too. He was as troubled by the laughter of those ridiculous, rather ludicrous young men, and their immodest mockery and jokes, as an Indian elephant is troubled by a mosquito. In fact, he rather prided himself on them and beautified himself, since he believed that they gave him the opportunity to conduct himself like a philosopher.

12

But anger led those delirious and wicked men to such a pitch of madness that they would not stop their rabid behavior until they managed to remove the saint from his bishopric, by piling up their villainies, contriving wickedness, and strengthening their murderous ranks. They

πολέμων ἐκείνων τῶν πολλῶν θέμενοι, ὅμοιον οἶμαί τι ποιήσαντες, ὥσπερ εἰ καὶ παῖδες ὑβρισταὶ καὶ ἀτάσθαλοι ἐς
τὸν σφῶν αὐτῶν πατέρα ἐκτραχυνθεῖεν καὶ ἐκποδὼν
θεῖναι βουλεύσαιντο τὰς πατρικὰς ἐπιπλήξεις ὡς μάστιγάς
τινας βαρυτάτας καὶ ὡς πληγὰς τοὺς ἐλέγχους καὶ ὡς
τομὰς τὰς ἐπιτιμίας οἰόμενοι, κἀντεῦθεν αὐταῖς ἐκείναις
τὸν σωφρονιστὴν τοῦ βίου καὶ τῶν καλλίστων διδάσκαλον ἀποσκευαζόμενοι.

2   Τί δέ, βάρβαρον μὲν ὀφθαλμὸν ἀρετὴ ἀνδρὸς εἴωθε
κατακλᾶν καὶ εἰς ἡμερότητα μετάγειν, ἐκείνους δὲ οὐκ
ἔμελλεν αἰδοῖ κατακάμπτειν ὁ πολὺς ταύτην Θεόκλητος;
Ἀμέλει καὶ τοῦ πνεύματος τῆς ὀργῆς λήξαντος, ὡς ἐν
γαλήνῃ λογισμῶν γεγονότες, συνῆκαν οἷον ἔργον διεπρά-
ξαντο καὶ ὅπως ὠμὸν καὶ ὅπως θηριῶδες, καὶ τοῖς τῆς
μεταμελείας εὐθὺς ἐβάλλοντο βέλεσι καὶ σφοδροὶ ἦσαν
τὴν μετάνοιαν, καὶ ὑφ' ἑνὶ συνθήματι συνελθόντες, ἱκέται
προσέπιπτον ἐλεεινοί, γονάτων ἐκείνου τῶν ἱερῶν καὶ
ποδῶν ἁπτόμενοι, λυθῆναι μὲν αὐτοῖς ἐξαιτούμενοι τὸ
ἁμάρτημα, ἐπανελθεῖν δὲ αὖθις αὐτὸν εἰς τὸ οἰκεῖον ποίμνιον (ἃ δὴ καὶ ἀμφότερα πεπείκασι τὴν φιλάρετον ἐκείνην καὶ ἀμνησίκακον ψυχήν), ἀληθῆ μετάνοιαν ἐπιδειξά-
μενοι. Καὶ πῶς γὰρ οὐκ ἔμελλον, εἰ μὴ λιθίνην εἶχον τὴν
σκληρότητα, εἰ μὴ θῆρες ἦσαν, εἰ μὴ φύσις τις τῶν ἀνθρώπων ὑπερόριος; Ὅπου γὰρ ὄψις ἀνδρὸς θεοφορήτου καὶ
θηρίων ἀπήνειαν κάμπτειν εἴωθε, ἡμεροῦν καὶ πραΰνειν
καὶ εἰς προβάτων μεταβάλλειν ἀτεχνῶς ἐπιείκειαν, πῶς
ἔμελλον ἀνίατον ἔχειν τὴν ἀπόνοιαν, οἱ καὶ Χριστὸν
ἐπεγνωκότες καὶ ὁσημέραι τηλικαύτης ἀρετῆς θεαταὶ

considered this the end of those many wars, behaving, in my opinion, like wicked and reckless children who become exasperated with their father and conceive the idea of ridding themselves of his paternal reproaches, because they regard his rebukes as akin to grievous floggings, his censures as physical blows, and his punishments as cuts to the flesh. Thus they manage to free themselves from all these things and also from him who moderated their life and taught them what was best for them.

But what happened next? If virtue can soften even the glare of a barbarian, transforming him into a civilized man, was it possible for them not to bend the knee to the great virtue that Theokletos possessed? After their spirited anger abated and their thoughts calmed down, they realized what a cruel and brutal crime they had committed, and they were immediately struck by the arrows of repentance. Full of remorse, they gathered together by agreement and prostrated themselves before him as his pitiable suppliants. They clasped his holy knees and feet, asking him to forgive them their trespasses and return to his own flock. They managed to persuade that virtuous and forgiving soul to fulfill both these wishes, since the repentance they showed was sincere. And how could it have been otherwise, unless they were as hard as rocks, or were wild beasts, or their nature was situated beyond the bounds of humanity? For the visage of a man of God may calm even the ferocity of wild beasts, appeasing and taming them and making them gentle as sheep. How, then, would it have been possible for them to go on behaving like incurable madmen? After all, they were Christians and beheld on a daily basis such virtue, which God

γενόμενοι, ἦν καὶ Θεὸς τοῖς ἰδίοις ἔστελλε χαρίσμασι;
Κατεπλούτισε γὰρ καὶ τοῦτον ὡς οἰκεῖον αὐτοῦ θεράποντα μεγάλαις καὶ ἀξίαις τῆς ἐκείνου πρὸς αὐτὸν ἀγάπης
δωρεαῖς καὶ τοῖς θαύμασιν αὐτὸν κατεκάλλυνε καὶ τὴν
ἀρετὴν ἀνεκήρυξεν.

13

Εἰ δὲ δεῖ τι καὶ τῶν θαυμάτων εἰπεῖν εἰς σαφῆ τῆς ἐνοι-
κούσης τῷ ἁγίῳ χάριτος μαρτυρίαν καὶ φανέρωσιν, ἑνὸς ἢ
δύο τῶν τῷ μεγάλῳ διαπραχθέντων ἐπιμνησθέντες, ὅσον
ἐκ τοῦ κρασπέδου φασὶ δεῖξαι τὸ ὕφασμα, ἐκ τούτων καὶ τὰ
λοιπὰ ταῖς πισταῖς καὶ φιλοκάλοις ψυχαῖς κατανοεῖν δώσομεν. Καιρὸς ἐνειστήκει τοῦ θέρους καὶ αἱ ἄρουραι μεσταὶ
τῶν ληΐων καὶ τοὺς ὁρῶντας εὐφραίνουσαι τῷ θεάματι.
Ἀλλὰ δὴ καὶ γεωργὸς τὴν ἄρπην ἤδη παρέθηγε καὶ τὴν
ἅλω ὠνειροπόλει καὶ τὰ σιτοδοχεῖα ἐξεκάθηρε, μονονουχὶ
τὸν σωρὸν τῶν ἀγαθῶν ἐν χερσὶν ἔχειν φανταζόμενος καὶ
γλυκείαις βλέπων ἐλπίσι καὶ μηδὲν πλέον ἐνδέον τὸ τῆς
εὐτυχίας ἢ ἄχρι δρεπάνης καὶ ἅλωνος εἶναι οἰόμενος. Ἀλλ'
ὁ μὲν καλοῖς οὕτως ἔβλεπεν ὄμμασι καὶ ἀποθήκας περι-
ενόει καὶ σίτου ταμιεῖα καὶ εὐθηνίας θάλασσαν, οὐκ ᾔδει
δὲ τοῦτο δὴ τὸ θρυλλούμενον, ὅτι πολλὰ μεταξὺ κύλικος
καὶ χείλεος <ἄκρου>. Οὐ πολὺ γὰρ τὸ ἐν μέσῳ καὶ ἀκρίδων
νέφος, ἀριθμοῦ τε ἅμα καὶ ὀφθαλμοῦ ἐκφεῦγον κατάληψιν, τοῖς ληΐοις ἐπικαταπτάν, χαλεπὸν θέαμα θεῖναι τὰς

himself had endowed with his own gifts. As the saint was his own servant, God enriched him with great endowments, worthy of his own love for him, adorned him with the grace of wonderworking, and proclaimed his virtue everywhere.

13

If, moreover, it is necessary for me to speak about his miracles so as to provide a clear testimony and proof of the grace dwelling within the saint, I will mention one or two that were performed by that great man, just enough to reveal the quality of *the robe from its hem*. Through them we will allow the faithful and those who love the good to infer the rest. Summer had arrived and the fields were filled with grain, a sight gladdening to onlookers. The farmer was sharpening his sickle and dreaming of the threshing. He was cleaning out the granaries, imagining that he already had a good harvest in his hands. He was full of sweet hopes and thought that nothing was needed for his happiness beyond a sickle and threshing floor. But gazing at them full of happiness, imagining granaries and storerooms full of grain and, so to speak, an ocean of prosperity, he was unaware of the proverb *there's many a slip between the cup and the lip*. Shortly thereafter, a cloud of locusts, immeasurable in number, greater than our eyes can see, fell upon the harvest. They were soon to transform those beautiful, rich, and fruitful

καλὰς ἐκείνας καὶ λιπαρὰς καὶ εὐκάρπους ἔμελλε πεδιά-
δας, ἀκαλλεῖς ἐξαίφνης ἀποδεικνυμένας καὶ τὴν οἰκείαν
ἀποκειραμένας εὐπρέπειαν, οὐ χερσὶ γηπόνων ἀλλ᾽ ἀγρί-
οις στόμασι περιτεμνομένας, οὐδὲ εἰς ἅλω συναγομένας,
ἀλλ᾽ εἰς φθορὰν ἀπερχομένας, εἰ μὴ τοῦ καλοῦ ποιμένος ἡ
ταχεῖα ἔφθασε βοήθεια.

2   Καὶ ὅρα τὸν τρόπον. Καὶ οὗτος γὰρ καὶ ἀκοῇ ἥδιστος
καὶ γλώττῃ φθεγγομένῃ γλυκύτατος. Ὁμοῦ γὰρ ἤκουσε
τὴν τοῦ πονηροῦ ἔθνους ἐπέλευσιν, καὶ οἷος ἐκεῖνος εἰς
ἔλεον θερμὸς καὶ ἀνυπέρθετος, παρευθὺ δίδωσιν ἀντὶ
παντὸς ἄλλου βοηθήματος τὴν οἰκείαν ῥάβδον εἰς ἄμυναν
καὶ ἵστησι τὴν ἀπὸ τῶν ἀκρίδων μάστιγα. Ἅμα γὰρ ἐνε-
πάγη πρὸ τῶν κακῶς θεριζομένων ληΐων ἡ ῥάβδος καὶ
ἀφανὴς ἦν ὁ ἀφανίζων ἐκεῖνος καὶ ὀλοθρεύων στρατὸς καὶ
εἰς μάστιγα ἡμῶν τῶν ἀνεπαίσθητα πταιόντων ἐπιπεμπό-
μενος, τοῖς δὲ γεωργοῖς πάλιν ἐλύετο τὰ σκυθρωπὰ καὶ
πάλιν ἦσαν ἐν χαρᾷ καὶ ταῖς πρότερον ἐνετρύφων εὐθυμί-
αις καὶ τοὺς οἰκείους καμάτους μεθ᾽ ἡδονῆς ἔβλεπον, οὓς
ἤδη ἀποδύρεσθαι παρεσκευάζοντο, καὶ οἱ ὕμνοι ἤδοντο
θερμοὶ καὶ εὐχαριστίαι συχναὶ αἱ μὲν Θεῷ, αἱ δὲ τῷ τούτου
θεράποντι.

fields into a wretched spectacle: they suddenly became ugly, stripped of their comeliness not by the hands of farmers, but cut down by the wild mouths of the locusts. That good harvest was not to be transferred to the threshing floor but was gone to ruin. The good pastor, however, rushed to their aid.

Look at how it happened: it is very pleasant to hear, but an even sweeter pleasure for the tongue to tell it. As soon as he heard of the attack of that frightful horde, his compassion became ardent and immediate, and without delay he offered no other help but his own staff as a weapon against them and stopped the plague of the locusts: as soon as he plunged his staff into the soil in front of the wheat that was being destroyed, that destructive and harmful army disappeared. It had been sent as a plague upon us who sinned without realizing it. The sorrow of the farmers disappeared once more, they were joyful again, and their former high spirits were restored to them; they looked upon their harvest labors full of joy, although just before they were ready to mourn their loss. Filled with ardor, they sang hymns and many prayers of thanksgiving both to God and his servant.

14

Κ̀αὶ ἕτερον δὲ ἡμῖν ὁ λόγος διεξιέτω τῆς ἐπισυνούσης τῷ Θεοκλήτῳ θείας χάριτος ἐναργὲς γνώρισμα. Γυνή τις, Λάκαινα τὸ γένος, πενιχρὰ τὴν τύχην, ἀνδρὶ συνοικήσασα ἰδιώτην ἕλκοντι βίον, ἀφαιρεθεῖσα δὲ καὶ τοῦτον, οἷα τὰ τοῦ Θεοῦ κρίματα, ὑπέμενε μὲν τὰ τῆς χηρείας δυσχερῆ, ἐπορίζετο δὲ τὰ πρὸς τὸ ζῆν ἀναγκαιότατα ταῖς οἰκείαις χερσί, πρὸς ἃς μόνας μετὰ Θεὸν ἑώρα, καὶ ἀνδρὸς ἔρημος καὶ συγγενείας πάσης καὶ βοηθείας. Ἀλλ᾽ ὦ τῆς τοῦ Δαίμονος ἐπηρείας. Βάσκανον ἐπιβάλλει τῷ γυναίῳ ὀφθαλμόν, ὁρῶν φέρουσαν γενναίως καὶ εὐχαρίστως τὰ τῆς χηρείας λυπηρὰ καὶ τῶν χειρῶν θατέραν (ἡ δεξιὰ δὲ αὕτη ἦν), διαφθείρει, φεῦ, καὶ πάρετον ποιεῖ, καὶ μὴ ὅτι ἄχρηστον, ἀλλὰ καὶ ἀκίνητον. Ἡ δὲ ὁρῶσα τὰς πρὸς τὸ ζῆν αὐτῇ περικλεισθείσας ἀφορμὰς καὶ τὴν μόνην καὶ πρώτην καὶ τελευταίαν τοῦ βίου παραμυθίαν διαπεσοῦσαν καὶ φορτίον, φεῦ, περιττὸν τὴν τροφὸν χεῖρα γεγονυῖαν, βάλλεται πολλῇ τῇ ἀθυμίᾳ καὶ πλήττεται τὴν ψυχὴν λύπῃ δεινῇ καὶ πρὸς οὐδὲν ἢ δάκρυα καὶ στεναγμοὺς νύκτες καὶ ἡμέραι ἀνηλοῦντο τῇ γυναικί. Οἰμωγαὶ νύκτωρ, οἰμωγαὶ μεθ᾽ ἡμέραν, καὶ οὔτε ἥλιος φαιδρὸς ἀναλάμπων γλυκὺς ἐκείνῃ καὶ ἥδιστος, οὔτε ὁ τῆς εὐνῆς καὶ τοῦ ὕπνου καιρὸς καθαρὸν ἐκείνῃ δακρύων ἐτίθει τὸ κλινίδιον. Ὠδύρετο τὴν μόνωσιν, τὴν τοῦ συζύγου στέρησιν, τὸ τελευταῖον καὶ πρῶτον ἀνιαρόν, τὴν τῆς χειρὸς πάρεσιν.

14

Let my account mention another miracle, yet clearer proof of the divine grace possessed by Theokletos. A poor woman, who was a native of Lakonia, lived together with a man of private station, but she lost him too, for such was God's decision. Thus she suffered the hardships of widowhood, earning the necessities of life with her own hands. Those hands were her only hope after God, since she had no husband, no relatives at all, no other assistance. But how wicked is the Devil! His eye, full of envy, turned upon the woman. He saw her enduring the hardships of widowhood with patience and grace, so he injured one of her hands, the right one, paralyzing it. Alas, she was not only unable to use her hand, she could not even move it. The woman realized that the only way of earning her living and her only, foremost, and last consolation in life was lost, and that her hand which had fed her had now become a useless burden. She was stricken with despondency and her soul was attacked by terrible sorrow. She spent her days and nights doing nothing else but weeping and groaning. She cried all night long, she cried all day long. The sunrise was not a sweet and happy sight for her, nor was the time for going to bed and sleeping pleasant for her, as it meant that she would wash her bed with tears. She bewailed her loneliness, the loss of her husband, and that which was her last and foremost misfortune, the paralysis of her hand.

2 Ὡς δέ ποτε μικρὸν τοῦ πένθους ἀνένευσε καὶ περιεσκόπει εἴ πού τι περιλέλειπται ζώπυρον ἀγαθῆς ἐλπίδος, βάλλεται κατὰ νοῦν τὸν κοινὸν τῶν θλιβομένων λιμένα, τὸν ὀξὺν εἰς βοήθειαν καὶ θερμὸν εἰς ἀντίληψιν, τὸν θεῖόν φημι Θεόκλητον, καὶ παρὰ τοῦτον ἀμελλητὶ προσελθοῦσα, τὰς οἰκείας ἐκτραγῳδεῖ συμφορὰς καὶ περιπαθεῖ ἄγαν καὶ περιωδύνῳ ψυχῇ ἄμα καὶ φωνῇ καὶ ὀφθαλμοῖς τετηκόσι προσβλέψασα τά τε τῶν δακρύων ῥεῖθρα ποταμηδὸν ἐκκενοῦσα κατὰ τῶν προσώπων, "Ἴδε," φησί, "τοῦ Θεοῦ ἄνθρωπε, ἴδε δυστυχὲς γύναιον καὶ ἴσως δαίμονός τινος παίγνιον. Ἴδε μου τὴν τῆς ψυχῆς ὀδύνην, δοῦλε τοῦ Θεοῦ," ἔλεγεν. "Οἴμοι, ὅτι γυνὴ γέγονα διήγημα γυναιξὶν ἄθλιον, οἶμαι δὲ καὶ ἀνδράσιν. Οἴμοι, ὅτι ἐνεχόρευσεν ἐν ἐμοὶ ἡ τῶν κακῶν Ἰλιὰς καὶ πᾶσάν μοι περιεῖλεν ὁ βίος παραμυθίαν. Οὐκ ἀνδρὸς κηδεμονία φίλην μοι ποιεῖ τὴν ζωήν, οὐ παιδὸς ὀφθαλμὸς κουφίζει μου τὰς συμφοράς, οὐ πρὸς γένους τις ὑπολέλειπται, ὥστε τούτῳ μόνῳ προσανακλαίειν τὴν πολλὴν συντριβὴν τῆς ψυχῆς καὶ τοῦ σώματος, ἀλλὰ πολλὰ μὲν τὰ τῶν λυπηρῶν κύματα, οὐδὲν δὲ καταφύγιον, πολλὴ ἡ θάλασσα τῶν ἀνιαρῶν, οὐδεὶς ὁ λιμήν."

3 Εἶτα καὶ ταῦτα τὰ τῆς γραφῆς ἐπισυνείρων, "Ἵνα τί μοι ἀπήντησε γόνατα, ἵνα τί δὲ μαστοὺς ἐθήλασα; Νῦν ἂν κοιμηθεῖσα ἡσύχασα. Ἵνα τί γὰρ δέδοται τοῖς ἐν πικρίᾳ φωνή, ζωὴ δὲ ταῖς ἐν ὀδύναις ψυχαῖς, αἲ ἱμείρονται τοῦ θανάτου καὶ οὐ τυγχάνουσιν;" Ὡς ἂν δὲ ἐπὶ πλέον τὴν συμπαθῆ ἐκείνην ψυχὴν πρὸς ἔλεον καταμαλάξῃ καὶ πείσῃ μέγα τι ἐπ᾽ αὐτῇ βουλεύσασθαι καὶ διαπράξασθαι (ᾔδει γὰρ ὡς ὅσον ἐκείνῳ

After she recovered a bit from her grief, she wondered 2 whether any spark of good hope was left for her. At that point, the common haven of those in distress, I mean the holy Theokletos, the quick helper, who was most ardent to assist everyone, came to her mind. She went to him without delay and described to him her hardships in tragic tones. She looked at him, her soul and voice full of sadness and mournful, her eyes melting, and tears flowing out of them like a river. "O servant of God," she said, "look here; look at an unfortunate woman, who in all probability is the plaything of a demon. O servant of God," she kept saying, "see the distress of my soul. Alas, I was born a woman, and my story will be a miserable narrative for other women to hear, and, I think, for men as well. *An Iliad of woes* dances around me and life has deprived me of all consolation. I have no husband to take care of me, reconciling me to life, no child's eye gives me comfort in my distress, I have no relatives to whom I may tearfully lament the great distress of my soul and body. The waves of my hardships are numerous, but there is no refuge; the sea of my distress is immense, but there is no safe harbor."

She also added these words of Holy Scripture: "*Why did* 3 *knees support me? Why did I suckle at my mother's breasts? Now I should have lain down and been quiet. Why do those in distress have* a voice? *Why is life given to souls, which grieve and desire death and obtain it not?*" She was holding out her paralyzed hand, supporting it with the other one, showing it in order to make this compassionate soul pity her the more and persuade him to think about her case seriously and do something great for her, for she knew well that, although he was

τὸ συμπαθὲς καὶ ἵλεων, τοσοῦτον καὶ τὸ πρὸς τὰς ἐπιδεί-
ξεις εὐλαβὲς καὶ ἀπώμοτον), τὴν πάρετον ἐκείνην χεῖρα τῇ
ἑτέρᾳ προέφερε κουφίζουσα χειρί, ἐδημοσίευε τὸ πάθος,
τὴν νέκρωσιν ταύτης ἀπωδύρετο, ἐξετραγῴδει τὰς ἐπ'
αὐτῇ συμφοράς. Ὁ δὲ τοῦ Χριστοῦ μιμητὴς ἀψευδέστατος
οἷς τε ἑώρα οἷς τε ἤκουε διαπονηθεὶς τὴν ψυχήν, ἅμα τε
δάκρυσι κατερρεῖτο καὶ εὐθὺς πρὸς ἱκετείαν ἠγείρετο,
χεῖρας ὑπὲρ τῆς γυναικὸς ἐπαίρων καὶ θερμῶς ἐκλιπαρῶν
ἀλαλήτοις στεναγμοῖς τὸν πάντα δυνάμενον καὶ φύσει φιλάνθρωπον, ὃς ἐπέχει πολλάκις εὐεργεσίας ἐφ' ἑτέραις
εὐεργεσίαις, τιμῶν μὲν μάλιστα τὴν ἀρετήν, οὐκ ἔλαττον
δὲ νομοθετῶν τὸ φιλάλληλον.

15

Ἀλλ' ἐνταῦθα μοι τὸ τῆς διηγήσεως τερπνὸν καὶ φιλαρέτοις ἀκοαῖς ποθεινότατον. Ὁ μὲν ἄνω εἶχε τὸν νοῦν, τὴν
ψυχήν, τὰς χεῖρας, ὅλον ἑαυτὸν μετὰ τῆς εὐχῆς ἐκ γῆς
μεταιρόμενον ὁ κἂν τῇ γῇ συμπολίτης τῶν ἀγγέλων καὶ
σύσκηνος, τὰ σκυθρωπὰ δὲ τῇ γυναικὶ διελύετο καὶ δάκρυα ἀνεστέλλοντο δάκρυσιν, τοῖς τοῦ ἁγίου τὰ περὶ τὴν
γυναῖκα λιμνάζοντα. Ἐφαψάμενος γὰρ τῆς ξηρανθείσης
χειρός, ἐκείνη μὲν τὴν προτέραν εὐρωστίαν ἐπανάγει καὶ
ἀποδίδωσι, τὴν γλῶτταν δὲ τῶν μακρῶν ἐκείνων κωκυτῶν
ἀπαλλάξας, ὑμνῳδὸν εὐθὺς καὶ εὐχάριστον ἀναδείκνυσι.

compassionately merciful, he avoided and resisted all display. She publicized her suffering, bewailed the paralysis of her hand, and described her hardships in tragic tones. That most true imitator of Christ was moved deep inside his soul by what he saw and heard, and was drenched with his own tears. Immediately he was aroused to pray, raising his hands for that woman's sake, *sighing, and unable to form distinct words,* and ardently entreating the all-powerful Lord, who is compassionate by nature. Sometimes, however, God does not display his mercy, in order to leave open other opportunities to display his benefactions. In this way, he honors virtue and teaches us to love each other.

15

But here comes the most gratifying part of my story, the most dear to the ears of all who love virtue: the saint had elevated his mind, his soul, his hands, his whole self, up to heaven. He who lived on earth, yet still conversed with and cohabited with the angels, now rose up from earth together with his prayer. At the same time, the woman's sorrow disappeared, and her swelling tears were dried up by the tears of the saint. Touching her withered hand, he restored and returned its former health, relieving her tongue from all that long wailing, and making it instead offer hymns of thanks to

Πλεονάζων δὲ αὐτῇ τὰς πρὸς εὐφροσύνην τε καὶ τὴν πρὸς Θεὸν εὐχαριστίαν ἀφορμάς, καὶ χρυσῷ τὴν ἄρτι ὑγιανθεῖσαν χεῖρα βαρύνει, φίλον καὶ ἥδιστον ἐκείνῃ φορτίον ἐπιφορτίζων καὶ ἡδέως ὁρώμενόν τε καὶ αἰρόμενον, ὥσπερ ὁ Χριστὸς τὴν κλίνην τῷ παραλύτῳ δεῖγμα τῆς προτέρας ἀναρρώσεως.

2   Ἀλλὰ ταύτην μὲν εὐθύμῳ ποδὶ καὶ χειρὶ οἴκαδε ἐπανατρέχειν ἐποίει, πολλαπλῆς εὐφροσύνης κρατῆρα κερασάμενος τῇ γυναικὶ ἢ μᾶλλον εἰπεῖν τὸν ποιητικὸν ἐκεῖνον κυκεῶνα κακῶν ἐπίληθον ἁπάντων. Αὐτὸς δὲ δριμυτέρῳ τῆς θείας ἀγάπης τῷ κέντρῳ νυττόμενος, ἀνθάμιλλον ἐδείκνυ καὶ τὴν σπουδὴν καὶ τὴν καθ᾽ ἡμέραν ἐπέτεινεν ἄσκησιν, ζημίαν ὥσπερ ἡγούμενος εἴ τι τῶν ἀγαθῶν καὶ ζήλου ἀξίων λάθοι διαδραμὸν αὐτὸν ἢ μὴ εἰς ἄκρον κατορθωθὲν ἄνευ τοῦ πρὸς ἐπίδειξιν ὁρᾶν. Οἱ γὰρ δι᾽ ἐπίδειξιν πόνοι οὔτε τὸ κατορθοῦν ἀκριβῶς οὔμενουν ἔχουσι καὶ Ἑλληνικῆς ὀδώδασιν ἀπονοίας ταὐτὸν εἰπεῖν καὶ ἀπιστίας. Ὁ δὲ ἄνω τείνων τὸ ὄμμα, πρὸς τὸ θυμῆρες Θεῷ καὶ εὐάρεστον ἵστη τὴν πολιτείαν, δόξαν μὲν ἡγούμενος τὸ πάσης προσκαίρου καταπτύσαι δόξης, τρυφὴν δὲ τὸ μὴ τρυφᾶν, μηδὲ ἡδονῇ ὑποχαυνοῦσθαι, τὸν καλὸν ὄντως καὶ ἐπαινετὸν φόβον φοβούμενος, ὡς μιμητὴς τοῦ εἰπόντος, "ὑποπιέζω μου τὴν σάρκα καὶ δουλαγωγῶ, μήπως ἄλλοις κηρύξας αὐτὸς ἀδόκιμος γένωμαι."

216

God. And then, multiplying her motives for happiness and gratitude to God, he weighed down her hand, the very one that had been recently cured, with a sum of gold. That weight was most beloved and desirable by her, and resembled *the bed* that Christ ordered *the paralytic* to carry on his shoulders as a sign of his previous healing. She was very happy to see it and very happy to carry it.

The saint made her run home with happy feet and hands, 2 mixing for this woman a drink full of all kinds of joy; or, rather, he gave her that poetic potion, which *makes us forget all our sorrows.* The saint, being even more strongly incited by the stimulus of divine love, showed a competitive zeal and *intensified his asceticism on a daily basis.* If he lost some good and enviable quality without noticing it, or if he did not manage to bring it to its perfection, he considered that a great misfortune. But he did not make a display of his virtue. For hardships that are endured for the sake of display do not lead us to a perfect accomplishment of our goals. Moreover, they reek of Greek madness, which is to say a lack of faith. But the saint, raising his eyes to heaven, tried to live in a way that pleased and satisfied God. He regarded his disdain for all perishable glory as his true glory, and *his pleasure was to avoid all pleasures* and not to be puffed up by them. He felt that fear which is truly good and praiseworthy, imitating the one who said, "*I discipline* my flesh *and make it my servant, so as not to become disqualified after preaching to others.*"

16

Ἀκούετε, ὅσοι περὶ τὰς λοπάδας καὶ τὰς τραπέζας κε-
χήνατε καὶ ἕνα τοῦτον ὅρον εὐδαιμονίας ἡγεῖσθε, γαστρί-
ζεσθαι καθ᾽ ἡμέραν καὶ ἐνευπαθεῖν ταῖς ἀποπτύστοις τρυ-
φαῖς καὶ τοῖς καταργουμένοις βρώμασιν, εἶτα μηδὲν
οἰόμενοι πλημμελεῖν. Ἀπόστολοι πάντες καὶ ποιμένες καὶ
διδάσκαλοι πεφρίκασι τὴν τρυφὴν ὡς τροφὸν τῆς αἰωνίου
φλογὸς καὶ ὑποπιέζουσι τὰς σάρκας καὶ ἄγχουσι τῷ τῆς
νηστείας χαλινῷ διὰ τὸν ἐκ τῆς ἀκρασίας ἐγειρόμενον
πόλεμον, σὺ δὲ οὐδὲ ἓν εἶναι φῂς παρὰ τῆς τρυφῆς τὸ
πλημμελὲς οὐδεμίαν τὴν βλάβην, οὐ μόνον δὲ ἀλλὰ καὶ
συνευδοκεῖς τοῖς τρυφῶσι, βέβηλος βεβήλου πράγματος
γινόμενος. <Εἰ οἱ> ὑπὲρ Χριστοῦ κινδύνοις ἐνομιλήσαν-
τες, οἱ τοσούτου πνεύματος ἀξιωθέντες ἐν αὐτοῖς τοῖς πειρασμοῖς, οἷς καθ᾽ ἡμέραν ἐπυροῦντο καὶ ὡσανεὶ ἐχαλκεύ-
οντο ἐν αὐτῷ τῷ κοσμικῷ, ἔτι καὶ τὸν ἐκ τῆς σαρκὸς
ὑπέφριττον πόλεμον καὶ τὸν κόρον ὡς ἐπίβουλον ἐδεδοί-
κεσαν, μήπου τι καὶ κακὸν αὐτοῖς ἀναρρήξῃ καὶ χείρονα
κίνδυνον τῶν ἔξωθεν κινδύνων ἐπαγάγῃ, ἢ που ἀξιόπιστος
ἡμῖν ὁ πράγμασι βιωτικοῖς περιπνιγόμενος καὶ ὀλίγα μὲν
τῆς ψυχῆς, πλείονα δὲ τῆς σαρκὸς φροντίζων καὶ διαμε-
ριμνῶν, εἶτα καὶ χλιδῶσαν καὶ περιρρέουσαν παρατιθέμε-
νος τράπεζαν καὶ ὡς οὐδεμία τις αὐτῷ ἐκεῖθεν ἡ βλάβη
πείθειν πειρώμενος, ὅθεν ἡ πολλὴ τῶν παθῶν ἔκκαυσις καὶ
ὁ περὶ τῆς σωφροσύνης κίνδυνος, τοὺς τῆς σαρκὸς ἀναρ-
ριπίζων ἄνθρακας; Οὔμενουν οὐκ ἂν εἴποι σωφρονῶν

16

Listen to me, you who are fond of culinary dishes and banquets, you who think that happiness consists only in stuffing one's belly all day long, delighting in abominable delicacies, and enjoying useless foods. And then you believe that this behavior is not sinful! All apostles, pastors, and teachers fear luxurious pleasure as a cause of the eternal hell fire, and so they subdue their flesh and squeeze it through fasting, in order to avoid the war caused by our immoderate desires. You say, however, that there is not a single sin at all to be found in excessive pleasure, that it does no harm, and you go so far as to give your approval to those who indulge in luxury, thus becoming an enabler of the unrestrained. Those men who ran such great risks for the sake of Christ, who were deemed worthy of that great spirit in the midst of their temptations, which burned them up like fire everyday as they were being forged, so to speak, upon the anvil of this world, they were afraid of the war that is caused by our flesh too. They also feared lest satiety, which is insidious, do them harm too, bringing them into a danger worse than those that come from the outside. Accordingly, a man who is immersed in the affairs of this life, who cares little for his soul and more for his flesh, cannot be trustworthy. When he prepares a luxurious and abundant table and tries to persuade us that he will not suffer any harm from all that, which naturally excites the passions, he endangers moderation and rekindles the fires of the flesh. No prudent man who is an

ἄνθρωπος καὶ κριτὴς ἀληθείας ἀδέκαστος, εἰ μή τις ἐξ-
απατᾶν ἑαυτὸν ἐθέλοι ἢ παίζειν κατὰ τῆς ἰδίας κεφαλῆς,
ἀπιθάνοις ψυχαγωγῶν ἑαυτὸν ῥήμασιν, ἐπειδὴ ὁ ταῖς φι-
ληδόνοις μαγγανείαις καταγοητευθεὶς δυσαπάλλακτον
τρέφει τὴν φαύλην συνήθειαν καὶ τῆς γαστρὸς δεσπόζειν
οὐ βούλεται. Οὐκοῦν χαλινὸς αὐστηροτέρας ἀγωγῆς πᾶσι
πιστοῖς τὰ τῆς σαρκὸς ἐγκοπτέτω σκιρτήματα καὶ ῥυθμιζέτω τὰς αἰσθήσεις, ὑποζευγνὺς αὐτὰς τῷ καλῶς ἄγοντι
λογισμῷ.

2   Εἴπερ εὐσεβῶς μεμαθήκατε ὡς ἡ τῆς βασιλείας τῶν
οὐρανῶν εἴσοδος στενὴ οὖσα καὶ θλιβερὰ ταῖς παχείαις
σαρξὶ καὶ πολυσάρκοις πάροδον οὐ δίδωσι, μᾶλλον δὲ καὶ
τὸν θεῖον ἀναλογιζόμενοι Θεόκλητον, ὥσπερ τῷ λόγῳ πάλαι, χρᾶσθε τῷ βίῳ νῦν ὁδηγῷ πρὸς ἐγκράτειαν, ὡς ἂν
κἀκεῖνος ἐν τῇ τῆς ἀνταποδόσεως ἡμέρᾳ ἐπὶ τῷ οἰκείῳ
ποιμνίῳ φαιδρὸς καὶ γεγηθὼς ὄρῷτο καὶ περὶ τὸν Κριτὴν
ἐστὼς βοᾷ παρρησίᾳ, "Οὓς δέδωκάς μοι ἐφύλαξα εἰς γενεὰς καὶ γενεὰς καὶ οὐδεὶς ἐξ αὐτῶν ἀπώλετο." Μηδὲ εἴη
τις ἀπωλείας υἱός, λάβοι δὲ πάντας ἡ δεξιὰ στάσις καὶ οἱ
τοῦ πατριάρχου Ἀβραὰμ κόλποι ταῖς τοῦ μεγάλου Θεοκλήτου πρεσβείαις, ὃς πολλὰς μὲν ὑπὲρ ἡμῶν νύκτας ἄγρυ-
πνος διετέλεσε, πολλὰ δὲ κατήνεγκε δάκρυα, πᾶσαν μὲν
τρυφὴν ἄλλην διωθούμενος καὶ ἀποπεμπόμενος, μίαν δὲ
καὶ ταύτην ἀδάπανον ἀνθαιρούμενος, τὴν ἐπίμονον τῶν
θείων γραφῶν ἀνάπτυξιν καὶ τὴν τῶν ἐν αὐτοῖς νοημάτων
μετὰ τοῦ Πνεύματος ἔρευναν, ἐξ ἧς τὸν τῆς ψυχῆς
ὀφθαλμὸν τηλαυγέστερον ἀπεδείκνυ θείαις θεωρίαις

impartial judge of the truth would agree with him, unless he wants to trick himself and risk his own life, deceiving himself with specious arguments. A man who is bewitched by pleasurable charms cannot easily liberate himself from that bad habit, and refuses to control his stomach. Therefore, a harsher bridle is necessary, which will tame the passions of the flesh for all the faithful and properly adjust their sensory perceptions by placing them under the control of their mind, which guides them correctly.

If, being pious persons, you have learned that the entrance leading into the kingdom of heaven is narrow, full of sorrow, and does not permit those who are fat and fleshy to pass through, or rather if you keep in mind the example of holy Theokletos, then use his life as a guide to continence, just as you used his words in the past. In this way, you will see him being joyful and happy on behalf of his flock on the day of the Last Judgment. Standing near the Judge, he will say with confidence, "I protected those whom you gave to me unto eternity, and none of them was lost." I hope none of them is a *son of perdition*. I wish them all to stand on the right-hand side and repose in *the bosom of* the patriarch *Abraham* through the intercessions of the great Theokletos, who kept vigil for our sake during many nights, shedding many tears, and avoiding and rejecting all other pleasures. His only relief, which cost nothing, was the constant study of the Holy Scriptures, exploring their meaning through the help of the Spirit. In this way, the eye of his soul became far-seeing, raised up and beautified by the contemplation of

2

ὑψούμενόν τε καὶ ὡραϊζόμενον καὶ τὸ τῆς διδασκαλίας νᾶμα δαψιλέστερον ἐπλούτει.

3 Ἄριστον μὲν γὰρ ὡς ἀληθῶς καὶ τὸ διαθρύπτειν τὸν ἐφήμερον ἄρτον τοῖς χρῄζουσι, μέγα δὲ τῷ ὄντι καὶ ἐπιεικῶς θειότατον τὸ διαθρέψαι ψυχὰς λιμῷ θείων λογίων ἐκτακείσας καὶ πρὸς τὸ τῆς ζωῆς ὕδωρ χειραγωγῆσαι καὶ ποτίσαι ταύτας καὶ ἀνθηροτέρας θεῖναι, τὸ τῶν παθῶν δύσμορφον ἀποτιναξαμένας ὥσπερ αὐχμηρίαν τινὰ ἐπιπολάζουσαν ταύταις. Ὅπερ ὁ μέγας Θεόκλητος ἔργον εἶχε διηνεκὲς καὶ ἀδιάλειπτον, τρέφων μὲν καὶ τὰ σώματα τῶν δεομένων ὥσπερ Ἰωσὴφ ὁ τῆς σωφροσύνης ὀφθαλμός, ἀφθόνῳ χειρὶ καὶ δαψιλεστέραις διαδόσεσι, τὸ πλέον δὲ αὐτῷ τῆς σπουδῆς περὶ τὰς ἐμπιστευθείσας ψυχὰς ἵστατο καὶ ἀέννιαος τῶν ἡδέων ἐκείνων ἀπέρρει χειλέων ὁ κρουνὸς καὶ οἱ τῆς ἁγνείας ἔπαινοι πολλοὶ καὶ ἡ ἐπ' αὐτὴν προτροπὴ πλείων. Ἐνομοθετεῖτο τὸ φιλάλληλον, ἡ ὁμόνοια, ἡ σύμπνοια, τὸ μέτριον, τὸ συμπαθές, τὸ φιλόπτωχον, τὸ γνήσιον τῆς ἀγάπης καὶ ἄδολον, τὸ ἀμνησίκακον. Παρήνει γοῦν μὴ δυσκαταλλάκτους εἶναι τοῖς παροξύνασι, μηδὲ ἐπίμονον τρέφειν τὸ βαρύμηνι, ἀλλ' εἰ δυνατόν, προφθάνοντας τὴν ὀργὴν διαλλάττεσθαι, εἰ δ' οὖν, ἀλλὰ μὴ μακρῦναι τὴν διάστασιν, μηδὲ κατήγορον τῆς ἀμαλάκτου φρενὸς καὶ ἀγρίας ψυχῆς καταδῦναι τὸν ἥλιον, μηδὲ ζημιοῦν ἑαυτὸν μηδένα, πᾶσαν δέησιν καὶ εὐχὴν καὶ νηστείαν ἐν μνησικακίᾳ βδελυκτὴν προσφέροντα τῷ Θεῷ καὶ ἀπόβλητον.

things divine, and the streams of his teaching flowed more copiously.

True, it is an excellent thing to give daily bread to those 3 who need it, but it is much more important and really divine to nourish those souls who are wasted with hunger for the words of God, to lead them toward *the water of life,* water them, and make them blossom, after stripping off the ugly passions that lie on the surface like a desiccation. This was the great Theokletos's constant, unending concern: to feed the bodies of those in need with a generous hand and abundant portions, as did Joseph, that paragon of moderation, but above and beyond that his concern was for the welfare of the souls entrusted to him. Streams of words flowed from his sweet lips continuously and he praised purity continually, exhorting the people to be pure. He taught them brotherly love, concord and harmony, moderation and compassion, love of the poor, sincere and unpretentious love, and forgiveness of past injuries. He urged them not to resist reconciliation with those who irritated them and not to nurture grievous wrath continuously. It was better, if possible, to be reconciled with their enemies before becoming angry; at any rate, they should not postpone reconciliation. We should not allow the setting sun to witness and indict our unyielding mind and savage soul. We should not do any harm to ourselves, since all prayers, vows, and fasts are abominable to God and worthless in the midst of our vindictiveness.

17

Ταῦτ' οὖν ἐνουθέτει καὶ παράδειγμα ἐξ ὑπογύου τὸν οἰκεῖον παρείχετο βίον, μήτε τινὶ τὴν ἔχθραν διατηρῶν, μήτε ὅλως ἐχθραίνων, εἰ μήπου πρὸς σωφρονισμὸν τῶν ἀδιόρθωτα πταιόντων σχηματίσαιτο τὸν ὀργιζόμενον καὶ χαλεπαίνοντα. Ἀλλὰ καὶ τῆς ἐλεημοσύνης εἰσηγητής, καὶ σιγῶν πολλάκις, ὑπῆρξεν ἀσίγητος, ἄφθονον οὕτω ῥέων τὴν πρὸς τοὺς πένητας εὐποιΐαν, ὡς μηδὲ καιρὸν παρατρέχειν τινὸς εὐεργεσίας ἀμέτοχον καὶ πλείω σχεδὸν τοῖς ἔργοις διδάσκειν ἢ τοῖς ῥήμασι. Τί δέ, οὕτως ὢν πρὸς ἔλεον ταχύς, οὕτως εὐμετάδοτος καὶ τὴν χεῖρα δαψιλὴς καὶ τὸ φιλάνθρωπον μεγαλόδωρος, ἔπαθέ τι ἀνθρώπινον καὶ ἐνηβρύνετο ταῖς τηλικαύταις μεγαλοψυχίαις καὶ ἐπιδόσεσιν ἢ τὸ φιλότιμον τῆς χειρὸς ἐξεπόμπευεν ἢ μακαριζόμενος ἐπὶ τούτῳ ὑπεχαυνοῦτο τοῖς ἐγκωμίοις; Οὔμενουν, ἀλλ' ὥσπερ αἰσχύνην νομίζων τουτονὶ τὸν μακαρισμὸν ἢ μᾶλλον παγίδα τοῖς ποσὶ καὶ βάραθρον κατασπῶν ἐφ' ἑαυτὸ τοὺς μὴ προσέχοντας, ἐδίδου μὲν ἐλευθέρᾳ χειρὶ καὶ ἐσκόρπιζεν ἀφθόνως τὸν πλοῦτον καὶ ἀφειδῶς, οὐ μὴν ἐνελαμπρύνετο ταῖς πτωχοτροφίαις καὶ φιλοξενίαις καὶ τοῖς πολυωνύμοις τῆς φιλοθεΐας γνωρίσμασιν, οὐδ' ἀνελεύθερόν τι καὶ μικροπρεπὲς ἐπὶ τούτοις ἐφθέγξατο, ὥσπερ οἱ ἐπίδειξιν τὴν δοκοῦσαν μεγαλοψυχίαν ποιούμενοι καὶ παραπολλύντες ἢ τὸ πᾶν τῆς ἄνω μισθαποδοσίας ἢ τά γε πλείονα.

17

Those were his admonitions, offering his own life as an immediate model. He did not bear anybody malice, nor was he anyone's enemy, unless he was pretending to be angry and hostile so as to chasten those who sinned irremediably. He advocated mercy and could not be silenced in this endeavor, even though he often remained silent. Streams of generous beneficence for the poor poured out from him. In fact, he never let time pass him by without doing acts of benefaction, and he almost taught more through his deeds than through his speech. He was so quick to show mercy, so charitable with his generous hand, and so liberal and loving toward mankind, but did he ever, being human, commit a sin in this respect? I mean, did he ever boast of his benefactions and benevolence, did he ever show off the liberality of his hand? Was he ever conceited because of the praises that he earned for this behavior? Never. He considered all those praises shameful, or rather as a trap for his feet, a cleft into which would tumble all who were not careful. He gave liberally and distributed his wealth lavishly and unstintingly, but he did not boast of feeding the poor, of his hospitality, and of his many other demonstrations of love for God. He never uttered an illiberal or petty word, as do those who make their supposed benefactions a cause for display, thereby losing the greater part or even the whole of their heavenly reward.

2 Ἔμελε δὲ αὐτῷ διαφερόντως τῆς τῶν ἀδελφῶν εὐδοκι-
μήσεως, καὶ τῷ καλῷ τούτῳ πυρὶ ἐκκαιόμενος, τοὺς μὲν
εὐδοκιμοῦντας ἐπ᾽ ἀρετῇ καὶ τὴν ἀγαθὴν ἅμιλλαν ἁμιλλω-
μένους ὑπερφέρειν τοῖς τῆς φιλοθέου πολιτείας προτερή-
μασιν ἐφίλει τε καὶ ἡδέως ἑώρα καὶ προσεπτέρου τούτοις
τὸ πρόθυμον, τοὺς δὲ χαυνοτέρους τὴν ψυχὴν καὶ μαλακώτερον ἔχοντας ὑπέθηγε μελιγλώττοις τισὶ παραινέσεσι
πρὸς εὐσεβῆ ζῆλον καὶ ἔνθεον καὶ πολλὴν ἐπὶ τούτοις
εἰσήγετο τὴν σπουδὴν καὶ ἐπίτασιν, κέντρον ὢν διηνεκὲς
καὶ ἐπίμονον, ὑπονύσσων καὶ ἀνεγείρων πρὸς τὴν τῆς ψυχῆς ἐπιμέλειαν, "Ἀδελφοί," λέγων, "ἐκεῖνο μετὰ τῶν ἄλλων
ὑμῖν ἔστω ἀνεπίληστον, ὥστε μηδένα τὸ ἑαυτοῦ ζητεῖν
συμφέρον, ἀλλὰ τὸ τοῦ πλησίον ἕκαστον. Ἴσως βαρὺ δο-
κεῖ τὸ ἐπίταγμα καὶ ἐπαχθές, ἀποστερῆσαι ἑαυτὸν καὶ
βρώματος καὶ πόματος, ὥστε θρέψαι τὸν πεινῶντα, γυμνη-
τεῦσαι, ὥστε ἐνδῦσαι τὸν γυμνητεύοντα, παραδοῦναι ἑαυτὸν εἰς πῦρ, εἰς μάστιγας, εἰς δεσμά, ὥστε ἐλευθερῶσαι τὸν
ἐπὶ τούτοις κατάκριτον. Ταῦτα καὶ ἀκοῦσαι χαλεπόν, καὶ
ὑπουργῆσαι χαλεπώτερον.

3 "Ἀλλ᾽ οὐκ ἐμὸν τὸ ἐπίταγμα, Παύλου δέ, ἐγὼ δὲ τὸ κου-
φότατον ἐπιτάττω πᾶσιν ὑμῖν καὶ ἐλαφρότατον, κήδεσθαι
τῶν ἀδελφῶν ὡς ἑαυτῶν, ἀπομερίζειν ἑαυτοῖς καὶ τοῖς πέ-
νησι τὰς κτήσεις, κοινὰς ποιεῖν <ἑαυτῶν> καὶ τῶν θλιβομένων τὰς οἰκίας, προΐστασθαι τῶν καταπονουμένων ὅλῃ
προθυμίᾳ, ὅλῃ χειρί. Τί τούτων δυσχερές, τί φορτικόν;
Οὐδὲν ἀπαιτῶ τῶν ὑψηλῶν ἐκείνων καὶ μεγάλων (οἶδα τὸ
νωθρὸν ὑμῶν καὶ χαῦνον καὶ ἔκλυτον καὶ πρὸς τοῦτο

He paid great attention to the reputation of his fellow   2
men, and was definitely consumed by this good fire, namely
he loved those who had a good reputation for virtue and
who competed with their brethren in a proper way in order
to surpass them in the virtues of the God-loving life. He
looked kindly upon them and encouraged their eagerness.
He also stimulated those who were dispirited and soft with
his honeyed admonitions, urging them toward a pious zeal,
inspired by God. He instilled great zeal and intensity in
them, acting in this like a horse goad, constantly and assidu-
ously pricking them and urging them to look after their
souls. "My brethren," he said, "remember this especially
along with all the rest, that no one should seek his own
profit, but everyone must seek what is profitable for his fellow men. That commandment may seem harsh and hateful,
namely to deprive yourself of your own food, drink, and
clothing in order to feed the hungry and dress the naked,
that you must surrender yourself to be burned, whipped,
and imprisoned in order to free your brethren who have
been condemned to these punishments. Even to hear that
commandment may be very hard, and to follow it is even
harder.

"This commandment, however, is not my own, it is Paul's.   3
For my part, I urge you all to do something easier and not so
burdensome, namely to take care of your fellow men as you
take care of yourselves. Divide up your goods among yourselves and the poor. Share your homes with those in distress,
protect those who are downtrodden with all your eagerness
and strength. What is so difficult about this, or unduly
burdensome? I do not demand anything of those people
who are lofty and important, since I am well aware of your

σκοπῶν μέτρια εἰσηγοῦμαι καὶ ἄπονα καὶ παντὶ κατορ-
θωθῆναι ῥᾴδια), μᾶλλον δὲ πρὸ τῶν ἄλλων τὸ κήδεσθαι
τῆς ἀλλήλων πρὸς ἀρετὴν προκοπῆς καὶ ἐπιδόσεως, ὡς
οὐδὲν οὕτω Θεῷ περισπούδαστον ὡς ἐνάρετος βίος καὶ
θείοις θελήμασι κατηρτισμένος. Λέγεις φιλεῖν τὸν Χριστόν; Δεῖξόν σου τὸ φίλτρον, δεῖξόν σου τὸν θερμὸν
ἔρωτα. Ἀγώνισαι ὑπὲρ τῶν ἐκείνου προβάτων, ἔλασον εἰς
τὴν ἐκείνου μάνδραν χορὸν σεσωσμένον, ποίμνιον ἐκλεκτόν. Ὁδήγησον ὅσους ἂν δυνηθῇς συμβουλαῖς, παραινέσεσιν, παρακλήσεσιν, ἐπιπλήξεσιν, εἰ καὶ τούτου δεήσειε,
πάσαις ἰδέαις καὶ λόγων καὶ ἔργων.

4   "Εἰ δὲ ἑτέρους ἀδυνατεῖς προσαγαγεῖν Θεῷ, μὴ δῆτα
καὶ τῶν σῶν ἀμελήσῃς, μήτε εἰ διδάσκαλος εἶ, τῶν μαθητῶν, μήτε εἰ δεσπότης, τῶν δούλων, ἀκριβῶς εἰδὼς καὶ
πεπεισμένος ὡς αἱ τούτων πλημμέλειαι τὴν σὴν μετελεύ-
σονται ψυχὴν καὶ ποινηλατήσουσιν, εἰ παρὰ τὴν σὴν ῥα-
θυμίαν καὶ ἀμέλειαν ἐς τὰ τῆς κακίας βάραθρα ἐκτραχηλι-
σθήσονται. Ὁ γὰρ Πατὴρ ἡμῶν ὁ οὐράνιος καὶ διδάσκαλος
καὶ Δεσπότης καὶ πατέρα πατρικῶς προεστάναι τῶν παίδων ἀπαιτεῖ καὶ διδάσκαλον μᾶλλον ῥυθμίζειν ταῖς ἀρεταῖς τὸν μαθητευόμενον βούλεται ἢ προβιβάζειν πρὸς τὴν
ἄλλην παιδείαν καὶ αὔξησιν, ἀλλὰ καὶ δεσπότην πάσης
ἀρετῆς εἶναι εἰσηγητὴν καὶ διδάσκαλον τοῖς ὑπὸ τὴν αὐτοῦ χεῖρα τελοῦσιν, εἴτε δοῦλοί τινες εἶεν, εἴτε ἐλεύθεροι.

5   "Καὶ μήτοι γε σεαυτὸν ἐξαπατήσῃς, ὡς καταρρᾳθυμῶν
τῆς τῶν ὑπηρετούντων βιοτῆς, νηποινεὶ τὴν δίκην διαδρά-
σεις καὶ ἀνεύθυνος τὸ ἐπ' αὐτοῖς ἔσῃ. Ἐγώ σοι τούτου
μάρτυς ἀψευδής, ὡς οὐ μόνον τῆς ἄλλης εἰς αὐτοὺς

feebleness, frivolity, and dissolute lives. With that in mind, I give you more moderate commandments, which are not burdensome and can easily be carried out by anyone. But what is more important than anything else is concern for the progress and advancement of our brethren in virtue. More than anything else, God loves a virtuous life that is led according to his own divine wishes. Do you say that you love Christ? Then prove your love for him, show him your ardent desire, struggle on behalf of his sheep, lead into his fold the select flock of those who have been saved. Guide those whom you can by your counsels, admonitions, entreaties, and rebukes (if there is need of them too), and do so by using all manner of words and deeds.

"If you are unable to lead others to God, at least do not 4 neglect your own people—I mean your students if you are a teacher, or your slaves if you are a master. You must know and be fully convinced that if they have fallen into the clefts of villainy because of your laziness and indifference, your own soul will be prosecuted and punished for their crimes. For our heavenly Father, teacher, and Lord demands that a father protect his children in a fatherly manner; he also demands that a teacher train his students in virtue. This is more important than to advance them in the rest of their instruction and progress. He also asks the master to be a teacher and instructor of the whole of virtue to his subordinates, whether they are slaves or freemen.

"Do not delude yourself that, if you neglect your servants' 5 way of life, you will escape punishment with impunity and give no accounting to God on their behalf. I myself bear true witness to you that you will have to answer to the

ὕβρεως ὑφέξεις εὐθύνας οὐ μεμπτὰς παρὰ τῷ ἀλαθήτῳ
Κριτῇ, εἴτε κολάζων ἀφειδῶς καὶ πληγαῖς ἀμέτροις, οὐ
πλημμέλειαν διορθουμέναις, ἀλλ' ὠμότητα ψυχῆς ἐξελεγ-
χούσαις, εἴτε λιμαγχονῶν, εἴτε τῷ κρυμῷ πήγνυσθαι ὑπὸ
γυμνῷ σώματι περιορῶν, ἀλλὰ καὶ εἰ τοῖς πάθεσι ἐκδότους
αὐτοὺς φέρεσθαι παραχωρήσειας καὶ ταῖς τῆς ψυχῆς κη-
λίσι καταρρυπαίνεσθαι καὶ τῷ βορβόρῳ τῶν ἡδονῶν ἐγκυ-
λίεσθαι, οὗ μείζων οὐκ ἔστι φροντὶς καὶ περὶ οὗ πᾶς τοῦ
Σωτῆρος λόγος καὶ ἅπαν μυστήριον. Τὰ γὰρ αἵματα τούτων ἐκ τῆς σῆς ὁ ἀψευδὴς ἀπαιτήσει χειρὸς καὶ προσθήκη
σοι γενήσεται βαρυτέρας τιμωρίας τὰ τῶν οἰκετῶν
ἁμαρτήματα, κἂν τὴν σὴν πλημμελοῦντες διαλανθάνωσι
γνῶσιν. Εἰ γὰρ σπουδαίως ἐκήδου τῆς αὐτῶν ζωῆς, εἰ τὴν
ἀνήκουσαν ἐτίθης πρόνοιαν, εἰ πρὸς ἀρετῆς ἀνεβίβαζες
παραίνεσιν, οὐκ ἂν οὕτως ἦσαν πρὸς τὸ ἁμαρτάνειν πρό-
χειροι, οὐδὲ ἄνετοι ταῖς ὁρμαῖς, ἀλλὰ τὸ μὲν τοῖς λόγοις,
τὸ δὲ τοῖς φόβοις δεσμούμενοι, τὸ τῆς σωφροσύνης
ἀγαθὸν ἄσυλον διετήρουν.

6   "Σὺ δὲ ἔστιν ὅτε καὶ τῶν δούλων ἐπαισθανόμενος τὴν
ἔκθεσμον καὶ βδελυρὰν διαγωγὴν καὶ ἀναστροφήν, μεγα-
λοψυχεῖς κακῶς καὶ περιφρονεῖς ἀπευκτῶς καὶ ὑπερβαί-
νεις θεομισῶς, ἄνθρακας ἐπὶ τὴν σεαυτοῦ σωρεύων κεφα-
λήν. Φεῦ τῆς πολλῆς πωρώσεως, φεῦ τῆς παραπλήκτου
φρενός, ὡς οἰκτείρω σε, ἄθλιε, τῆς ἐκδεχομένης σε μετὰ
μικρὸν ὀργῆς, ὡς ἀποκλαίομαι τὴν ἀναισθητοῦσαν τῶν
οἰκείων συμφορῶν ἠλιθιωτάτην ψυχήν. Ἄνθρωπον ἐνεπι-
στεύθης, ἄνθρωπε, ὁμοιοπαθῆ, ὁμόδουλον, ὁμόσκηνον,
καὶ τῷ θείῳ βαπτίσματι υἱὸν ἐποίησω τοῦ ὑψίστου Θεοῦ,

infallible Judge for punishing them excessively, or beating them beyond measure in a way that does not correct their mistakes but only reveals the cruelty of your soul, for weakening them by hunger, or abandoning them naked to freeze in the cold. Beyond that, you will also be held responsible for allowing them to surrender to their passions, polluting themselves with the stains of their soul and rolling around in the filth of their desires. The Savior's teaching and the whole of his mystery are precisely about this and have no greater concern. That infallible Judge will demand an accounting for the blood of these men from your hand. The sins of your dependents will make your punishment more severe, even if you are ignorant of their crimes since, if you had seriously watched over their lives and given the requisite forethought, lifting them up to virtue through your admonitions, they would not have been so prone to committing such sins and so vulnerable to their impulses. They would have been restrained either through your words or through fear, and would have maintained the treasure of their prudence inviolate.

"And sometimes you showed false magnanimity when 6 you perceived the monstrous and heinous behavior and conduct of your servants, overlooking those sins in a criminal way and thereby sinning in a way that is abominable to God, *heaping up coals on* your own *head!* Oh, how insensibly and madly you behaved! O wretched one, I feel pity for you, since prompt wrath awaits you. I bewail that most stupid soul which is not aware of its own suffering. O man, another person was entrusted to you, who is subject to the same passions as you, a servant of God like you, who inhabits the same place as you. You made him a son of the highest God

εἶτα καταναρκῶν τῆς ἐπιμελοῦς εἰς αὐτὸν προνοίας, ποιεῖς
υἱὸν ἀπωλείας, μήτε λόγον ἐφιστῶν χαλινοῦντα, μήτε φόβον ἀνακρούοντα, ὅλως δὲ ἐφιεὶς πορνείαις αὐτὸν καὶ
ἀτίμῳ πάσῃ διαγωγῇ, εἰ βούλοιτο, καταφθείρεσθαι. Ὢ τῆς
παροίνου φρενός, ὦ τῆς ἀναλγήτου ψυχῆς!

7   "Ὡς σπαράττομαι τὰ σπλάγχνα καὶ αὐτὰ τὰ αἰσθητή-
ρια καὶ διακόπτομαι τὴν ψυχήν, μόνον ταῦτα καὶ λογιζόμενος, καὶ διὰ τὸ φιλάδελφον καὶ συγγενὲς τῆς φύσεως
καὶ συμπαθὲς τῆς οἰκειώσεως, ἐπὶ τοῖς σοῖς ὡς ἐπὶ τοῖς
ἐμοῖς ἀλγῶ, μᾶλλον δὲ ὡς πατὴρ ἀληθὴς τοῖς σοῖς ἐπιστε-
νάζω κακοῖς, προανιστορῶν ἤδη τὸ ἀφόρητόν σοι τῆς
κολάσεως, ὃ ἡ δικαία τοῦ Θεοῦ κρίσις ὑμῖν ἑτοιμάζει τοῖς
ἀνουθέτητα καὶ ἀσωφρόνιστα παραπικραίνουσι, τοῖς ποι-
οῦσι σκεύη ἀτιμίας τὰ τιμιώτατα καὶ ἀπωλείας τέκνα τοὺς
ἐπὶ σωτηρίᾳ κτηθέντας καὶ περιποιηθέντας τῷ τιμίῳ τοῦ
Σωτῆρος ἡμῶν αἵματι. Ἀλλ᾽ ὀψέποτε ἀνανήψατε, τὴν
πολλὴν ἀποθέμενοι ἀμβλυωπίαν, καὶ ἑαυτοὺς κἀκείνους
τοῦ αἰωνίου πυρὸς τῆς φοβερᾶς ἐξαρπάσατε Γεέννης, ὡς
ἔγωγε λοιπὸν τὸ ἐφ᾽ ὑμῖν ἀθῷος τε καὶ ἀνέγκλητος.

8   "Οὐ γὰρ ὑπεστειλάμην *τὴν ἐρχομένην εἰς ὑμᾶς ῥομφαίαν*
δηλῶσαι ὑμῖν. Εἴθε δέ μοι παρῆν καὶ πάντας πειθηνίους
λαβεῖν τῷ θείῳ στοιχειουμένους φόβῳ καὶ ταῖς ἀρίσταις
ἐντολαῖς ἄριστα καὶ τελειουμένους. Ἀλλ᾽ ἐπείπερ εἰπεῖν
μὲν καὶ συμβουλεῦσαι καὶ παρακαλέσαι δυνατόν, τὸ μὲν
ἐμὸν ἅπαν γέγονε, ὑμῶν δὲ ὅσαι μὲν εὐγενεῖς ψυχαὶ καὶ

through holy baptism, but afterward you neglected your responsibility toward him, transforming him into a *son of perdition*. You neither kept a tight rein on him through your speech, nor inspired him with fear. You allowed him, if he should so wish, to destroy himself through fornication and a conduct that was in all ways disgraceful. What madness, what an insensible soul!

"My guts, and even the organs of my senses, heave violently and my soul is cut into pieces, merely by thinking about all this. Since I love my brethren and am made of the same nature as you, feeling compassion because of our relationship, I feel pain for your sins as if they were mine, or, rather, like a true father I bewail your hardships, imagining in advance your unbearable punishment in hell, which is prepared by the just verdict of God for all of you who embitter him imprudently and immoderately. You do so by turning the most honorable things into vessels of dishonor, by taking those who were taken to be saved and turning them into children of perdition, men for whom the precious blood of our Savior atoned. Repent even at this late hour, set aside your great blindness, and snatch both yourselves and them from the eternal fire of frightful Gehenna. As far as I am concerned, therefore, I am innocent of your crimes. 7

"For I did not hesitate to reveal to you *the sword that is coming* for you. I wish you were all obedient to me, being taught by the fear of God and becoming perfect in an excellent manner through those perfect commandments. Since, however, I am able to speak to you, give you my advice, and beseech you, and in doing this I have done all that I can, I am certain that those among you whose souls are noble and 8

τοῦ μέλλοντος κριτηρίου ἐπαισθανόμεναι, συνήσουσιν, εὖ
οἶδα, καὶ τῆς τῶν παίδων ἅμα καὶ τῶν οἰκετῶν καὶ τῶν ὑπὸ
χεῖρα πάντων ἐπιμελήσονται σωτηρίας, μέγα ἑαυτοῖς ἐκ
τῆς ἐπιμελείας ποριζόμενοι κέρδος ὅσην ἐκ τῆς ῥαθυμίας
τὴν κατάκρισιν, οἱ δὲ τῆς ῥαθυμίας υἱοί, καὶ μετὰ τοσαύ-
την διαμαρτυρίαν τοῖς αὐτοῖς ἐπιμένοντες, κακοὶ κακῶς
ἐκκαύσουσι καθ᾽ ἑαυτῶν δριμυτέραν τὴν τῆς κολάσεως
κάμινον."

18

Ταῦτα λέγων, πολλοὺς εἷλκε πρὸς ἐπιστροφὴν καὶ συνιέναι παρεσκεύαζεν. Εἰ δέ τις ταῖς φιλαρέτοις ταύταις ὑπο-
θήκαις μὴ ἐκρύπτετο, ἀλλὰ τὸ ἔκλυτον ἀνεπαίσθητον εἶχε
καὶ τὸ ῥάθυμον ἀσωφρόνιστον, οὐδὲ ἐπιπλήξεων, οὐδὲ
σφοδροτέρων ἐφείδετο ῥημάτων πρὸς τὸν τοιοῦτον, ἀλλὰ
βαρύτερός τις ὡρᾶτο καὶ φοβερωτέραν παρέτεινεν αὐτῷ
τὴν ἀπὸ τῶν λόγων μάστιγα, κατατρέχων τῆς ἀμαλάκτου
ψυχῆς πληκτικώτερον καὶ ὑπομιμνήσκων τῆς φρικώδους
ἐκείνης καὶ ἀλαθήτου ἐτάσεως, ἐν ᾗ πάντα γυμνὰ τῷ Κριτῇ
καὶ τετραχηλισμένα παρίστανται, ἡνίκα πολὺς μὲν ὁ μετά-
μελος, τὸ ἐκ τούτου δὲ οὐδὲ βραχὺ ὄφελος. Φρονίμων οὖν
ἔλεγε καὶ νουνεχῶν ὡς ἀληθῶς προφθῆναι τὴν ἐκεῖ πικρί-
αν καὶ ἰαθῆναι τὴν κακίαν διὰ τῆς ἐνταῦθα μετανοίας καὶ
ἐξομολογήσεως καὶ πρὸ τοῦ θανάτου ἐπιόντα τὸν θάνατον

perceive the future tribunal will understand and will care for the salvation of your children, your servants, and all who are under your authority. They will derive great profit from this solicitude, as great, in fact, as their condemnation will be from their indifference otherwise. But the sons of sluggishness who persist in this behavior will surely remain adamant and will go on behaving in that way even after these anxious entreaties; they will wickedly kindle the fires of hell in a more painful manner for themselves."

18

With these words he managed to bring many people back into the fold and make them aware of their sins. But if these virtuous admonitions did not lead someone to suppress his urges, and instead he allowed his depravity to casually slide by and failed to correct his lazy attitude, the saint did not refrain from using strong words to rebuke him. He appeared terrifying to them and the whip of his words became more frightening. He hounded and chastised them, inveighing against their intractable souls more effectively, reminding them of that frightful and infallible judgment, when *all* will be *open and laid bare* before our Judge. There will be much to repent over at that time, but to no avail, not even a bit. He said that prudent and sensible men should take care to mend their sins before that time in order to preempt the pain there through repentance and confession of their sins in this life. Thus, if death comes before death,

ἡμερώτερον ἑαυτοῖς κατασκευάσαι καὶ ὡς δυνατὸν κου-
φότερον. Οὐ γὰρ πᾶσιν ὁμοίως πικρός, οὐδὲ πάντας ταῖς
αὐταῖς κατατείνων ὀδύναις, ἀλλ' ἔνθα συνειδὸς ἐγκλήμασι
βαρυνόμενον καὶ ψυχὴ κατάστικτος ἁμαρτήμασι, πολλῷ
πικρότερα ἐκεῖ καὶ δριμύτερα τὰ τοῦ θανάτου βέλη, οὐ
χωρισμὸν μόνον ψυχῆς καὶ σώματος ἐργαζόμενα, ἀλλὰ
τὴν προσδοκίαν τῶν μελλόντων ἐπεγείροντα πικρὰν καὶ
ἄλλην καὶ πρὸ τῆς κολάσεως κόλασιν.

19

Οὕτω μὲν περὶ τὴν ὑψηλὴν τῆς ἀρχιερωσύνης διέκειτο
ἐπιστασίαν ὁ δεξιὸς ποιμὴν καὶ προθύεσθαι τῆς ποίμνης,
εἰ δεήσειεν, ἕτοιμος, καὶ ταῦτα φιλοπονῶν οὐκ ἐπαύετο,
οὐδ' ὑπανεδίδου, οὐδ' ὤκλαζεν, ἡ *Τυρσηνικὴ* ὢν μικροῦ
σάλπιγξ ἐν τῷ καταγγέλλειν ἀσιγήτως τοῖς λαοῖς τὰ σωτήρια, ἄξιον ἑαυτὸν τοῦ καλέσαντος ἀποδεικνύων καὶ εἰδὼς
ἐφ' ᾧ παρὰ τῆς Χάριτος ἐκλήθη καὶ τί τὸ ἔργον τῆς ἐμ-
πιστευθείσης αὐτῷ προστασίας εἴτε προεδρίας.

2   Ἐπεὶ δὲ ἔδει κἀκεῖνον, ἄνθρωπον ὄντα, μὴ ἀγνοῆσαι
τὴν κοινὴν τῆς φύσεως λειτουργίαν, μᾶλλον δὲ ἀναλῦσαι
πρὸς τὸν ἡδὺν Δεσπότην καὶ ἐπέραστον καὶ τῆς ἐκείνου
μετέχειν γλυκύτητος, πῶς τοῦτο γίνεται; Ἤδη μὲν γὰρ καὶ
γῆρας αὐτῷ ὑπὸ τοῖς τῆς ἀρετῆς ἱδρῶσι τὴν τοῦ σώματος

236

they will have made it gentler and lighter, as far as possible. For death is neither frightful nor painful to all men in equal measure, as its arrows cause much more pain and suffering to those whose conscience is burdened with crimes and whose soul is stained with sins. These arrows not only separate the soul from the body, but implant into the soul a bitter awareness of those trials that lie ahead, thus creating another hell before hell itself.

19

That was how the good pastor managed his high office of bishop. If there was need, he was ready to sacrifice himself for his flock. He did not ever pause in his labors; he did not withdraw from the fight; his eagerness did not abate; he was almost that *trumpet of the Tyrrhenians,* since he did not stop proclaiming to the people the road of their salvation. In this way, he proved that he was worthy of the one who had summoned him, that he knew why he had been summoned by Holy Grace, and understood the tasks of that high office entrusted to him, that is, of his bishopric.

But since he was a human being too, he could not fail to 2 perform the service that is common to us all, or rather to return to his sweet and beloved Lord, in order to participate in his ineffable sweetness. How did that take place? When he was already old, and the labors that he had undertaken for the sake of virtue had deprived his body of vigor, an

εὐτονίαν παρείλετο, ἔτι δὲ καὶ νόσος τῷ γήρᾳ συνεπιθε-
μένη πρὸς τὸ κοινὸν καὶ ἀναπόδραστον ἐξεκαλεῖτο χρέος
καὶ τὴν ὀφειλὴν ἀπῄτει τῆς φύσεως. Ὁ δέ, ὡς ᾔσθετο ὅσον
οὔπω τέλος αὐτῷ τὴν ἐφήμερον ἔξουσαν ζωήν, ἵνα μηδὲ
τῆς τελευταίας προσρήσεως, μηδὲ τῆς ὀφειλομένης παραινέσεως μηδ᾽ ἐν ἐσχάτοις τὴν οἰκείαν ἀποστερήσοι ποίμνην,
μετακαλεῖται μὲν ὅσον τοῦ βήματος, μετακαλεῖται δὲ καὶ
ὅσον τῆς ἱερᾶς κιγκλίδος ἐκτός, οἱ δέ (οὐδὲ γὰρ οὕτω φόβος προθυμίαν ἐγείρει κινήσεως, ὡς πόθος πόδας πτεροῖ
καὶ σχεδὸν ἵπτασθαι ποιεῖ πρὸς τὸ ποθούμενον), θᾶττον ἢ
ἐκλήθησαν παρῆσαν, προοφθῆναι τῶν πλησίον ἕκαστος
καὶ πρῶτος τῆς θεοφιλοῦς γλώττης τὴν εὐλογίαν κομίσα-
σθαι περιφανῶς ἀξιόμαχόν τι κρίνοντες.

3   Ὡς δὲ περιστάντας ἀθρόους ἔγνω καὶ μονονουχὶ χαί-
νοντας καὶ ὅλους ἐκκρεμεῖς τῆς ἡδίστης ἐκείνης καὶ συνήθους φωνῆς, ἀναπτύσσει τὸ μελίγλωττον ἐκεῖνο καὶ πολλῶν χαρίτων ἀνάμεστον στόμα καὶ τὰ τελευταῖα καὶ ὡς
ἔπος εἰπεῖν ἐξιτήρια ὑπὸ ἠρεμαίᾳ καὶ γαληνῇ προσφθέγ-
γεται φωνῇ, "Σώζοι σθέ μοι," λέγων, "ἱερὰ συναυλία, ὅση
τε ἐν πατράσι καὶ γέρουσι καὶ ὅση ἐν παισὶ καὶ ἀκμάζουσι,
σώζοισθε ἐπὶ πᾶσι τοῖς σωτηρίοις καὶ χριστοτερπέσιν
ἔργοις καὶ τὴν κατὰ Θεὸν εὐδοκίμησιν φέρουσι. Ταῦτα
ὑμῖν τελευταῖα προσλαλῶ ῥήματα, συνταττόμενος ὁμοῦ
καὶ παρεγγυώμενος τὴν πολλὴν ἐκείνην καὶ φιλόπονον
διδασκαλίαν, τὴν ἐμὴν παρακαταθήκην, ἄχραντον τηρεῖν
καὶ ἀμείωτον, ὡς ἂν καὶ ὑμεῖς τῆς ἄνω τιμῆς ἀξιωθείητε,
ἀρίστης πολιτείας μισθὸν τοῦτον εὑράμενοι, κἀμοὶ εἴη
ἐγκαυχᾶσθαι τῇ ὑμῶν λαμπρότητι καὶ ἐλλαμπρύνεσθαι

illness came upon him as an additional affliction to his old age, calling him to the common and inescapable debt of us all, asking him to pay back our debt to nature. As soon as he realized that his mortal life would soon come to a close, he summoned *all the clergy who stand in the sanctuary* and the laymen who stand outside the chancel barrier in order not to deprive his flock in his final hours of his farewell address and obligatory exhortation. They came to him almost before they were summoned, for love, far more than fear, excites our eagerness to run and causes wings to sprout on our feet that allow us to fly to the one we love. Each one of them was eager to arrive ahead of his fellows, in order to be the first to obtain the blessing of that mouth that was beloved by God. They clearly deemed it a matter worth competing over.

When he realized that all were gathered around him, full of excitement, waiting in suspense to hear his sweet and familiar voice, the saint opened his honey-tongued mouth, which was full of graces, and began his final and, so to speak, valedictory speech in a quiet and calm voice. "O blessed company, fathers and elders, grown men and children, God bless you, as you perform all those salvific deeds that satisfy Christ and guarantee God's approbation. This is the last speech that I address to you. I bid you farewell and at the same time exhort you to carry out the numerous, arduous teachings that I entrusted to you, without adulterating or diminishing them. In this way you too will be rewarded with a heavenly honor, finding this reward for your excellent behavior, and I will boast of and be proud of your splendor

3

παρὰ τῷ δικαίῳ καὶ φιλοτίμῳ μισθαποδότῃ Χριστῷ, οὗ τῇ
δεξιᾷ νῦν ὑμᾶς παρατίθημι, τὴν ἀφ' ὑμῶν πορείαν ποιούμενος καὶ πρὸς ἑτέρας μονὰς καὶ σκηνὰς καλούμενος,
ἀλλὰ καὶ μαρτυρόμενος ἐνώπιον Θεοῦ καὶ ἀγγέλων καὶ
παρεγγυώμενος, ἵν', εἴ τι τῶν οἰκείων κήδεσθε ψυχῶν, εἴ
τι τῶν ἄνω μονῶν ἐφίεσθε, τὸ μεῖζον εἰπεῖν καὶ τὸ πᾶν ἐν
βραχεῖ, εἴ τι ἑαυτοὺς στέργετε καὶ τὴν οἰκείαν περιέπετε
σωτηρίαν, ὡς ἐδιδάχθητε, ὡς ἐπαιδεύθητε, οὕτως ἀναστρέ-
φοισθε, οὕτως πολιτεύοισθε, ἀκόλουθον ὑμῶν τὴν ζωὴν
δεικνύντες καὶ ταῖς ἐμαῖς συμβαίνουσαν διδασκαλίαις,
μᾶλλον δὲ ταῖς τοῦ Πνεύματος. Οὐδὲν γὰρ ἡμέτερον
ἀνηγγείλαμεν, ἀλλ' ὅσα αἱ θεῖαι ἡμᾶς ἐμυσταγώγησαν
γραφαί.

4   "Προσέχετε ἑαυτοῖς, ἀδελφοί, καὶ μηδὲν μηδενὶ τὴν
ἀρετὴν ἐγκοπτέτω, μὴ πλοῦτος, μὴ δόξα, μὴ ἑτέρα τις
παρεμπεσοῦσα φροντὶς δούλη καὶ νόθος καὶ πόρρω Θεοῦ
βάλλουσα, μὴ μόνον ὅτι ὑψηλοτέροις εἶναι τούτων ὀφειλόμενον ὑμῖν ἐστι καὶ δίκαιον, ἀλλ' ὅτι μηδὲ ἔχει μηδὲν
αὐτῶν τὸ βέβαιον καὶ μόνιμον, ἀλλὰ κἂν τρυφὴν εἴπῃς, ὡς
καπνὸς ἐκλείπει, κἂν εὔκλειαν, ὡς ὄναρ παίζει, καὶ χρῆμά
τι ἀπατηλὸν καὶ ἀστάθμητον ὁ πᾶς τῶν ἀνθρώπων βίος,
καὶ τὰ μὲν τῶν ἡδονῶν ἰνδάλματα, ὅσα καὶ οἷα, μικρὸν εὐ-
φράναντα ταχὺ διέπτη καὶ διέρρευσεν, αἱ δὲ ἐπ' αὐτοῖς εὐθύ-
ναι καὶ τιμωρίαι παραμένουσι, φεῦ, ἀϊδίως τῇ ψυχῇ, καὶ
αὐτὸ τοῦτο ἐγκαλουμένῃ, ὅτι τῷ μοχθηρῷ τούτῳ σαρκίῳ
προστεθεῖσα καὶ προσηλώσασα ὅλην ἑαυτὴν καὶ ὡσανεὶ
ἐντήξασα τοῖς πλάνοις καὶ ταπεινοῖς καὶ πολὺ τὸ κίβδηλον
καὶ ἀπατηλὸν ἔχουσι, τῶν ὄντως ὄντων ὑπερεφρόνησεν,

before Christ, who distributes his rewards justly and liberally. Now that I am leaving you, being called to another abode and dwelling place, I entrust you to his right hand. I testify *before God and the angels* and give you a last commandment: if you care for your souls, if you wish to advance to the heavenly abode, or—let me here say in a few words the most important thing, indeed everything—if you love yourselves and care about your own salvation, be careful to behave and conduct yourselves in the way that I taught and educated you, showing that you live according to my instructions, or rather the instructions of the Spirit. For I did not teach you anything that was my own invention, but rather only the mysteries into which Holy Scripture initiated us.

"My brethren, take care of yourselves; your virtue should 4 not be diminished by anything, whether by wealth, glory, or any other servile, spurious, and incidental concern that alienates you from God. Not only is it obligatory and righteous to be above those cares, but you must also remember that there is nothing permanent and stable about them. Luxury, you say? *It vanishes like smoke.* Glory? It cheats us like a dream. Man's entire life? It is deceptive and unstable. What really are those illusions created by pleasure? They give us a small satisfaction and then quickly vanish and flow away. But alas, the guilt and the punishment of our souls for all of them are eternal. Woe! Our soul will be accused too: that it has attached itself to this wretched flesh, that it has nailed the whole of itself to it and was absorbed by all those deceptive, unworthy, spurious, and illusory things, while neglecting what is real. We resemble those who go walking in

ὥσπερ οἱ ἐν ἀσελήνῳ νυκτὶ καὶ βαθεῖ σκότῳ πορευόμενοι
καὶ τοὺς κάχληκας ὡς μαργαρίτας συλλέγοντες. Μὴ γοῦν
τῇ περὶ ταῦτα σπουδῇ καὶ ἀλογίστῳ φορᾷ καὶ συννεύσει
ζημιωθῆτε τὸ ἀΐδιον χρῆμα καὶ ἀθάνατον, τὰς ὑμετέρας
ψυχάς, μή, τεκνία ἀγαπητὰ ἐν Κυρίῳ καὶ ποθούμενα, μὴ
τῆς ἐμῆς ποίμνης ὁ σκολιὸς κατακαυχήσηται Δράκων, ὁ
ποικίλος τὴν κακίαν καὶ δόλιος καὶ οὐδὲν ἔχων ἀνεπινόη-
τον εἰς πονηρίαν, ἵν᾽ ἐν ἑνί τινι τρόπῳ λάθῃ σαγηνεύσας
καὶ τῆς αἰωνίου ἀποβουκολήσῃ ζωῆς, ἀλλ᾽ ἕκαστος ἑαυτὸν
ὁράτω καὶ τὸν βίον ῥυθμιζέτω πρὸς ἀρετὴν καὶ τῶν πλησίον τὴν εὐδοκίμησιν οἰκείαν λογιζέσθω.

5   "Μᾶλλον δὲ πρὸ τῶν ἄλλων οἱ τῷ καταλόγῳ τῷ ἱερα-
τικῷ ἐγκατειλεγμένοι, ὅσῳ μείζων ἡ τιμή, τοσούτῳ μείζω
καὶ τὴν ἀρετὴν ἐπιδείκνυσθε. Δότε τῷ πλήθει καλὰ παραδείγματα καλοῦ βίου καὶ Θεῷ πλησιάζοντος, καὶ τοῦτο
ὑμῖν εἰς κέρδος, τοῦτο ὑμῖν εἰς προσθήκην ἀμοιβῆς παρὰ
Θεῷ. Συμμερίτης ἔσῃ τῶν μισθῶν τῷ ἐκ τῆς σῆς πολιτείας
βελτιουμένῳ καὶ πρὸς ἀρετὴν ἀνατρέχοντι, κοινωνὸς τῶν
στεφάνων, κοινωνὸς τῶν ἀντιδόσεων. Ὀκνῶ γὰρ μνημο-
νεῦσαι τῶν ἐναντίων, ἵνα μὴ βαρύνω σου τὴν ἀκοὴν βαρεῖ
καὶ φορτικῷ ἀκούσματι, οἵαν σεαυτῷ προξενεῖς τὴν ζημίαν, ὅπως διπλοῦν τὸ κατάκριμα, φαύλης πολιτείας ἀρχέτυπον τῷ λαῷ γινόμενος.

6   "Ἀλλ᾽ ἐπεὶ τοῦτο καὶ σιωπῶντος ἐμοῦ συνίης, ἁγνὰς
χεῖρας, ἁγνὰς φρένας τῇ φρικτῇ πρόσαγε θυσίᾳ, εἰδὼς ὅτι
μετὰ τῶν χερουβεὶμ ἕστηκας, μετὰ τῶν σεραφεὶμ τέταξαι
τὴν ἁγίαν ἐκείνην καὶ μακαρίαν ἀναφέρειν φωνὴν καὶ τὴν
φρικώδη μυσταγωγίαν ἀποπληροῦν. Οἱ ψάλλοντες, οἱ

pitch darkness on a moonless night, and collect pebbles, mistaking them for pearls. Do not lose what is eternal and immortal, I mean your souls, by devoting yourselves eagerly to those things in an irrational manner. My children, beloved in the Lord, do not let the evil Dragon boast of destroying my flock. He devises all kinds of villainy, is treacherous, and devises all sorts of evil tricks in order to trap us, unawares, in a net, and deprive us of eternal life, one way or another. Each one of you must look to yourself and adjust your life so that it leads toward virtue, and consider the good repute of your fellows to be your own also.

"You who are registered among the clergy must be more 5 ardent in cultivating virtue, to the same degree as your honor is nobler. Provide for people good examples of a virtuous life that draws near to God. That will be to your advantage and you will obtain a greater reward from God. You will share in the rewards of that man who becomes better and more virtuous as a result of your conduct. You will receive the same crown and the same repayment. I hesitate to mention what will happen in the opposite case, so as not to burden your ears with words that are hard to bear and disturbing. This will be harm that you will inflict on yourself; your punishment will be double if you give an example of bad conduct to your people.

"In any case, even if I remain silent, you understand all 6 these things. Therefore, raise high your chaste hands and your chaste mind and then proceed to the performance of the awesome sacrifice. Know that you stand alongside the cherubim and are entitled to sing that holy and blessed hymn together with the seraphim, performing that awesome mystery. As for the singers, readers, and all who per-

ἀναγινώσκοντες, οἱ πᾶσαν ἱερὰν λειτουργίαν ὑπηρε-
τοῦντες, ἁγίως ἀναστρέφεσθε ἐν ἁγίῳ οἴκῳ Θεοῦ ἡμῶν.

7   "Λαός μου, ὃν ἠγάπησεν ἡ ψυχή μου, ὃν εὔχομαι γενέσθαι ποίμνιον ἐκλεκτόν, κλῆρον εὐλογημένον, μερίδα σε-
σωσμένην, λαός μου, γένεσθέ μοι καὶ ὑμεῖς εἰς καύχημα,
εἰς εὐφροσύνην, εἰς δόξαν, εἰς τιμὴν ἐν ἡμέρᾳ ἐπισκοπῆς τοῦ
μεγάλου καὶ μόνου Κριτοῦ, μὴ ἐγκληθῆτε παρ' ἐκείνῳ τῷ
ἀδεκάστῳ δικαστῇ ὡς ἀπειθεῖς, ὡς ἀνήκοοι, ὡς τέκνα μω-
μητά, ὡς υἱοὶ ἄνομοι. 'Πείθεσθε τοῖς ἡγουμένοις ὑμῶν,'
Παῦλος ὑμῖν διακελεύεται. 'Αὐτοὶ γὰρ ἀγρυπνοῦσιν ὑπὲρ
τῶν ψυχῶν ὑμῶν ὡς λόγον ἀποδώσοντες.' Μὴ παροξύνητε
τὸ Πνεῦμα τὸ ἅγιον ταῖς ἐπιμόνοις ὑμῶν κακίαις, διὰ τὴν
τοῦ βίου ματαιότητα πάντα κυκῶντες καὶ ταράσσοντες,
κατεπαιρόμενοι ἱερέων τε καὶ ἀρχιερέων καὶ κακὰς ἑαυτοῖς ἐν τῷ μέλλοντι δικαστηρίῳ ἀποθησαυρίζοντες τὰς
ἀμοιβάς. Μὴ κατεχέτω ὑμᾶς ὁ πηλός, μηδὲ ἡ κόνις τὰ
φρονήματα ὑμῶν τρεφέτω, μηδὲ τὴν πολλὴν σαπρίαν καὶ
τὸν βαθὺν βόρβορον καὶ τὴν ἄτιμον ἰλὺν τιμῆς ἄξια
ἡγεῖσθε. Τίς γὰρ οὐκ οἶδε τὸ κίβδηλον τῶν τοῦ βίου πραγμάτων καὶ ἀπόπτυστον; Τίνι οὐχὶ γνώριμον τοῦ βίου τὸ
πολυπλανὲς καὶ μάταιον; Τίνι οὐχὶ δῆλον τὸ τῆς ζωῆς ἄδη-
λον καὶ ἀβέβαιον; Ἧς ἓν μόνον ἐστὼς καὶ πάγιον, τὸ πάντας θανάτῳ προδιδόναι, τὸ μηδένα δύνασθαι συντηρῆσαι
ἑαυτὸν κρείττονα θανάτου καὶ τῶν ἐκείνου βρόχων ἐλεύ-
θερον.

8   "Τὸ δὲ πάντων χαλεπώτατον καὶ πολλῶν δακρύων
ἐπιεικῶς ἄξιον, ὅτι οὓς ἂν ἑαυτῇ ἐξαπατήσασα προσδήσῃ
καὶ πολλοὺς ἑαυτῆς τοὺς πόθους κακῶς ἀναρρήξειε καὶ τῷ

form various holy services during the liturgy, *you should behave* in a holy manner *inside the* holy *house of* our *God.*

"O my people, whom my soul has loved and who I wish   7
will become an excellent flock, a blessed company that is
saved: my people, become a source of pride, happiness, *glory,*
and honor for me *on the day of our judgment* by the great and
only true Judge. Do not be accused by that impartial judge
of being disobedient, ignorant, villainous, and lawless sons.
'*Obey your leaders,*' Paul admonishes you, '*for they are keeping
sleepless watch over our souls and will give an account on* our
behalf.' Do not make the Holy Spirit angry against you by
persisting in sin, by disturbing and turning all things upside
down through the vanity of your life, through which you will
also bring blame down upon the priests and the bishops,
since you will store up bad rewards for yourselves at that future tribunal. Be not slaves to filth, nor let the dust feed your
mind. Do not regard decayed matter, the deep and muddy
pit, and ignoble materials as something prestigious. For who
does not know the fraudulent and disgusting character of
worldly affairs? Who is not familiar with the deceit and vanity of life? To whom is the uncertainty and unreliability of
life not clear? Only one thing is certain and permanent, that
life delivers all of us to death; nobody can prevail over death,
nobody can escape its nets.

"What is much more grievous and worthy of tears is that   8
after giving them a small satisfaction, life delivers those
whom it has deceived and made captive over to an eternal

λίχνῳ δελεάσῃ καὶ τῷ λείῳ καταγοητεύσῃ, μικρὰ τέρψασα, αἰώνια, οἴμοι, κολάζει, ἀσυνέτων δὲ καὶ κομιδῇ ἠλιθίων ὀλιγοχρονίου τέρψεως ἀνταλλάξασθαι πικρὰν οὕτω καὶ ἀδιεξίτητον κόλασιν. Ἧς μηδενὶ μὲν ὑμῶν γένοιτο πεῖραν λαβεῖν, Κύριε καὶ Θεέ μου, εἰ δέ τις, ὡς ἀπεύχομαι, ἐμπεσεῖται, εἴσεται σαφῶς, ὡς μὴ ὤφελεν, ὡς παιδιά τις τὰ ἐνταῦθα κολαστήρια πρὸς τὰ μέλλοντα. Εἰ γὰρ ἄνθρωποι τηλικούτων εἰσὶν ὀργάνων εὑρεταὶ καὶ οὕτως ἀφορήτων εἰς κόλασιν, ἡ τοῦ Θεοῦ ὀργὴ πηλίκην ἑτοιμάσει τιμωρίαν τοῖς παροργίζουσι καὶ μὴ ζητοῦσι μετάνοιαν; Ἀκούομεν δὲ ὅτι κατὰ τὸ ἔλεος αὐτοῦ οὕτω καὶ ὁ θυμὸς αὐτοῦ.

9   "Μηδεὶς οὖν, ἀδελφοί, θελήσῃ πειραθῆναι Θεοῦ ἀγανακτήσεως, ἀλλ᾽ ἕκαστος τὰ οἰκεῖα εὖ τιθέσθω, καὶ μήτε νεότης εἰς μακροὺς χρόνους τὰς ἐλπίδας ταμιευέσθω, ἀλλὰ τὰ σκιρτήματα τῆς σαρκὸς ἐπεχέτω, τοῖς τῆς ἐγκρατείας κατάγχων χαλινοῖς (οὐδὲ γὰρ οἶδε ποίᾳ φυλακῇ ἔρχεται κλέπτης, μήτε νέου μήτε γηραιοῦ φειδόμενος), μήτε τὸ γῆρας ἀναπιπτέτω καὶ ἀπελπιζέτω τὴν ἐπανόρθωσιν, εἴ τί που παρεσφάλη τοῦ πρέποντος, μηδὲ ῥηγνύτω μείζονα τὴν πληγήν, μηδὲ τὸ σύντριμμα χαλεπώτερον ἐργαζέσθω. Τί γὰρ δεῖ ἐπιξαίνειν τὰ ἕλκη καὶ προστιθέναι ἀνομίαν ἐπ᾽ ἀνομίᾳ; Ἄλλη δὲ τοῦ Κριτοῦ ἀγανάκτησις ἀναπίπτειν τινὰ καὶ ἀναβάλλεσθαι τὴν ἰατρείαν καὶ ἐκλύεσθαι, δέον προφθάνειν τὸ πρόσωπον αὐτοῦ ἐν ἐξομολογήσει. Τί πολλὰ λέγω; Πλείω καὶ ταῦτα τῆς παρούσης δυνάμεως. Τὰς ἐντολὰς οἴδατε, ὑπὸ ταύταις ὡς ὑπὸ μεγάλῳ φωτὶ πορεύεσθε

condemnation. Seduced by gluttony, they burst out in evil longings, bewitched by its softness. But only foolish and stupid men take bitter and eternal punishment as a reward for a short-lived pleasure. O my Lord God, I wish that none of you may experience such a thing! If, God forbid, this fate befalls someone, he will realize that the torments of this life are child's play compared to the torments of the future. For if mere men are able to devise such dreadful instruments of unbearable torture for punishment, can we imagine what dreadful torments the wrath of God is preparing for those who anger him and do not seek to repent? We hear that *his* wrath *is equal to his mercy.*

"My brethren, I hope that none of you wishes to test   9
God's wrath, but each should conduct his own affairs in a just manner. Those who are young should not postpone their hopes for long, but should tame the disorderly urges of their flesh, restraining it with the reins of continence (since they do not *know at what time of night the thief will come,* and he spares neither youths nor old men). Those who are old should not lose heart or despair of correcting themselves, if they have somehow strayed from the right path, nor should they rip open the wound, nor worsen their affliction. Is there any need to aggravate their wounds, or to add new sins to the previous ones? The Judge will also be angered if we lose heart, postpone healing our wounds, and relax, when our duty is *to rush to confess our sins before him.* But why am I speaking at such great length? Even what I have already said surpasses my strength. You know the commandments. Follow them now, as under a great light: you will shine, and

καὶ φωτίζεσθε καὶ τὰ πρόσωπα ὑμῶν οὐ μὴ καταισχυνθῇ ἐκεῖθεν αὐγαζόμενα, ἀλλὰ καὶ εἰς τὰ τοῦ φωτὸς σκηνώματα, εὖ ἴστε, καταντήσετε, τῆς ἀτελευτήτου χαρᾶς μεθέξοντες."

20

Καὶ ὁ μὲν ἐνταῦθα καταπαύει τὸν λόγον, οὐ μετὰ μακρὸν δὲ καὶ τὴν πρόσκαιρον ζωήν, ἧς ἐκ πολλοῦ τὴν διάζευξιν ἠγάπα, ὡς ἂν τὸ γεῶδες βάρος καὶ τὸ βρῖθον ἐπὶ τὰ κάτω σκῆνος ἀποσεισάμενος, πρὸς τὸν μόνον ἀναλύσῃ καὶ ἐπὶ τὰς ἀλύπους καὶ μακαρίας ἀποκατασταίη σκηνάς. Ὁ δὲ πᾶς λαὸς τῆς Λακεδαίμονος, τότε μᾶλλον αἰσθόμενοι τῆς ζημίας (πέφυκε γὰρ τὸ ἀγαθὸν οὐχ οὕτω παρὸν ὡς ἐκ χειρῶν ἁρπασθὲν τοῖς πολλοῖς καὶ παχυτέροις ἐπιγινώσκεσθαι), πρὸς οἰμωγὰς καὶ ἀνακλήσεις γοερὰς ἐξενικῶντο καὶ μετὰ θρήνων ὁμιλαδὸν συνέτρεχον ἔκθαμβοι ἐπὶ τῷ ἀκούσματι, παραπλῆγες μικροῦ καὶ ἔκφρονες. Οὕτω γὰρ αὐτοὺς διετίθει τὸ πάθος. Ἄλλοι γε μὴν ἄλλα διεθρήνουν καὶ ἄλλοι ἐπ᾽ ἄλλοις ἐκόπτοντο καὶ ἦν πολύθρους τις ὁ θρῆνος καὶ πολύγλωσσος.

2   Ἤκουσας ἂν γερόντων τὸν τροφέα, τὴν βακτηρίαν, τὴν παράκλησιν ἀποδυρομένων καὶ ἑαυτῶν ὅλην δυστυχίαν τὴν ἐκείνου ἀποβίωσιν ἀποκαλούντων καὶ τὸ γῆρας λοιπὸν βαρυνομένων καὶ ἀποστεργόντων τὴν ζωὴν καὶ ταῖς οἰκείαις ἐπαρωμένων πολιαῖς, ὅτι τοσούτῳ πάθει καὶ

your faces will not be ashamed but enlightened. Know well that you will reach the dwelling places of light where you will participate in eternal joy."

20

The saint concluded his speech at this point and, after a short while, concluded his transient life as well. He had long wished to depart from this life so that, by shaking off his earthly burden and his body that weighed him down, he might reach our only God and be restored to those blessed dwelling places, where there is no grief. Only then did all the people of Lakedaimon became aware of what they had lost. For the value of a good thing is recognized by the dimwitted masses only when it is taken away, not when it was present. Therefore, they were overwhelmed with wailing and mournful invocations. They gathered all together with lamentation, stupefied by what they had heard. They were almost paralyzed and out of their minds: that was how deep their grief ran. All were engaged in different lamentations, and beating different parts of their bodies, and those cries were uttered by many tongues in a clamor.

You could hear old men mourning the one who had nurtured them, who had been their staff of support, their consolation, and they called his death a total misfortune for them all. They could no longer endure the burden of old age and loved life no more. They cursed their white hair, since they had lived long enough to see this calamity and horrible

τοιούτῳ θεάματι ἐφυλάχθησαν, ἀλλ' οὐ προέφθησαν τῇ ἀποτόμῳ τοῦ θανάτου τομῇ τὰς πολλὰς τῶν συμφορῶν τρώσεις καὶ τὰς ἀμυθήτους τῶν ἀνιαρῶν πληγάς. Οὐδὲν ἄλλο οὐδὲ τὰ τῶν χηρῶν πρόσωπα ἢ συνεχεῖ κατερρέοντο τῇ τῶν δακρύων λιβάδι, κἀκεῖναι τὴν ζωὴν ἀπελέγοντο, κἀκείναις εὐκταῖος ὁ πᾶσι φευκτὸς ἐνομίζετο θάνατος καὶ ἀρχὴν ζόφου, ἀρχὴν τῆς ἀφωτίστου νυκτὸς τῶν θλίψεων, ἀρχὴν συμφορῶν ἀπαραμυθήτων τὴν παροῦσαν τότε ἡμέραν καὶ ἐδέχοντο καὶ ὠνόμαζον, ἀρχὴν ὄντως χηρείας, τῆς σιδηρᾶς καμίνου τῆς δυστήνου βιοτῆς, ἣν ἐν ταῖς τῶν συζύγων ἀποβολαῖς ἐπιγνῶναι παρὰ τῆς ἐκείνου δεξιᾶς ἐκωλύθησαν. Καὶ ὀρφανοὶ τὰ αὐτὰ ἀπωδύροντο, τὸν πατέρα περιπαθῶς ἄγαν τὸν φιλόστοργον ἀνακαλούμενοι.

3   Καὶ πᾶσα ἡλικία ἐλεεινῶς τὰ προπεμπτήρια ἐκόπτετο. Οὐδὲ γὰρ ὁ πλούτῳ κομῶν ἔλαττον ὡρᾶτο κατηφιῶν τοῦ πένητος, ἀλλ' ὁ μὲν τὸν σωφρονιστὴν ἐν νῷ βαλλόμενος, τὸν πρὸς Θεὸν μεσίτην, τὸν ἥμερον παιδευτὴν καὶ εὐμέθοδον, ὅπως χρὴ μεταχειρίζεσθαι τὸν πλοῦτον καὶ οἰκεῖον ποιεῖν τὸν ἀλλότριον, ὁ δὲ ὅπως τὰ τῆς πενίας ἀνιαρὰ εὐχαρίστως φέρειν, καὶ ἀμφότεροι ὁμοίῳ κέντρῳ τῆς ἀθυμίας νυττόμενοι, ὁμοίως εἰς δάκρυα κατεφέροντο καὶ ὁμοίως γοερὰν ἀνέπεμπον φωνὴν καὶ μύχιον ὑπεστέναζον, ἀποβαλόντες, φεῦ, τὸν τεχνίτην καὶ γνήσιον ἰατρὸν καὶ φιλάνθρωπον.

4   Ὦ, τίς ἂν τοῦ τότε καιροῦ τὰ πάθη ἐκτραγῳδήσειε; Δάκρυα ἐν ἀνδράσι, δάκρυα ἐν γυναιξί, καὶ ταῦτα θερμὰ καὶ ταῦτα κρουνηδὸν ἐκχεόμενα, ἀφ' ὧν περιδήλως ἐδηλοῦτο τὸ φίλτρον καὶ ἡ ἐγκάρδιος στοργὴ πάντων καὶ ἡ θερμὴ

spectacle and had not been prevented by the relentless dissolution of death from seeing these numerous wounds caused by their hardships and terrible afflictions. The same could be seen on the faces of widows, with tears streaming from their eyes continuously; they too did not want to live anymore. Death, which is avoided by all people, was most desirable to them too. They considered and called that day the beginning of darkness, the beginning of the lightless night of their sorrows, the beginning of their inconsolable hardships, the real beginning of their widowhood, the iron furnace of their miserable lives, for at the time of their husbands' deaths they were prevented from truly experiencing it by the saint's helpful hand. Orphans too mourned him in a similar way, passionately invoking their affectionate father.

People of all ages piteously bade him farewell. The rich 3 man was seen to be distressed no less than the poor man. The former mourned the one who corrected him, who acted as an arbitrator between himself and God, who taught him calmly and properly the right way to use his wealth and make another's property his own. The poor man, by contrast, mourned the one who taught him how to endure the hardships of poverty by thanking God. Both were stung by sadness in the same way and shed tears, crying and groaning deeply, since they had lost, alas, a skillful, genuine, and benevolent physician.

Who can properly describe the passions that were un- 4 leashed at that time? Tears among the men, tears among the women—both hot and gushing out like streams. Those tears were a clear proof of the affection, the heartfelt love of all people for the saint and their fervent faith in him who was

πίστις ἡ πρὸς τὸν ἑαυτῶν ποιμένα καὶ διδάσκαλον. Καὶ συνέρρεον ἐπὶ τὴν κηδείαν ἡλικία πᾶσα καὶ πᾶσα ἰδέα βίου καὶ πᾶν ἐπιτήδευμα. Οὐ δοῦλος ὑστέρει, οὐ δεσπότης. Καὶ ἄρχων τῷ ἰδιώτῃ συνέτρεχε, προληφθῆναι ὑπ᾽ ἐκείνου ζημίαν ἡγούμενος. Ὅλοι περιφανῶς ἐξεκενοῦντο οἴκοι, καὶ παρθένος θαλαμευομένη χρόνῳ καὶ ἀρρένων ὄψιν ἐκκλίνουσα, κατετόλμα τότε τῆς ἐξόδου καὶ τὴν αἰδῶ μικρὸν ἀπετίθετο, ὡς οὐδὲν τοσοῦτον ζημιωθησομένη τῷ ὀφθῆναι βραχύ, ὅσον καρπωσομένη κέρδος ἐκ τῆς τοῦ ἱεροῦ σώματος προσψαύσεως, εἴπερ τυχεῖν τούτου γένοιτο. Ἐπτέρου καὶ τὰς γηραιὰς σάρκας καὶ μαρανθείσας τῷ χρόνῳ ἡ τῆς εὐλογίας ἐλπὶς καὶ πᾶσαι ἀγυιαὶ καὶ πᾶσαι ἄμφοδοι ἐστενοῦντο τῷ πλήθει, οὐ τὸ προσελθεῖν μόνον καὶ ψαῦσαι τοῦ παναγίου σώματος, ἀλλ᾽ ἤδη καὶ τὸ προσιδεῖν τὴν ἰσάγγελον ἐκείνην πολιὰν ἁγιασμὸν ἡγουμένων πάντων καὶ στερρὰν εὐλογίαν καὶ μεγίστων τινῶν ἀπόλαυσιν.

21

Ἀλλ᾽ ἡμεῖς μέντοι ταῦτα, ὦ θεία καὶ ἱερὰ κεφαλὴ καὶ πατριαρχῶν σύσκηνε, μικρὰ μέν, οὐκ ἀρνούμεθα, καὶ τῆς σῆς μεγαλειότητος πολύ τι ἐκπίπτοντα, ὅμως δ᾽ οὐκ ἐλάττω τῆς δυνάμεως, εἰ καὶ τῆς προθυμίας ἐλλιπέστερα. Σὺ δέ, ὁ περὶ Θεὸν ὢν καὶ περὶ τὴν ἄνω χορεύων χαρὰν καὶ τῷ ἀνεσπέρῳ φωτὶ αὐγαζόμενος, μηδὲ ἡμῶν τῶν ἐν τῷ σκοτεινῷ τούτῳ σαρκίῳ ἐνειργμένων ἐπιλάθοιο, ἀλλὰ καὶ

their pastor and teacher. People of all ages, habits of life, and trades gathered together at his funeral: no servant was absent, no official neglected to attend. The magistrates came together with ordinary men, the one trying to arrive before the other, thinking that a later arrival would give a bad impression. All the houses were left manifestly empty. Young maidens who had been raised inside the house for a long time, avoiding being seen by men, dared now to come out, setting their modesty aside for a short while. They did not worry about being seen by men for a short time, a small evil compared to the great benefit of touching the saint's body, if they managed to do so. The hope of that blessing made the flesh of old men that had withered due to age fly toward the saint. All streets and roads were congested by the crowd. Everyone thought not only to come and touch the holy body, but also to see his angelic white hair, considering even that to be a sanctification, a great blessing, and a delight of the highest order.

21

O holy and divine man, who now dwells in the same tent as the patriarchs, I offer to you this text. I do not deny that my offering is small and most unworthy of your greatness. It is not, however, inferior to my own powers, although it is not equal to my eagerness. But you who are now before God, dancing and sharing in the joy of heavenly beings, you who shine with an eternal light, do not forget us who are

τῷ ἱερῷ τῆς σῆς ποίμνης ποιμένι συμποιμαίνοις καὶ κοινω-
νοίης τῶν φροντίδων γνησίως, ταύτην ἀμοιβὴν τῆς εἰς σὲ
θερμῆς ἀγάπης ἀντιδιδούς, καὶ αὐτὴν τὴν ὑπὸ τῇ σῇ φίλῃ
δεξιᾷ ποιμανθεῖσαν ἀγαπητῶς ποίμνην περιέποις ὡς πρότερον ἢ καὶ ἔτι θερμότερον καὶ ἐν εὐσεβείᾳ συντηροίης
καὶ βίου καθαρότητι, ἁγνοὺς τὰς ψυχάς, ἁγνοὺς τὰ σώματα παριστῶν Θεῷ καὶ τῇ κάτω ταύτῃ σκηνῇ καὶ τῶν
οὐρανίων ἀντιτύπῳ καὶ εἰς αὐτὴν εἰσάγων τὴν οὐράνιον
μάνδραν ἄξια τοῦ ἐκεῖ νυμφῶνος περικειμένους ἐνδύματα.

2   Κἀμοὶ δὲ ταῖς θερμαῖς σου πρεσβείαις ἁμαρτημάτων
ἄφεσιν πρυτανεύοις καὶ ἀμείψαιο τὸν μικρὸν τοῦτον πό-
νον εὐλογίαις σαῖς καὶ ταῖς διὰ βίου προστασίαις, μηδὲ τι
δυσχεράνοις, ὅτι μακράν που τῆς ἀξίας ἐκτετοπίσμεθα.
Οὐδὲ γὰρ ἐπεπηδήσαμεν σου τοῖς ἐγκωμίοις, ὡς δοκοῦντες ἔχειν τι εἰπεῖν τῆς σῆς ἀνεφίκτου ἀρετῆς ἐφικνού-
μενον, ἀλλ' ἐπιταγῇ δουλεύοντες καὶ πατρὶ πειθόμενοι
Πνεύματι ἀγομένῳ καὶ ᾧ ἀπειθεῖν κίνδυνος οὐ μικρός,
τοῦτον ὑπήλθομεν τὸν ἀγῶνα. Εἰ δὲ καὶ *παίδων ψελλί-
σματα πατράσιν εἰσὶ φίλτατα,* δέξαι καὶ ταῦτα προσηνῶς,
κἀμοῦ τοῦ ἐπιταχθέντος εἰπεῖν καὶ πάντων τῶν τὰς ἀκοὰς
ἡδέως τῷ περὶ σὲ πόθῳ ὑπεχόντων τούτοις τοῖς διηγήμασι
θερμῶς προΐστασο, πάσας κοιμίζων συμφοράς, πᾶσαν γαλήνην δωρούμενος καὶ εἰς τὴν μέλλουσαν χαρὰν ποδηγῶν,
ἧς γένοιτο πάντας ἡμᾶς ἐπιτυχεῖν χάριτι καὶ φιλανθρωπίᾳ
τοῦ Κυρίου ἡμῶν Ἰησοῦ Χριστοῦ, ᾧ ἡ δόξα καὶ τὸ κράτος
σὺν τῷ Πατρὶ καὶ τῷ ζωοποιῷ καὶ παναγίῳ καὶ ἀγαθῷ
Πνεύματι πάντοτε, νῦν καὶ ἀεὶ καὶ εἰς τοὺς αἰῶνας τῶν
αἰώνων, ἀμήν.

prisoners of this dark flesh. Help our holy bishop to shepherd his flock by truly sharing in his cares. That will be a proper reward for his ardent love for you. Go on protecting, with the same loving care, the flock that was once under your most beloved right hand, and do so now as before, or even more ardently than before. May you preserve this flock in faith and purity of life, and present them to God pure in soul and body for as long as they are here in this earthly tent, which is an imitation of its heavenly counterpart. Then introduce them to the heavenly sheepfold, and dress them in garments worthy of the bridal chamber there.

Through your ardent intercessions, secure for me the forgiveness of my sins and reward this small product of my labors by blessing me and by protecting me for life. Do not be angry because my text is unworthy of you. For I did not rush to praise you of my own will, as if I could really say something equal to your unattainable virtue. Rather, I undertook this laborious task so as to carry out an order and remain obedient to my father, who was led by the Spirit, and whom it is a great danger to disobey. If it is true that *fathers love the babblings of their children,* accept my offering graciously. Fervently protect both me, who was ordered to speak, and all who listen happily to these stories because of their love for you. Alleviate their suffering and grant them spiritual tranquility, leading them to the eternal joy of the future. May we all attain it through the grace and compassion of our Lord Jesus Christ who loves mankind. Glory and power be always to him, to his Father, and to the most Holy, life-giving, and good Spirit, now and forever more, unto the ages of ages, amen.

LIFE OF THEODORE
OF KYTHERA
BY LEO

Βίος καὶ πολιτεία τοῦ ὁσίου πατρὸς ἡμῶν Θεοδώρου τοῦ ἐν τῇ νήσῳ Κυθηρίᾳ ἀσκήσαντος. Ποίημα Λέοντος

Εὐλόγησον.

I

Τὰς τῶν μεγάλων ἀνδρῶν ἀριστείας καὶ τοὺς γενναίους ἀγῶνας καὶ τὰ παλαίσματα, εἰ καὶ δι᾽ ὀλίγου τῶν ὧδε μετατεθῶσιν, οὐκ ἐν μήκει χρόνου ἀλλὰ προθυμίᾳ ψυχῆς καὶ ζέσει πίστεως ἐτάζειν οἶδεν ὁ δικαίως πάντα τὰ ἡμέτερα ἐτάζων Χριστὸς ὁ Θεὸς ἡμῶν. Εἰ γὰρ κατὰ τὸν θεολόγον Γρηγόριον *τοῦ ὕστερον εἰσελθεῖν εἰς τὸν ἀμπελῶνα τὸ καὶ ὕστερον κληθῆναι πρὸς τὴν ἀμπελουργίαν αἴτιον,* πάντως καὶ τὸ μὴ ἐπὶ πολὺ ἐμμεῖναι τῇ ἐργασίᾳ οὐχ ἡμέτερον ἔγκλημα, ἀλλὰ τοῦ δικαίως καὶ φιλανθρώπως πάντα τὰ ἡμέτερα οἰκονομοῦντος κρίμα Χριστοῦ τοῦ Θεοῦ ἡμῶν. Διὸ πολλάκις δι᾽ ὀλίγου προθύμῳ σπουδῇ καμών τις τῶν ἴσων τοῖς ἐκ πολλοῦ κοπιάσασιν ἢ καὶ μειζόνων ἠξιώθη δωρεῶν, καὶ μάρτυς τῶν λεγομένων αὐτὸς ὁ μισθαποδότης Χριστὸς τὴν τοῦ ἀμπελῶνος περὶ τούτου εἰσάγων

The life and conduct of our holy father Theodore, an ascetic on the island of Kythera: a work by Leo

Bless this reading.

I

Christ our God, who examines everything that we do in a righteous manner, evaluates the heroic feats, brave efforts, and struggles of great men, taking into account not the duration of their struggles but the eagerness of their souls and the ardor of their faith, even in those cases when some of them swiftly depart from this world. For if, in the words of Gregory the Theologian, *our late invitation to the vine dressing is the reason for our belated entrance* into the vineyard, the short duration of our efforts can likewise be imputed not to us but to the decision of Christ our God, who settles all our affairs in a humane and just manner. For this reason, a man who has toiled with eager zeal for a short time often is deemed worthy of the same reward as those who have worked longer, or even greater gifts. Christ himself, our paymaster, bears testimony to my words when he introduces the parable of the

παραβολὴν καὶ τοῖς ὀψέ ποτε δι' ὀλίγου κοπιάσασι τοῦ ἴσου τοῖς δι' ὅλης ἡμέρας διὰ τὸ πρόθυμον τῆς σπουδῆς ἀξιώσας μισθοῦ.

2   Εἰ δὲ καὶ ἔτι σαφέστερον εἰς ἐναργῆ πραγμάτων ἔκβασιν τὴν τοῦ λόγου βούλει μαθεῖν ἀλήθειαν, εἰσὶ καὶ ἐν μάρτυσι καὶ ἐν ἀσκηταῖς πλεῖστοι, εἷς δὲ ἐκ πολλῶν ἡ κορωνὶς τῶν μαρτύρων, ὁ μέγας Δημήτριος, ὃς εἰς μέσον παρελθών, σαφέστερον δείξει τὸν λόγον. Δι' ὀλίγου γὰρ λόγχαις μόνον τρωθείς, τῶν ἄλλων τῶν διὰ πολλῶν χρόνων ποικίλως βασανισθέντων καὶ κατακοπέντων καὶ καέντων μειζόνως τοῖς θαύμασιν ὑπερέλαμψεν, ἐκ προθέσεως δηλονότι τὸ σπουδαῖον τοῦ ἀγῶνος ἐπιδειξάμενος. Ὁ καὶ εἰδὼς ὁ ἐτάζων καρδίας καὶ νεφροὺς Χριστὸς ὁ Θεὸς ἡμῶν, τὸ ζέον καὶ τὸ διάπυρον τοῦ πρὸς αὐτὸν πόθου μᾶλλον ἐστεφάνωσεν ἢ τὰς ποινὰς καὶ πλέον τῶν ἄλλων χαρίσμασι κατεκόσμησε.

3   Τοιοῦτός ἐστι καὶ ὁ παρ' ἡμῶν εἰς διήγησιν νῦν προτεθείς, ὁ μέγας ἐν ἀσκηταῖς Θεόδωρος, προθύμῳ σπουδῇ καὶ ζέσει πίστεως δι' ὀλίγου ἀσκήσας τῇ τῶν μεγίστων δωρεῶν κατεπλουτίσθη χάριτι, οὗ τὸ σεπτὸν τοῦ βίου καὶ πρὸ τῆς ἀσκήσεως καὶ τοὺς ἀποκρύφους πόνους μετὰ τὴν ἄσκησιν ἡ τῶν θαυμάτων ἔδειξε πηγή. Ἀμυδρῶς γὰρ ἡμῖν ἔδειξε τῶν κατορθωμάτων τοὺς πόνους, καὶ τούτους ὅσους οὐκ ἦν δυνατὸν λαθεῖν τοῖς συνήθως πρὸς αὐτὸν ἔχουσι ἢ καὶ συναναστρεφομένοις, τοὺς μείζονας τῶν ἔργων ἱδρῶτας ὁ Χριστὸς διὰ τῶν ἰάσεων ἐκήρυξε. Καὶ οὐ θαυμαστόν. Ὥσπερ γὰρ ὁ τῆς οἰκουμένης φωστὴρ καὶ διδάσκαλος, ὁ μέγας ἀπόστολος Παῦλος, ἀριθμῶν τὰ οἰκεῖά

vineyard: he thought that those who came late and worked for a short time were worthy to receive the same fee as those who labored throughout the whole day because of their zeal and readiness.

If you want to verify the truthfulness of my words even further, in order to see the matter clearly, there are many witnesses among the martyrs and ascetics. One among those many witnesses was the great Demetrios, the crown among martyrs, who, coming into our midst, makes what I am saying clearer. Although he was quickly executed with spears alone, through his miracles he outshone all the other saints who had been tortured in many ways for a longer time, mutilated, and burned. This was obviously due to the inner disposition of the saint, who gave proof of the great eagerness of his struggles. Christ, our *God who searches our hearts and emotions,* was aware of this and crowned the saint's burning love for him, rewarding it more than the punishments suffered by the others, and adorned him with more numerous gifts.

One such man is the saint whose life is the subject of my present narrative, the great ascetic Theodore. By leading a short ascetic life in eager zeal and with ardent faith, he was enriched with the grace of the greatest gifts. The fountain of his miracles gave proof of the pious life that he lived, even before he became an ascetic, and then of his hidden struggles, after he took up the ascetic challenge. For he himself revealed to us only a faint notion of his laborious achievements; I am referring to those labors which could not be kept secret from those who were close to him and spent their time with him. But Christ revealed to us his even greater toils through his acts of healing. This should not be a source of amazement. For once when Paul, the great apostle

ποτε κατορθώματα, εἰς ζῆλον ἡμῖν ἐπήγαγεν ὅτι "χωρὶς τῶν παρεκτός," δεικνὺς διὰ τοῦ λόγου πλείονα ἢ καὶ μείζονα εἶναι τὰ παρασιωπηθέντα.

4   Πάντως καὶ οὗτος τὸ κενὸν τῶν ἀνθρώπων φεύγων δοξάριον, ὅσους λαθεῖν ἀγῶνας οὐκ ἠδυνήθη ἢ καὶ ἀμυδρῶς, ὡς ἔφημεν, ἐξηγήσατο, ταῦτα τῷ λόγῳ προτέθεικεν εἰς διήγησιν, τὰ μείζονα δὲ τῶν ἀγώνων, ἃ Θεῷ μόνῳ νυκτὸς καὶ ἡμέρας δεικνύων ἦν, αὐτὸς ἐκεῖνος ὁ στεφοδότης Χριστὸς ἀνακηρύττει σήμερον διὰ τῆς τῶν δωρεῶν παροχῆς. Τὴν γὰρ ἑκάστου τῶν ἁγίων πρὸς Θεὸν παρρησίαν οὐδὲν ἡμῖν ἄλλο ἐμφαίνειν εἴωθεν, ἀλλ᾽ ἡ τῶν αἰτήσεων ἄφθονος παροχὴ καὶ τὸ ἐν ἀνάγκαις ἑτοίμως προΐστασθαι, εἰς ἃ καὶ μᾶλλον οὗτος δεύτερος ἢ καὶ ἴσος ἀνεδείχθη Νικόλαος.

2

Πατρίδα τε αὐτοῦ καὶ γένος οὐκ ἐβουλόμην διαγράψαι (τί γὰρ ὄφελος ἐκ τῆς κάτω πόλεως περιγράφεσθαι τοὺς τῆς ἄνω Σιὼν πολίτας, ἐξ ἧς οὐκ ἔστι τινὰ σπουδαῖον φανῆναι ἢ φαῦλον ἢ ἄσημον ἢ λαμπρόν), ἀλλ᾽ ἵνα δειχθείη καὶ ἐν τούτῳ τὸ περιφανὲς τοῦ ἀνδρὸς καὶ ὁ πρὸς Θεὸν αὐτοῦ πόθος, οὐδὲ αὐτὸ παρασιωπήσω. Ἦν δὲ αὐτοῦ πατρὶς ἡ περιφανὴς τῶν πόλεων Κορώνη, ἡ ἐν τῷ θέματι

who enlightened and taught the entire world, was enumerating his own achievements, he added the phrase *"except for those I omit,"* infusing us with zeal, for with those words he indicated that his omissions were more numerous or even greater.

In the same way, my speech will deal only with those few 4 contests which the saint could not hide, because he wanted to avoid human vainglory, as well as with those to which he himself vaguely referred. But the greatest among his contests, which he revealed only to God day and night, are proclaimed publicly today by Christ himself, who crowned him, through the great gifts with which he has been rewarded. Nothing can disclose to us the degree of a saint's access to God other than God's prompt fulfillment of the saint's requests and the saint's eagerness to help us in difficult circumstances. In this respect, Theodore became a second Saint Nicholas, or rather equal to him.

2

It was not my intention to write anything about his fatherland and his family. For is there really any profit in describing the citizens of the heavenly Zion in terms of their earthly city, through which no one can be glorified, vilified, or made famous or obscure? However, I am not going to pass over those topics in silence either, in order to show the man's eminence and love of God in this respect as well. His fatherland was the illustrious city of Korone, which is in the

Πελοποννήσου διακειμένη, γονεῖς δὲ οὐκ ἄσημοι, ἀλλὰ
τῶν ἐπ᾽ εὐλαβείᾳ μᾶλλον λαμπρυνομένων ἢ πλούτῳ. Οἳ
καὶ τεκόντες τοῦτον, πενταετῆ ὄντα τοῖς μαθήμασιν ἐκδί-
δωσι, καὶ ἄλλοις δύο ἔτεσι τοῖς μαθήμασιν ἐνδιατρίψαντα,
ὡς εἶναι αὐτὸν ἑπταετῆ, τῷ ἐπισκόπῳ τῆς πόλεως προσά-
ξαντες τῷ κλήρῳ ἐγκαταλέγουσιν. Ἔδει γὰρ τὸν τοιοῦτον
καὶ ἐν τῷ βίῳ ἔτι ὄντα ἱερὸν ἀνάθημα εἶναι, τὴν ψυχὴν καὶ
τὸ σῶμα Θεῷ καθιερώσαντα καὶ φωτὸς οἰκητήριον γεγο-
νότα.

2   Δι᾽ ὀλίγου δὲ τῶν γονέων αὐτοῦ τὸν βίον ἀπολιπόντων,
ἔτι αὐτοῦ ὀρφανοῦ καὶ ἀνηλίκου τυγχάνοντος ὁ πρωτοπαπᾶς τοῦ Ἐναυπλίου, συνήθης ὢν τῶν αὐτοῦ γονέων καὶ
φίλος εἴτε καὶ συγγενής, ἀκριβῶς οὐδεὶς ἐδίδαξε—ταῦτα
γὰρ ἡμεῖς οὐκ εἰδότες, οἱ ὄντες ἐν ταῖς ἡμέραις ταύταις οὐ
συνεγράψαμεν, ἀλλ᾽ ὡς ὁ μακάριος οὗτος Θεόδωρος, μετὰ
τὸ καταλεῖψαι τὸν βίον καὶ ἀποκαρῆναι ἐπανιὼν ἀπὸ Ῥώ-
μης εἰς Μονεμβασίαν διηγήσατό τινι, ταῦτα μόνα συνετά-
ξαμεν καὶ ταῦτα μετὰ τὸ δοξασθῆναι αὐτὸν παρὰ Θεοῦ καὶ
δεῖξαι τὸ θεάρεστον τοῦ βίου αὐτοῦ διὰ τῶν γενομένων
ἰάσεων. Ὅθεν τὰ πλεῖστα αὐτοῦ, λέγων δὴ ἀναστροφὴν
βίου καὶ γένους περιφάνειαν καὶ ἀσκητικοὺς ἀγῶνας τοὺς
πλείους οὐκ ἴσμεν—ἐλθὼν δέ, ὡς ἔφημεν, ὁ πρωτοπαπᾶς
καὶ λαβὼν αὐτὸν ἐν τῇ ἰδίᾳ, ἐν τῷ Ναυπλίῳ ἀπήγαγεν, καὶ
ἐκεῖσε τοῦτον ἀναθρέψας καὶ γράμμασιν ἐκπαιδεύσας
μετὰ τὴν ἐνηλικίωσιν καὶ γυναικὶ συζεῦξαι ἠθέλησεν. Ὁ
δέ, ὡς ἡ ἀλήθεια ἔδειξεν, οὐκ ἠβούλετο. Πῶς γὰρ καὶ
θελῆσαι τοῦτο εἶχεν, ὁ καὶ μετὰ τὴν συνάφειαν ὅλως τῷ
λογισμῷ μὴ πεδηθείς, μὴ γυναικὸς πόθῳ, μὴ τέκνων

administrative district of the Peloponnese. His parents were not obscure people, but they were more renowned for piety than for wealth. When their son was five years old, his parents sent him to school. After completing two years of study up to the age of seven, his parents presented him to the bishop of that city and enrolled him in the ranks of the clergy. It was proper for such a man to be offered as a holy gift to God while he was still in this life, since he had dedicated himself body and soul to God and had become an abode of light.

After a short time, his parents departed from this life, and the saint, who was still a minor, was orphaned. Then the senior priest of Nauplion came to Korone. He knew the saint's parents well, being either their friend or kinsman; no one really explained this to me. Not knowing these matters, since I was not present at the time, I have refrained from writing them down. I confine myself to those events narrated by the blessed Theodore to someone after he renounced the world and became a monk, at the time of his return from Rome to Monemvasia. These events took place after God glorified Theodore and revealed that his life was pleasing to him, through his miraculous healings. That is why I do not know many details concerning the conduct of his life, the glory of his family, and the majority of his ascetic struggles. As I said, the senior priest came and took the saint away to Nauplion, his own city, where he raised him and educated him in letters. When he reached maturity, the priest wanted to marry him off, but the saint had no such wish, as was truly revealed afterward. How could he want such a thing? Even after he was married, his mind was not attached to it; he was bound neither by love for his wife, nor

2

στοργῇ, οἷς εἴωθε καὶ αὐτὰ τὰ θηρία στέργειν, ἀλλὰ τῇ τοῦ θανάτου ἐννοίᾳ τὸν νοῦν ἐνασχολῶν *πάντα ἡγεῖτο ὡς σκύβαλα·* Ὅμως ἐκράτησεν ἡ τοῦ ἀναθρεψαμένου βουλὴ καὶ γυναικὶ συζευχθεὶς δύο ἐξ αὐτῆς ἀπογεννᾷ παῖδας, ἡ δὲ τοῦ θανάτου μνήμη ἔνδον σμύχουσα ἐν τῇ καρδίᾳ αὐτοῦ οὐκ ἠρεμεῖ, ἀλλὰ μᾶλλον ηὔξανεν.

3

Ὁ δὲ ἐν τῷ τότε ἐπισκοπεύων τῆς Ἀργείων ἐκκλησίας, ὁ θεοφιλέστατος ἐπίσκοπος Θεόδωρος, μαθὼν τὰ κατ᾽ αὐτὸν καὶ κατανοήσας τὸ τοῦ ἀνδρὸς καὶ ἀπ᾽ αὐτοῦ τοῦ σχήματος (διαδείκνυται γὰρ ὡς ἐπὶ τὸ πολὺ τὸ κάλλος τῆς ψυχῆς καὶ ἐν τῇ ἐπιφανείᾳ τοῦ προσώπου καὶ μαρτυρεῖ τῷ λόγῳ ὁ πρωτομάρτυς Στέφανος τὴν μορφὴν ὡς ἀγγέλου δεικνὺς ἐν τῷ συνεδρίῳ τῶν θεοκτόνων Ἰουδαίων. Οὕτω γὰρ καὶ οὗτος χαριεστάτην εἶχε τὴν ὅρασιν καὶ ἀγγελικὴν) χειροτονεῖ τοῦτον διάκονον, ἀλλ᾽ οὐκ ἦν ἠρεμεῖν πάντως τοῦ θείου πόθου τὸ κέντρον, ἀλλ᾽ ἐν τῇ καρδίᾳ αὐτοῦ νῦττον καὶ ὡς πῦρ κηρὸν κατεσθίον, καὶ τὸ πρόσωπον αὐτοῦ σκυθρωπὸν καὶ τὸ ὄμμα κατάξηρον τοῖς ὁρῶσιν ἐδείκνυ, ὡς πληροῦσθαι ἐπ᾽ αὐτὸν τὸ παροιμιακὸν λόγιον, τὸ φάσκον *"Καρδίας εὐφραινομένης θάλλει πρόσωπον, ἐν δὲ λύπαις οὔσης, σκυθρωπάζει μᾶλλον."* Ἐν τοιαύτῃ οὖν ἀδολεσχίᾳ ὁρῶντες αὐτὸν τινὲς τῶν συνήθων καὶ φίλων

by affection for his children. Even wild animals love their offspring, but he, constantly occupying his mind with the thought of death, *considered all other things as refuse.* However, the one who raised him managed to impose his will: the saint was married to a woman and had two children by her. However, the thought of death, which was hidden inside his heart, did not remain quiet, but became even stronger.

3

Theodore, the man beloved by God who was bishop of the church of Argos at the time, learned about the saint and understood the man's piety even from his appearance, since the beauty of the soul is generally reflected even on a man's face. Testimony for what I am saying is offered by Stephen, the first martyr, whose face appeared like that of an angel *at the council* of the god-murdering Jews. In the same way, Theodore's visage was most graceful, like that of an angel. Therefore, the bishop ordained him a deacon. However, the love of God, which was like a goad, would not leave him in peace, but went on stirring the saint's heart, devouring it as fire melts wax. His face was gloomy and his eyes were completely dry, plain for all to see. The passage from the book of Proverbs was proved true in him: *"The face of a man whose heart is happy is bright,* but *if someone is in distress, his face is gloomy."* Some of his friends and acquaintances, seeing him in such a meditative state, asked him the reason for this

ἐπύθοντο τὴν αἰτίαν, ὁ δὲ ἀπεπέμπετο αὐτοὺς λόγοις χρηστοῖς, μηδὲν ἀνιαρὸν λέγων ἔχειν.

2 Ἀλλ' οὐκ ἦν εἰς τέλος λαθεῖν. Ἡ γὰρ ἐπιφάνεια τοῦ προσώπου καὶ τὸ κατηφὲς ἦθος καὶ οἱ ἐκ βάθους στεναγμοὶ ἄγγελοι τοῦ λογισμοῦ τοῖς παρατυχοῦσιν ἐγίνοντο. Διὸ καί τινες τῶν οἰκειοτέρων ὡς ἐξ ἀγάπης τυχὸν πλέον τῶν ἄλλων θαρρεῖν ἔχοντες, διὰ σπουδῆς ἐποιοῦντο μαθεῖν τὰ κατ' αὐτόν, καὶ ἰδίᾳ λαβόντες αὐτὸν ἐν ὅρκοις τὰ τῆς λύπης καὶ κατηφείας εἰπεῖν ἠνάγκαζον, "Εἰπὲ ἡμῖν, ὦ φίλε," λέγοντες, "τίς ἡ συνέχουσά σε τοσαύτη ἀθυμία καὶ λύπη; Οἶδας γὰρ καὶ αὐτός, συνετὸς ὤν, ὅτι ὥσπερ νέφος ἀποτίθεται ζάλην ζόφου τῇ κενώσει τῶν ὀμβρίων ναμάτων, οὕτω καὶ ψυχὴ ἐξειποῦσα τὴν ἐγκάρδιον λύπην, βάρους καὶ ἀθυμίας κουφίζεται.

3 "Οὕτω γὰρ ὁ Θεὸς ᾠκονόμησε τὰ ἀνιαρὰ τοῦ βίου ἀναψύχεσθαι, διὰ διδασκάλων καὶ γραφῶν παραινέσεως, διὰ φίλων καὶ συγγενῶν παρακλήσεως, δι' ὑπομονῆς καὶ εὐχαριστίας. Τί δέ σοι ταῦτα παραμυθήσεται μὴ εἰδὼς ὃ ἔχεις; Τίς δὲ καὶ οὐ καταμέμψεται ἐπὶ πολὺ οὕτω τηκομένου σου καὶ μηδενὶ θαρροῦντος τὰ κατὰ σέ; Εἰπὲ οὖν ἀνενδοιάστως, καὶ εἰ μὲν δυνάμεως ἔχ ομεν δι' ἔργων παραμυθήσεσθαί σοι, γνώσῃ ἐξ ἔργων τὸ τῆς ἀγάπης γνήσιον. Εἰ δ' ἀδυνατοῦμεν πρὸς τοῦτο, κἂν διὰ λόγου, διὰ συμβουλῆς, δι' εὐχῆς, καὶ ὁ Θεὸς μεταβαλεῖ τὰ λυπηρὰ καὶ δωριεῖται παράκλησιν. Εἰπὲ οὖν ἡμῖν, παρακαλοῦμεν, καὶ μὴ ἀποκρύψῃς."

behavior, but the saint sent them away, telling them some pleasantries and denying that he was unhappy at all.

But in the end it was impossible for him to escape atten- 2 tion. His gloomy face, his sulking, and his heavy groaning revealed his thoughts to all who happened to meet him. Some of those most familiar with him, who were on more intimate terms with the saint than others because they loved him, made an effort to learn what was wrong with him. They took him aside and, putting him under oath, pressed him to reveal the reason for his sadness and low spirits, saying: "O friend, tell us what is this great despondency and sadness that oppresses you? You are intelligent, so you know that a man confessing the dejection that lies in his heart may be relieved of his burden and depression just as a cloud expels the gloom of its inner darkness by releasing the rain water that it holds inside.

"This is a dispensation by God: the sorrows of this life are 3 alleviated through the admonitions of our teachers and of Scripture, through the consolation of our friends and relatives, and through our own patience and gratitude. But how can someone provide that consolation to you, if he does not know what is wrong with you? Who will not find blame with you for not entrusting your secrets to someone, even though you have been dejected for such a long time? Reveal them now without any hesitation, and if we are in a position to bring you solace through our deeds, you will realize that our love is genuine because of them. But if we are unable to do so, even with our words, our advice, and our prayers, then God will turn your distress into happiness, giving you comfort. Please tell us, we beg of you, and hide nothing."

4   Ὁ δὲ πρότερον κατασφαλισάμενος αὐτοὺς μηδενὶ ἐξειπεῖν, εἶτα ἐκ βάθους στενάξας καὶ τοὺς ὀφθαλμοὺς δακρύων πλήσας ἀπεκρίνατο. "Ὦ ἀδελφοὶ καὶ φίλοι, ἐμὲ οὐδὲν τῶν ἀνιαρῶν τοῦ βίου τούτου λυπεῖ, ἀλλ᾽ οὐδὲ λυπῆσαι δύναται. Πῶς γὰρ καὶ λυπήσει τὸν ἐν μηδενὶ θελγόμενον ἢ ὅλως προσκείμενον τοῖς τοῦ βίου πράγμασιν; Ἀλλ᾽ ἓν μόνον ἐστὶν ὃ λυποῦμαι, ἡ τοῦ θανάτου μελέτη. Ἐννοῶ γὰρ πῶς ἐκ τῶν τοῦ βίου πάντων γυμνὸς εἰς Ἅιδου πορεύσομαι καὶ ἐκ τοῦ φόβου τήκεταί μου ἡ καρδία. Ἐννοῶ πῶς πάντων ἡ ἀγάπη καὶ πάντα τὰ ἡδέα τοῦ βίου ἕως ἐπικαλύψεως λίθου καὶ τήκεταί μου ἡ καρδία. Ἐννοῶ πῶς πᾶσα δόξα καὶ πλοῦτος καὶ ἡδονὴ σώματος ὡς σκιὰ καὶ ὄναρ καὶ τήκεταί μου ἡ καρδία. Ἐννοῶ πῶς πάντες ἐν πᾶσι κοινῇ συνερχόμεθα, μόνοι δὲ καὶ γυμνοὶ τῷ τάφῳ παραδιδόμεθα καὶ τήκεταί μου ἡ καρδία. Ἐννοῶ πῶς πᾶσαν φύσιν βροτείαν καὶ πᾶσαν ἡλικίαν λαβὼν ὁ θάνατος βορὰν σκωλήκων τίθησι καὶ τήκεταί μου ἡ καρδία. Ἐννοῶ πῶς ἐν τῷ τάφῳ οὐκ ἔνι γνωσθῆναι κάλλος μορφῆς ἢ δόξα βίου, ἀλλὰ πάντες σῆψις καὶ φθορὰ καὶ τήκεταί μου ἡ καρδία. Ἐννοῶ πῶς πᾶσα φύσις βροτεία ὡς φύλλα δένδρου οἱ μὲν πίπτουσι καὶ εἰς ἀφανισμὸν χωροῦσιν, ἕτεροι δὲ φύονται καὶ τήκεταί μου ἡ καρδία.

5   "Ταῦτα ἐννοῶν καὶ τὸ προφητικὸν λόγιον εἰς νοῦν ἔχων, τὸ φάσκον ὅτι 'Ὡς οἱ ἰχθύες οἱ θηρευόμενοι ἐν ἀμφιβλήστρῳ κακῷ καὶ ὡς ὄρνεα τὰ θηρευόμενα ἐν παγίδι, ὡς ταῦτα παγιδεύονται οἱ υἱοὶ τῶν ἀνθρώπων εἰς καιρὸν πονηρόν, ὅταν ἐπιπέσῃ ἐπ᾽ αὐτοὺς ἄφνω,' καὶ λέγω τῇ ψυχῇ μου, 'Ἀθλία ψυχή, εἰ ἄφνω παρ᾽ ἐλπίδα παγιδευθῇς καὶ σὺ τῷ

270

Theodore, after making them swear under oath not to say   4
anything to anyone, groaned heavily, filled his eyes with
tears, and spoke to them: "O my brethren and friends, it is
no sorrow of this world that saddens me, nor would such a
thing even be able to sadden me. How could it cause pain to
a man who is not attracted by any of those things, who pays
no attention at all to the affairs of this world? My sadness is
caused by just one thing, meditation on death. For I am con-
templating how I will go to Hades, stripped of all worldly
possessions, and my heart wastes away with fear. I realize
that the love of others and all the pleasures of life will last
only until the gravestone is set above one, and my heart
wastes away. I realize that all glory, wealth, and the pleasures
of the flesh are like shadows and dreams, and my heart
wastes away. I realize that we are all in this together, but we
are delivered to the grave alone and naked, and my heart
wastes away. I realize how death carries away every mortal
and all ages of men, and turns them into food for worms,
and my heart wastes away. I realize that no beauty of the
body or glory of life can exist in the grave, but that we all rot
away and decay, and my heart wastes away. I realize that all
nature is mortal and falls down and decomposes quickly like
the dead leaves of a tree, and then others are born to take
their place, and my heart wastes away.

"Realizing all this and remembering that saying of the   5
prophet, '*Like fish captured in a cruel net, and like birds caught in
a snare, so mortals are snared in a time of calamity, when it suddenly falls upon them*,' I say to my soul: 'O miserable soul, if
you too are trapped by death unexpectedly, what will you say

θανάτῳ, τί ἀπολογήσει, ἢ ποῖον ἄλλον καιρὸν εἰς μετάνοιαν εὑρήσεις, τίς δέ σου καὶ μνείαν ποιήσει ποτὲ τοῦ χρόνου τῇ λήθῃ τὰ σὰ ἐπικαλύψαντος; Τίς δέ σοι καὶ τῶν φίλων ἢ συγγενῶν ἢ οἰκείων παραστήσεται τότε ἐν Ἅιδῃ κολαζομένῃ; Ποῦ δὲ τότε παραμυθία φίλων ἢ προστασία ἀρχόντων ἢ παρατροπὴ λόγων τὴν ἀλήθειαν ὑποκλέπτουσα; Ποῦ δὲ οἱ ἀνωφελεῖς καὶ καθημερινοὶ τοῦ βίου κόποι; Τί δὲ τῶν βιωτικῶν ἐξελεῖταί σε τότε τῆς κολάσεως; Τί δὲ τῶν ἁπάντων ἐλευθερῶσαι δυνήσεται;'

6 "Ταῦτά εἰσιν, ἀδελφοί, τὰ κατεσθίοντά μου τὴν καρδίαν, ἐν τούτοις νυκτὸς καὶ ἡμέρας μελετῶντί μοι, προφητικῶς εἰπεῖν, 'Ἐξηράνθη ὡς ὄστρακον ἡ ἰσχύς μου καὶ τὸ ὀστοῦν μου ἐκολλήθη τῇ σαρκί μου.' Ἐννοήσας δὲ ὡς μηδὲν ἄλλο εἶναι ταύτης τῆς λύπης ἴαμα καὶ ψυχῆς σωτηρία, εἰ μὴ ἡ τοῦ βίου ἀναχώρησις καὶ τὸ κατὰ μόνας Κυρίῳ δουλεύειν, βούλομαι ὑποχωρῆσαι τοῦ βίου καὶ τοῦ ποθουμένου τυχεῖν."

7 Ταῦτα ἀκούσαντες οἱ ἄνδρες καὶ ὥσπερ κατανυγέντες, ὑπέσχοντο καὶ αὐτοὶ ἀκολουθῆσαι αὐτῷ. Ἀλλ' ἐκείνους μὲν ὁ τοῦ βίου δεσμὸς ὑπερθέσεσιν ματαίαις εἶργε τοῦ ἀγαθοῦ, αὐτὸς δὲ πλοῖον εὑρὼν λάθρᾳ τῶν οἰκείων ἀποδρὰς ἐπὶ Ῥώμην ἔπλευσε. Καλῶς δὲ τὸν πλοῦν διανύσας καὶ καταλαβὼν τὰ ἐκεῖσε, ἦν νηστείαις καὶ εὐχαῖς σχολάζων ἐν τοῖς πανσέπτοις ναοῖς τῶν ἁγίων καὶ κορυφαίων ἀποστόλων. Καὶ ποιήσας ἐκεῖ χρόνους τέσσαρας καὶ διελθὼν πάσας τὰς ἐκκλησίας καὶ τὰ μοναστήρια, συντυχὼν τότε καὶ ἁγίοις ἀνδράσι καὶ ὥσπερ ἐφόδιον τὰς τιμίας αὐτῶν εὐχὰς κομισάμενος, διὰ τὸ μὴ εὑρεῖν ἐκεῖσε τόπον

to defend yourself? Will you find another time in which to repent? Who will commemorate you when time has covered everything of yours in oblivion? Which of your friends or relatives or member of your household will stand by your soul at the time of its torments in Hades? Where will the consolations of your friends be then, or the protection promised by magistrates? No elaborate speech will be able to distort the truth. Where will those daily labors be which bring us no profit at all? Will any aspect of this life save you from hell, will anything at all be able to liberate you?'

"These, my brethren, are the thoughts that consume my 6 heart, as I *turn* these things *over in my mind day and night* like the prophet who said, '*my power is dried up like a potsherd, and my bone has cleaved to my flesh.*' Realizing that the only remedy for my distress and the only salvation for my soul is to abandon this life and to serve the Lord in solitude, I want to leave this world and obtain what I so dearly desire."

Hearing these words, the others were deeply moved and 7 promised to follow him. But their attachments to the affairs of this life prevented them, through their dilatory tactics, from fulfilling this good purpose. The saint, however, found a ship and, escaping the attention of his relatives, sailed off to Rome. Arriving there after a safe voyage, he devoted himself to fasting and prayer in the all-sacred churches of the holy and chief apostles. He spent four years there, visiting all the monasteries and churches. He met many holy men and collected their precious blessings like provisions for the future. But failing to find a quiet place there to live in

ἥσυχον τοῦ κατὰ μόνας ἀσκῆσαι, ὑπέστρεψεν ἐν Μονεμβασίᾳ, ποθῶν τοῦ ἀπελθεῖν εἰς Κυθηρίαν τὴν νῆσον, ἔρη-
μον καὶ ἀοίκητον τότε οὖσαν διὰ τὰς ἐπιδρομὰς τῶν τότε
Ἀγαρηνῶν. Ἐκεῖσε γὰρ ὥσπερ ἐν φωλεῷ οἱ ἐν Κρήτῃ τότε
οἰκοῦντες ἐγκρυπτόμενοι τοῖς διερχομένοις ἐπετίθεντο,
ἀλλὰ καὶ ἐν ἄλλοις, ἐν οἷς ἂν ἀπήρχοντο ληΐζεσθαι, τὰς
διόδους ἐκεῖθεν ἐποιοῦντο καὶ διὰ τοῦτο οὐδεὶς ἐτόλμα
οἰκῆσαι ἐκεῖ.

4

Ἐλθὼν δὲ ἐν τῇ Μονεμβασίᾳ ἔμεινεν ἐν τῷ ναῷ τῆς
ὑπεραγίας Δεσποίνης ἡμῶν Θεοτόκου τῆς λεγομένης
Διακονίας ἐν κελλίῳ ἡσυχάζων καὶ ἀεὶ τὸ ψαλτήριον στι-
χολογῶν νύκτα καὶ ἡμέραν, τὸ δὲ ἔνδυμα αὐτοῦ ἦν ῥάκος
τρίχινον. Ἐν νηστείᾳ δὲ καὶ κατανύξει τῇ ἐκκλησίᾳ σχολάζων σύννους ἵστατο κάτω νεύων. Χρονίζοντος δὲ αὐτοῦ ἐν
τῇ Μονεμβασίᾳ ἐν τῷ ῥηθέντι ναῷ διὰ τὸ μὴ εὑρίσκειν ἐξ
ἑτοίμου πλοῖον, ἡ γυνὴ αὐτοῦ μαθοῦσα παρά τινος τὰ κατ᾽
αὐτὸν ἀπέστειλε διὰ γραφῆς παράκλησιν αἰτοῦσα τῷ ἐπισκόπῳ Μονεμβασίας, ὅπως ἀποστείλῃ αὐτὸν καὶ μὴ βου-
λόμενον ἐκεῖσε, τοῦτο λέγουσα ὅτι "δι᾽ οὐδὲν ἕτερον, ἀλλ᾽
ὅπως ἀποκείρῃ κἀμέ. Οὐδεὶς γάρ με ἄνευ προτροπῆς
ἐκείνου ἀποκεῖραι τολμᾷ." Ὁ δὲ ἐπίσκοπος δεξάμενος καὶ
ἀναγνοὺς τὰ γράμματα, ἀπέστειλεν αὐτὰ πρὸς τὸν μακάριον Θεόδωρον, δηλώσας αὐτῷ καὶ τοῦτο, ὅτι "Ἴδε τὰ
γράμματα καὶ ὃ νοεῖς εἶναι κάλλιον, τοῦτο καὶ ποίησον."

solitude as an ascetic, he returned to Monemvasia. His wish was to go to the island of Kythera, which was desolate and uninhabited at the time due to the raids of the Hagarenes. For the people who were then inhabiting Crete hid out there as if in a lair, attacking those who passed by. Even when they attacked other places in order to plunder them, they sailed past Kythera and so no one dared to live there.

4

As soon as he came to Monemvasia, he settled in the church of our all-holy Lady, the Theotokos, who is called Diakonia. He practiced the life of spiritual tranquility in a cell, constantly reciting the Psalter, day and night. He was dressed in a ragged garment made of hair. He devoted himself to a life of fasting and contrition in the church, always deep in thought and with downcast eyes. While he was delayed in Monemvasia in the aforementioned church, because he could not find an available ship, someone informed his wife about him and so she sent a letter to the bishop of Monemvasia asking him to send Theodore back to her, even against his will. She added, "Do it, for no other reason but that he may tonsure me too, for no other man dares to do that without his consent." After the bishop received and read this letter, he sent it to the blessed Theodore, saying to him, "Read this letter and do whatever you think best."

Δεξάμενος δὲ ταῦτα ὁ μακάριος Θεόδωρος καὶ ἀναγνούς, πρὸς τὸν ἀποκομίσαντα ἔφη, "Ταῦτα τὰ γράμματα οὐκ εἰσὶ τῆς γυναικός. Γνωρίζω γὰρ τὸν γράψαντα καὶ ὁ Κύριος νὰ τὸν σώσῃ, ἀλλ᾿ οὐκ ἐμποδίσει ὁ Διάβολος τὴν ὁδόν μου."

2   Τούτοις τοῖς λόγοις ἀποπέμψας τὸν ἀποσταλέντα παρὰ τοῦ ἐπισκόπου τῆς συνήθους ἀσκήσεως εἴχετο, μηδὲν ὅλως περὶ τροφῆς ἢ ἐνδύματος φροντίζων ἢ αἰτῶν παρά τινός τι καίπερ χειμῶνος σφοδροτάτου ὄντος αἱ σάρκες αὐτοῦ ἐκ τοῦ κρύους πηγνύμεναι ἀπελιθοῦντο, οἱ ὀφθαλμοὶ πελιδνοὶ καὶ ὕφαιμοι καθωρῶντο. Ἀλλ᾿ οὐκ ἐδεήθη ὅλως τινός, ἀλλὰ μᾶλλον ἀποστειλάντων αὐτῷ τινῶν φιλοχρίστων σαγίον καὶ ἱμάτιον καὶ ὑποδήματα διὰ τὴν τῆς ψύξεως ἀνάγκην, τοὺς μὲν ἀποστείλαντας, ἀποδεξάμενος τῆς προαιρέσεως ὑπερηύξατο, τὰ δὲ ἀποσταλέντα οὐκ ἔλαβεν, ἀλλ᾿ ἦν ἀρκούμενος τῷ τριχίνῳ ῥακίῳ, ὃ περιεβέβλητο, τοῦτο ποιούμενος καὶ νυκτὸς ἐγκοίτιον καὶ ἡμερινὸν περιβόλαιον. Ἄρτον δὲ ἢ καί τι ἄλλο ἀπέστειλεν αὐτῷ τις, μετρίως ἐξ αὐτοῦ ἀπογευσάμενος, τὰ λοιπὰ τοῖς δεομένοις ἐδίδου.

3   Ἐν δὲ τῷ ναῷ τῆς ὑπεραγίας Δεσποίνης ἡμῶν Θεοτόκου, τῷ ὄντι ἐν τῷ χωρίῳ τὰ Τέρεα, ἦν προσμονάριος μοναχός τις λεγόμενος Ἀντώνιος. Οὗτος συχνοτέρως ἤρχετο πρὸς τὸν μακάριον Θεόδωρον ὠφελείας χάριν (ἦν γὰρ οὐ μόνον διὰ λόγου ὁ ἀοίδιμος ὠφελῶν τοὺς παρατυχόντας, ἀλλὰ καὶ ἐκ τῆς διαίτης καὶ ἐκ τῆς ταπεινώσεως καὶ καταστάσεως). Οὗτος μαθὼν ὅτι βούλεται ἐν τῇ Κυθηρίᾳ περᾶσαι ὁ ὅσιος, παρεκάλει ἀπιέναι σὺν αὐτῷ, ὁ δὲ συνέθετο.

Once the blessed Theodore had taken the letter in his hands and read it, he said to the letter carrier, "This is not my wife's handwriting. I know who wrote the letter, and may the Lord save him. The devil will not prohibit me from following the road I have chosen."

With these words he dismissed the bishop's messenger 2 and went on with his habitual ascetic life, not caring at all about food or clothes. He did not ask for anything from anyone, although the winter was extremely harsh and his flesh had frozen like stone from the cold, while his eyes were dull and bloodshot. But he did not beg from anyone. Even when some Christ-loving people sent him a cloak, a shirt, and a pair of shoes so that he might cope with the cold, he commended those who had sent these things for their good intentions and prayed for them, but he did not accept the gifts, being content with the ragged hair garment he was wearing, which served as both his blanket at night and his garment during the day. If someone sent him some bread or something else to eat, he just tasted the food and sent the leftovers to those in need.

The keeper of the church of our all-holy Lady, the Theo- 3 tokos, in the village of Terea was a monk called Antony. This man used to visit the blessed Theodore quite often in order to gain some spiritual benefit, since the famous man benefited those who came to him not only through his speech, but also through his way of life, his humility, and his conduct. As soon as Antony learned that the saint wanted to cross over to Kythera, he asked to go with him, and the saint agreed.

5

Ποιήσαντος δὲ αὐτοῦ ἐν τῇ Μονεμβασίᾳ ἐνιαυτὸν ἕνα, ἧκεν ὁ τουρμάρχης Μελίτων μετὰ τεσσάρων χελανδίων ἀποσταλεὶς παρὰ τοῦ διέποντος τότε τὴν βασίλειον ἀρχὴν Ῥωμανοῦ τοῦ γέροντος, ἀπιὼν κατὰ τῶν τὴν Κρήτην τότε οἰκούντων Ἀγαρηνῶν. Καὶ μαθὼν τοῦτο ὁ μακάριος Θεόδωρος, ἀπελθὼν προσέπεσεν αὐτῷ τοῦ ἀναλαβεῖν αὐτὸν καὶ ἀπαγαγεῖν ἐν τῇ νήσῳ. Συνθεμένου δὲ τοῦ τουρμάρχη, σπουδαίως αὐτὸς ἀπελθὼν εἰς τὸ χωρίον, ἀνελάβετο τὸν δηλωθέντα μοναχὸν καὶ ταχέως ὑποστρέψαντες ἐνέβησαν εἰς ἓν τῶν διήρων, ἔχοντες καὶ βιβλία τὰ ἀναγκαῖα, Ψαλτήριον, Ὀκτώηχον, Ἀπόστολον καὶ Εὐαγγέλιον.

2 Ὡς δὲ καιροῦ γενομένου, ἀπήεσαν ἐν τῇ νήσῳ καὶ οἱ μοναχοὶ ἀπέβησαν εἰς τὴν γῆν. Μικρὸν δὲ ἀναστάντες ἀπ' αὐτῶν οἱ πλευστικοὶ πρὸς τὸ ἕτερον μέρος τῆς νήσου, εὗρον πλοῖον Ἀγαρηνῶν ἔχον ἐνενήκοντα ἄνδρας, οἳ καὶ ἀντέστησαν τῇ Ῥωμαϊκῇ πλευσίᾳ γενναίως, ἀλλὰ τῇ ὁρμῇ τοῦ πυρὸς ἡττήθησαν. Ἅμα γὰρ τῷ ῥῖψαι κατ' αὐτῶν πῦρ καί τινας ἐξ αὐτῶν καταφλεχθῆναι, οἱ λοιποὶ βαλόντες ἑαυτοὺς εἰς τὴν θάλασσαν, τῇ νήσῳ προσερρύησαν. Οὓς καὶ καταδραμόντες οἱ πλευστικοὶ μετὰ ὅπλων, τοὺς μὲν ἀπέκτειναν, ἄλλους συλλαβόμενοι τῷ τουρμάρχῃ αὐτῶν ἀπήγαγον. Εἴκοσι δὲ ἐξ αὐτῶν ἄνδρες, τοῖς ἄλσεσι τῆς νήσου ἐγκρυβέντες, εἰς τέλος διέλαθον. Οὓς καὶ πλειστάκις καὶ ἐμπόνως ψηλαφήσαντες, οὐδὲν πλέον ἤνυσαν ἢ κόπους. Ὡς δὲ ἀπέκαμον ψηλαφῶντες, ὑπέστρεψαν ἐν τῇ

5

After the saint spent a whole year in Monemvasia, the *tourmarch* Meliton came to the city with four ships. He had been sent by Romanos the Elder, who was emperor at the time, and was headed against the Hagarenes who were then living on Crete. As soon as the blessed Theodore learned this, he went and begged the *tourmarch* to take him and bring him to the island. When the *tourmarch* agreed, the saint hurried to the village, to fetch the aforementioned monk. They came back quickly and boarded one of the biremes, taking with them the necessary books: the Psalter, the *Oktoechos,* the Apostle, and the Gospel.

As soon as the weather permitted, they sailed to the island and the two monks went ashore. When the fleet left them behind and sailed to the other part of the island, it came across a ship with ninety Hagarenes, who put up brave resistance to the Roman ships, but were defeated by the force of the fire. For as soon as they attacked the Hagarenes with fire, some of them were burned alive, while the others threw themselves into the sea and swam toward the island. The sailors attacked them with their weapons and killed some of them, while others were taken prisoner and led to the *tourmarch.* In the end, only twenty of the Hagarenes were able to escape, hiding in the forests of the island. They tried to track them down repeatedly, sparing no effort, but had nothing to show for their labors. After they wearied of searching for them, they returned to Monemvasia full of joy

Μονεμβασίᾳ μετὰ χαρᾶς καὶ νίκης, ἓν λυπούμενοι πάντες, περὶ τῶν μοναχῶν ὡς ἀδύνατον εἶναι λέγοντες τὸ μὴ ἐμπεσεῖν αὐτοὺς εἰς χεῖρας τῶν καταλειφθέντων τῇ νήσῳ Ἀγαρηνῶν, καὶ μάλιστα μὴ μαθόντων τῶν μοναχῶν περὶ τούτων ὅλως. Ἀλλὰ τὰ παρὰ ἀνθρώποις ἀδύνατα παρὰ τῷ Θεῷ δυνατά. Ὁ γὰρ φυλάξας τὸν Δανιὴλ ἐν τῷ λάκκῳ τῶν λεόντων καὶ τοὺς ὁσίους αὐτοῦ διεφύλαξεν. Οἶδε γὰρ Κύριος εὐσεβεῖς ἐκ πειρασμοῦ ῥύεσθαι. Διὰ τοῦτο καὶ χρονισάντων αὐτῶν ἐν τῇ νήσῳ καὶ πᾶσαν αὐτὴν διὰ τὴν τῶν ἀναγκαίων συλλογὴν πολλάκις διελθόντων, οὐ συνεχωρήθησαν εὑρεῖν τοὺς ἀοιδίμους τούτους.

3   Ὁ δὲ μοναχὸς Ἀντώνιος, ποιήσας ἐκεῖ ἀπὸ τῆς ἑπτὰ καὶ δεκάτης τοῦ Ἰουλίου μηνός (τότε γὰρ ἐνέβησαν εἰς τὸ διήριν οἱ μακάριοι) διὰ τὸ ἀπαραμύθητον τοῦ τόπου καὶ διὰ τὸ μὴ δύνασθαι αὐτὸν ὑπομένειν τὴν ἐκ πείνης καὶ κακουχίας, ἔτι δὲ καὶ κρύους ἀνάγκην (ἤδη γὰρ καὶ προβεβηκὼς ἦν ὁ Ὀκτώβριος μήν), εὑρὼν πλοῖον ἐνέβη εἰς αὐτὸ καὶ ὑπεχώρησε, καθὼς αὐτὸς ἐξηγήσατο. Πυνθανομένων δέ τινων πῶς κατέλιπε τὸν κῦριν Θεόδωρον καὶ ὑπεχώρησε, ἔφη ὅτι "Κεράτια συνήξαμεν τοῦ ἔχειν εἰς διατροφὴν ἡμῶν, καὶ δι᾽ ὅλης τῆς ἡμέρας τῇ εὐχῇ σχολάζοντες, τῇ ἑσπέρᾳ μόνον ἐξ αὐτῶν τὸ σῶμα παρεμυθούμεθα, καὶ ὁ μὲν κῦρις Θεόδωρος ὀλίγα ἐξ αὐτῶν ἤσθιεν, ἐγὼ δέ, γέρων ὢν καὶ μὴ δυνάμενος ἐγκρατεύεσθαι, ἤθελον ἔτι φαγεῖν, αὐτοῦ δὲ μὴ ἐσθίοντος, ἐπεῖχον ἐμαυτὸν καὶ μὴ βουλόμενος. Ὡς δὲ καὶ χειμὼν ἤγγιζε, δεδιὼς τὴν ἐκ τοῦ κρύους ἀνάγκην, ὡς εὗρον ἐπ᾽ εὐθείας τὸ πλοῖον, ὑπεχώρησα." Καὶ αὐτὸς μὲν ἀπελθὼν καὶ ἐπικλείσας ἑαυτὸν ἐν κελλίῳ, ἐκαρτέρησεν

for their victory. But they all had one regret, saying that it would be impossible for those two monks to escape the hands of the Hagarenes who remained on the island, especially since the monks were not aware of their existence. But *what is impossible for men is possible for God.* For he who had protected Daniel inside the lions' den kept his saints intact too, since the Lord knows how to protect pious men from their trials. Although the Hagarenes stayed on the island for a long time and roamed all over it many times in order to collect the necessary provisions, God did not allow them to find those men of blessed memory.

The monk Antony had been there on Kythera since July 3 17, the date when the two blessed men boarded the bireme. But because of the island's lack of comforts and because he was not able to endure hunger, deprivation, and cold (seeing as it was toward the end of October), after finding a ship he embarked on it and left, as he himself related. To those who asked him how he abandoned master Theodore and left the place, he answered, "We gathered the pods of the carob tree for our food and devoted our day to prayer. Only at night did we offer our bodies some comfort by eating those seeds. Master Theodore ate very few, but I, being an old man and unable to control myself, wanted to eat more. But since Theodore did not eat, I restrained myself, even against my will. But since winter was coming and I was afraid of the cold weather, I left as soon as I found a ship." He left and enclosed himself in a cell, persevering there for twenty-

ἐκεῖσε χρόνους εἴκοσι καὶ τρεῖς, καὶ εἰς βαθὺ γῆρας ἐλάσας, διὰ τὸ τὴν ἐγκλείστραν ἀπειλεῖν πτῶσιν ἐξῆλθε καὶ ἐν τῷ ναῷ αὖ τοῦ Προδρόμου μικρὸν διακαρτερήσας, πρὸς Κύριον ἐξεδήμησεν.

4 Ὁ δὲ ὅσιος Θεόδωρος ποιήσας ἐν τῇ νήσῳ ἐν τῷ ναῷ τῶν ἁγίων καὶ ἐνδόξων τοῦ Χριστοῦ μεγάλων μαρτύρων Σεργίου καὶ Βάκχου μῆνας ἕνδεκα, τῷ κρύει πηγνύμενος καὶ ἐν πείνῃ καὶ κακουχίᾳ καὶ μονώσει νύκτα καὶ ἡμέραν μετὰ δακρύων τὸν Θεὸν ἐξιλεούμενος, τῷ ἑνδεκάτῳ μηνὶ πρὸς Κύριον καὶ αὐτὸς ἐξεδήμησε. Σεπτεμβρίου δὲ μηνός, χελανδίου κατὰ πάροδον σταθέντος ἐν τῇ νήσῳ, ἀπῆλθον οἱ πλευστικοὶ προσκυνῆσαι τῷ ναῷ τῶν ἁγίων μαρτύρων καὶ εὗρον τοῦτον ἔξω τῆς ἐκκλησίας κείμενον ἀδιάφθορον, πρὸς κεφαλὴν δὲ αὐτοῦ εὗρον ὄστρακον γεγραμμένον οὕτως, "Ἐγὼ Θεόδωρος, ἐλάχιστος διάκονος, κατεκλίθην ἐν τῇ ἀρρωστείᾳ μηνὶ Ἀπριλίῳ ἑβδόμῃ καὶ ἰδοὺ ἀποθνήσκω μηνὶ Μαΐῳ δωδεκάτῃ, ἐν ἡμέρᾳ τοῦ ἁγίου Ἐπιφανίου." Ταῦτα οὖν ἀναγνόντες καὶ προσκυνήσαντες τοῦ ἁγίου τὸ λείψανον, ὑπέστρεψαν καὶ τῆς νήσου ὑπεχώρησαν, καταλείψαντες αὐτὸν ἐν ᾧ εὗρον τόπῳ. Τοῦ δὲ βασιλέως ἀποστείλαντος εἰς Κρήτην καὶ ἀλλάγιον ποιήσαντος μετὰ ἔτη τρία, Μονεμβασιῶταί τινες ἀπελθόντες εἰς Κυθηρίαν τοῦ θηρεῦσαι ὀνάγρους καὶ αἰγάγρους, ὡς πρὸς τὸν ναὸν τῶν ἁγίων μαρτύρων ἐγένοντο, ὁρῶσι τὸν ὅσιον ἔμπροσθεν τοῦ ναοῦ κείμενον σῶον ὅλως καὶ ἀσινῆ. Προσκυνήσαντες δὲ αὐτὸν μετὰ δακρύων καὶ ἐν τῷ ναῷ προσενέγκαντες, ἔθαψαν.

three years. But because his hermitage was ready to collapse and he had become hoary with old age, he abandoned it. After spending a short time in the church of the Forerunner, he departed to God.

Saint Theodore spent eleven months on the island, in the church of the holy and glorious great martyrs of Christ Sergios and Bakchos. Frozen by the cold and suffering from hunger and all deprivations, completely isolated, and asking God's forgiveness with tears day and night, he too departed for the Lord, in the eleventh month of his sojourn there. In September, a passing ship happened to anchor off the island and the sailors went to pay due honors to the holy martyrs in their church. There, outside the church, they found his body intact. By his head they found a potsherd where the following was written: "I, the humble deacon Theodore, fell ill on the seventh of April, and behold, now, on the twelfth of May, the feast of Saint Epiphanios, I am dying." After reading this and kissing the saint's remains, they went back and departed from the island, leaving Theodore's body behind in the place where they found it. Three years later, the emperor sent men to Crete for an exchange of prisoners. Then some citizens of Monemvasia went to Kythera to hunt wild asses and goats, and came to the church of the holy martyrs. There they saw the holy man lying in front of the church, still completely intact. They paid due honors to him with tears, brought the body into the church, and buried it there.

6

Οὗτος ὁ βίος τοῦ μακαρίου Θεοδώρου, αὕτη ἡ πολιτεία τοῦ κατὰ Θεὸν ζήσαντος καὶ τὸν κόσμον μισήσαντος. Ταῦτά τις, τὰ μὲν παρ᾽ ἐκείνου τοῦ ἀοιδίμου ἀκούσας, τὰ δὲ καὶ παρὰ τῶν εἰδότων αὐτὸν μαθών, ἰδιωτικῶς ἀπεγράψατο, ἡμεῖς δὲ μετὰ τὸ δοξασθῆναι αὐτὸν παρὰ Θεοῦ διὰ τῆς τῶν θαυμάτων ἀφθόνου δωρεᾶς, χάριν ἀφοσιώσασθαι τῷ ἁγίῳ βουλόμενοι καὶ μηδὲν ἄλλο ἰσχύοντες, μικρὸν ὅσον καὶ ἡμεῖς κατὰ ἀγροικίαν καλλωπίσαντες τὰ γεγραμμένα, μηδὲν τῆς ἀληθείας καταλείψαντες ἢ οἴκοθεν προστιθέντες, τοῖς βουλομένοις εἰς σωτηρίαν ψυχῆς μιμήσασθαι τὸν ἐκείνου ἐκτεθείκαμεν βίον.

2 Καὶ τὰ μὲν τῆς ἀσκήσεως καὶ πολιτείας τοῦ ἀοιδίμου Θεοδώρου τοῦτον ἔχει τὸν τρόπον. Ἡμεῖς δὲ πρὸς αὐτὸν τὸν λόγον τρέψωμεν. Ποίοις δὲ λόγοις ἐγκωμιάσω, παμμάκαρ Θεόδωρε, πῶς δὲ καὶ τὴν σὴν ἐπαινέσω νουνεχίαν, ὅτι πόνοις βραχέσι τὴν μακαρίαν ἠλλάξω ζωήν; Τί δὲ καὶ ὀνομάσω σε Ἀβραὰμ ὡς μετανάστην τῶν οἰκείων γενόμενον ἢ Ἐλισσαῖον τῇ φωνῇ τοῦ διδασκάλου εὐθὺς ἐπακούσαντα; Ἀντώνιον ἐρημοπολίτην καὶ σημειοφόρον ἢ ἄλλον θρηνητὴν Ἰερεμίαν στεναγμοῖς καὶ δάκρυσι τοῦ λαοῦ τὴν σωτηρίαν ἐξαιτούμενον; Μάρτυρα ὡς τῇ προαιρέσει μαρτυρήσαντα καὶ μέσης ὁδοῦ τῶν μιαιφόνων διὰ πόθον θεῖον οἰκήσαντα ἢ ἀπόστολον, ὡς ὀλιγοχρονίῳ ἀσκήσει καὶ προθύμῳ σπουδῇ τὴν σωτηρίαν εὐράμενον καὶ ῥαθύμους διεγείραντα πρὸς μετάνοιαν;

6

That was the life of the blessed Theodore. That was the conduct of a man who lived according to God's commandments and detested this world. Someone wrote all this down in a simple style, obtaining part of the information from this man of blessed memory and part of it from those who knew him. After the saint was glorified by God through the gift of abundant miracles, wishing to confer a favor upon the saint and not being in a position to do anything else, I have tried to embellish this text to a small degree, although my style is rough and uncouth. Neither omitting anything that was true, nor adding anything myself, I have expounded his life for the sake of all those who want to imitate it and save their souls.

This, then, was the ascetic life and conduct of Theodore 2 of blessed memory. Let us now address him directly. Most blessed Theodore, what words may I use to praise you? How can I praise your prudence? Your labors were brief, but you obtained the blessed life. How should I address you? Shall I call you a new Abraham, because you departed from your fatherland, or shall I call you a new Elisha, because you immediately obeyed the commandment of your teacher? Are you a new Antony, a citizen of the desert and wonderworker, or a new Jeremiah, he of the lamentations, who begged God for the salvation of his people by moaning and crying? Shall I call you a martyr, since your intention was to become a martyr, choosing to dwell amid killers out of your love of God? Or an apostle, because through your brief ascetic life and your eager zeal you found your salvation and roused the indolent to repentance?

3   Ὄντως τῶν ἀμφοτέρων τοὺς τρόπους ἐζήλωσας. Ὡς
μὲν Ἀβραὰμ οὐ πατρίδος μόνον, ἀλλὰ καὶ τῶν οἰκείων
μελῶν ἀπαρνησάμενος τῷ Χριστῷ ἠκολούθησας καὶ οὐκ
ἐμαλακίσθης τῇ τῶν οἰκείων στοργῇ, οἷς εἴωθαν καὶ αὐτὰ
τὰ θηρία στέργειν. Ὡς Ἐλισσαῖος ἀνεπιστρόφως πάντα
καταλιπὼν ἠκολούθησας τῷ καλέσαντι, καὶ τῷ ἀρότρῳ
τοῦ σταυροῦ τὸν αὐχένα συνδήσας ἀποστολικῶς, ἐνεκρώ-
θης τῷ κόσμῳ καὶ κόσμος σοί. Ὡς ὁ μέγας Ἀντώνιος, ἔρη-
μον κατὰ μόνας οἰκήσας καὶ δαίμονας ἡττήσας, ἰδοὺ δι-
ώκτην οὐ μόνον δαιμόνων, ἀλλὰ καὶ παθῶν ἀνιάτων ὁ
Χριστός σε ἀνέδειξεν. Ὡς Ἰερεμίας ἄλλος τοῦ Ἰσραήλ
(λέγω δὴ τοῦ χριστιανικοῦ λαοῦ, τοῦ ἐν γνώσει Θεὸν εἰδότος) νυκτὸς καὶ ἡμέρας οὐ μόνον μετὰ δακρύων, ἀλλὰ καὶ
τῷ κρύει πηγνύμενος καὶ πείνῃ καὶ δίψῃ καὶ κακουχίᾳ πιε-
ζόμενος, ὁλονύκτοις στάσεσι τὴν σωτηρίαν ἐζήτεις. Ὡς
μάρτυς κέρδος τὸ διὰ Χριστὸν θανεῖν ἡγούμενος, καὶ
νῆσον, ἣν πάντες ὡς φωλεὸν τῶν ἀθέων Ἀγαρηνῶν οὐδὲ
πλησιάσαι ἐτόλμων, σὺ διὰ Θεὸν καὶ οἰκήσας μέχρι τέλους
διεκαρτέρησας, πληρῶν καὶ ἐν τούτῳ τὸ ἀποστολικὸν λόγιον, τὸ λέγον "Τίς ἡμᾶς χωρίσει ἀπὸ τῆς ἀγάπης τοῦ Χριστοῦ;", καὶ τὰ ἑξῆς. Ἀπόστολον δέ, ὅτι ὀλιγοχρονίως
ἀσκήσας προθύμως διὰ τῆς πρὸς Θεὸν παρρησίας καὶ τῆς
τῶν αἰτήσεων παροχῆς πάντας ἐγείρεις πρὸς ζῆλον. Ἡ
γὰρ πολυήμερος κάκωσις τοῖς ῥαθύμοις ὄκνον ἐμποιεῖ, καὶ
δειλίᾳ πολλῇ συσχεθέντες, τοῦ ἀγαθοῦ βίου ἀμελοῦσι. Σὺ
δὲ δι' ὀλίγου τὸ πρόθυμον ἐνδειξάμενος καὶ Θεὸν θερα-
πεύσας, διὰ τῆς τῶν ἰάσεων παροχῆς πᾶσι κηρύττεις
τὴν τοῦ Θεοῦ φιλανθρωπίαν, καὶ ὁδὸν σύντομον τῆς

Your manner of life imitated them all. Like Abraham you 3
not only renounced your country, but renounced the members of your family as well and followed Christ. You did not
let love of your own kin soften you, which happens even to
wild beasts. Like Elisha, you left everything behind, not
looking back, following the one who called you. Like an
apostle you bound your neck to the plow of the cross, you
died for this world, and the world was as dead for you. Like
the great Antony, you inhabited the desert in solitude, defeating the demons. And behold, you became not only a persecutor of demons, but were also appointed by Christ to be
a healer of incurable illnesses. Like a new Jeremiah, *day and
night* in your standing vigils you asked for the salvation of Israel (I mean of the Christian people, who knew God consciously). You not only *shed tears,* you were frozen from the
cold and suffering from hunger, thirst, and other deprivations. Like a martyr, you considered your death for Christ to
be a personal gain: you inhabited the island that no one else
dared approach because they considered it a nest of the godless Hagarenes, and you managed to live there until your
death, persevering for the love of God. In this way, you fulfilled the words of the apostle, *"Who is going to separate us
from Christ's love?"* and what follows in that text. You were an
apostle, because after zealously leading an ascetic life for a
short time, through your frankness toward God and by fulfilling people's requests you managed to incite everyone to
zeal. For long hardships tend to make those who are lazy
even more sluggish: constrained by their cowardice, they
neglect the virtuous life. However, by exhibiting your zeal
and worshipping God for a short time, you reveal God's philanthropy to all, giving them healing cures. By showing them

σωτηρίας ὑποδεικνύς, ῥαθύμους διεγείρεις εἰς μετάνοιαν. Σὲ ἄλλον Θεόδωρον καθηγητὴν καὶ ποιητὴν εἰπεῖν οὐκ ὀκνήσω. Εἰ γὰρ ἐκεῖνος ὑπερορίας καὶ ὕβρεις ὑπέστη διὰ Χριστὸν καὶ λαοῦ καθηγήσατο καὶ συγγράμματα κατέλιπεν, ἀλλὰ σὺ ἑκουσίως, οὐ μόνον ἐκ τόπου τινὸς ἀλλὰ καὶ τοῦ κόσμου παντὸς μέχρι τέλους ἔξω γενόμενος, ὡς ἄλλα συγγράμματα τὸν σὸν κατέλιπες βίον καὶ καθηγεῖται λάμπων ἡλίου φαιδρότερον τοῖς διὰ μετανοίας ὁδεύειν προαιρουμένοις.

4   Ταῦτά σοι τὰ ἐγκώμια παρ' ἡμῶν, εἰ καὶ ἀνάξια τῶν πόνων σου, παμμάκαρ Θεόδωρε, σὲ θεῖον δώρημα καλέσαι ἄξιον. Ἐκ Θεοῦ γὰρ τῇ ἐλαχίστῳ ταύτῃ νήσῳ πεμφθείς, διὰ τῆς τῶν θαυμάτων πηγῆς λαμπρὰν ταύτην καὶ καταφανῆ τοῖς πᾶσι πεποίηκας. Σὺ γὰρ ταύτης οὐ μόνον οἰκιστής, ἀλλὰ καὶ κόσμος τῇ τῶν ἰάσεων ἀνεδείχθης ἀφθόνῳ παροχῇ. Οὐχ οὕτως γὰρ ἐγκαλλωπίζεται βασιλεὺς διαδήματι, ὡς αὕτη τοῖς σοῖς ὡραΐζεται θαύμασι. Σὺ ταύτην ἀκαταγώνιστον ἐκ τῶν ἀθέων βαρβάρων διατηρεῖς. Τὸ γὰρ σὸν καρτερικώτατον σῶμα καὶ τὴν σὴν πρεσβείαν ὡς τεῖχος καὶ φύλακα ἔχουσα, τὰς αὐτῶν καταδρομὰς οὐ πτοεῖται. Σὲ ὅπλον κατ' ἐχθρῶν προβαλλομένη, τὰς παρατάξεις αὐτῶν φοβερὰς οὔσας καὶ τὰ στρατόπεδα αὕτη καταγελᾷ ὡς μειρακίων ἀθύρματα. Τὸ γὰρ σὸν ὄνομα ὡς ῥομφαίαν δίστομον κατ' ἐχθρῶν ἔχοντες οἱ δοῦλοί σου, ὁρμῇ καὶ μόνῃ καταγωνίζονται τούτους καὶ πλήθη μαχίμων ἐνόπλων ὡς θηρίων ἀγρίων λίθοις καὶ ξύλοις

a shortcut to salvation, you incite to repentance those who are indolent. I will not hesitate to call you a new Theodore, the guide and author. For while the latter endured exile and abuse for the sake of Christ, guided the people, and left a legacy of writings, you of your own free will departed not only from a particular place, but abandoned the whole world, until your death, and you left behind your own life as if it were your written works. That life, shining more brightly than the sun, guides those who wish to take the road of repentance.

O most blessed Theodore, these are my praises for you; 4 although they are unworthy of your struggles, it is right to call you a gift from God. God indeed sent you to that very small island, which, through your fountain of miracles, you made illustrious and well-known to all people. You not only became its founder, but also its adornment through the abundant stream of cures that you provide. The island is more adorned by your miracles than an emperor takes pride in his crown. You keep it safe from the attacks of the godless barbarians. The island, having your most long-suffering body as a protective wall and your intercessions to God as its guardians, does not fear their invasions. Holding you before itself as a weapon against our enemies, our island mocks their frightful military formations and armies as if they were children's toys. Your servants use your name as a double-edged sword against the enemy, and defeat them solely through their own spirited rush: they manage to put to flight a multitude of well-armed fighters, as if they were wild beasts, by throwing rocks and sticks at them. The island has

καταδραμόντες διώκουσι. Σέ, ἅγιε, ὡς ἄγκυραν ἀσφαλῆ ἔχουσα, τὴν τοῦ βίου ζάλην καὶ τὰς τρικυμίας ἀκαταπον-τίστως περᾷ.

5 Σοὶ πᾶς πιστὸς ὁλοψύχως προστρέχων, τὴν τῶν αἰτή-σεων χάριν λαμβάνει καὶ λιμένα καὶ καταφύγιον πάσης βιωτικῆς περιστάσεως καλεῖ ἄξιον. Τίς γάρ σου τὸ ὄνομα ἐν θαλάσσῃ πλέων καὶ ἐν ζάλῃ καταποντούμενος, ἐκ ψυχῆς ἐπικαλεσάμενός σε, σωτηρίαν οὐχ εὕρατο; Τίς δὲ νόσοις καὶ ὀδύναις βαλλόμενος καὶ τῷ ναῷ σου προστρέ-χων ἐκ ψυχῆς οὐ λαμβάνει τὴν ἴασιν; Τίς δέ σε καὶ θεασά-μενος καὶ τῷ τιμίῳ σου προσψαύσας λειψάνῳ οὐκ ἔχει σε ἀρωγὸν καὶ φύλακα ἐν παντὶ καιρῷ καὶ τόπῳ; Σὺ νοσούν-των ἴασις, λυπουμένων παράκλησις, χειμαζομένων λιμήν, τῶν ἐν ἀνάγκαις λύτρον. Σὲ πᾶσα ἡ νῆσος παραμύθιον ἔχουσα, τὸ ἀπαράκλητον τοῦ τόπου καὶ τὰς τῶν ἐπιβού-λων ἐπιθέσεις καὶ πᾶσαν βιωτικὴν θλίψιν ἀνωδύνως φέρει. Ἅμα γὰρ ἔρχεταί τις λυπούμενος, τῇ τιμίᾳ σου προσκυνή-σας σορῷ καὶ τῷ ἁγίῳ σου προσψαύσας λειψάνῳ, πᾶσαν ἀθυμίαν ἀποθέμενος καὶ λύπην, ὅλος χάριτος καὶ ἡδονῆς καὶ εὐφροσύνης πνευματικῆς πληροῦται.

6 Καὶ νῦν, παναοίδιμε Θεόδωρε, μὴ παύσῃ πρεσβεύων ὑπὲρ ἡμῶν πρὸς τὸν Κύριον. Μέμνησο τῆς γῆς ταύτης. Ἐν ταύτῃ γὰρ τὸν Θεὸν ἐξεζήτησας καὶ εὗρες καὶ τῆς αὐτοῦ βασιλείας ἔτυχες. Ἐν ταύτῃ τοῖς στεναγμοῖς τῶν δακρύων σου καὶ ἱδρῶσι τῶν πόνων σου ὡς πτεροῖς κουφιζόμενος εἰς τὰς αἰωνίους καὶ μακαρίας μονὰς ἀνέδραμες, ἔνθα οἱ τῶν ἁγίων δῆμοι σκηνοῦσι καὶ ἡ ἄληκτος εὐφροσύνη ἀνα-πέμπεται. Τοιγαροῦν εὐαρεστήσας Θεῷ καὶ ἐν αὐτῷ

you, my saint, as a secure anchor, and thus it crosses the tempestuous sea of this life safely, weathering its storms.

All the faithful take refuge in you with all their heart, and 5 they are rewarded with the fulfillment of their requests, calling you a haven and a worthy refuge from all the adverse circumstances of this life. Is there anyone traveling by sea and in danger of being wrecked by a tempest who invoked your name with all his heart and did not find salvation? Is there anyone who is attacked by illnesses and pain and is not cured after running to your church with all his heart? Is there anyone who, after seeing and touching your holy relics, is not helped by you and does not enjoy your protection in all times and places? You are the cure for those who are ill, a comfort for those who are in distress, a haven for those who endure hardships, a deliverance for all in their hour of need. Since the entire island has in you a consolation, it can endure its own unforgiving nature and the attacks of its enemies, and can bear the various adverse circumstances of life without pain. As soon as someone in distress comes to pay due honors to your reliquary and touch your holy relic, he is delivered from all distress and sadness and is filled with pleasure, delight, and spiritual joy.

O Theodore of most blessed memory, do not now stop 6 praying to the Lord on our behalf. Remember this land. It was here that you sought to find God and found him, being rewarded with his kingdom. It was here that you managed to reach the eternal and blessed abodes, being lifted up on the wings of your sobbing tears and the sweat of your hard labor. There dwell all the saints, and their happiness that has no end rises upward. Since you have pleased God and have

κλῆρον ἁγίων λαβών, ἱκεσίαν ποίει πάντοτε ἀσίγητον ὑπὲρ ἡμῶν, τῶν ἐπταισμένων λυτρωθῆναι καὶ καταταγῆναι ἐν μερίδι τῶν δικαίων, ὅτι τῷ Πατρὶ καὶ τῷ μονογενεῖ αὐτοῦ Υἱῷ σὺν τῷ παναγίῳ καὶ ἀγαθῷ καὶ ζωοποιῷ αὐτοῦ Πνεύματι πρέπει πᾶσα δόξα, τιμὴ καὶ προσκύνησις εἰς τοὺς αἰῶνας τῶν αἰώνων, ἀμήν.

earned from him an abode suitable for a saint, pray to him unceasingly on our behalf: ask him to forgive us our trespasses and allow us to settle in the abodes of the righteous, since to the Father, to his only-begotten Son, and to the all-Holy, good, and life-giving Spirit are due all glory, honor, and worship, now and forever and ever, amen.

COMMEMORATION
OF ARSENIOS,
ARCHBISHOP OF KERKYRA

Μνήμη τοῦ ἐν ἁγίοις πατρὸς ἡμῶν Ἀρσενίου ἀρχιεπισκόπου Κερκύρας

Κοσμήσας Ἀρσένιος ἡμῖν τὸν θρόνον,
νῦν πρὸς αἰθέριον ἀπέβη πόλον.
Ἐννέα καὶ δεκάτῃ κῦρ Ἀρσένιον νόες ἦραν.

I

Ὁ ἀοίδιμος οὗτος καὶ μέγας ἡμῶν πατὴρ Ἀρσένιος ἐν
τοῖς χρόνοις ἦν Βασιλείου τοῦ εὐσεβοῦς βασιλέως τοῦ ἐκ
Μακεδονίας, γεννηθεὶς ἐκ γονέων εὐσεβῶν καὶ θεοφιλῶν,
τοῦ μὲν πατρὸς αὐτοῦ ἐκ τῆς ἁγίας πόλεως Ἱερουσαλὴμ
ὁρμωμένου, τῆς δὲ μητρὸς ἐκ Βηθανίας. Οἵτινες νομίμως
συναφθέντες, ἐν ἀπαιδίᾳ τὸν βίον διήνυον, πάσῃ δὲ ἀρετῇ
καὶ ἀγαθοεργίᾳ τὸν Θεὸν θεραπεύοντες, καρπὸν ηὔχοντο
δοθῆναι αὐτοῖς. Καὶ δὴ τῆς εὐχῆς αὐτῶν ἐπακούσας ὁ
Θεός, ἄξιον ὄντως τῆς αἰτήσεως τὸν καρπὸν αὐτοῖς ἐδω-
ρήσατο. Τὸν καλὸν οὖν τοῦτον Ἀρσένιον ἐν Βηθανίᾳ
γεννήσαντες, τῷ Θεῷ ἐκ σπαργάνων ἔγνωσαν ἀναθεῖναι.
Ὅθεν καὶ τριετῆ γενόμενον, αἴρουσι μεθ' ἑαυτῶν, καὶ
πρὸς ἓν τῶν ἐκεῖσε μοναστηρίων γενόμενοι, τῷ Θεῷ καὶ

Commemoration of our father among the saints, Arsenios, archbishop of Kerkyra

Arsenios adorned our episcopal throne, and now he has departed to the vault of heaven. On the nineteenth of the month, lord Arsenios was taken up by the celestial minds.

I

Our great father, the famous Arsenios, lived in the time of the pious emperor Basil from Macedonia. He was born to pious and God-loving parents. His father came from the holy city of Jerusalem, while his mother was from Bethany. They were legally married, but life passed without them having any children. They worshipped God through all their virtues and good deeds, and prayed to be given offspring. God heard their prayer and granted them offspring truly worthy of their request. They gave birth to that excellent Arsenios in Bethany and decided, from his early infancy, to give him as an offering to God. Therefore, as soon as he was three years old, they took him with them and, going to one of the monasteries in that area, they delivered him to God

τῷ τῆς μονῆς προεστῶτι ἀνέθεντο, εἰς δωδεκαετίαν αὐτῷ τὰ τῆς μοναδικῆς πολιτείας ταμιευσάμενοι. Καὶ αὐτοὶ μὲν τὸ μοναδικὸν ἀμφιεσάμενοι σχῆμα καὶ κατὰ Θεὸν ἐκεῖσε πολιτευσάμενοι, τὸν βίον ἀπέλιπον.

2   Ὁ δέ γε τίμιος παῖς Ἀρσένιος, γράμμασι παιδευόμενος καὶ καλῶς ἀνατρεφόμενος, πάσῃ προέκοπτεν ἐναρέτῳ πο-λιτείᾳ. Τὸν δωδέκατον δὲ πεφθακὼς χρόνον, καὶ αὐτὸς ἤδη τὸν μονότροπον ὑπέδυ βίον. Ἀλλὰ πλείονος ἐφιέμε-νος τῆς ἐκ τῶν μαθημάτων παιδεύσεως, τὴν Σελεύκειαν κατέλαβεν, ἔνθα τὸ τῆς ἱερωσύνης ἀξίωμα ἐδέξατο, βιασα-μένου αὐτὸν τοῦ ἐκεῖσε ἀρχιερέως διὰ τὴν ἀρετὴν τὴν αὐτῷ ἐπιλάμπουσαν. Θελήσαντος δὲ αὐτοῦ τὴν Ἱερου-σαλὴμ αὖθις θεάσασθαι, πλοίῳ ἐντυγχάνει πειρατικῷ καὶ χερσὶν Ἀγαρηνῶν περιπεσών, χάριτι Θεοῦ λυτροῦται τῆς αἰχμαλωσίας, λόγοις προσηνέσι τε καὶ εὐσεβέσι τοὺς ἀθέ-ους ἐκμειλιξάμενος.

2

Ἀπολυθεὶς δὲ καὶ τοὺς ἁγίους καταλαβὼν καὶ προσκυ-νήσας τόπους καὶ τὸν πόθον ἀφοσιωσάμενος, τὴν Κων-σταντινούπολιν καταλαμβάνει καὶ παρὰ τοῦ ὁσιωτάτου Τρύφωνος δεξιοῦται. Ἐκείνου δὲ πρὸς τὸν πατριαρχικὸν ἀναβάντος θρόνον, τῶν ἐκκλησιῶν οὗτος τὴν φροντίδα πιστεύεται. Καὶ μετὰ μικρόν, Τρύφωνος τὸν βίον ἀπολιπόν-τος, Θεοφύλακτος ἐπὶ τὸν θρόνον ἀνάγεται. Ὃς δὴ τὸν

and to the abbot of the monastery, arranging for him to become a monk when he reached the age of twelve. Then they too took the monastic habit and, after living there according to the laws of God, they departed from this life.

Their precious child Arsenios learned his letters and was raised well; he advanced in all aspects of the virtuous life. As soon as he reached his twelfth year, he too entered the monastic life. But wishing to obtain a better education, he went to Seleukeia, where he accepted the office of the priesthood, since the bishop there put pressure on him because of the virtue that shone upon him. Wishing to see Jerusalem once more, he fell into the clutches of a pirate ship and became prisoner of the Hagarenes. But he was saved from captivity through the grace of God: the saint managed to appease those godless men with his gentle and pious words.

2

2

After his release, he visited the Holy Places, to which he paid due honor, thereby fulfilling his desire. He then went to Constantinople and was welcomed by the most holy Tryphon. As soon as Tryphon had ascended the patriarchal throne, Arsenios was entrusted with the guardianship of the churches. After a short while, Tryphon left this life and Theophylaktos was raised to the throne. He realized that the

μακάριον εὑρὼν Ἀρσένιον ἀρετῆς ὕψει μαρτυρούμενον, ψήφῳ Θεοῦ κινηθείς, τῆς μεγάλης Κερκυραίων ἐκκλησίας ἀρχιερέα χειροτονεῖ καὶ τὸν τοῦ φωτὸς ἄξιον ἐπὶ τὴν λυχνίαν τίθησιν. Ἐντεῦθεν Ἀρσένιος ἐπὶ τὸν θρόνον ἀναβάς, τὰ τοῦ βήματος πρῶτον κατακοσμεῖ καὶ τὴν χειροτονίαν καθαρὰν καὶ ἀνεπίληπτον ἐπισπεύδει ποιεῖσθαι. Εἶτα καὶ τὰ κοινὰ πατρικῶς προμηθούμενος, ὀρφανῶν γίνεται πατήρ, χηρῶν ὑπερασπιστής, ἀδικουμένων προστάτης, πεινώντων τροφεύς, πενήτων χορηγός, καταπονουμένων βοηθός, λυπουμένων παράκλησις, ἀσθενούντων ἰατρός, καὶ ἁπλῶς τοῖς πᾶσι γέγονε τὰ πάντα κατὰ τὸν θεῖον ἀπόστολον.

2   Διὸ καὶ ὁ Θεὸς χάρισι θαυμάτων αὐτὸν ἀντημείψατο. Σκυθῶν γάρ ποτε τῇ πέραν καταδραμόντων γῇ καὶ πρὸς τὴν νῆσον διαπερασάντων, ὁ μακάριος, μηδὲν μελλήσας, πρὸς αὐτοὺς παραγίνεται, τὴν ἐκείνων ὁρμὴν εἰρηνικῶς παρεμποδίσαι πραγματευόμενος. Ἀλλ’ οἱ Σκύθαι ληστρικῶς τοῦτον κρατήσαντες, διὰ μονοξύλων τῇ θαλάσσῃ ἐπέβησαν. Ὅπερ γνόντες οἱ Κερκυραῖοι καὶ αὐτοὶ διαπλευσάμενοι, κατὰ πρόσωπον αὐτοῖς συνήντησαν, καὶ ταῖς τοῦ ποιμένος εὐχαῖς θαρρήσαντες, θαρσαλέως κατ’ αὐτῶν ὥρμησαν, καὶ σὺν Θεῷ τούτους τροπωσάμενοι, οὓς μὲν μαχαίρας ἔργον ἀπέδειξαν, οὓς δὲ τῇ θαλάσσῃ ἐβύθισαν, τοὺς δὲ λοιποὺς καταδιώξαντες, ἐν τῇ λεγομένῃ Τετρανήσῳ πάντας ἀπώλεσαν. Ἔνθα δὴ καὶ διὰ προσευχῆς ὁ ἅγιος ὕδωρ ἐξαγαγὼν ἐκ πέτρας, ὅπερ καὶ νῦν ἐστὶ βρύζον, τὸν ἑαυτοῦ διψῶντα λαὸν ἐκόρεσε.

blessed Arsenios was recognized as a man who had reached the peak of virtue and, moved by the decision of God, he ordained him archbishop of the great church of Kerkyra; he thus *placed on the lampstand* one who was worthy to carry the light. So Arsenios, ascending the throne, adorned the affairs of the clergy with due order; he first strove to ensure that ordinations were pure and blameless. Afterward, managing public affairs in a paternal manner, he became a father for orphans, a defender of widows, a protector of those who were treated unjustly, a source of food for the hungry, a provider for the poor, a helper of those who were crushed, a consoler of those in distress, a healer of the sick, and, in one word, *he became everything for everyone,* in the words of the divine apostle.

Hence God rewarded him with the grace of miracles. For once when the Scythians invaded the region opposite Kerkyra and crossed over to the island, the blessed man went to them without delay, trying peacefully to prevent their advance. But the Scythians, after taking him prisoner like pirates, went out to sea in their dugout canoes. As soon as the inhabitants of Kerkyra realized this, they sailed out too, confronted them, and, having confidence in the prayers of their shepherd, bravely attacked them. With God's assistance, they put them to flight, killing some with the sword, while drowning some others in the sea. They chased the rest away and destroyed them all in the region of the so-called Four Islands. There the saint used his prayers to produce water from a rock, which is still flowing, and thereby slaked the thirst of his people.

3   Λαμπρῶς οὖν πρὸς τὸν ἴδιον ἐπιστρέψας θρόνον, πολλῶν καὶ ἑτέρων θαυμάτων αὐτουργὸς ἐγένετο. Αὐχμὸν γὰρ ἰσχυρότατον, τοὺς κατὰ πᾶσαν νῆσον καρποὺς κατ᾽ ὀλίγον διαφθείροντα, δι᾽ ἐντεύξεως ἔλυσε καὶ ὑετὸν εὐχῇ κατήγαγε. Παιδίσκην δέ τινος τῶν κατὰ τὴν νῆσον περιφανῶν, ὑπὸ δαίμονος δεινῶς ὀχλουμένην, εὐχῇ μόνῃ καὶ ἀπὸ νάματος τοῦ συνήθους ῥαντισμῷ, τοῦ δαίμονος ἠλευθέρωσεν. Ἑτέρᾳ δὲ γυναικὶ Ἀνδρονίκου τινὸς κληρικοῦ δυστοκούσῃ καὶ πρὸς τὸ θανεῖν ἤδη προσεγγιζούσῃ, δι᾽ εὐχῆς τὸ ζῆν ἐχαρίσατο καὶ τὸ βρέφος ἀποτεκεῖν ἐποίησε. Γυναῖκα δὲ ἄλλην ἡμίξηρον οὖσαν, ἐλαίου χρίσματι ἁγίου ὑγιᾶ καὶ ἄρτιον ἀποκατέστησε, καὶ ὀργὴν κατὰ τῶν λογάδων Κερκύρας παρὰ τοῦ βασιλέως Κωνσταντίνου τοῦ Πορφυρογεννήτου, υἱοῦ Λέοντος τοῦ σοφωτάτου, κηρυχθεῖσαν, πάντας κελεύουσαν ἀχθῆναι εἰς τὴν Κωνσταντινούπολιν, αὐτὸς ἐντέχνως ταύτην διέλυσεν. Ὁ γὰρ τὴν ἀρχὴν Κερκύρας παρὰ βασιλέως δεξάμενος, φιλοχρήματος ὤν, κατ᾽ αὐτῶν ἀδίκως ἐψεύσατο. Ὁ δέ γε θεῖος πατήρ, ὑπὲρ αὐτῶν τὴν ψυχὴν θέμενος καὶ γήρως καὶ θαλάσσης καὶ χειμῶνος ἐπιλαθόμενος, πρὸς τὸν βασιλέα παρεγένετο, καὶ τὸν ἐκείνου καταπραΰνας θυμόν, συμπαθείας γραμμάτιον ἐδέξατο.

He returned to his throne triumphantly and worked 3 many other miracles in person. Through his intercession he ended a great drought which had gradually destroyed the crops throughout the whole island, and he also brought down rain with his prayer. He liberated the maidservant of one of the prominent men of the island from the demon that was viciously tormenting her, simply by using his prayer and by sprinkling her with the usual spring water. He also saved, again through his prayers, the life of the wife of a clergyman called Andronikos, who was experiencing a difficult labor and was near death, and enabled her to give birth to her baby. He also restored to health another woman who was all but withered away by anointing her with holy oil. In a skillful way, he appeased the wrath of the emperor Constantine Porphyrogennetos, the son of the most wise Leo, which was directed against the prominent men of Kerkyra. The emperor had ordered all of them to be brought to Constantinople. The man entrusted by the emperor with the government of Kerkyra was greedy and had unjustly lied about them. But the holy father, who risked his life for them, paid no heed to his old age, to the sea, or the winter, and went to the emperor, calming his anger and receiving a letter of pardon.

3

Κἀκεῖθεν φιλοφρόνως ἐξελθών, πρὸς τὴν ἰδίαν ποίμνην ἐρχόμενος καὶ κατὰ τὴν λεγομένην Σκύρον φθάσας
νῆσον, νόσῳ περιπίπτει. Πλησίον δὲ Κορίνθου γενόμενος,
τῷ Θεῷ τὴν μακαρίαν ψυχὴν παρέθετο. Ἐντίμως οὖν
ἐκεῖσε παρά τε τῶν ἰδίων καὶ τῶν συνελθόντων κηδεύεται.
Ὕστερον δὲ οἱ τῆς πόλεως Κερκύρας παραγενόμενοι,
μετὰ τοῦ ἱεροῦ λειψάνου πρὸς τὴν ἰδίαν ἐπανιέναι πόλιν
ἐφώρμουν. Ἔνθα δὴ καί τι θαύματος ἄξιον συνέβη γενέσθαι, τοῦ Θεοῦ τὸν οἰκεῖον δοξάζοντος θεράποντα. Τὴν
ἀρετὴν γὰρ τοῦ ἀνδρὸς οἱ τῆς ἐπαρχίας ἐκείνης ἀκούοντες
καὶ τοῦτον διὰ θαύματος ἔχοντες, ἐτόλμησαν ἁγιασμοῦ
χάριν τῆς ἱερᾶς αὐτοῦ γενειάδος λάθρᾳ μέρος λαβεῖν, ὃ
καὶ ποιήσαντες ἐγνώσθησαν. Ὅμως τὸ τίμιον αὐτοῦ σῶμα
ἀνακομισθέν, εὑρέθη πάλιν σῶον τῇ τοῦ Θεοῦ χάριτι, τὴν
γενειάδα ἔχον ὁλόκληρον, ὃ καὶ κατετέθη εὐλαβῶς ἐν τῇ
Κερκυραίων ἁγιωτάτῃ μητροπόλει, θαύματα καὶ ἰάσεις
βρύον ἑκάστοτε εἰς αἶνον Χριστοῦ τοῦ Θεοῦ ἡμῶν. Ὧι ἡ
δόξα καὶ τὸ κράτος σὺν τῷ ἀνάρχῳ Πατρὶ καὶ τῷ παναγίῳ
καὶ ἀγαθῷ καὶ ζωοποιῷ αὐτοῦ Πνεύματι εἰς τοὺς αἰῶνας,
ἀμήν.

3

While returning from there in a gracious way to his own flock, he fell ill when he arrived at the island called Skyros. When he approached Corinth, he entrusted his blessed soul to God and was honorably buried there by his own men and those who had come to meet him. Afterward, the inhabitants of the city of Kerkyra went there and hastened back to their own city with his sacred relic. At the time, a miracle took place, since God wanted to glorify his servant. The inhabitants of the province of Corinth had heard about that man's virtue, and held him in such admiration that they dared to steal secretly a part of his beard, in order to receive his blessing, but their deed was revealed. However, when his holy body was brought back, it was found to be intact through the grace of God, his beard undamaged. His body was laid to rest in the most holy cathedral of the Kerkyrians, and since then it gushes forth miracles and cures every day, to the glory of Christ our God. To him, to his Father who has no beginning, and to the all-Holy, good, and vivifying Spirit are due all power and glory, unto the ages, amen.

Abbreviations

AASS = *Acta Sanctorum,* 71 vols. (Paris, 1863–1940)

BHG = *Bibliotheca hagiographica graeca* (Brussels, 1909)

CPG = Ernst L. von Leutsch and Friedrich W. Schneidewin, eds., *Corpus Paroemiographorum Graecorum,* 2 vols. (Göttingen, 1839–1851); repr., 3 vols. (Hildesheim, 1958–1961)

LSJ = Henry G. Liddell, Robert Scott, and Henry Stuart Jones, eds., *A Greek-English Lexicon,* 9th ed. with Supplement (Oxford, 1968)

ODB = Alexander P. Kazhdan et al., eds., *Oxford Dictionary of Byzantium,* 3 vols. (New York, 1991)

PG = Jacques-Paul Migne, *Patrologiae cursus completus, Series graeca,* 161 vols. (Paris, 1857–1866)

PmbZ = Ralph-Johannes Lilie et al., eds., *Prosopographie der mittelbyzantinischen Zeit: Erste Abteilung (641–867),* 6 vols. (Berlin, 1999); *Zweite Abteilung (867–1025),* 8 vols. (Berlin, 2013)

SynaxCP = Hippolyte Delehaye, ed., *Synaxarium ecclesiae Constantinopolitanae e codice Sirmondiano nunc Berolinensi: Propylaeum ad Acta sanctorum Novembris* (Brussels, 1902)

Note on the Texts

The Greek text of the first five works constitutes a revised version of an earlier edition by Ioannis Polemis, published in *Βυζαντινὰ ὑμνογραφικὰ καὶ ἁγιολογικὰ κείμενα,* edited by Ioannis Polemis and Evelina Mineva (Athens, 2016). The critical apparatus has been omitted, typographical errors have been corrected, and some changes have been made to the capitalization, punctuation, and readings of the text. The edition of the *Life of Theodore of Kythera* revises the 1967 edition of Nikolaos Oikonomides with some corrected readings based on a new inspection of the manuscripts. The text of the *Commemoration of Arsenios, Archbishop of Kerkyra* is based on the 1909 edition of Sevastianos Nikokavouras, with some revised readings by Polemis after consultation of the single manuscript. Changes in capitalization and punctuation have been introduced as well in the two latter texts to conform to the style of the Dumbarton Oaks Medieval Library. Below, we list details on manuscript sources and previous critical editions.

Martyrdom and *Encomium of Nicholas the Younger* (Polemis-Mineva, 440–65): Demetrios Z. Sophianos, ed., Ἅγιος Νικόλαος ὁ ἐν Βουναίνῃ: Ἀνέκδοτα ἁγιολογικὰ κείμενα. Ἱστορικαὶ εἰδήσεις περὶ τῆς μεσαιωνικῆς Θεσσαλίας (Γ´ αἰών) (Athens, 1972), 139–51 *(Anonymous Life)*, 152–60 *(Encomium)*.

Each of these hagiographic texts is preserved in a single manuscript: the *Martyrdom* [no *BHG* no.] in Meteora, Metamorphosis 81, fols. 139v–146v (fifteenth century); the *Encomium,* written by the presbyter Achaïkos [*BHG* 2309], in Zoodochos Pege (Andros) 94, fols. 53r–59v (twelfth century).

Funeral Oration for Athanasios, Bishop of Methone (Polemis-Mineva, 466–83): Konstantinos Kyriakopoulos, ed., Ἁγίου Πέτρου ἐπισκόπου Ἄργους Βίος καὶ Λόγοι: Εἰσαγωγή-κείμενον-μετάφρασις-σχόλια (Athens, 1976), 44–66; earlier editions: Angelo Mai, *Nova Patrum Bibliotheca,* vol. 9/3 (Rome, 1888), 31–51; and Chrestos Papaoikonomou, Ὁ πολιοῦχος τοῦ Ἄργους ἅγιος Πέτρος ἐπίσκοπος Ἄργους ὁ θαυματουργός (Athens, 1908), 91–106. The edition of the oration [*BHG* 196] is based on Messina, San Salvatore 15, fols. 51v–61v (twelfth century): see Enrica Follieri, "Santi di Metone: Atanasio vescovo, Leone taumaturgo," *Byzantion* 41 (1971): 378–451, at 402n1; Alexander Sideras, *Die byzantinischen Grabreden: Prosopographie, Datierung, Überlieferung: 142 Epitaphien und Monodien aus dem byzantinischen Jahrtausend* (Vienna, 1994), 106. On the manuscript, see Augusto Mancini, *Codices graeci monasterii Messanensis S. Salvatoris* [= *Atti della R. Academia Peloritana,* vol. 23, fasc. 2] (Messina, 1907), 23–26; Maria Teresa Rodriquez, *Bibliografia dei manoscritti greci del fondo del SS. Salvatore di Messina* (Rome, 2002), 19–20. Three other later manuscripts of the sixteenth to eighteenth centuries (Palermo, Biblioteca centrale, Qq H 46 and II. E. 15, and the Bollandist Library in Brussels, 0194 [286]) were not consulted.

Life of Peter, Bishop of Argos (Polemis-Mineva, 483–501): Konstantinos Kyriakopoulos, ed., Ἁγίου Πέτρου ἐπισκόπου Ἄργους Βίος καὶ Λόγοι: Εἰσαγωγή-κείμενον-μετάφρασις-

σχόλια (Athens, 1976), 232–54; earlier editions: Angelo Mai, *Nova Patrum Bibliotheca*, vol. 9/3 (Rome, 1888), 1–17; Chrestos Papaoikonomou, Ὁ πολιοῦχος τοῦ Ἄργους ἅγιος Πέτρος ἐπίσκοπος Ἄργους ὁ θαυματουργός (Athens, 1908), 59–74. The *Life* [*BHG* 1504] is preserved in two manuscripts, anonymously in Vaticanus Palatinus gr. 27, fols. 25v–31v (eleventh century) and under the name of Theodore of Nicaea in Athens, National Library of Greece, 278, fols. 286r–94v (fourteenth century).

Life and Miracles of Theokletos, Bishop of Lakedaimon (Polemis-Mineva, 501–35): Nikos Vees, ed., "Vie de saint Théoclète évêque de Lacédémoine, publiée d'après le manuscrit n. 583 de la bibliothèque Barberine," *Revue byzantine/ Vizantiiskoe Obozrenie* 2 (1916): suppl. 1–55; and Agesilaos Sgouritsas, "Ὁ Λακεδαιμονίας ἅγιος Θεόκλητος," Θεολογία 27 (1956): 567–93, who did not know the edition of Vees. Some useful corrections were suggested by Eduard Kurtz in *Revue byzantine/Vizantiiskoe Obozrenie* 3, section 2 (1917), 27–29. The *Life* [*BHG* 2420] is preserved in a single manuscript, Vaticanus Barberinianus gr. 583, pp. 684–707 (late fourteenth century). For a description of the manuscript, see Sofia Kotzabassi, *Die handschriftliche Überlieferung der rhetorischen und hagiographischen Werke des Gregor von Zypern* (Wiesbaden, 1998), 201–7.

Life of Theodore of Kythera: Nikolaos Oikonomides, ed., "Ὁ Βίος τοῦ Ἁγίου Θεοδώρου Κυθήρων (10ος αἰ.) (12 Μαΐου-*BHG*, ἀρ. 2430)," in Τρίτον Πανιόνιον Συνέδριον: Πρακτικά (Athens, 1967), 264–91, repr. *Byzantium from the Ninth Century to the Fourth Crusade: Studies, Texts, Monuments* (Brookfield, Vt., 1992), no. 7. Oikonomides's edition of the *Life* [*BHG* 2430] was based on two manuscripts, (*A*) Athos,

Iviron 804 (formerly 356), fols. 116r–130v (sixteenth century) and (*B*) Patriarchate of Jerusalem 66, fols. 312v–24r.

Commemoration of Arsenios, Archbishop of Kerkyra: Sevastianos Nikokavouras, ed., Ἀκολουθίαι τῶν ἁγίων Ἰάσωνος καὶ Σωσιπάτρου, τῆς παρθενομάρτυρος Κερκύρας τῆς Βασιλίδος, τοῦ ἁγίου Ἀρσενίου μητροπολίτου Κερκύρας, τῆς ὁσίας Θεοδώρας τῆς Αὐγούστης καὶ τοῦ ἁγίου ἱερομάρτυρος Βλασίου (Kerkyra, 1909), 60–62. The *synaxarion* notice [*BHG* 2044] is found only in a manuscript from Grottaferrata, Biblioteca Statale del Monumento Nazionale, B.α.022 (gr. 048) of the seventeenth century.

SIGLA

A = Athos, Iviron 804 (formerly 356)

B = Patriarchate of Jerusalem 66

AK = Anthony Kaldellis

IP = Ioannis Polemis

Kurtz = Eduard Kurtz

Nik = Sevastianos Nikokavouras

Oik = Nikolaos Oikonomides

< > = added by editor

[ ] = secluded by editor

<...> = lacuna

†† = corrupt passage

Notes to the Texts

FUNERAL ORATION FOR ATHANASIOS, BISHOP OF METHONE

1.1 τὸν ἑαυτῶν βίον *IP*: τὸν ἑαυτὸν βίον *Polemis-Mineva*

7.1 *After* τετύχηκε, *probably one should add* μαρτυρίας *or something similar.*

LIFE AND MIRACLES OF THEOKLETOS, BISHOP OF LAKEDAIMON

3.1 Τί γάρ τοι *corrected by Kurtz*: Τί γάρ τι *Polemis-Mineva*
ἐξ αὐτῶν τῶν σπαργάνων *IP*: ἐξ αὐτῶν σπαργάνων *Polemis-Mineva*
εἰς προσθήκην *corrected by Kurtz*: ὡς προσθήκην *Polemis-Mineva*
τὴν αἰθέριον χωροβατῶν *corrected by Kurtz*: τὴν αἰθέριον χορο-βατῶν *Polemis-Mineva*

6.1 ἀπεπλήρου *corrected IP*: ἀνεπλήρου *Polemis-Mineva*

8.1 *After* ὑπ' αὐτῷ τὴν ψυχὴν, *a page and a half have been left blank in the Barberini manuscript.*

9.1 καὶ τὰ ῥάκια *IP*: ῥακία *Polemis-Mineva*

10.1 ἀπαναισχυντοῦντας *IP*: ἀπαναισχυνοῦντας *Polemis-Mineva*
πολλῆς τούτων πονηρίας *IP*: πολλῆς τούτων πονηρίαις *Polemis-Mineva*

12.1 Ἐς τοσοῦτον *IP*: Εἰς τοσοῦτον *Polemis-Mineva*

14.2 οἶμαι δὲ καὶ ἀνδράσιν *IP*: οἴμοι δὲ καὶ ἀνδράσιν *Polemis-Mineva*

16.1 βέβηλος βεβήλου πράγματος *Polemis-Mineva*: σύμβουλος βε-βήλου πράγματος *emendation proposed by Kurtz*
αὐτοῖς τοῖς πειρασμοῖς *IP*: τοῖς *omitted by Polemis-Mineva*

17.1   τῆς ἄνω μισθαποδοσίας *IP*: τῆς ἄνω μισθοδοσίας *Polemis-Mineva*

17.5   τῷ βορβόρῳ τῶν ἡδονῶν *IP*: τῷ βορβόρῳ τῶν παθῶν *Polemis-Mineva*

17.7   ταῦτα καὶ λογιζόμενος *IP*: καὶ ταῦτα λογιζόμενος *Polemis-Mineva*

        ἐπὶ σωτηρίᾳ κτηθέντας *corrected by Kurtz*: κτισθέντας *Polemis-Mineva*

18.1   συνιέναι παρεσκεύαζεν *IP*: συνιέναι παρεσκεύαζε *Polemis-Mineva*

        ἡνίκα πολὺς μὲν *IP*: ἡνίκα μὲν πολὺς *Polemis-Mineva*

20.1   αἰσθόμενοι τῆς ζημίας *IP*: αἰσθόμενοι τὴν ζημίαν *Polemis-Mineva*

20.4   τοσοῦτον ζημιωθησομένη *corrected by Kurtz*: τοσοῦτον ζημιω-θησομένην *Polemis-Mineva*

        ὅσον καρπωσομένη *corrected by Kurtz*: ὅσον καρπωσομένην *Polemis-Mineva*

LIFE OF THEODORE OF KYTHERA

1.1   τοῦ ὕστερον *IP*: τὸ ὕστερον *Oik*
       τὸ καὶ ὕστερον *A*: καὶ τὸ ὕστερον *BOik*
       πάντως καὶ τὸ *A*: καὶ παντὸς τὸ *B*, πάντως καὶ τοῦ *Oik*

1.3   δεικνὺς διὰ τοῦ λόγου *AB*: ἐδείκνυ διὰ τοῦ λόγου *Oik*

2.1   ἐξ ἧς οὐκ ἔστι *IP, AK*: ἐξ ὧν οὐκ ἔστι *ABOik*
       οὐδὲ αὐτὸ παρασιωπήσω *IP*: οὐδὲν αὐτὸ παρασιωπήσω *ABOik*

2.2   οὐ συνεγράψαμεν *A*: συνεγράψαμεν *BOik*
       ἀναστροφὴν βίου *IP*: ἀνατροφὴν βίου *ABOik*

3.1   τὸ ὄμμα κατάξηρον *IP*: τὸ σῶμα κατάξηρον *ABOik*

4.3   τὰ Τέρεα *A*: Ταίρεα *BOik*

5.3   χρόνους εἴκοσι καὶ τρεῖς *A*: χρόνους εἴκοσι τρεῖς *BOik*

6.3   καὶ κόσμος σοί *IP*: καὶ κόσμος σὺ *ABOik*

COMMEMORATION OF ARSENIOS,
ARCHBISHOP OF KERKYRA

1.1   ἔγνωσαν ἀναθεῖναι *IP*: ἔγνωσαν ἀναθῆναι *Nik*

2.3   κατήγαγε *IP*: κατήγαγεν *Nik*

         ἀποτεκεῖν ἐποίησε *IP*: ἀποτεκεῖν ἐποίησεν *Nik*

         ἄρτιον ἀποκατέστησε *IP*: ἄρτιον ἀποκατέστησεν *Nik*

Notes to the Translations

Martyrdom of Nicholas the Younger

title   *Bless this reading, master*: This phrase (and similar expressions in the other texts in this volume) is not actually part of the *Life,* but a liturgical rubric added later, when the text would have been read aloud in church or in a monastic refectory. The "master" would have been the presiding priest, bishop, or abbot.

1.1   *brought praise upon himself through his own deeds*: The distinction between praise through words and deeds was a commonplace since ancient times; see, for example, Isocrates, *Panathenaicus* 124.19.

    For whatever overcomes a man, to that he is enslaved: 2 Peter 2:19.

1.2   *the Muses nor the Graces of Helikon*: See Hesiod, *Theogony* 1.

    the tongue of stammerers: Isaiah 35:6.

    opened the donkey's mouth: Numbers 22:28, a reference to the story of Balaam and the donkey.

    gave unlettered fishermen . . . in their nets: See Matthew 4:18–19; Mark 1:16–17; Luke 5:1–11.

2.2   *the emperor of that time, Leo, the brother of Alexander*: Leo VI (r. 886–912); see *PmbZ* 2, no. 24311. On his brother Alexander, who ruled as coemperor and succeeded Leo in 912, see *PmbZ* 2, no. 20228.

    his strong moral convictions: Gregory of Nazianzos, *Oration* 43, ch. 64, lines 16–17 (Bernardi, p. 266).

    nor did he like jokes . . . vulgar manner: Gregory of Nazianzos, *Oration* 43, ch. 64, lines 29–30 (Bernardi, p. 266).

his appearance was serene: Gregory of Nazianzos, *Oration* 7, ch. 3, line 7 (Calvet-Sébasti, p. 186).

3.1   *Avars*: The Avars were a nomadic people from Central Asia who first encountered Byzantines in the sixth century in the area north of the Black Sea. They became more sedentary over time. See *ODB* 1:237. For speculation on the actual identity of the people here called Avars, see Introduction, subsection on Nicholas the Younger.

3.2   *The emperor Leo . . . in the eastern part of the empire*: There is no other reference in extant sources to Leo leading an expedition in Asia Minor: Kazhdan, "Hagiographical Notes (5–8)," 180.

heirs to the curse: Possibly the curse of Cain; see Genesis 4:11.

4.1   *Ternavon*: This toponym probably refers to Mount Meluna, near the modern town of Tirnavos, nine miles northwest of Larissa.

4.2   *transformed themselves into God's mirrors*: 2 Corinthians 3:18.

all-night stations: A reference to the psalms and antiphons *(staseis)* of the night office *(pannychis)*.

whoever endures . . . will receive salvation: Matthew 10:22.

6.1   *Vounaina*: In all probability it is to be identified with modern Vounaina, between Karditsa and Larissa.

a tall oak: Homer, *Iliad* 14.398. Perhaps also an allusion to the oak of Mambre beside which Abraham dwelled: see Genesis 13:18.

7.1   *the father of lies*: John 8:44.

a spectacular downfall: Job 20:5.

just as he had insinuated himself into Eve's mind secretly in the past: See Genesis 3:2–7.

8.1   *your religion*: Little is known about the religion of the Avars, who did not convert to Christianity; see *ODB* 1:237.

worshipping the living God: Hebrews 9:14.

for at the time . . . pierced in his side: See John 19:34.

after his servant Nicholas was wounded in his side: See John 19:34. The saint was executed in a manner similar to Saint Demetrios. Therefore, the author employs a commonplace of the texts referring to Saint Demetrios: see Isidoros Glavas, *Homily 1 for Saint Demetrios*, ed. Basil Laourdas, "Ἰσιδώρου ἀρχιεπισκόπου Θεσσαλονίκης ὁμιλίαι εἰς τὰς ἑορτὰς τοῦ ἁγίου

Δημητρίου," Ἑλληνικά 5 (1954): 19–65, at 22.37–23.4, who draws the comparison between Saint Demetrios and Christ.

tall oak: Homer, *Iliad* 14.398.

9.1   *Philip*: On Philip, the metropolitan bishop of Larissa, see *PmbZ* 2, no. 26607. His dates are unknown.

10.1   *the pearl of great value*: Matthew 13:46.

11.1   *governor of Thessalonike, Euphemianos*: The Greek term *doux,* here translated as "governor" and derived from the Latin *dux,* indicated the military commander of a theme, an administrative district. Euphemianos is not attested outside the hagiographic tradition for Nicholas; see *PmbZ* 2, no. 21790. The name Euphemianos has been added to the Greek text by its first editor, Demetrios Sophianos, on the basis of the relevant passage of the *Encomium of Nicholas the Younger by the Presbyter Achaïkos,* chapter 7.1.

Horation, who held consular rank: Consul *(hypatos)* was an honorific title, typically associated with administrative and fiscal officers; see *ODB* 2:963–64. Horation is not recorded elsewhere; see *PmbZ* 2, no. 22630. Ὁρατίων or ὡρατίων is an attested word for an address by an official (emperor, consul, etc.), and our author may have misunderstood the term for an official address or decree as the name of a person.

bring glory to him: This could also be rendered "bring glory to itself," that is, to divine justice.

12.1   *Demetrios*: Demetrios was the patron saint and protector of the city of Thessalonike. On his cult, see *ODB* 1:605–6.

wonderworker Achilleios: A local saint of Larissa and allegedly the first bishop of that city. He supposedly lived in the fourth century and took part in the First Ecumenical Council of Nicaea (325 CE). On his true identity and cult, see Anna Avramea, "Ἅγιοι ἐπίσκοποι τοῦ ἑλλαδικοῦ χώρου ποῦ ἔζησαν ἤ καθιερώθηκαν κατά τοῦς 8°–10° αἰώνες, μὲ εἰδική ἀναφορά στον ἅγιο Ἀχίλλιο Λαρίσης," in *Οι ήρωες της ορθόδοξης εκκλησίας: Οι νέοι άγιοι, 8ος–16ος αιώνας,* ed. Eleonora Kountoura-Galake (Athens, 2004), 47–64, at 54–61. For the church of Saint Achilleios in Larissa, see *ODB* 2:1180.

13.1   *who both smites and cures*: Deuteronomy 32:39.

14.1 *recounted his dream . . .* : A substantial part of the text is missing in
the manuscript.

The next morning at dawn . . . : A part of the text is missing in the
manuscript.

without spot or wrinkle: Ephesians 5:27.

15.1 *recorded in the book of those who live*: Revelation 21:27.

Encomium of Nicholas the Younger

1.1 *chosen people*: Titus 2:14; Exodus 19:5 and passim.

the sound of the feasting company: Psalms 41:5.

to both take pleasure . . . the blood of their martyrdom: Gregory of
Nazianzos, *Oration* 24, ch. 3, lines 21–22 (Mossay, pp. 44–46).

dark multitudes: probably demons; see Ephesians 6:12.

what is seen for what is invisible: See 2 Corinthians 4:18. We take
the Greek expression τοῖς μὴ οὖσιν as referring to those things
that are not here on earth but in heaven.

rational sacrificial offerings . . . offerings that were acceptable: Gregory of Nazianzos, *Oration* 24, ch. 4, lines 13–14 (Mossay, p. 46).

1.2 *yet another one of our precious and notable possessions*: Gregory of
Nazianzos, *Oration* 24, ch. 8, lines 10–11 (Mossay, p. 54).

Nicholas of Myra: For his cult, see *ODB* 2:1469–70.

bloodless sacrifice: That is, the Eucharist.

sanctify Israel with . . . blood: See Leviticus 16:19 (that is, of animal
blood).

He made his death count as the last mystery: Gregory of Nazianzos,
Oration 15, ch. 10, in PG 35:929B.

a new Abraham: Gregory of Nazianzos, *Oration* 43, ch. 37, lines
10–11 (Bernardi, p. 208).

he did not sacrifice his son . . . as a test by God: See Genesis 22:1–13.

he lay down . . . on the latter's behalf: John 10:11.

*go out with his household to battle . . . save Lot together with his whole
family*: Abraham's actions in Genesis 14:14–15.

2.1 *Christ-loving emperor Leo*: On Leo, see the note to the *Martyrdom
of Nicholas the Younger,* chapter 2.2 above. For Leo and Alexander's eastern expedition, see the *Martyrdom of Nicholas the
Younger*, chapter 3.2.

2.2 *the Avar nation*: See the note to the *Martyrdom of Nicholas the Younger*, chapter 3.1 above.

the ninth plague of Egypt: Locusts are the eighth plague in Exodus 10:13–15, so this appears to be a mistake by the author.

the locust and the grasshopper: Psalms 104:34.

Noah's ark: See Genesis 6:14–8:19.

3.1 *renamed Larisos . . . level and flat*: Achaïkos relates a fanciful etymology for Larisos (that is, Larissa) based on its phonetic similarity with the words "merry" *(hilaros)* and "level" *(isos)*.

The saint entered the city: According to the *Martyrdom of Nicholas the Younger*, chapter 4.1, the saint did not enter the city, but moved on to Mount Ternavon as soon as he reached Thessaly.

Ternavon: It probably refers to Mount Meluna, which is near the modern town of Tirnavos, nine miles northwest of Larissa.

3.2 *even the just fall into the hands of sinners*: Matthew 26:45; Mark 14:41; and Gregory of Nazianzos, *Oration* 21, ch. 17, lines 2–3 (Mossay, p. 144).

3.3 *If only we had one or two such men to intercede with God on his behalf*: The meaning of this sentence is unclear.

the heavenly Jerusalem, the new Zion: See Hebrews 12:22.

the spirits of the righteous: Hebrews 12:23.

4.1 *the crown . . . according to the rules*: 2 Timothy 2:5.

5.1 *considered that wound a proof of . . . virtue*: Gregory of Nazianzos, *Oration* 21, ch. 17, lines 28–29 (Mossay, p. 146).

Into your hands . . . I commit my spirit: Luke 23:46.

7.1 *He was a distinguished and handsome man . . . honored by the citizens*: It is noteworthy that Achaïkos presents the governor *(doux)* of Thessalonike as a decent man, contrary to the author of the *Martyrdom of Nicholas the Younger*, who presents him as an arrogant and difficult person, susceptible to flattery.

he resorted to the great Demetrios: Demetrios was the patron saint and protector of the city of Thessalonike. On his cult, see *ODB* 1:605–6.

7.2 *Saint Achilleios*: A local saint of Larissa and allegedly the first bishop of that city. He supposedly lived in the fourth century and took part in the First Ecumenical Council of Nicaea (325 CE). On his true identity and cult, see Avramea, "Ἅγιοι

ἐπίσκοποι τοῦ ελλαδικού χώρου," 54–61. For the church of
Saint Achilleios in Larissa, see *ODB* 2:1180.

he was eager . . . to be tormented: An allusion to Job's suffering; see
in particular Job 1:13–2:10.

8.1   *The inhabitants of Larissa . . . recognized the saint*: Another differ-
ence from the *Martyrdom of Nicholas the Younger:* the citizens of
Larissa in the latter text knew nothing of the saint, since the
saint had not entered their city at all.

9.1   *psalms and hymns and spiritual songs*: Ephesians 5:19.
washed seven times in the Jordan River: 4 Kings 5:10–14. The end
of the text is missing in the manuscript.

FUNERAL ORATION FOR ATHANASIOS, BISHOP OF METHONE

1.1   *tend to switch . . . either way*: Gregory of Nazianzos, *Oration* 42, ch.
16, line 1 (Bernardi, p. 82).
preconceptions: The meaning of the Greek word πρόσληψιν (provided the text is sound) is unclear to us.

2.1   *he who bears the name of immortality*: Athanasios means "immortal" in Greek.
the servant who had hidden . . . under the earth: See Matthew 25:25.

2.2   *I fear being convicted of disobedience*: As at the end of this para-
graph, the author Peter implies that he writes the funeral oration at the insistence of another, who remains unnamed.
to give to those who beg: Matthew 5:42; Luke 6:30.
gives the gift of speech . . . our mouth: Ephesians 6:19.

3.1   *The streams of fire . . . stood still in awe before that body*: That miracle
of Saint Agatha, the great martyr of Sicily killed during the persecution of Decius, is referred to in the *Encomium of Patriarch
Methodios of Constantinople:* see Elpidio Mioni, "L'encomio di S.
Agata di Metodio patriarca di Costantinopoli," *Analecta Bollandiana* 68 (1950) [= *Mélanges Paul Peeters,* vol. 2]: 58–93, at 91.
*those grateful sons who were carrying their elderly fathers on their
shoulders*: This is an allusion to a legend concerning two brothers of Catania who abandoned their treasures in order to carry

their parents away from an eruption of Mount Etna. See, for example, Lycurgus, *Against Leocrates* 95; Pausanias, *Description of Greece* 10.28.4.

4.1 *the dwelling of all who rejoice*: Psalms 86:7.

the tree by getting to know its fruit: Luke 6:44; see also Matthew 7:16–20.

in the same way . . . tests the quality of gold: Wisdom 3:6.

wind, rain, hail . . . a house: See Matthew 7:27.

Ishmaelites, the descendants of Hagar: See Genesis 16:11.

invaded that island: A reference to the invasion of Sicily led by Arab Muslims from North Africa. The Aghlabid dynasty, based in Ifriqiyya (Tunisia), gained complete control of Sicily during the course of the ninth century.

4.2 *that holy nation and royal priesthood*: Exodus 19:6; 1 Peter 2:9.

he who had summoned his brother . . . who had summoned him: See John 1:41–42.

after long travels . . . he was crucified: For the travels of Andrew the Apostle and his martyrdom in Patras, see *ODB* 1:92.

the divine commandment given to . . . Abraham . . . land and hearth: See Genesis 12:1–4.

divine judgment: See, for example, Numbers 11:1.

all things that do not depend on us: This is based on an old commonplace of Stoic philosophy, adopted by early Christian authors: the distinction between those things that depend on us (τὰ ἐφ' ἡμῖν), things that are within our power to affect through choice, and those that do not depend on us (τὰ οὐκ ἐφ' ἡμῖν).

5.1 *forgets what lies behind . . . lies ahead*: Philippians 3:13.

stillness, knowing that he is God: Psalms 45:11.

From the time of his youth he wished . . . to live alone: Lamentations 3:27–28.

5.2 *fighting not against . . . hosts of wickedness*: Ephesians 6:12.

The bishop . . . appointed him leader of a community of monks: Anna I. Lambropoulou, "Ὁ μοναχισμὸς στὴν Ἀχαΐα κατὰ τὴ μεσοβυζαντινὴ περίοδο: Συνθῆκες ἐξάπλωσης καὶ ἀνάπτυξης," in Ὁ μοναχισμὸς στην Πελοπόννησο 4^{ος}–15^{ος} αι., ed. Voula Konte (Athens, 2004), 87–112, at 94–95, believes that the bishop in

question was Theodore II of Patras, and that the monastery belonged to the metropolitan's jurisdiction.

the prize of the upward call: Philippians 3:14.

Let your light . . . who is in heaven: Matthew 5:16.

6.1 *the bishop considered the possibility of elevating him . . . without blame*: Is this an implied criticism of Photios of Constantinople, who was swiftly elevated through the ranks to the dignity of patriarch in 858, although he had been a layman a few days before?

in a small corner: Possibly a reference to Acts 26:26.

6.2 *like the good shepherd . . . lay down his own life*: John 10:11.

he became everything . . . to win over: 1 Corinthians 9:22.

the one who had entrusted: This could refer either to Christ or to the bishop of Patras.

those who slaughter . . . wear their wool: Ezekiel 34:3.

Blessed be the Lord . . . become rich: Zachariah 11:5.

7.1 *deviate from the straight and narrow*: Literally, "from the royal path of moderation."

He placed all parts of his soul . . . at the proper time: The whole passage is ultimately inspired by the teaching of Plato on the distinctions among the parts of the soul and the four cardinal virtues: see, for instance, *Republic* 441e–45b.

to untie . . . quarrels: Isaiah 58:6.

the feet of those who were lame: Job 29:15.

door . . . open to all: Job 31:32.

he received God's . . . . : Probably one should add here something like "witness."

blameless, righteous, and true: Job 1:1.

7.2 *easy yoke*: Matthew 11:30.

He also described the angels . . . grim and fiery eyes: The idea of angels accompanying Christ on the Day of Judgment is suggested in Matthew 16:27 and 25:31, and 2 Thessalonians 1:7.

8.1 *multiply the sum that he was given by God*: See Matthew 25:20.

a faithful servant . . . preside over numerous cities: See Luke 19:17–19.

entered into the joy of his Lord: Matthew 25:23.

showing both himself and the children . . . unblemished and safe: See Hebrews 2:13; Isaiah 8:18.

all men into men taught by God: John 6:45.

Zamolxis: Described by Plato as a king and god of the Thracians, who taught the holistic healing of body and soul (*Charmides* 156d–e); see also Herodotus, *Histories* 4.94. The entire passage that follows (down to "were not persuaded to keep them forever") is based on Theodoret of Cyrrhus, *Graecarum affectionum curatio* 1.25 and 9.7–12: ed. Pierre Canivet, *Théodoret de Cyr: Thérapeutique des maladies helléniques*, Sources chrétiennes 57 (Paris, 1958), 110, 337–39.

Anacharsis: Described by Herodotus (*Histories* 4.76–77) as a Scythian wise man who came to Greece.

Mnesion for the Argives: According to Theodoret of Cyrrhus, the source of our text, Mnesion was a lawgiver of the Phokaians, not the Argives. It is possible that Peter confuses Pheidon, the ancient king of Argos, with the Mnesion of his source. See Laniado, "Ἅγιος Πέτρος," 129–38.

Nestor: The Homeric king of Pylos.

sweeter than honey: Homer, *Iliad* 1.249.

Solon: The famous Athenian lawgiver (early sixth century BCE).

Cleisthenes: The politician credited with the introduction of democracy to Athens (late sixth century BCE).

crowned their lawgivers . . . oil like swallows: See Plato, *Republic* 398a.

blessed man . . . the fear of God: Psalms 111:1.

does not merely introduce . . . perfects us in it: This distinction appears in Dorotheos, *Various Teachings* (*Doctrinae Diversae*) 4.51, lines 26–27, in *Dorothée de Gaza: Oeuvres spirituelles*, ed. Lucien Regnault and Jacques de Préville (Paris, 1963).

8.2   *his discussion with Peter . . . that particular virtue*: See John 21:15–17.

delighted greatly in the commandments: Psalms 111:1.

his seed put down roots in the earth: Psalms 111:2.

there is glory and great wealth in his house . . . justice abides eternally: Psalms 111:3.

that kind of wealth . . . from doing so: See Matthew 19:23–24; Mark 10:23–25; Luke 18:24–25.

who reposes among the saints: Isaiah 57:15.

pledges the future glory of the saints: Ephesians 1:14.

stolen by thieves: Matthew 6:19.

8.3   *Blessed indeed . . . and committed sins*: Psalms 1:1.

flow out of the belly of those who believe: John 7:38.

No guile was found on his lips: 1 Peter 2:22; Isaiah 53:9; Revelation 14:5.

That thrice-blessed father may be compared . . . New Jerusalem: Psalms 124:1.

Lifting up his eyes: Psalms 120:1.

he himself looked upon the example of those who had satisfied God: Here begins the comparison *(synkrisis)* of the saint with the great figures of the past. It was an obligatory part of any Byzantine encomium.

9.1   *his sincere and blameless faith . . . the patriarch Abraham*: An allusion to the praise for Abraham's faith to be found in Romans 4:9–16.

the authenticity of his character: See Genesis 25:27.

reconciling himself . . . had sold him off: See Genesis 45:4–15.

the zeal of Phinees . . . killing sinners with his spear: See Numbers 25:7–11.

He did not make the earth open up . . . all that they were holding illegally: See Numbers 16:31–35.

using prayer alone . . . deprived of his hair: It is evident that Peter of Argos draws this detail from a lost *Life of Athanasios*, where there was a reference to the saint's miraculously depriving of his hair a man who had insulted him or the priesthood.

shave it off: "Shave off pollution" is presumably a pun on the punishment imposed by the saint.

9.2   *he subdued not only demons through his song*: See 1 Kings 16:23.

as he had always yearned for his death . . . enjoy the company of Christ: Philippians 1:23.

He did not bring fire down from heaven, burning up the impious: See 4 Kings 1:10.

nor did he turn those who insulted him . . . for their supper: See 4 Kings 2:23–24.

speech, seasoning it with the salt: Colossians 4:6.

a man truly desirous: The phrase "a man truly desirous" (ἀνὴρ ἐπιθυμιῶν) occurs in the Theodotion version of Daniel 9:23 and 10:11; see the Rahlfs edition of the Septuagint.

Like the three young men . . . as if it was ashes: See Daniel 3:13–27.

9.3 *no one greater has arisen among those born of women*: Matthew 11:11; the reference is to John the Baptist or Forerunner.

baptized him in the Jordan River: See Matthew 3:15–16; Mark 1:9; Luke 3:21–22.

the frankness with which his speech was filled . . . rebuked those in power: See Matthew 14:4.

his admonitions to repentance: See Matthew 3:2.

reward everyone according to his deeds: Matthew 16:27; Psalms 61:12.

10.1 *Christ's disciples in him*: The text is obscure at this point. Possibly the Greek word τῳ is corrupt.

find and gain Christ: An allusion to Philippians 3:8–9.

he carried the cross: Matthew 16:24; Mark 8:34; Luke 9:23.

considering all other things to be as refuse: Philippians 3:8.

11.1 *he was raised above the abasement of his body*: See Philippians 3:21.

to turn inward: Gregory of Nazianzos, *Oration* 2, ch. 7, lines 2–3 (Bernardi, p. 96). What follows is a typical farewell speech delivered by a saint before his death. On the origins of that genre, see Raymond E. Brown, *The Gospel according to John (XIII–XXI)* (Garden City, N.Y., 1970), 598–600.

you will become dwelling places and living sanctuaries of God: See 1 Corinthians 3:16–17; 2 Corinthians 6:16.

whose throne is heaven and whose footstool is the earth: Isaiah 66:1; Acts 7:49.

My Father and I will come to that man . . . and we will make our home with him: John 14:23.

12.1 *to love God with our entire soul . . . as we love ourselves*: Matthew 22:37–39; Mark 12:30–31; Luke 10:27. See also Galatians 5:14.

The first and most encompassing of the commandments . . . follow upon this one: See Matthew 22:40; also Mark 12:31.

to love our enemies: Matthew 5:44; Luke 6:27.

to sacrifice our life for our friends: John 15:13.

to forgive our debtors: Matthew 6:12.

our heavenly Father may forgive our own debts too: Matthew 6:14.

the horrible condemnation of the servant . . . had been discharged: See Matthew 18:23–35.

the one who needs our mercy: See Matthew 25:35–36.

into the eternal fire . . . and his angels: Matthew 25:41. Peter has substituted "Satan" for "the devil."

12.2   *sitting . . . on a throne*: Matthew 19:28.

before a river of . . . fire: Daniel 7:10.

laid bare: Probably a reference to Hebrews 4:13; compare chapter 18.1 in the *Life and Miracles of Theokletos*.

As many of us . . . have put on Christ: Galatians 3:27.

Let us not toss that garment aside . . . thrown out of the wedding chamber: See Matthew 22:12–13.

Let no foul word . . . that are edifying: Ephesians 4:29.

we will have to render an accounting . . . the words that came out of our mouth in vain: See Matthew 12:36.

Let each of us please his neighbor for his good: Romans 15:2.

13.1   *the cock sacrificed to Asklepios*: Plato, *Phaedo* 118a. Before he died, Socrates told his followers that he owed a cock to Asklepios, a sacrifice that one normally performed after recovering from an illness. The meaning of Socrates's words is still debated today, and it is unclear how this Byzantine author understood them.

the pandering words he addressed . . . Anytos and Meletos: Anytos and Meletos were two of the main prosecutors in the trial against Socrates (Plato, *Apology* 23e); Socrates was convicted of impiety and moral corruption and sentenced to death. The "pandering words" here might allude to the final exchange between Socrates and his followers in Plato's dialogue *Phaedo*. Socrates's followers urge him to delay his execution, but he dismisses their pleas, orders hemlock brought to him, and drinks it (Plato, *Phaedo* 116e–18a).

14.1   *beautiful feet*: Romans 10:15; also Isaiah 52:7.

into your hands I commend my soul: Luke 23:46; also Psalms 30:6.

full of the days: Job 42:17.

he left regret behind him: Proverbs 11:3. The authorship of the book of Proverbs was traditionally ascribed to Solomon.

the ripe grain . . . the storehouses of God: See Matthew 3:12; Luke 3:17.

the reward . . . is great indeed: Matthew 5:12; Luke 6:23.

He blossoms like a palm tree . . . like a cedar: Psalms 91:13.

his remembrance will be everlasting: Psalms 111:6.

his glory inextinguishable: Homer, *Odyssey* 4.584.

14.2   *at the hands of the powerful*: Jeremiah 38:11; also Psalms 34:10.

him who becomes everything for everyone: 1 Corinthians 9:22.

a new Siloam: See John 9:7. Siloam was a pool with healing powers in the southeast corner of Jerusalem.

LIFE OF PETER, BISHOP OF ARGOS

1.1   *to incur such a great risk*: Marinos, *Life of Proklos* 1.8–9, in *Marinus: Proclus ou sur le bonheur*, ed. Henri D. Saffrey and Alain-Philippe Segonds (Paris, 2002), 1.

unholy for me to remain silent: Marinos, *Life of Proklos* 1.25–26 (Saffrey and Segonds, p. 2).

I decided to make the attempt and compose his life: Marinos, *Life of Proklos* 1.33–34 (Saffrey and Segonds, p. 2).

whatever my memory prompts me to write offhand: Gregory of Nazianzos, *Oration* 21, ch. 5, line 8 (Mossay, p. 118).

2.1   *the great city of Constantine*: That is, Constantinople.

large and beautiful churches: Gregory of Nazianzos, *Oration* 43, ch. 63, line 12 (Bernardi, p. 262).

3.1   *It would be hard to exaggerate . . . thought of greed*: Marinos, *Life of Proklos* 4.27–28 (Saffrey and Segonds, p. 6).

3.2   *Paul, who was the oldest and the first to emerge from his mother's womb*: On Paul, the older brother of Peter of Argos, see *PmbZ* 2, no. 26292, and Athanasios D. Kominis, "Παρατηρήσεις καὶ διορθώσεις εἰς τοὺς ἐπισκοπικοὺς καταλόγους Ἀργολοκορινθίας," Πελοποννησιακά 13 (1978–1979) [= Πρακτικὰ Α΄ Συνεδρίου Ἀργολικῶν Σπουδῶν]: 22–27, at 23 (Παράρτημα).

that famous Peter: According to *PmbZ* 2, no. 26429, the identity of this Peter (not to be confused with Peter of Argos, the subject of the *Life*) is obscure. He should perhaps be identified with Peter of Galatia, a monk on Mount Olympos who was invited

by the emperor Basil I (r. 867–886) to settle near Constantinople. The emperor built the monastery of Saint Phokas on the Stenon on the European shore of the Bosporos strait (R. Janin, *Les églises et les monastères,* vol. 1, pt. 3 of *La géographie ecclésiastique de l'empire byzantin,* 2nd ed. [Paris, 1969], 499), for his sake, and the saint died there in old age: *PmbZ* 2, no. 26426. The *Life* of the saint referred to below in the text is now lost.

4.1   *Although his secular knowledge was abundant . . . did not boast of it*: Almost the same phrase is used in the *Life of Saint Athanasios the Athonite (Vita A)* 22.9–10, in *Vitae duae antiquae sancti Athanasii Athonitae,* ed. Jacques Noret (Turnhout, 1982), 12.

   good a friend . . . of . . . temperance: Marinos, *Life of Proklos* 4.19–21 (Saffrey and Segonds, p. 6).

4.2   *His bearing, gait . . . may also be admired*: Plutarch, *How a Man May Become Aware of His Progress in Virtue* 84e.

   an unruly colt: Possibly an allusion to the image of the chariot in Plato, *Phaedrus* 246a–54e.

   strove to become a good man: Possibly an echo of the prayer of Socrates in Plato, *Phaedrus* 279b.

   many depraved persons possessed the former assets: That is, good birth and a proper education.

   It may be pointless . . . prolific: Marinos, *Life of Proklos* 5.1–5 (Saffrey and Segonds, p. 7).

5.1   *Nicholas of Italy*: On the Italian origin of Nicholas I Mystikos, patriarch of Constantinople (901–907, 912–925), see *PmbZ* 2, no. 25885.

   because of which he was exiled: Nicholas was exiled in 907.

   he succumbed to . . . the emperor's view concerning the fourth marriage: This is not accurate. Nicholas, while recognizing the young Constantine VII as emperor, persecuted those who had supported the emperor Leo VI in his endeavor to have his fourth marriage recognized. His relations with Zoe Karbonopsina, Leo's fourth wife, were strained; see *ODB* 3:2228.

   others had defected from his side: Such as Arethas, metropolitan of Caesarea; see *PmbZ* 2, no. 20554. Peter was offered a metropolitan see probably after 912, when Nicholas was reinstated to

his throne: Nikos A. Vees, "Zur Sigillographie der byzantinischen Themen Peloponnes und Hellas," *Vizantijskij Vremennik* 21 (2014): 90–110, 192–235, at 98–99. *PmbZ* 2, no. 26292, places this offer and the subsequent election of Peter's brother Paul as metropolitan of Corinth in Nicholas's first patriarchate, between 901 and 907, following Athanasios D. Kominis, Γρηγόριος Πάρδος μητροπολίτης Κορίνθου καὶ τὸ ἔργον αὐτοῦ (Athens and Rome, 1960), 44–45.

praising many of the divine martyrs . . . with his encomia: On Peter's writings, see *PmbZ* 2, no. 26428. The only speech by Peter on a martyr that is still preserved is his *Oration on Saint Barbara*. Probably he wrote others, which are now lost.

6.1   *Argos and Nauplion*: At that time both cities were under the jurisdiction of the bishop of Argos: see Yannopoulos, "Ἱστορικές πληροφορίες," 168; Alexios Savvidis, "Τα προβλήματα σχετικά με το βυζαντινό Ναύπλιο," in Yannopoulos and Savvides, *Μεσαιωνικὴ Πελοπόννησος*, 129–49, at 131–34; and Voula Konti, "Το Ναύπλιο και οι σχέσεις του με την επισκοπή Άργους κατά τη μέση βυζαντινή περίοδο," *Σύμμεικτα* 15 (2002): 131–48.

the speech that he composed regarding his flight: This speech is now lost.

7.1   *followers of Asklepios*: That is, physicians, Asklepios being the god of medicine.

He did not wait for the wheat . . . the pressures brought to bear by the tax collectors: On the significance of this passage, see Maria Gerolymatou, "Πελοποννησιακὲς μονὲς καὶ ἐξουσία," in *Ο μοναχισμὸς στην Πελοπόννησο 4^{ος}–15^{ος} αι.*, ed. Voula Konti (Athens, 2004), 37–53, at 51–52.

7.2   *He steered . . . toward whichever craft they liked*: This is proof of the existence of handicrafts in the area of Argolis (and Corinth): Michael S. Kordosis, *Συμβολὴ στὴν ἱστορία καὶ τοπογραφία τῆς περιοχῆς Κορίνθου στοὺς μέσους χρόνους* (Athens, 1981), 232.

thrown to the poor from above: Probably from a balcony in the episcopal palace.

8.1   *A famine was pressing hard upon the Peloponnese . . . full of dead bod-*

ies: Constantelos, "Ἡ ἱστορικὴ σημασία," 354, believes that the description of the devastation of the Argolid at this time is exaggerated.

our new Joseph: Compare Gregory of Nazianzos's description of Basil of Caesarea as a new Joseph in *Oration* 43, ch. 36, lines 1–2 (Bernardi, p. 204). In the biblical narrative, Joseph provides food to the Egyptians in a time of famine in exchange for the ownership of their land and property; see Genesis 47:13–26.

he created life for them . . . according to the proverb: An ancient proverb: Diogenianos, *Proverbs* 1.17 (*CPG*, vol. 1, p. 183, lines 13–14).

8.2   *measure*: The *medimnos* was a unit of measurement of varying quantity for both grain and land: see *ODB* 2:1388. It is also commonly called a *modios*.

In the case of Elijah of Thisbe . . . the widow of Sidon and her children: See 3 Kings 17:7–16.

9.1   *These stories . . . attracted even some barbarians to him*: Probably a reference to remnants of Slav tribes in the Argolid; see Yannopoulos, "Ἱστορικές πληροφορίες," 172.

the inhabitants of Crete . . . lived like robbers: On other references to pirate raids in the Saronic Gulf, see Kordosis, Συμβολὴ στὴν ἱστορία, 89. Crete had been conquered by Arab Muslims from Spain led by Abu Ḥafs between 824 and 828. The island remained a base for Arab raids within the Aegean until its capture by Nikephoros II Phokas in 961. See *ODB* 1:546.

9.2   *hurled fire*: This is a reference to the so-called Greek fire used by the Byzantine navy. The "fire" was a liquid incendiary propelled from a metal instrument; its exact composition and means of ignition are uncertain; see *ODB* 2:873.

Cretans speak like Cretans to Cretans, as the proverb says: An ancient proverb about those who lie to other liars, sometimes rendered as "diamond cuts diamond": Makarios, *Proverbs* 7.35 (*CPG*, vol. 2, p. 205, lines 5–6).

10.1   *the story of the young freedwoman who was dragged into slavery*: There is a similar story in Gregory of Nazianzos, *Oration* 43, ch. 56, lines 1–30 (Bernardi, pp. 242–44).

the general of that time: Yannopoulos, "Ἱστορικές πληροφορίες,"

173–74, points out that the headquarters of the *strategos* of the administrative district of the Peloponnese at the time were not at Argos, but Corinth. That is an indication that the episode might be an invention of our author, Theodore of Nicaea.

the stronger arm: Psalms 34:10 and Jeremiah 38:11.

11.1   *he urged them to anoint the girl with the blessed oil*: Following the biblical precedent in James 5:14. On the sacrament of unction, see *ODB* 3:2142.

12.1   *the three parts of his soul*: That is, reason, the spirited part of the soul, and desire, as distinguished by Plato in the *Republic*, Book 4.

    he had a luminous mind: Compare the phrase of Diadochos of Photike, *Centuries* 40, in *Diadoque de Photicé: Oeuvres spirituelles,* ed. Edouard des Places, 3rd ed. (Paris, 1966), p. 108, lines 5–6.

    he was able, through its operations . . . in a simple way: See a similar passage in John Philoponos, *On Aristotle's De anima*, in *Ioannis Philoponi in Aristotelis de anima libros commentaria,* ed. Michael Hayduck (Berlin, 1897), p. 2, lines 12–15.

12.2   *John, the beloved disciple*: Saint John the Evangelist.

    of the Word who was in the beginning: The author here alludes to the Gospel of John, whose first chapter refers to the Word being present "in the beginning" (John 1:1), but also as being the "only-begotten" (John 1:14, 18).

    you had leaned upon the pure chest of Christ: See John 13:25.

12.3   *we had in mind another man . . . "protected by God"*: The proper name Theophylaktos means "protected by God." The reference is to either the *protospatharios* Theophylaktos, governor of the Peloponnese, or the patriarch Theophylaktos, who died in 956. But John the evangelist referred to Peter himself, whom he described as "a man protected by God"; that is, he did not employ the word *theophylaktos* as a personal name but as an adjective. See also Alexander Kazhdan, *A History of Byzantine Literature (850–1000)*, ed. Christine Angelidi (Athens, 2006), 114n3.

    a plain of destruction: Joel 2:3 and 4:19.

14.1   *the bed on which the holy man was lying*: Gregory of Nazianzos, *Oration* 43, ch. 80, line 3 (Bernardi, p. 300). The concluding pas-

sage of the *Life* contains several quotations from Gregory's funeral oration for Basil of Caesarea, a text which was in many ways the archetype for *Lives* of sainted bishops.

a quarrel broke out between the citizens of Argos and those of Nauplion: On the (often troubled) relations between the two cities, see Alexios Savvidis, "Τα προβλήματα σχετικά με το βυζαντινό Ναύπλιο," in Yannopoulos and Savvides, *Μεσαιωνικὴ Πελοπόννησος*, 133–34; Panayotis A. Yannopoulos, "Η περιστασιακή επισκοπή Ναυπλίου κατὰ τον Θ΄ και τον Ι΄ αιώνα," in *Μεσαιωνικὴ Πελοπόννησος*, 315–41, at 323–41.

15.1   *disinterested generosity*: Gregory of Nazianzos, *Oration* 43, ch. 36, line 6 (Bernardi, p. 204).

    He contended against some . . . not left behind by any: Gregory of Nazianzos, *Oration* 21, ch. 4, lines 1–2 (Mossay, p. 116).

16.1   *May you watch . . . from above*: Gregory of Nazianzos, *Oration* 43, ch. 82, lines 6–7 (Bernardi, p. 304).

    Now that your outer shell has fallen away: That is, his body.

    In a way worthy of your prophecy: Apparently Peter had predicted to the author of our text that he would become a bishop.

LIFE AND MIRACLES OF THEOKLETOS, BISHOP OF LAKEDAIMON

title   *Lakedaimonia*: Sparta in the southern Peloponnese.

1.2   *the old tales about Lakedaimon . . . the virtue of this man*: The following contrast is probably based on the preface to Book 5 of Eusebios's *Ecclesiastical History*.

    that flower of virtue, exemplar of the priesthood: Gregory of Nazianzos, *Oration* 1, ch. 7, line 3 (Bernardi, p. 80).

2.1   *"gift of God" to Lakedaimon*: The phrase "gift of God" (*doron Theou* in Greek) is possibly a reference to bishop Theodosios of Lakedaimon; see *PmbZ* 2, no. 27950. However, it is possible that another name is hidden under those words (for example, a Theodoretos, Theodoros, or Dorotheos).

2.2   *he builds holy churches, such as this one which adorns Lakedaimon*: We do not know to which church the author refers.

whatever he could ascertain was written down: The author refers here to his own writing of the *Life*.

3.1   *pass judgment on the tree based on the fruit that it produced*: Matthew 12:33; see also Luke 6:43–44.

preferred the solitude of the desert to the society of men: For similar wording, see Gregory of Nazianzos, *Oration* 21, ch. 19, lines 20–21 (Mossay, pp. 148–150).

dwelling alone on a roof: Psalms 101:8.

3.2   *His wealth consisted of the hopes that he placed in God*: Gregory of Nazianzos, *Oration* 15, ch. 5 (PG 35:920B).

exchanging all these for the precious pearl: Matthew 13:46.

4.1   *Stricken with love*: See Song of Songs 2:5.

good merchant: Gregory of Nazianzos, *Oration* 17, ch. 7 (PG 35:975.36), derived from Matthew 13:45.

through the fire . . . came to resemble authentic gold: Perhaps an allusion to 1 Peter 1:7.

let him be hidden . . . on a pedestal: See Matthew 5:15; Mark 4:21; Luke 11:33.

for the whole Peloponnese and the major part of Greece as well: The distinction between the Peloponnese and Greece implies that the former was a distinct administrative district at the time of the text's composition.

4.3   *do not care at all*: Diogenianos, *Proverbs* 3.46 (*CPG*, vol. 2, p. 43, lines 14–15).

clay and brickmaking: Exodus 1:14.

4.4   *fearing things that should cause a justifiable fear*: Psalms 13:5; the author contrasts Theokletos with those mentioned by the Psalmist, the people who fear things that should *not* cause fear.

6.1   *the eye of the blind and the foot of the lame*: Job 29:15.

became all things to all people, in order to win over everyone: 1 Corinthians 9:22.

6.2   *mourned like Jacob for his son Joseph*: See Genesis 37:34.

as David mourned for Jonathan: See 2 Kings 1:17.

7.2   *a single Creator*: Gregory of Nazianzos, *Carmina moralia,* in PG 37:938A.

loftier, suspended in the air . . . on the earth: This may be an allusion

to Aristophanes's satirical depiction of Socrates suspended in a basket in midair (*Clouds* 225–27). Aristophanes was a standard classroom text in Byzantium.

the parable of Lazarus and the rich man: See Luke 16:19–31.

8.1   *their soul that was concealed by it . . .* : After this phrase half a page is left unwritten in the Barberini manuscript.

9.1   *ignominious suffering for the sake of Christ*: Gregory of Nazianzos, *Oration* 4, ch. 58, lines 3–4 (Bernardi, p. 164).

9.2   *possible that envy . . . could endure all this*: Gregory of Nazianzos, *Oration* 21, ch. 32, line 1 (Mossay, p. 176).

11.1   *Imitating that Jewish assembly*: The author is referring to the supposed machinations of the Jews against Christ as narrated in the Gospels. No polemic of the saint against the Jews living in Lakedaimon at the time survives: Ilias Anagnostakis, "Μονεμβασία-Λακεδαίμων: Για μία τυπολογία αντιπαλότητας και για την Κυριακή αργία στις πόλεις," in *Οι βυζαντινές πόλεις 8ος–15ος αιώνας: Προοπτικές της έρευνας και νέες ερμηνευτικές προσεγγίσεις*, ed. Tonia Kiousopoulou (Rethymno, 2014), 101–38, at 110.

of the same make: See *LSJ,* under κεραμεία.

knaves-market: Diogenianos, *Proverbs* 1.3 (*CPG*, vol. 1, p. 181, lines 3–6). Literally, "a market of Kerkopes," or "man-monkeys," a race of mischievous dwarves connected in legend to Herakles; see *LSJ,* under Κέρκωψ.

During the day they shot . . . like arrows: Psalms 90:5.

11.2   *an Indian elephant is troubled by a mosquito*: Apostolios, *Proverbs* 10.37 (*CPG*, vol. 2, p. 495, line 2).

13.1   *the robe from its hem*: Diogenianos, *Proverbs* 5.15 (*CPG*, vol. 1, p. 252, lines 2–3).

there's many a slip between the cup and the lip: Diogenianos, *Proverbs* 7.46 (*CPG*, vol. 1, p. 294, lines 6–7).

14.1   *Lakonia*: That is, the region of Sparta.

14.2   *An Iliad of woes*: Gregory of Cyprus, *Proverbs* 2.29 (*CPG*, vol. 2, p. 72, line 6).

14.3   *Why did knees . . . been quiet*: Job 3:12–13.

Why do those in distress have a voice . . . and obtain it not?: Job 3:20–

21. The author uses "voice" (*phone*) here in place of the biblical "light" (*phos*).

sighing, and unable to form distinct words: Romans 8:26.

15.1   *the bed that Christ ordered the paralytic to carry*: Matthew 9:6. See also Mark 2:11; Luke 5:24; John 5:8.

15.2   *that poetic potion*: A reference to the potion that Circe gave Odysseus to bewitch him; see Homer, *Odyssey* 10.290, 316.

makes us forget all our sorrows: Homer, *Odyssey* 4.221.

intensified his asceticism on a daily basis: Athanasios of Alexandria, *Life of Antony* 45.1, ed. Gerhard J. M. Bartelink (Paris, 1994).

his pleasure was to avoid all pleasures: Gregory of Nazianzos, *Oration* 43, ch. 61, lines 8–9 (Bernardi, pp. 256–58).

I discipline . . . to others: 1 Corinthians 9:27. The author uses "flesh" (*sarx*) instead of the Pauline "body" (*soma*).

16.2   *the entrance . . . narrow, full of sorrow*: See Matthew 7:14; also Luke 13:24.

son of perdition: John 17:12; 2 Thessalonians 2:3.

stand on the right-hand side: See Matthew 25:33–34, on the righteous being placed on the right-hand side of Christ.

the bosom of . . . Abraham: Luke 16:22.

16.3   *the water of life*: John 4:10.

that paragon of moderation: See Genesis 39:12.

We should not allow the setting sun . . . savage soul: See Ephesians 4:26.

17.2   *acting in this like a horse goad . . . urging them to look after their souls*: See Plato, *Apology* 30e–31a.

you must surrender yourself . . . condemned to these punishments: See Hebrews 10:33–34.

17.5   *with impunity*: The Greek term for this, νηποινεί, is rare and otherwise unattested in texts of the Byzantine period.

17.6   *heaping up coals on your own head*: Proverbs 25:22.

son of perdition: John 17:12; 2 Thessalonians 2:3.

17.7   *turning the most honorable . . . into vessels of dishonor*: See Romans 9:21; 2 Timothy 2:20.

the eternal fire of frightful Gehenna: See Matthew 5:22.

17.8   *the sword that is coming*: Ezekiel 33:3, 6.

18.1   *all . . . laid bare*: Hebrews 4:13.

19.1   *trumpet of the Tyrrhenians*: Aeschylus, *Eumenides* 567; Euripides, *Phoenician Women* 1377–78, that is, a loud trumpet. The Tyrrhenians were an ancient people of Italy, usually identified with the Etruscans.

19.2   *all the clergy who stand in the sanctuary*: Gregory of Nazianzos, *Oration* 43, ch. 81, lines 1–2 (Bernardi, p. 302).

19.3   *I will boast of and be proud of your splendor*: Possibly an allusion to 2 Thessalonians 1:4.

            I testify before God and the angels: 1 Timothy 5:21.

19.4   *It vanishes like smoke*: Psalms 67:3.

            it has nailed the whole of itself to it: A common metaphor for how the soul is united with the body, which goes back to Plato, *Phaedo* 83d.

            collect pebbles, mistaking them for pearls: See Gregory of Nazianzos, *Oration* 33, ch. 1, lines 5–9 (Moreschini, p. 156).

19.6   *that holy and blessed hymn*: That is, the *Trisagion*.

            the seraphim: An allusion to the angelic cry, "Holy, holy, holy," in Isaiah 6:3, echoed in the Byzantine *Trisagion*.

            awesome mystery: A reference to the divine liturgy.

            you should behave . . . inside the holy house of God: 1 Timothy 3:15.

19.7   *glory . . . on the day of our judgment*: 1 Peter 2:12.

            Obey your leaders . . . give an account on our behalf: Hebrews 13:17.

19.8   *his wrath is equal to his mercy*: Sirach 16:12.

19.9   *they do not know at what time of night the thief will come*: Matthew 24:43.

            to rush to confess our sins before him: Psalms 94:2.

            Follow them now, as under a great light: See Proverbs 6:23.

            your faces will not be ashamed: Psalms 33:6.

20.2   *Orphans too mourned . . . their affectionate father*: Gregory of Nazianzos, *Oration* 43, ch. 81, line 14 (Bernardi, p. 304).

21.1   *its heavenly counterpart*: See Hebrews 8:2.

            the bridal chamber: See Matthew 9:15; Mark 2:19; Luke 5:34.

21.2   *fathers love the babblings of their children*: John of Damascus, *Oration on Saint John Chrysostom* 1.9, in *Die Schriften des Johannes von Damaskos*, ed. Bonifatius Kotter, vol. 5 (Berlin and New York, 1988), 359–70, at 359.

LIFE OF THEODORE OF KYTHERA

1.1   *our late invitation to the vine dressing is the reason for our belated entrance*: Gregory of Nazianzos, *Oration* 40, ch. 20, lines 19–20 (Moreschini, p. 242).

    the parable of the vineyard . . . their zeal and readiness: See Matthew 20:8–16.

1.2   *Demetrios*: This was the famous patron saint of the city of Thessalonike, who, according to Byzantine tradition, was executed with spears by the emperor Maximian.

    Christ, our God who searches our hearts and emotions: Psalms 7:10; see also Psalms 26:2.

1.3   *"except for those I omit"*: 2 Corinthians 11:28.

1.4   *a second Saint Nicholas*: He refers to Saint Nicholas of Myra. For his cult, see *ODB* 2:1469–70.

2.1   *the administrative district of the Peloponnese*: From the early ninth century, the Peloponnese was a *thema,* or theme (a military and administrative district), in its own right: see *ODB* 3:1621. Korone, located in southeastern Messenia, was a suffragan bishopric of Patras.

    When their son was five years old, his parents sent him to school: This is the so-called *propaideia,* or preliminary education, beginning around the age of six.

    his parents presented him to the bishop of that city: This is a practice attested in other lives of saints, for example the *Life of Saint Demetrianos of Cyprus,* who was enlisted among the clergy from a tender age: see *AASS,* November 3 (1910), 302A. Such children were educated by clergymen, their fathers being unable to hire tutors for financial reasons.

2.2   *senior priest*: It appears that the senior priest *(protopapas)* of Nauplion was under the jurisdiction of the bishop of Argos: see Oikonomides, "Ὁ Βίος τοῦ ἁγίου Θεοδώρου Κυθήρων," 269; see also *PmbZ* 2, no. 30756.

    Korone: The town is not actually mentioned in the text but is clearly meant.

    considered all other things as refuse: Philippians 3:8.

3.1   *Theodore . . . who was bishop of the church of Argos*: We know little

about this Theodore; see Oikonomides, "Ό Βίος τοῦ ἁγίου
Θεοδώρου Κυθήρων," 269, and *PmbZ* 2, no. 27680.

Stephen . . . council of the god-murdering Jews: See Acts 6:15.

The face of a man . . . his face is gloomy: Proverbs 15:13.

3.4 *we are delivered to the grave alone and naked*: See Ecclesiastes 5:14;
Job 1:21.

decomposes quickly like the dead leaves of a tree: Possibly a reminiscence of Homer, *Iliad* 6.146.

3.5 *Like fish . . . when it suddenly falls upon them*: Ecclesiastes 9:12.

3.6 *turn . . . over in my mind day and night*: Psalms 1:2.

my power is dried up . . . my flesh: Psalms 21:16 and 101:6.

3.7 *the saint . . . sailed off to Rome*: On pilgrimage to Rome in this period, see Oikonomides, "Ό Βίος τοῦ ἁγίου Θεοδώρου
Κυθήρων," 270.

the holy and chief apostles: That is, the apostles Peter and Paul.

Hagarenes: A term applied to Arabs, referring to their supposed
descent from Hagar, the mother of Ishmael (see Genesis 16:11).
The nearby island of Crete had been conquered by Arab Muslims from Spain led by Abu Ḥafs between 824 and 828. The island remained a base for Arab raids in the Aegean until its reconquest by Nikephoros II Phokas in 961. See *ODB* 1:546.

no one dared to live there: The island of Kythera was repopulated
after 961; see Panayotis A. Yannopoulos, "Τα μεσοβυζαντινά
Κύθηρα. Μεθοδολογική προσέγγιση των πηγών και ιστο-
ρική πραγματικότητα," in Yannopoulos and Savvidis, *Μεσαιωνικὴ Πελοπόννησος*, 201–18, at 211.

4.1 *the church of our all-holy Lady, the Theotokos, who is called Diakonia*:
Theotokos, "Mother of God," was a title of Mary that was defined at the Council of Ephesus in 431. The epithets *diakonos*
and *diakonousa* are attested for the Virgin, but not *diakonia*,
to the best of our knowledge. The church in Monemvasia is
known only from this text.

he could not find an available ship: That is, he could not find a ship
to take him to Kythera.

4.3 *the village of Terea*: This village is mentioned in an imperial letter
of the year 1301: Oikonomides, "Ό Βίος τοῦ ἁγίου Θεοδώρου
Κυθήρων," 271.

monk called Antony: This monk is known only from the *Life of Theodore;* see *PmbZ* 2, no. 20493.

5.1 *the tourmarch Meliton*: See *PmbZ* 2, no. 25048. On the title *tourmarches,* a high military officer serving immediately under the general in command of each province, see *ODB* 3:2100–1.

four ships: The Greek term *chelandion* can refer either to transport vessels or to warships; see *ODB* 1:417.

Romanos the Elder: The Byzantine emperor Romanos I Lakapenos (r. 920–944); see *PmbZ* 2, no. 26833.

one of the biremes: A bireme was a ship with two banks of oars.

Oktoechos: The *Oktoechos* was a book containing the hymns of daily services, except for Lent, Easter, and Pentecost. Anthologies of *oktoechos* hymns for Sundays date from the eighth century: *ODB* 3:1520.

the Apostle: A collection of New Testament epistles of the apostles used by the Orthodox Church only at the Eucharistic liturgy.

5.2 *defeated by the force of the fire*: For Greek fire, see note above to chapter 9.2 of the *Life of Peter, Bishop of Argos.*

what is impossible for men is possible for God: Luke 18:27; see also Matthew 19:26.

he who had protected Daniel inside the lions' den: See Daniel 6:14–22.

5.3 *his hermitage*: The Greek term is *enkleistra* (literally, "enclosure"), or recluse's cell, a word used to describe the abode of a solitary in which he remains constantly, never going out.

the church of the Forerunner: The Forerunner (*Prodromos*) is John the Baptist.

5.4 *a passing ship*: For the Greek term *chelandion*, see note above on chapter 5.1.

Saint Epiphanios: Bishop of Salamis on Cyprus, a prominent Church Father of the late fourth century, he died en route to Salamis from Constantinople on May 12, 403: *ODB* 1:714.

6.2 *Your labors were brief, but you obtained the blessed life*: The author is alluding here to the theme with which the *Life* began, that you can still win everything even if only with a brief burst of effort at the end.

a new Abraham, because you departed from your fatherland: See Gen-

esis 12:1–5. Chapters 6.2–3 of the *Life* contain the *synkrisis,* that is, a comparison of the saint to his predecessors that is typical of the closing paragraphs of many hagiographical works.

a new Elisha . . . the commandment of your teacher: See 3 Kings 19:20.

a new Antony: On Saint Antony the Great of Egypt, see *ODB* 1:125–26.

6.3   *you died for this world, and the world was as dead for you*: See Galatians 6:14.

day and night . . . You not only shed tears: Jeremiah 14:17

Who is going to separate us from Christ's love?: Romans 8:35.

a new Theodore: He is referring to Saint Theodore the Stoudite (d. 826), an influential monastic reformer. See *ODB* 3:2044–45.

6.4   *it is right to call you a gift from God*: A pun on the name Theodore, which means "gift of God."

they manage to put to flight . . . throwing rocks and sticks at them: The author is possibly referring to a real event.

COMMEMORATION OF ARSENIOS, ARCHBISHOP OF KERKYRA

title   *archbishop of Kerkyra*: The well-known island in the Ionian Sea, known also by the name Corfu. Although the bishop of Kerkyra was a suffragan of Nikopolis, then later of Kephallenia, and only in the eleventh century was elevated to the rank of metropolitan, Arsenios is constantly referred to in the sources as an archbishop.

On the nineteenth of the month: Arsenios died on January 19, in an unknown year in the second half of the tenth century.

celestial minds: That is, angels.

1.1   *the pious emperor Basil from Macedonia*: Basil I (r. 867–886), founder of the Macedonian dynasty; see *PmbZ* 2, no. 20837.

Bethany: This is a village near Jerusalem.

1.2   *Seleukeia*: Possibly the port city in Isauria, since it was a metropolitan see, but the author might have in mind as well Seleukeia Pieria, the port of Antioch.

2.1   *the most holy Tryphon*: Tryphon was patriarch of Constantinople (928–931); see *PmbZ* 2, no. 28374.

Theophylaktos: Theophylaktos was patriarch of Constantinople (933–956); see *PmbZ* 2, no. 28192.

placed on the lampstand: Luke 8:16. See also Matthew 5:15; Mark 4:21; Luke 11:33.

he became everything for everyone: 1 Corinthians 9:22.

2.2   *Scythians*: The term "Scythians" referred to nomadic tribes of the Eurasian steppe and was applied by Byzantine writers to a wide range of nomadic peoples; see *ODB* 3:1857–58. This *Life* seems to be the only source for an attack on Kerkyra at this time; see *ODB* 2:1124.

    Four Islands: Four small islands off the coast of Epiros, about two and a half miles northwest of Bouthrotos; see Peter Soustal (with the assistance of Johannes Koder), *Nikopolis und Kephallenia* (Vienna, 1981), 269, under Tetranesa.

2.3   *the emperor Constantine Porphyrogennetos, the son of the most wise Leo*: The references are to Leo VI the Wise (r. 886–912) and Constantine VII Porphyrogennetos (r. 945–959); see *PmbZ* 2, nos. 24311 and 23734.

3.1   *the most holy cathedral of the Kerkyrians*: We do not know whether the text refers to the church of Jason and Sosipatros or to the basilica of Jovian in the old city; see *ODB* 2:1124.

Bibliography

EDITIONS AND TRANSLATIONS

Nicholas the Younger

Sophianos, Demetrios Z., ed. Ἅγιος Νικόλαος ὁ ἐν Βουναίνῃ· Ἀνέκδοτα ἁγιολογικὰ κείμενα· Ἱστορικαὶ εἰδήσεις περὶ τῆς μεσαιωνικῆς Θεσσαλίας (Ι΄ αἰών), 139–51 (Life), 152–60 (Encomium). Athens, 1972.

Athanasios of Methone

Kyriakopoulos, Konstantinos, ed. Ἁγίου Πέτρου ἐπισκόπου Ἄργους Βίος καὶ Λόγοι· Εἰσαγωγὴ-κείμενον-μετάφρασις-σχόλια, 44–67 (Greek text and modern Greek translation), 275–316 (commentary). Athens, 1976.
Mai, Angelo. Nova Patrum Bibliotheca, vol. 9, no. 3, 31–51. Rome, 1888.
Papaoikonomou, Chrestos. Ὁ πολιοῦχος τοῦ Ἄργους ἅγιος Πέτρος ἐπίσκοπος Ἄργους ὁ θαυματουργός, 91–106. Athens, 1908.

Peter of Argos

Kyriakopoulos, Konstantinos, ed. Ἁγίου Πέτρου ἐπισκόπου Ἄργους Βίος καὶ Λόγοι· Εἰσαγωγὴ-κείμενον-μετάφρασις-σχόλια, 232–55 (Greek text and modern Greek translation), 415–98 (commentary). Athens, 1976.
Mai, Angelo. Nova Patrum Bibliotheca, vol. 9, no. 3, 1–17. Rome, 1888.
Papaoikonomou, Chrestos. Ὁ πολιοῦχος τοῦ Ἄργους ἅγιος Πέτρος ἐπίσκοπος Ἄργους ὁ θαυματουργός, 59–74. Athens, 1908.

Theokletos of Lakedaimon

Kurtz, Eduard. "Neskol'ko popravok k tekstu zitiia sv. Theoklita, izdannomu Nik. A. Veisom v 1-m prilozhenii ko 2-mu tomu Vizantiiskago

Obozrenija." *Revue byzantine/Vizantiiskoe Obozrenie* 3 (1917): II, 27–29. [Important corrections were made by Kurtz.]

Sgouritsas, Agesilaos. "Ὁ Λακεδαιμονίας ἅγιος Θεόκλητος." *Θεολογία* 27 (1956): 567–93. [Sgouritsas did not know Vees's edition.]

Vees, Nikos, ed. "Vie de saint Théoclète évêque de Lacédémoine, publiée d'après le manuscrit n. 583 de la bibliothèque Barberine." *Revue byzantine/Vizantiiskoe Obozrenie* 2 (1916): suppl. 1–55.

Vlachakos, Petros K. *Ἅγιος Θεόκλητος Λακεδαιμονίας.* Thessalonike, 2015. Modern Greek translation.

———. *Ὁ Βίος τοῦ ἁγίου Θεοκλήτου Λακεδαιμονίας. Ἱστορική, γλωσσική καὶ ὑφολογικὴ διερεύνηση.* Thessalonike, 2015. [Analysis of the text.]

Theodore of Kythera

Oikonomides, Nikolaos, ed. "Ὁ Βίος τοῦ Ἁγίου Θεοδώρου Κυθήρων (10ος αἰ.) (12 Μαῖου - *BHG*, ἀρ. 2430)." In *Τρίτον Πανιόνιον Συνέδριον: Πρακτικά*, 264–91. Athens, 1967. Reprint, *Byzantium from the Ninth Century to the Fourth Crusade: Studies, Texts, Monuments*, no. 7. Brookfield, Vt., 1992.

Arsenios of Kerkyra

Nikokavouras, Sebastianos. *Ἀκολουθίαι τῶν ἁγίων Ἰάσωνος καὶ Σωσιπάτρου, τῆς παρθενομάρτυρος Κερκύρας τῆς Βασιλίδος, τοῦ ἁγίου Ἀρσενίου μητροπολίτου Κερκύρας, τῆς ὁσίας Θεοδώρας τῆς Αὐγούστης καὶ τοῦ ἁγίου ἱερομάρτυρος Βλασίου*, 60–62. Kerkyra, 1909.

THE ORATIONS OF GREGORY OF NAZIANZOS

Editions of Byzantine texts are cited in full in the Notes to the Translation where they occur, with the exception of texts available in the Loeb Classical Library. The *Orations* of Gregory of Nazianzos, however, are cited with a frequency that make it more practical to give full citations all together and only once.

Orations 1–3 = Bernardi, Jean, ed. *Grégoire de Nazianze: Discours 1–3*. Sources chrétiennes 247. Paris, 1978.

Orations 4–5 = Bernardi, Jean, ed. *Grégoire de Nazianze: Discours 4–5. Contre Julien*. Sources chrétiennes 309. Paris, 1983.

Orations 6–12 = Calvet-Sébasti, Marie-Ange, ed. *Grégoire de Nazianze: Discours 6–12.* Sources chrétiennes 405. Paris, 1995.

Orations 20–23 = Mossay, Justin, and Guy Lafontaine, eds. *Grégoire de Nazianze: Discours 20–23.* Sources chrétiennes 270. Paris, 1980.

Orations 24–26 = Mossay, Justin, and Guy Lafontaine, eds. *Grégoire de Nazianze: Discours 24–26.* Sources chrétiennes 284. Paris, 1981.

Orations 32–37 = Moreschini, Claudio, and Paul Gallay, eds. *Grégoire de Nazianze: Discours 32–37.* Sources chrétiennes 318. Paris, 1985.

Orations 38–41 = Moreschini, Claudio, and Paul Gallay, eds. *Grégoire de Nazianze: Discours 38–41.* Sources chrétiennes 358. Paris, 1990.

Orations 42–43 = Bernardi, Jean, ed. *Grégoire de Nazianze: Discours 42–43.* Sources chrétiennes 384. Paris, 1992.

RELEVANT STUDIES

Anagnostakis, Ilias, and Anthony Kaldellis. "The Textual Sources for the Peloponnese, A.D. 582–959: Their Creative Engagement with Ancient Literature." *Greek, Roman, and Byzantine Studies* 54, no. 1 (2014): 105–35.

Caraher, William S. "Constructing Memories: Hagiography, Church Architecture, and the Religious Landscape of Middle Byzantine Greece: The Case of St. Theodore of Kythera." In *Archaeology and History in Roman, Medieval and Post-Medieval Greece: Studies on Method and Meaning in Honor of Timothy E. Gregory,* edited by William Caraher, Linda Jones Hall, and R. Scott Moore, 267–80. Aldershot, UK: Ashgate, 2008.

Chrestou, Eirene, and Katerina Nikolaou. "Στοιχεῖα γιὰ τὴν κοινωνία καὶ τὸν καθημερινὸ βίο στὴν περιοχὴ τῆς Λακωνίας (Θ´–ΙΒ´αἰ.) ἀπὸ ἁγιολογικὰ κείμενα." *Βυζαντιναὶ Μελέται* 2 (1990): 3–27.

Constantelos, Demetrios. "Ἡ ἱστορικὴ σημασία τῶν Βίων Πέτρου Ἄργους, Ἀθανασίου Μεθώνης καὶ Νίκωνος τοῦ Μετανοεῖτε διὰ τὴν Πελοπόννησον τοῦ 10ου αἰῶνος." In *Μνήμη Ἰωάννου Εὐ. Ἀναστασίου,* 349–64. Thessalonike, 1992.

Kazhdan, Alexander. "Hagiographical Notes (5–8)." *Byzantion* 54, no. 1 (1984): 176–92.

Koulouras, Georgios. "Σχετικά με τον Βίο του αγίου Νικολάου του Νέου (10ος αι.): Μία νέα προσέγγιση." *Βυζαντινά* 22 (2001): 113–22.

Kyriakopoulos, Konstantinos. "Προβλήματα περὶ τὸν Βίον καὶ τὸ ἔργον τοῦ ἁγίου Πέτρου ἐπισκόπου Ἄργους." *Πρακτικὰ Α´ Συνεδρίου Ἀργολικῶν Σπουδῶν,* 262–70. Athens, 1979.

Laniado, Avshalom. "Άγιος Πέτρος επίσκοπος Άργους, ο επιτάφιός του Εἰς τὸν Ἀθανάσιον ἐπίσκοπον Μεθώνης και η Ἑλληνικῶν Θεραπευτικὴ Παθημάτων του Θεοδωρήτου Κύρρου." In Μνήμη Τασούλας Οικονόμου (1998–2008), edited by Ioannes D. Varales and Giannes A. Pikoulas, 129–38. Volos, 2009.

Oikonomides, Nikolaos. "Ὁ Βίος τοῦ Ἁγίου Θεοδώρου Κυθήρων (10ος αἰ.) (12 Μαΐου - BHG, ἀρ. 2430)." In Τρίτον Πανιόνιον Συνέδριον: Πρακτικά, 264–91. Athens, 1967.

Orgels, Paul. "En marge d'un texte hagiographique (Vie de S. Pierre d'Argos, 19): La dernière invasion slave dans le Péloponnèse (923–925)." Byzantion 34, no. 1 (1964): 271–85.

Scholz, Cordula. Graecia Sacra: Studien zur Kultur des mittelalterlichen Griechenland im Spiegel hagiographischer Quellen. Frankfurt, 1997.

Sophianos, Demetrios Z. Άγιος Νικόλαος ὁ ἐν Βουναίνῃ: Ἀνέκδοτα ἁγιολογικὰ κείμενα, ἱστορικαὶ εἰδήσεις περὶ τῆς μεσαιωνικῆς Θεσσαλίας (Ι' αἰών). Athens, 1972.

Vasiliev, Alexander. "The 'Life' of St. Peter of Argos and Its Historical Significance." Traditio 5 (1947): 163–91.

Vees, Nikos A. "Vie de saint Théoclète évêque de Lacédémoine, publiée d'après le manuscrit n. 583 de la bibliothèque Barberine." Revue byzantine/Vizantiiskoe Obozrenie 2 (1916): suppl. 1–55.

Yannopoulos, Panayotis A. "Ιστορικές πληροφορίες του Θεοδώρου Νικαίας για την Αργολίδα." In Μεσαιωνικὴ Πελοπόννησος: Βυζάντιο, Λατινοκρατία, Τουρκοκρατία, edited by Panayotis A. Yannopoulos and Alexios K. G. Savvidis, 165–85. Athens, 2013.

Yannopoulos, Panayotis A., and Alexios K. G. Savvidis, eds. Μεσαιωνικὴ Πελοπόννησος: Βυζάντιο, Λατινοκρατία, Τουρκοκρατία. Athens, 2013.

Index